SANSKRIT CRITICISM

SANSKRIT CRITICISM

V. K. CHARI

MOTILAL BANARSIDASS PUBLISHERS
PRIVATE LIMITED • DELHI

First Indian Edition: Delhi, 1993

ISBN: 81-208-0956-4

FOR SALE IN INDIA ONLY

Also available at:
MOTILAL BANARSIDASS
41 U.A. Bungalow Road, Jawahar Nagar, Delhi 110 007
120 Royapettah High Road, Mylapore, Madras 600 004
16 St. Mark's Road, Bangalore 560 001
Ashok Rajpath, Patna 800 004
Chowk, Varanasi 221 001

PRINTED IN INDIA

BY JAINENDRA PRAKASH JAIN AT SHRI JAINENDRA PRESS, A-45 NARAINA INDUSTRIAL AREA, PHASE I, NEW DELHI 110 028 AND PUBLISHED BY NARENDRA PRAKASH JAIN FOR MOTILAL BANARSIDASS PUBLISHERS PVT. LTD., BUNGALOW ROAD, JAWAHAR NAGAR, DELHI 110 007

To

the late Professor T. R. V. Murti

and

the late Dr. V. Raghavan

with gratitude and affection

CONTENTS

ix
Acknowledgments

xi
Sanskrit Critical Schools and Writers

1
1 / Introduction

9
2 / *Rasa:* Poetry and the Emotions

29
3 / The Essentiality of the Emotions

48
4 / The Logic of the Emotions

75
5 / Modes of Meaning: Metaphor

95
6 / Suggestion

132
7 / Style and Meaning

161
8 / The Logic of Interpretation

195
9 / Poetic Apprehension and Poetic Truth

227
10 / The Validity of *Rasa* as a Theoretical Concept

253
Notes

283
Bibliography

297
Index

ACKNOWLEDGMENTS

This book owes its inspiration to the late T. R. V. Murti and to the late Dr. V. Raghavan, who initiated me into *śāstraic* studies. In gratitude, I dedicate the book to them. S. S. Janaki of the Kuppuswami Sastri Research Institute, Madras, with whom I read the Alaṃkāra texts, has offered me her unstinted support ever since I began work in this field. My special thanks to her.

Many other scholars also helped me in my studies in one way or another. K. K. Raja, director of The Adyar Library and Research Centre, Madras, read portions of this work and shared his thoughts with me. I benefited greatly by my discussions with Rewa Prasad Dwivedi of Banaras Hindu University, Professor Sriramachandrudu of Osmania University, Hyderabad, and Pandit Srivatsankacharya of Madras Sanskrit College. T. Venkatacharya of the University of Toronto clarified problematic passages of Sanskrit commentaries, and A. N. Aklujkar of the University of British Columbia offered helpful criticism. My uncle, Tiruvengadacharya, helped me to appreciate the nuances of Sanskrit poetry. To all these, my thanks. I owe a special debt to F. E. Sparshott for his benevolent patience in reading the earlier drafts of this manuscript and for offering helpful comments; and to Eliot Deutsch for his warm interest in my work and for the encouragement he offered toward its publication. I am also thankful to Dale M. Riepe and to my colleague Jack Healy for their comments on this work. I also want to thank Stuart Kiang of the University of Hawaii Press, under whose supervision this manuscript was revised for publication. I must also acknowledge my general debt to the many previous expositions of Sanskrit poetics, especially to the work of Raghavan, De, Krishnamoorthy, Raja, Gerow, Gnoli, and Masson/Patwardhan. I have often gone to their work for clarification and for interpreting and translating Sanskrit passages. Thanks are also owed to the Social Sciences and Humanities Research Council of Canada for leave fellowships in 1972–1973 and 1979–1980 that enabled me to carry out my research in India.

Some of the material included in this book is expanded from articles published earlier: "Decorum as a Critical Concept in Indian and Western Poetics," *Journal of Aesthetics and Art Criticism* 26 (1967); "The Concept of *Rasa-Dhvani* (Emotive Meaning)," *Adyar Library Bulletin* 39

(1975); "Poetic Emotions and Poetic Semantics," *Journal of Aesthetics and Art Criticism* 34 (1976); "Validity in Interpretation: Some Indian Views," *Journal of Aesthetics and Art Criticism* 36 (1978); "The Indian Theory of Suggestion (Dhvani)," *Philosophy East and West* 27 (1977); "The Nature of Poetic Truth: Some Indian Views," *British Journal of Aesthetics* 19 (1979). I thank the editors for permission to reproduce this material.

SANSKRIT CRITICAL SCHOOLS AND WRITERS

Literary Critics	
Bharata, *Nāṭyaśāstra*	ca. 5th century B.C. -3rd century A.D.
Commentators on Bharata	
Lollaṭa	A.D. 9th century
Śaṅkuka	9th century
Bhaṭṭanāyaka	9th–10th century
Abhinavagupta	10th–11th century
The Alaṃkāra school (Rhetoric)	
Bhāmaha	7th–8th century
Daṇḍin	8th century
Udbhaṭa	8th–9th century
Rudraṭa	9th century
The Rīti school (Style)	
Vāmana	8th–9th century
The Dhvani school (Suggestion)	
Ānandavardhana	9th century
Abhinavagupta	10th–11th century
Mammaṭa	11th century
Miscellaneous Writers on Poetics	
Rājaśekhara	10th century
Dhanaṃjaya	10th century
Kuntaka	10th–11th century
Kṣemendra	11th century
Bhoja	11th century
Mahimabhaṭṭa	11th century
Hemacandra	1088–1172
Ruyyaka	12th century
Viśvanātha	14th century
Appayya Dīkṣita	16th–17th century
Jagannātha	17th century

The Philosophical Systems

Mīmāṃsā

Jaimini, *Mīmāṃsā Sūtras*	ca. 200 B.C.
Śabara	ca. 1st century B.C.
Kumārila Bhaṭṭa (founder of the Bhāṭṭa school of Pūrva-Mīmāṃsā)	A.D. 7th century
Prabhākara (founder of the Prābhākara school of Pūrva-Mīmāṃsā)	7th century

Nyāya (Logic)

Gotama (Gautama)	ca. 6th century B.C.

Vyākaraṇa (Grammar)

Pāṇini	ca. 400 B.C.
Kātyāyana	ca. 300 B.C.
Patañjali	ca. 150 B.C.
Bhartṛhari	ca. 5th century A.D.

SANSKRIT CRITICISM

I

INTRODUCTION

In this book, I address myself to a twofold task: to present brief profiles of the major concepts of criticism in Sanskrit, together with a critique of them, and also, wherever possible, to review the Sanskrit theories in a comparative light to see how they stand up against critical thinking in the West, especially of our own age. When I set out to write this book, I felt that there was no need for another book of expositions or for a history of concepts, along traditional lines, after the many scholarly studies by Indian as well as Western Sanskritists. What cried out to be done, I felt, was to attempt a reevaluation of the Indian theories in the terms provided by the ancient systems themselves. It also seemed to me that most previous discussions (barring Edwin Gerow's *Glossary of Indian Figures of Speech,* which argues for a figurative aesthetic) were inconclusive in their assessment of the relative merits of the various concepts and schools of criticism; they seldom promised anything like a consistent general theory of literature.[1] Such a theory, if one were to be worked out, had, however, to come out of the very materials of traditional thought—it was not to be imposed from the outside. This consideration led me to look for a theoretical standpoint in the doctrine of *rasa* (roughly translated as "emotive aesthetics")—a standpoint from which I could evaluate all other theories and concepts and for which I could also find sufficient support in the texts and commentaries. *Rasa* is the most important concept in Indian aesthetics and may be seen as a pervasive influence in the theories of painting, sculpture, and dance in addition to poetry and dramaturgy.

Thus, of the four major concepts that dominated the critical scene in ancient India—namely, figuration (*alaṃkāra,* or poetry as figurative or deviant speech), style (*rīti,* poetry as structured expression), suggestion (*dhvani,* poetry as indirect expression), and *rasa* (poetry as emotive expression)—I take my stand on the *rasa* theory and criticize the other theories in that light. I argue that poetry is better defined by its evocatory aim than by any formal peculiarities or by any special semantics of its own. This, however, is not entirely my own conclusion but, as I show, what is stated explicitly or implicitly by the critics themselves. My criticisms, too, rest on a detailed examination of the relevant critical and philosophical texts.

Thus, while for the most part I derive my authority from what the Sanskrit critics themselves have to say, I also add something to traditional discussions. I present new arguments in support of or against the theories in question. Where the critics or their commentators seem undecided about the validity of a given theory or overly accommodating in treating rival theories, I force the issues to their logical conclusions and try to demonstrate their strengths or weaknesses. For instance, a sort of dubiety seems to characterize traditional discussions of the theory of poetic suggestion *(dhvani)*. But I take a hard look at this theory and question its claim that poetry is necessarily a "suggestive" use of language. I further argue that, in the final analysis, even according to the protagonists of *dhvani, rasa* rather than *dhvani* is the ultimate criterion of literariness. I defend the view of the opponents of the theory that suggestion is at best an aspect of poetic discourse, not what defines its nature.

In presenting a theory of style as ornamentation of meaning, I base my argument on what the Dhvani critics themselves state explicitly about the language of poetry as well as on some implications contained in their comments, although I reject their general position on the status of suggestion. I also use the traditional distinction between poetic form as ornament and poetic meaning as the ornamented and argue the nonessential, that is, nondefining, nature of the former. I reach the conclusion that literature is not, in the ultimate analysis, a type of language use but a type of meaning—emotive meaning, specifically. Some literary examples can be shown to exhibit no marked stylistic features, to be stylistically neutral. In this connection, I point out that one of the most valuable contributions of the *rasa* theory to literary criticism is its emphasis on the context of meaning being the determinant of style. The *rasa* theory does not of course deny the functionality of style or of figures. Formal features do serve an evocative function when there is a context for them. But meaning is what gives form its reason for being.

Some people may doubt the universal applicability of *rasa* as a principle of criticism. Arguing from the standpoint of the figurationists (the Alaṃkāra school), Gerow has expressed the view that, while *rasa* (the emotive element) is important for drama and its performance, it is certainly not essential for poetry as a verbal art. He writes, "The best that can be said of *rasa* in the context of verbal or poetic expression is that it is an aspect or element thereof."[2] Gerow points out that, in terms of its historical evolution, the *rasa* theory was first conceived by Bharata in the context of the theater and that it was only later, when the theatrical art ceased to be a living force and lyrical (strophic) poetry took its place, that the application of *rasa* was extended to all poetry. This may very well have been the case, but what is significant for aesthetics is that *rasa* was made into such a general principle and its application demonstrated by Ānandavardhana and Abhinavagupta. Gerow makes much of the generic distinction between drama and poetry. But, as Abhinavagupta asserts, poetry too is essentially drama, a verbal enactment of the emotions. Bharata too, it must be remembered, speaks of *rasa* in connection with the dramatic text *(kāvya)* as also in connection with the nonverbal representation in the theater. There is no "qualitative difference" between drama and theatrical representation, only a "quantitative difference of emotion."[3] This study will show that *rasa* is all pervasive and cuts across generic boundaries. It must be present, as a shaping principle, in all writing worth the name literature, be it a haiku, an epic, a novel, or a drama.

This is not of course to claim that, as a theoretical concept and principle of definition, *rasa* exhausts, or renders unnecessary, all other critical considerations—considerations of structure, style, generic mode, imagery, and so forth. This is only to say that such considerations become significant only insofar as they are guided by the principle of *rasa*. A general theory of poetry, it should be realized, can do no more than provide the guidelines for the practical business of criticism.

A book dealing with literary theory must naturally consider general problems of meaning, especially given the assumption of the Sanskrit critics that the semantics of literature must derive its sanction from the semantics of ordinary language, however different literary language may sometimes appear to be. A large part of this study is therefore taken up by the problems of general semantics—language, meaning, and interpretation (discussed in chaps. 5, 6, and 8)—for which I have drawn heavily on the theories of meaning formulated by the ancient philosophical schools, primarily the Mīmāṃsā school of thought. Interpretation is a central issue, not only in general semantics and philosophical analysis, but in aesthetic criticism as well (see Hirsch, Beardsley, and Sparshott, among others). Therefore, in chapter 8, I deal with this problem, outlining in some detail the *mīmāṃsā* rules of interpretation and also showing the application of some of them to literary examples.

Literary criticism, in the Sanskrit tradition, has been understood to be a *śāstra*—by which is meant any systematic, well-formulated body of knowledge. A "śāstraic" exposition is supposed to involve three different kinds of inquiry: (i) inquiry into the nature of substances or the categories of knowledge *(padārtha-mīmāṃsā);* (ii) inquiry into the nature of language *(śabda-mīmāṃsā),* since language is the invariable medium in which knowledge is formulated; and (iii) inquiry into the validity of critical statements *(prāmāṇya-mīmāṃsā).* Of these, the first and the third traditionally came under the purview of logic or *nyāya,* which is called *pramāṇa-śāstra,* whereas the second, language, came under grammar *(vyākaraṇa),* which dealt with words *(pada-śāstra). Pūrva-mīmāṃsā* stressed the sentence aspect of language and was known as *vākya-śāstra.* As an exegetical science, *mīmāṃsā* was concerned with the interpretation of the comprehensive meanings of the Vedic texts. As a scientific inquiry, literary criticism in Sanskrit borrowed its modes of procedure, its logic, and its conceptual language from these formalistic disciplines. Logic, grammar, and *mīmāṃsā,* rather than such metaphysical systems as Vedānta, Sāṃkhya, and Yoga, set the pattern for critical discussions in Sanskrit.

An important feature of this study is that the expositions of the various critical theories are set in their proper context of philosophical ideas. For dealing with any kind of text, scriptural or literary, we need to have a set of logical, semantic, and epistemological concepts. The Sanskrit critics take it as axiomatic that the problems of literary meaning are not a special class of problems but those that are common to all philosophical analysis. They assume that an understanding of the basic philosophical problems is a necessary prerequisite for the understanding of critical questions and a basis for a theory of poetics. Most manuals of poetics in Sanskrit, therefore, contain sections on theories of meaning and sometimes extended discussions of philosophical views concerning the nature of the word, the question of reference, modes of meaning, and so on. In settling points about the language of literature, these critics constantly draw on *mīmāṃsā,* logic, and grammar. In a very important sense, then, the science of literary criticism in India was but an extension of its philosophical, scholastic tradition and not in any way separate from it.

If there is any one philosophical standpoint that I constantly defend and draw on, it is that of the Mīmāṃsā school. Verbal autonomy, impersonality (anti-intentionalism and antiaffectivism), and unity of meaning are the three pillars on which the whole superstructure of *mīmāṃsā,* as a theory of language, rests. In essence, this theory states that the word is a self-luminous and self-explanatory symbol and a distinct source of knowledge *(pramāṇa).* No doubt, words give knowledge got from other sources by virtue of their referential function—that is, what they signify are meanings pertaining to a world (mental or material) that is outside the sign and known by other means of knowledge. But this does not mean that that knowledge is directly got from other sources; it is directly caused by the sign itself by virtue of its signifying capacity. The sign does not depend, for its own authority as an instrument of knowledge, on any external source—man or God. The *mīmāṃsā* maxim has it that, in the Veda, the word itself speaks *(śabde bruvati)*. Hence its autonomous character.

The Indian philosophy of grammar too maintains substantially the same position with respect to the authority of the word. Even as their counterparts in the West do (e.g., Saussure), the Indian theorists conceived of meaning as a referential relation between the audible word form *(śabda)* or the signifier and the inaudible, mentally perceived sense or object content *(artha)*—the signified. Unity of meaning is also an important axiom in all Indian theories. Since the spoken or written word is our only source of meaning, all meanings that a text can generate must flow from the words of the text directly, or indirectly as implications. However, meanings are not confined to the linguistic form alone, although they must be warranted by it; they are determined by what are known as the "contextual factors" *(prakaraṇādi)*. A sentence must be regarded as an "utterance," as a purposive speech act. The limits of the meaning of a sentence are set by the twin criteria of completeness and logical consistency. But for these two conditions, it is argued, no other, superfluous meaning can be got out of a sentence. I show that these principles were also the basic presuppositions of literary criticism in Sanskrit. To my knowledge, no previous modern writer has sufficiently emphasized the relevance of the *mīmāṃsā* principles to problems of criticism.

In defining literature by its aim rather than by its linguistic form, and in arguing that literature is a kind of "verbal prompting" or "evocation" of moods (chap. 3), I draw on the *mīmāṃsā* theory of *bhāvanā*. Through a subtle grammatical and logical analysis, the *mīmāṃsā* theorist shows that the Vedic texts are a form of verbal prompting, that prompting men to perform certain ritual acts is, in modern terminology, their illocutionary force. The application of this principle to literature is suggested by the critics themselves (Abhinavagupta, Bhaṭṭanāyaka, and Dhanika). But this idea has not been picked up by modern exponents, and its implications have not been explored.

"Generalization of meanings" is another semantic principle that is quite central to the Sanskrit theory of aesthetic experience. Abhinavagupta shows how this process of generalization is a feature of poetic apprehension. The authority for this, once again, comes from the *mīmāṃsā* theory of the import of propositions *(śābda-bodha)*. The implications of this idea for the problem of the poetic universal and poetic truth are discussed in chapter 9.

Some recent exponents, notably, A. K. Coomaraswamy, K. C. Pandey, and J. L. Masson, have given needlessly metaphysicized accounts of Indian aesthetics.[4] Following such accounts, many people in the West have the impression that Indian art and art theories have to be studied only in their religious, transcendental setting.[5] But, as it should become clear from this essay, Sanskrit criticism—at any rate, the mainstream of it—had nothing to do with religion or metaphysics. The various theories of poetry—*rasa, dhvani,* and so forth—were all based on purely aesthetic considerations and not put forward as theories of reality or world hypotheses.[6]

All the philosophical schools in India, including those espousing logic and *mīmāṃsā,* no doubt originated in theological disputations and had a metaphysical axe to grind. But what is often not appreciated is the fact that, in the process of defending their own systems, they also raise valuable philosophical questions concerning language, meaning, and truth that can be studied for their own importance, independent of their original contexts. The insights they offer into such problems and the discursive tools they developed can be fruitfully employed in any critical investigation, quite apart from the metaphysics. For example, the *mīmāṃsā* rules of interpretation and analysis of sentence types have their value even outside the Veda. Bhartṛhari's metaphysical doctrine of the Word as Brahman (Śabda-Brahma-Vāda) does not detract from the value of his analyses of word and sentence and of verbal cognition. In dealing with the phenomenon of language itself, his method is strictly empirical and analytic. As for the literary critics, while they use the insights of all these philosophers wherever they can, they generally remain metaphysically uncommitted as far as critical inquiry is concerned. A notable example is Abhinavagupta himself, who, though he was a follower of Kashmir Śaivism and may have read some of that mysticism into his account of aesthetic experience, never really allows his metaphysical interests to interfere with his critical analyses.

Some Western scholars may be inclined to think that the Indian theories are valuable only for understanding Indian literatures and culture. But this, I think, is not the right conception. There surely are some general principles in aesthetics and art, whether formulated by Eastern or Western thinkers, whose validity may be seen to extend beyond their native boundaries.[7] That the ideas discussed here apply cross-culturally is amply demonstrated in nearly every chapter of this book by the frequent examples I give from English literature.

Since my aim is also to present the Sanskrit materials in a comparative perspective, I discuss parallel strains in modern Western, chiefly Anglo-American, criticism. However, a systematic comparative study is not the aim. Such a study would have involved a far more thorough treatment of Western thought than could be undertaken within the limits of the present work. Therefore, I cite only those critics or critical ideas that have an immediate bearing on my discussions and can illuminate the issues at hand. My object is primarily to test the validity of the Sanskrit ideas and see how useful they are in theorizing about literature. The Western parallels are used for purposes of illustration, contrast, or confirmation. The comparisons also serve another purpose. They relate the issues raised in Sanskrit criticism to contemporary critical debates and thus show their relevance to the interests and concerns of our own time. The topics in terms of which this book is organized are at the center of modern aesthetic discussions.

I have profited a great deal from recent Anglo-American aesthetics, especially from the work of Beardsley, from the speech act theory of Austin and Searle, and generally from the analytic spirit of contemporary philosophical thought. Some of the critical terms I employ and the criteria of judgment are drawn from these sources. I am aware, though, that some of the conclusions reached here run counter to the established notions of our age; they may, in fact, seem reactionary to many. For one thing, an emotive theory of literature is likely to be viewed with suspicion, however one may argue its case. So is any theory that puts greater emphasis on meaning than on style and language or argues for an ornamental view of style. No doubt, this view has a long tradition in Western criticism too, from Aristotle down to the neoclassical age. But it goes against the grain of much modern thinking. Also, the rather absolutist, essentialist view of literature that I advocate would be resisted by many in an age committed to pluralism and open-endedness. Postmodernist criticism has sought to force a revision of the traditional notions of language and meaning, and deconstruction has even questioned the possibility of a meaningful critical discourse. Influential as these movements are with the present generation of critics, they do not, in my opinion, invalidate the classical argument for the objectivity, stability, and determinacy of verbal meanings and for the reliability of language as an instrument of knowledge and communication. Such notions are the very basis of human discourse and cannot be unsettled too easily, as the Hindu philosophers show in refuting the arguments of the Buddhist nihilists. They are also the basic presuppositions of philosophical thought in the West, down the ages, and still continue to be in the mainstream of Anglo-American criticism.

The discussions presented here are technical and involve subtle, and sometimes hairsplitting, logical and semantic distinctions. But while the logical subtleties could not altogether be avoided, I have tried to render them in the modern idiom, as far as possible. Critical discussions in Sanskrit are also conducted in an argumentative style, on the model of "the opponent's view" *(pūrva-pakṣa),* refutation, and "the established view" *(siddhānta)*. A critic could not be supposed to have established his own standpoint until he has refuted other standpoints and answered all possible objections. The same dialectical need dictates the somewhat argumentative spirit of my presentations and makes it necessary for me to take sides in the critical debates.

My concern, in this study, is with certain conceptual issues pertaining to the understanding of literature that are the same in both the Sanskrit and the English critical traditions. I therefore attempt merely to abstract from the Sanskrit texts certain general principles that have value in theorizing about literature. The study of Sanskrit literature itself is not one of my aims. On the other hand, in illustrating the various ideas, I depend to a large extent on English examples in order to facilitate the understanding of the non-Sanskritists.

Finally, I must caution the reader not to expect to find here any new theories or startling conclusions. The aim of this study has been to expound, clarify, and evaluate some very old ideas, purely in the spirit of critical investigation. However, I believe that the interest of Sanskrit criticism is not merely historical but theoretical as well. The arguments put forward by these ancient thinkers bear on matters that are basic to critical discussions at all times, and they may even be seen sometimes to bring clarification to our thinking about language and literature.

2

RASA: POETRY AND THE EMOTIONS

Because the object of this study is to approach literary theory centrally from the standpoint of the concept of *rasa,* it would be appropriate to begin by elucidating the meaning and scope of that term. As a general theory of literature, the *rasa* doctrine *(rasa-vāda)* is based on two premises: (i) that literary works, as verbal compositions, express emotive meanings and (ii) that all literature is typically emotive discourse or discourse that has to do with the portrayal of feelings and attitudes rather than with ideas, concepts, statements of universal truths, and so forth. The second premise relates to the problem of defining literature and will be taken up in chapter 3. But the first premise raises a host of philosophical questions. What kind of entities are the emotions, and what is their objective or ontological status? How are they recognized? How do they get expressed in words? If emotions can be expressed in language, what precisely is the sense in which they are said to be "expressed"? Where are the poetic emotions located, and what is the mode of their existence? Do they exist in the poet, in the reader or spectator, or, in some mysterious way, in the poem itself? These and other related questions, which have to be answered before our theory can be established on a sound footing, will be the concern of this chapter.

Rasa is the most important concept in Sanskrit criticism and one that is central to all discourse about literature. As we shall see, it also influenced the theories of dance and the visual arts as well. As a critical term, *rasa* is multifaceted and presents problems of translation. However, in its most basic sense, it means "aesthetic relish"[1] and comprehends two related ideas.

First, *rasa* is the relishable quality inherent in an artistic work—which, according to Bharata, the first known formulator of the *rasa* theory, is its emotive content. Every work—poem or play—is supposed to treat an emotive theme and communicate a distinct emotional flavor or mood, such as the tragic, comic, erotic, and so forth. In this sense, one can speak of the *rasa* of a work and also, since there are many such moods, of poetic or dramatic "moods" or "emotions" (to use these terms interchangeably)—of *rasas* in the plural. A distinction is also made between the common human emotions treated in the poem—which are termed *bhāvas*—and the art emotion or *rasa* that emerges from such a treatment, the assumption being that the raw stuff of the emotions presented as undergone by characters in a play or by the speaker of a lyric poem is transformed in the process into a universalized emotion and rendered fit for a contemplative enjoyment. Thus, every emotion treated in the poem is said to lead to or yield a corresponding aesthetic mood. I will not press this distinction here since the emotion treated in the poem and its resultant aesthetic state are qualitatively the same: that is, if a play deals with the tragic emotion, the aesthetic mood generated by it will also be tragic, although transformed in the way indicated. In any case, as we shall see in chapter 9, this transformation is in the way the work is apprehended rather than an ostensible feature of the work itself.

In the second sense in which the term is understood, *rasa* is the relishable experience occasioned by the work in the reader or spectator—which we may refer to as the "*rasa* experience." I shall therefore use the term *rasa* in both these senses, as the context requires, but most generally to signify "the poetic emotion." Where a distinction between types of meaning is implied, I shall translate the word as "emotive meaning."

Thus, although *rasa,* as originally propounded by Bharata, was purely an aesthetic concept, it has, through the centuries, been absorbed into theological discussions and consequently become strongly tinged with the language of one or another of the metaphysical cults. Bharata's commentators themselves sought, from time to time, to give a metaphysical twist to the *rasa* theory. Thus, Bhaṭṭanāyaka, who wrote under the inspiration of Sāṃkhya and Vedānta, attempted to spiritualize aesthetic experience in describing it as a blissful state of mind, comparable to the enjoyment of Brahman. He thought of drama as a means to the realization of the highest goal of life, namely, spiritual emancipation *(mokṣa).* The attempt to apply Hindu transcendental theories to aesthetic criticism is also seen in Abhinavagupta's definition of *rasa* as a supramundane *(alaukika)* experience, quite distinct from ordinary modes of knowledge.[2] This metaphysicized account of *rasa,* which came to be known as *rasa-brahma-vāda,* became the standard explanation of that concept in the manuals of poetics. With the rise of the devotional schools in the medieval period, the *rasa* concept received an out-and-out religious interpretation. The Vaiṣṇava mystics of Bengal offered a completely revamped theory of *rasa* and sought to deify poetic emotion by making it a form of god realization. The modern Indian exponents of the subject, the most influential among them being Coomaraswamy, have also contributed to the general impression, prevalent in the West, that the aesthetics of the Hindus is but an extension of their mystical speculations, that it is a "theological aesthetics." For Coomaraswamy, the *rasa* theory is "essentially metaphysical and Vedantic in method and conclusion."[3] Coomaraswamy is not alone in connecting the *rasa* theory with metaphysics. K. C. Pandey, in his volume on Indian aesthetics, reads Abhinavagupta's theories in the light of Kashmir Śaivism.[4] He observes that, in Abhinavagupta's transcendentalist view, aesthetic contemplation becomes a form of meditation on the Self itself, in which, with all objective reference suspended and the aesthetic object disappearing from view, the Self rests in its own luminous consciousness. The art object becomes thus a mere focus for meditation. *Rasa* is the experience of the Self itself as pure and unmixed bliss.[5]

Abhinavagupta's language no doubt lends itself readily to this kind of interpretation. The influence of the metaphysical doctrines is also unquestionably present. It seems that, in his anxiety to secure for aesthetic experience a unique status, Abhinavagupta needlessly subtilizes the concept of *rasa*. His attempt to expatiate on the mysticism of aesthetic enjoyment would seem unnecessary because it does not help the practical business of criticism. But, despite the transcendentalist vocabulary, neither Abhinavagupta nor the other exponents actually seek to subsume aesthetics under theology or illuminist metaphysics of one brand or another. Again, although these critics tend to describe *rasa* experience in mystical terms, they never fail to seek validation for their theories at the logical, phenomenological level and to secure for criticism an objective aesthetic basis. Paradoxical as it may seem, the metaphysical preoccupation of these critics does not hurt their aesthetics. For, whatever the metaphysical or religious values aesthetic experience may be supposed to afford to the spiritual aspirant, the doctrine of the *rasas* or dramatic emotions, as originally enunciated by Bharata and expounded at length by Ānandavardhana and Abhinavagupta, takes its stand squarely on the material, instinctual nature of man. Abhinavagupta himself is quite explicit in pointing out that *rasa* experience is distinct from religious attitude or Yogic experience.[6] Poetry *(kāvya)* is simply a dramatization of human emotions and is of the form of pleasure and pain.[7]

It should therefore be recognized that *rasa* is not an esoteric doctrine but, as I hope to demonstrate, a strenuously argued theory of the nature of poetic discourse and much more respectable critically than it is often taken to be. Reduced to its simplest form, the *rasa* theory states that the aim of poetry is the expression and evocation of emotions and that a poem exists for no other purpose than that it should be relished by the reader.[8] Aesthetic experience is this act of relishing or gustation *(rasana)*. The object that induces this experience in the reader or spectator is a *rasa-kāvya*—a work that manifests *rasa*. In other words, the poem arouses certain feelings in the reader because it is itself the concrete objectification of those feelings. Thus, it is assumed that the *rasa* apprehended by the reader is the *rasa* manifested by the poem.

The idea that poetry expresses emotions and moves us is not of course new to Western criticism. It is implicit in Aristotle's *Poetics,* in the Greco-Roman rhetorical tradition generally, in Longinus particularly, in Romantic expressionistic aesthetics down to Croce, and in such modern critics as Richards and Eliot. But the Western prejudice against emotions in poetry, too, is as old as Plato and the Puritans. Traditionally, Western criticism has reflected a division of loyalties between the opposite principles of *dulce* and *utile,* so much so that a complete aesthetics of the emotions was not possible unless it was also justified by moral, cognitive, or philosophical values. This is true even of Aristotle. In the Indian tradition, on the other hand, one finds a more consistent and systematic theorizing about poetry in terms of the emotions and an attempt to explain the whole area of poetic semantics as well as aesthetic psychology centrally from the standpoint of the emotions.

The emotive theory was not by any means the only theory to be advanced by the classical Sanskrit critics. Sanskrit poetics had its school of metaphor *(alaṃkāra),* which thought of figurative or deviant expression as the special characteristic of poetic language, and its school of style *(rīti),* which believed that a special arrangement of words, of phonetic and syntactic features, constituted the essence of poetry. Then there was the most influential school, that of suggestion *(dhvani),* led by Ānandavardhana, author of the classic *Dhvanyāloka* (The light of suggestion), and his commentator Abhinavagupta. This school argued that poetic indirection was a special, supernumerary activity of words, outside both literal and metaphoric functions. While these two critics advanced a novel theory of suggestion, they were also responsible for developing Bharata's doctrine of the emotions, which Bharata himself applied mainly to dramatic literature, into a unified theory of poetry. At their hands, the concept of *rasa* became the central criterion of poetic semantics; it subsumed even the principle of suggestion.

A few other preliminary remarks will be necessary for a correct understanding of the scope of this theory and of its basic assumptions. The *rasa* theory implies that there are a number of specific emotions, each with its distinct tone or flavor, and not an anonymous aesthetic emotion or a host of nameless emotions. Poetic works are not merely emotionally charged in some vague sense like music or nonrepresentational painting, but they treat a specific number of emotions as their subject matter. Psychic states, attitudes, and reactions are the stuff of poetry, their representational content. As Bharata said, "Drama is the representation of the mental states, actions, and conduct of people."[9] Thus, Bharata lists as many as forty-nine emotional states *(bhāvas),* of which eight are primary or durable states *(sthāyins),* with their corresponding *rasas* or aesthetic moods; thirty-three are transitory states *(vyabhicārins);* and eight are involuntary expressions, like tears, horripilation, trembling, and so on, which are also thought to be mental states even though they appear as physical conditions. The eight basic emotions are erotic love, comic laughter, grief, fury, heroic spirit, fear, wonder, and disgust or revulsion. Only these basic emotions can be developed into distinct aesthetic moods, whereas the other, transient emotions come and go according to their affinity with the durable emotions. Later commentators, however, added a ninth emotion to Bharata's list of eight basic states, namely, subsidence or serenity *(śānta).* The final number of basic emotions in the *rasa* tradition is therefore taken to be nine.[10]

This theory of poetic emotions is, again, a theory mainly of poetry in its broadest, Aristotelian sense, not a general theory of the arts. For the language of the emotions best suits poetry, which is a representational art. No doubt, Bharata, in his *Nāṭyaśāstra,* assigned specific emotional or suggestive values to musical notes *(svaras)* and melodic patterns or *jātis* (later called *rāgas*) when they were used in stage presentation for evocative purposes. But there is no suggestion in Bharata that the musical notes by themselves express any particular emotions.[11]

A *rāga* is so called because, etymologically, it produces a mood, albeit in a vague way, or is colored by it. Any given *rāga* may be adapted to a variety of moods. A *rāga* can become the vehicle of a mood when it is employed in an expressive context, when, for instance, a lyric is set in a *rāga.* It then takes on the feeling tone of the meanings of the verbal text with which it is combined. But it cannot be said to express or signify that feeling as its subject matter, its referential content. Nor is a *rāga* sad, joyful, arousing, depressing, and so on in itself, in the sense that it possesses those qualities; it is felt to be so only in association with meanings that are sad, joyful, and so on. Therefore, melody is related to the meanings of the song, not as an expressor *(vācaka),* but as a suggestor *(vyañjaka),* in the sense that, when music is combined with the words of the song, it somehow seems to become fused with the meaning and evokes the very mood that is conveyed by the meaning. Both Ānandavardhana and

Abhinavagupta recognize that musical sounds too can be suggestive of *rasa* in this way, although they are nonmeaningful or nonexpressive *(avācakaśabda)*. Abhinavagupta states explicitly that the power of conveying *rasa* inheres only in the expressive situation of the play or poem.[12]

Indian dance is no doubt predominantly expressive and expository and is employed largely in dramatic or narrative contexts to interpret through gesture the theme and mood of the accompanying song. The elaborate language of hand gestures *(mudrās),* glances, and body movements, which are the paraphernalia of Indian dancing, is designed to enact the mood of the song as well as translate into the visual medium the meanings of the verbal text. The great emphasis placed on *abhinaya* or gestural enactment is a clear indication of the influence of the *rasa* concept on Indian dancing and on playacting as well. Bharata dealt with both dance and music in connection with drama, and so both these arts were for him natural adjuncts of the theater and vehicles of dramatic expression. *Rasa* is no doubt conveyed directly by the verbal meanings of the drama or song, but music, both vocal and instrumental, and dance are valuable aids to mood building in any stage performance. Indian dance is composed of two distinct elements: gestures, including facial expressions, hand and leg positions and their movements, gaits, and stances; and pure dance movements consisting of footwork, poses, and rhythmic movements of hands and legs in combination. Of these, gestures directly express feelings and other mental states, as they can be understood as signals or indicative signs of inner states. Even the pure dance movements are described by Bharata and by subsequent writers in terms of their uses in appropriate expression contexts.

But Abhinavagupta points out that pure dance movement must be distinguished from dramatic expression proper. Dance is a gestureless movement of hands and legs based on rhythm *(tāla)* and tempo *(laya),* whereas dramatic enactment *(abhinaya)* is a gestural interpretation of verbal meanings and their concomitant emotions *(bhāvas)* through the visible physical medium of facial expressions and body movements. Dance consists in transcribing the musical patterns into corresponding patterns of bodily movements. Although it may sometimes form part of an expository situation—drama or song—it is not dependent on the verbal meanings as it flows directly from the rhythm of the song. Moreover, it need not necessarily accompany a song, for there could be a dance based on instrumental music or simply on the sounds of drums. Thus, it is related neither to the meaning nor to the emotions expressed by the song. Emotions are expressed either through speech *(vācika)* or through physical gesture *(āṅgika)*. In both forms, there is the notion of an expresser *(vācaka)* and an expressed content *(vācya)*. But, in dance, there is no direct apprehension of a cognitive or narrative content.

This was also the view established by Bharata against the contention of those who held that even pure dance movements can be expressive of meanings and that emotional experiences can express themselves directly through rhythmic movements.[13] Bharata says, "Dance (when it is employed in drama or song) is occasioned by no specific need except that its use adds to the beauty (of the presentation)."[14] Abhinavagupta admits, however, that dance can become a vehicle of *rasa,* even as music is, even though it is not directly expressive of it. He explains, "*Rasa* is manifested by dramatic action *(nāṭya);* but the dramatic action itself arises from the play or song (that is, from the meanings of the verbal text) which is expressive of *rasa.* And, as a dance, introduced in the context of *rasa,* becomes the means of its evocation, it also acquires a dramatic quality."[15] It is thus established that both dance and music are formally different from any mode of expression that has to do with the objectification of emotions. Whatever emotive values they acquire can be attributed to their use in specific expression contexts.

The relation of the *rasa* doctrine to the arts of painting and sculpture is, however, more intimate since these arts are understood by the ancient Indian writers as being essentially representational. According to the *Viṣṇudharmottara Purāṇa,* painting and sculpture, like expressive dance, "reproduce all that is the object of experience in the three worlds." They employ the same eye expressions, hand gestures, and body postures that are found in dance. Expressiveness is considered to be the very essence of image making. Even as one speaks of the dramatic emotions *(nāṭya-rasas),* one can also speak of the *rasas* expressed in painting or sculpture *(citra-rasas).*[16] Emotion *(bhāva)* is thus accepted as one of the criteria of painting, together with symmetry, similarity, proper disposition of colors, and so on.

Yet there will be objections to an emotive theory of poetry from the point of view of the formalist critic that must be answered before *rasa* can be established as a valid critical theory. As is well known, modern criticism, especially Anglo-American criticism, has, with its strong scientific bias, moved away from all affective theories and emotive vocabulary to an almost uncompromisingly objective, formalistic approach to art. It believes in isolating the poetic object as a unique entity and fixing the focus hard on its objective, demonstrable features. In this view, theories that are based on either the psychology of composition or the reader's affective responses would not be valid theories of criticism. But this objection cannot be leveled against Sanskrit poetics, which, like its classical counterpart in the West, was predominantly an empirical, rhetorical tradition, showing no interest in the author's personal psychology or in the psychology of the creative process. Rather, it addressed its inquiry to the finished product and to the nature of the effects it produces on the reader. Thus, it avoids the personal and genetic heresies, against which the New Criticism in the West has rightly revolted.

Sanskrit poetics also avoids the pitfalls of the various transcendental revelatory theories associated with Romanticism and traceable largely to Platonic and neo-Platonic doctrines as well as to the Hebraic-Prophetic tradition. Theorists in this tradition believe that the artist has a vision of a reality hidden behind the appearance of things and makes the revelation of this vision the object of his art.[17] The trouble with this view is that the critic has no means of knowing this vision of ultimate reality except through the work itself and that, when he does come to know about it, he cannot ascertain whether it has been faithfully reproduced or embodied by the work. The Sanskrit critics speak of art as an object of enjoyment rather than as a medium for transmitting inspired visions of ultimate reality. Although for them art occasions a supernal delight, its matrix is the common stuff of human emotions. Aesthetic experience is simply the apprehension of the created work as delight, and the pleasure principle cannot be separated from aesthetic contemplation. This delight is regarded as its own end and as having no immediate relation to the practical concerns of the world or to the pragmatic aims of moral improvement or spiritual salvation.[18] Sanskrit theory is thus opposed to a didactic, hortative view of literature. Abhinavagupta declares that poetry is fundamentally different from ethics or religion and that the principal element in aesthetic experience is not knowledge but delight, although poetry may also lead to the expansion of our being and enrich our power of intuition.[19]

Nevertheless, this preoccupation with emotions and with affective experience rather than solely with the formal properties of the work makes the *rasa* theory vulnerable to the charges of expressionism and psychologism. The language of emotions and all expressionistic doctrines, stemming mainly from Romantic philosophy, has been under attack in recent years, especially from the followers of Wittgenstein. People as diverse as Susanne Langer, Clive Bell, T. S. Eliot, Middleton Murry, Yvor Winters, Northrop Frye, and F. R. Leavis have all been found to be tainted in some degree by the sin of expressionism.[20] The expressionistic doctrine corresponds to the earlier picture theory of language propounded by Wittgenstein in his *Tractatus* and rejected by him later in *The Philosophical Investigations* in favor of his theory of language games.

The whole problem concerning the language of poetic emotions centers on the question, Can emotional qualities be tested as they are normally taken to reside in the subjective experience of the writer or reader? The answer to this question hinges on our being able to describe the connection between the work of art and the feeling in such a way that one can locate the feeling in the work of art itself and, in a sense, make it testable.[21] The approach in the light of Wittgenstein's logic seeks to avoid the dangers of both expressionist and affective theories by locating the feelings squarely in the work of art itself instead of imputing them to any actual person, artist, or observer. It does not evaluate the work either by inquiring whether it has faithfully expressed the author's alleged feelings or by examining its effects on the minds of the audience. The feelings we find in the poem or play are objective qualities present in the work. They are not the feelings of anybody in particular; they are just feelings defined by their objects and situational contexts. The language of feelings is not then a private language; it is more a system of symbols, a language game that is understood by those who have learned its conventions and usages.

But this objective emphasis is, in fact, quite congenial to the Indian theorist. The *rasa* theory itself, as formulated by Bharata in his *Nāṭyaśāstra,* deals with the emotions in an entirely objective way. In his famous *rasa sūtra* (formula), Bharata explains how emotions are expressed in poetry: "Emotions in poetry come to be expressed through the conjunction of their causes and symptoms, and other ancillary feelings that accompany the emotions."[22] Here Bharata stipulates three conditions or situational factors that must be present together for an emotion to become manifested: (i) that which generates the emotion, which includes *(a)* the object to which the emotion is directed (i.e., the intentional object, *ālaṃbanavibhāva*), for example, Juliet, and *(b)* other exciting circumstances *(uddīpanavibhāva),* for example, youth, privacy, moonlight, etc.; (ii) the overt expressions (actions and gestures) that exhibit the emotion, called *anubhāvas,* for example, tears, laughter, etc.; and (iii) other ancillary feelings, such as depression, elevation, agitation, etc., that normally accompany that emotion. The object, thus set forth by Bharata, of representing the various emotions in terms of their attendant conditions makes the poetic situation very much a public situation.

Bharata's commentators, who followed him, were careful to point out that the emotions treated in poetry are neither the projections of the reader's own mental states nor the private feelings of the poet; rather, they are the objective situations abiding in the poem *(kāvyagata),* as its cognitive content. The sorrow presented in the *Rāmāyaṇa* is to be taken not as the personal sorrow of the poet but sorrow itself in its generalized form and identified by its criteria.[23] If it were only a feeling personal to the poet, it would not attain the status of a poem *(ślokatva)* and would not be fit for the reader's contemplation. It is further stated that the possibility of the poetic emotions being objectified in the work is dependent on their representation in words. *Rasa* is apprehended as residing in the work, in the situational factors presented in an appropriate language.[24] A poet chooses a theme because he sees a certain promise for developing its emotional possibilities and exploits it by dramatizing its details. It is immaterial whether he felt any emotion, although it is likely that he did. Poetry, then, is composed of words and sentences. The represented emotion, or *rasa,* is the meaning of the poetic sentence. The purport of the poetic sentence consists in the conveying of the basic emotions—for example, love or grief—through words descriptive of the actions and gestures that are invariably associated with those emotions.[25]

That poetic emotions have their "life in the poem" and arise only in relation to their formal representation in the poem is also the conclusion of T. S. Eliot.[26] Speaking of Ezra Pound's poetry, Eliot says that Pound's verse is always definite and concrete because "he has always a definite emotion behind it," and he quotes Ford Madox Hueffer's statement that "poetry consists in so rendering concrete objects that the emotion produced by the objects shall arise in the reader.[27] Feelings and passions, Eliot further argues, are not merely subjective but objective and public. Hate, envy, admiration, and so on can be named and the naming is important.

> It is obvious that we can no more explain a passion to a person who has never experienced it than we can explain light to the blind. But it would be obvious also that we can explain the passion equally well: it is no more "subjective" because some persons have never experienced it than light is subjective because the blind cannot see. We can explain it by its relations, by its effect upon the heart beat, its toxic alterations of the system, by its effects on conduct and social intercourse. Without these relations, which give the feeling its whatness, the feeling could not be said to exist.[28]

Bharata's *rasa sūtra* affirms as much. Emotions exist and are manifested in inalienable association with their causes and circumstances. As they are known in life by their objective signs, so also are they apprehended from the language that describes them. It would therefore be wrong to bring the charge of subjectivism or naive emotionalism against the *rasa* theory.

But, as Harold Osborne asks pertinently, can emotional qualities like anger, sorrow, fear, and so on, which are only experienced by sentient beings as psychological effects, be properly attributed to works of art?[29] What do we mean when we say that feelings are properties of the work itself or that they may be predicated of the work directly? The Sanskrit critics too ask this question, and their answer is precisely the one suggested by Osborne: only in a secondary or metaphoric sense can we speak of the work as being the locus of *rasa,* on the strengh of the maxim that the quality of the effect is extended to the cause. As the commentators on the *Daśarūpaka* explain, "Although rasa is the relish enjoyed by the reader it is also the relishable quality manifested by the work. Hence the work too may be spoken of as possessing rasa *(rasavat)* in the way that one says 'Clarified butter is longevity itself' because it is conducive to that state. A relishable object becomes relish itself, just as it is said of Brahman, 'Brahman is relish indeed.' "[30]

Here of course *rasa* is understood in its general sense as aesthetic relish. A work is called tragic or comic because it is an object of emotion to the reader. Similarly, too, we attribute vaguely defined affective qualities called "aesthetic emotions" to arrangements of shapes, colors, sounds, and so on and speak of them as though they were the formal properties of the work itself. While in the case of nonrepresentational arts, however, we can attribute emotional qualities to them only metaphorically, in the case of a verbal representation these qualities are seen not only as properties of our response but as messages signified by means of the symbolism of words, by verbal descriptions of situations, actions, and gestures. Thus, the persons represented in a work, the poet himself or a character, are also shown as having an emotion or as being objects of emotion to other people in the story or to the poet. Otherwise, they would not become objects of emotion to the reader and arouse the corresponding emotion in him. It is in this sense that emotions are the meaning or the representational content of a literary work.

The objectivist has no difficulty in admitting that poetry may express an emotion through its objects and situations. However, for him, it must do so without its having to arouse that emotion in the reader because there is no way of ascertaining that the emotion aroused in the reader is the same as that expressed by the work. Besides, pleasure and emotion in the reader are not sufficient criteria for discriminating works of art. They do not advance criticism beyond the statement that works of art give pleasure or that they evoke a peculiar emotion. We cannot judge the relative worth of works of art by the degree of pleasure that they give because we do not have a public measuring rod for the purpose. No two persons experience the same emotional reactions and in precisely the same degree.

A critic poses the problem as follows. Meanings and ideas are of course objectively present in the work; they can, for instance, be adequately and most often unambiguously specified. "But since there can be no equally sensitive control of emotional response we are here in the realm of the subjective."[31] This difficulty is fully appreciated by the *rasa* theorist. Hence Bharata and, following him, Ānandavardhana set up an elaborate logic of the emotions and a body of criteria for situation appraisal, called *rasaucitya* (propriety in the treatment of the emotions), based on public norms and standards (*lokadharmī, lokapramāṇa).* It must not be forgotten that what the Sanskrit critics are talking about are not the elusive inner happenings of the Cartesian theory but "meanings" of emotive situations and behavior as they enter into human discourse. Emotions in poetry are as objective and public as "meanings and ideas" are and can be specified as adequately as the others can be.

If this is so, then it would seem to follow that, in order to recognize emotions in poetry, it is not necessary to have emotions oneself. Granted that a poem or drama expresses emotions by representing people in emotional situations and attitudes, which will serve as signs to the reader of those emotions. But, as Osborne remarks, "When we see a 'natural' sign of an emotion, whether in real life or in art, the emotion signified to us is not necessarily or usually experienced by us. What occurs is direct observation that such and such a person is displaying signs of emotion and knowledge by inference that he is experiencing the emotion displayed. We have not direct knowledge by acquaintance of his emotion."[32] Another critic argues, "One recognizes feelings without oneself having those feelings. . . . We can recognize the presentation of grief without being grief-stricken ourselves."[33]

But such a conclusion seems to strike at the very root of the conception of *rasa* as aesthetic relish. For, concerned though they are about the essential objectivity of the poetic emotions, the Sanskrit critics do not wish to banish the affections altogether from the poetic experience. Nor do they entirely dispense with mental concepts. On the other hand, they insist that emotions are inner psychic states, but known by their criteria. Bharata, whose approach to aesthetics was more practical than philosophical, naively assumed that the emotions expressed in poetry are the emotions felt by the poet and shared by the audience. But Śaṅkuka, an early commentator on Bharata, saw the difficulty implicit in Bharata's formula for emotional expression and stated that emotions, being mental states, cannot be directly known or expressed; the knowledge of them is made possible only by their perceptible causes and effects, which are their logical signs. The emotions, he maintained, are inferred from their signs, and poetic representation (imitation, according to him) is only of these external signs, not of the intrapsychic states themselves, which cannot be expressed even by the power of poetry.[34]

Abhinavagupta, too, recognizes this distinction between inner mental states and their external conditions and signs and points out that, while these signs serve to manifest or make known the emotions, they are not identical with the emotions themselves. The two belong to two different orders of existence (the one is physical and insentient and the other mental and sentient), and they are apprehended by different organs of perception.[35] The spectator, no doubt, learns to recognize the emotive situation by observing the behavior of people in ordinary life, but he does so as much through a direct knowledge of his own emotions.[36] The adult person has a fund of personal memories and psychic impressions *(saṃskāras)* that enable him not only to recognize and interpret others' behavior but sometimes also to participate in these feelings. It is not true, as has been suggested, that we do not usually experience the emotions we recognize in others. There is such a thing as the power of sympathy, which we have all felt at one time or other. Śaṇkuka's view that poetic emotions are only inferred does not therefore account fully for aesthetic experience. It is true that the spectator must recognize the objective signs, but then he does not merely infer the emotions as being present in others, in which case he cannot feel any sympathetic vibration of the heart, which is essential to aesthetic experience. Therefore, Abhinavagupta says that, in the final analysis, it is one's own mental states that one perceives, the objective situation presented in the work serving simply to awaken the latent impressions or dispositions.[37] When one reads a poem, after one has grasped the verbal meaning that a character, Umā or Hara, felt joy or grief, there appears a direct perception of a mental order in which the meanings of the poem are lived as intimate personal experiences.

The Sanskrit theorist's assumption that there are these inner psychic states or preexisting conditions as distinct from their perceptible signs or symptoms and that they are unapproachable except through a direct experience of them at the interpersonal level of sympathy seems like a regression to the private language argument, which the language philosophers are so worried about. In recent years, theorists like J. L. Austin have tended to deny the existence of subjective states such as anger, grief, and the like apart from their behavioral manifestations.[38] Both Śaṇkuka and Abhinavagupta agree that emotions are mental entities that are not identical with their natural expressions or with their verbal representations. Thus, they both assume that they are logically and epistemologically prior to their outward manifestations while at the same time they admit that they can become known to others only through their external signs.

The ambiguity of this position seems to bear a close resemblance to that of Wittgenstein's. In his anxiety to avoid the extremes of the Cartesian and behaviorist positions, Wittgenstein was compelled to admit that feelings and sensations exist as nonbehavioral and nondispositional mental states but that they cannot be named and investigated independently of the circumstances that produce them and the behaviors by which they are naturally expressed. What Wittgenstein denied was not the internality of sensations but their incommunicability and unteachability. Inner experiences may well and do exist, but what enters our language is what is naturally expressed by behavior. Wittgenstein grants that pain, for instance, is more private than pain behavior, but inasmuch as it is private it plays no part in the language game. But does this mean that pain, this private accompaniment of pain behavior, "drops out of consideration as irrelevant" and no reference is made to it?

At least some of his exponents believe that Wittgenstein did not mean to abolish this inner reference.[39] Chris Gudmunsen has shown that what Wittgenstein as well as Mahāyāna Buddhism meant to deny was not the occurrence of "mental processes"—sensations and feelings like hope, pain, etc.—but the notion that words designate or refer to these entities and are bound together with them in a one-to-one correlation. Words derive their meanings from their use, not from their referents. The final upshot of this is that there is a gap between words and experience: "On the one hand there are inner experiences, and on the other statements about them. The statements, however, are not about the experiences in the way we feel we would like them to be." Private sensations cannot be designated by words except indirectly. Gudmunsen cites the following statement by Wittgenstein: " 'But I do have a real *feeling* of joy (Freude).' Yes, when you are glad you really are glad. And of course joy is not joyful behavior, nor yet a feeling around the corners of the mouth and eyes. 'But "joy" surely designates an inward thing.' No. "Joy" designates nothing at all. Neither any inward nor any outward thing."[40] The Sanskrit critics, including some schools of Indian philosophers, recognized this separation between language and experience; they did not subscribe to the picture theory. But, at the same time, they were emphatic in stating that inner experiences do exist, that they are directly perceived by the mind, and that their perception is their only proof. The *rasa* experience, similarly, brings its own validity *(svataḥ pramāṇa)* and does not demand any external proof by other means of knowledge.

But, even if the case for inner feelings is granted, a problem still remains for the literary critic. If poetry, as Wimsatt and Beardsley put it, "is a way of fixing emotions,"[41] in other words, of presenting the logic of the emotions or the structure of the emotive situation according to Bharata's formula, then would not all reference to its affective quality "drop out of consideration as irrelevant"? Emotions in poetry are presented as meanings inhering in an objective situation, not as private sensations. From this it would seem to follow that a cognitive understanding of these meanings is all that is needed for an understanding of the work. The Sanskrit critics, including Bharata, did not want to admit this because of their concern for setting up the aesthetic object as a source, not so much of knowledge, as of delight. For Bharata, *rasa* is so called because of its relishability, and poetic meaning is something that moves or evokes emotions.[42] Bharata speaks of the emotional thrill that a poem produces in the reader: "When a meaning, charged with emotion, strikes the heart of the sympathetic reader, it courses through his body like fire through a dry log."[43] We seem to have here a familiar variety of affective criticism—a testimony to what Wimsatt and Beardsley call "goose-flesh experience" that one has often met with, for example, in Emily Dickinson's statement that if she felt "physically as if the top of my head were taken off, I know that is poetry," or in Housman's accounts of "shivers down the spine" and the sensation in "the pit of the stomach."[44]

Some commentators on Bharata's doctrine, such as Śaṅkuka and Mahimabhaṭṭa, who followed the school of the logicians, sought to establish the *rasa* theory on a firm cognitive footing and explored the semantic and epistemological basis of poetic meaning rather than merely its affective qualities. But even they attested implicitly to the power of poetry to communicate a valuable affective experience to the reader. For Śaṅkuka, no doubt, the poetic perception is an inferential process—emotions are inferred from their characteristic signs. But he admitted that delight alone would result from this process owing to the very nature of the objects depicted in the poem or play. To both Bhaṭṭanāyaka and Abhinavagupta, despite their differences, *rasa* perception is neither simple inferential knowledge nor a neutral semantic perception but essentially a form of relishing. Abhinavagupta says that the sensitive reader who apprehends the emotive situation does not do so in a neutral frame of mind but is drawn into it owing to the power of sympathy.[45] Thus we do not merely become aware of fear in somebody else when a fear situation is presented in a drama; we also experience the mood of fear, however remotely, as a vibration of the heart. It is not enough that the emotions are inferred in others or that emotive meanings are understood from the words of the poem in the way that factual statements are understood; they must also be found delectable. Otherwise, there would be little incentive to contemplate a work of art, much less to seek a repetition of that experience.

Both Bhaṭṭanāyaka and Abhinavagupta are quite emphatic in stating that poetic apprehension, whether in the poet or in the reader, does not result merely from the ordinary modes of knowledge like inference and verbal cognition, for these modes do not by themselves induce a repeated contemplation of the literary work, which is the very life of the aesthetic attitude.[46] If emotions are merely inferred as existing in others *(paragatatvena)*—in the character or actor—there would be no imaginative identification *(tanmayībhāva)* and no aesthetic delight. If the spectator merely had a clinical perception, as it were, that "This is Rama who is in love with Sita because his circumstances and his behavior are those of a man who is in love," there would not arise any sympathetic response in him because the objects and circumstances that produced love in Rama are not present in him.

Again, poetic apprehension is not inferential knowledge because once an inference is made another inferential act concerning the same object cannot be initiated in the absence of the desire to infer *(sisādhayiṣā)*. In inference, the mind comes to rest once the object is inferred, but not so in aesthetic perception. The same holds for verbal understanding: once a statement is understood, it becomes useless—as an object of knowledge, that is—and there is no reason why you should want to understand it a second time. Hence, poetic messages are different from the injunctions contained in the scriptures or the statements in historical treatises in that they not only convey information but also make that information worthy of repeated contemplation *(carvaṇāviṣaya)*.[47]

Nor do poetic meanings serve any ulterior end as do the meanings of scriptures. The perception of poetic meanings is not of the form "I have been commanded to do this," "I want to do this," "I have done what I had to do," and so on. The gustation of the emotions *(rasāsvāda)* has no reference to what has gone before or what comes after, but like a magical flower it has its essence solely in the moment of its experience. Hence it is quite distinct from ordinary modes of knowledge or from Yogic perception.[48]

Similar considerations led Bhaṭṭanāyaka to assert that *rasa* is neither perceived, produced, nor manifested and to posit a special capacity of poetic language called "evocation" *(bhāvakatva)*, which is a power assumed by words, distinct from their significative capacity *(abhidhā)*, by which the emotions presented in the poem are realized by the reader in a generalized form. He also proposed a second process called "enjoyment" *(bhogīkaraṇa)*, apart from verbal understanding, whereby poetic meanings are enjoyed by the reader.

Abhinavagupta, however, rejects this hypothesis of a distinct aesthetic faculty called enjoyment. He argues that the apprehension of poetic emotions is a form of cognition because that which is not cognized cannot, like a goblin, be discoursed about.[49] There is also nothing called enjoyment that is different from perception or knowledge.[50] His conclusion is that *rasa* experience is a form of direct inner perception that consists of relishing and that the relishing is only a particular type of perception. Poetic apprehension is a form of feeling response *(bhāvanā)* because it induces a repeated contemplation of the object.[51] It (emotional perception) is called by another name, *rasana* or *carvaṇā,* owing to the particular means by which it is called into existence, even as other modes of knowledge like sense perception, inference, and verbal cognition are given different names owing to differences in their means.[52] The difference in this case consists in the fact that emotions are relished even while they are cognized.[53]

Rasa experience is, in other words, a type of emotional perception, not accounted for by other modes of knowledge, but implicit in them. As Viśvanātha explains, it is of the nature of cognizing the aggregate of the situational signs and is identical with the apprehension of the emotion embedded in them.[54] When an emotion is rendered delectable through a representation of its appropriate conditions in poetry, it attains *rasa*-hood.[55]

Thus, the *rasa* theory would be opposed to a purely cognitive view that argues that poetry is a mode of knowledge and contemplated as a pattern of knowledge and that valid cognitive knowledge rather than emotional thrills is the proper aim and mode of existence of poetry.[56] Recent critical theory in the West has had a stake in exalting poetry above the mere matter of emotions and sympathy, or entertainment (a low aim!), to a mode of knowledge. While still maintaining a fundamental difference between the poetic and scientific ways of knowledge, it argues that the end of poetry is no less than the apprehension of reality—to bring greater self-knowlege, to convey an authentic vision of the structure of the mind, and so on. Poetry is set up as a rival to science in that a knowledge function is claimed for it, but it is pointed out that this sensuous, experiential knowledge given by poetry is radically different from the propositional knowledge of science. Science gives us but an emasculated version of the world, and so we need poetry to restore to us "the world's body"—its concrete organic content.

The emphasis on the concrete, presentational, rather than the discursive, aspect of poetry would of course be congenial to the *rasa* theorist. But he would insist that this quality of poetry is what pertains to the very nature of the emotive presentation itself. Emotive presentation is necessarily of a particular situation, character, and action, not of emotions in the abstract. The *rasa* theorist would also deny that it is the function of poetry to make a contribution to our knowledge of the world. Poetry gives us no new knowledge of ourselves—this function is perhaps better served by philosophy and psychology. It rather mirrors the psychic states that are already known to us and dramatizes them or presents them as something experienced. Poetic knowledge is more accurately described as a type of "recognitive" knowledge *(pratyabhijñā)* because it most generally presents what we have already known before but would like to experience again.

It is also argued from the point of view of the cognitive theory that, if poetry is to express emotion, it should do so only in the way in which words like "cat" or "unicorn" may be said to denote certain objects. "Poetry refers denotatively to emotions." It only "denotes" or "signifies" emotions rather than "evoking" them.[57] This is, in a way, admitted by the *rasa* theorist. The objects and other conditions of the emotive situation are denoted by the words that describe them. These words may also be said to "signify" the emotive state, through its objective conditions, that is. But, then, it must be pointed out that, in poetry, objects and facts (cats and unicorns) are presented, not as things to be cognized for their own sake, but as objects of emotion to people. And they are "cognized" as such by the reader. However, the *rasa* theorist sees no harm in admitting that poetic presentations, being emotive statements, can and do also arouse feeling responses in the readers and that these responses are felt as a vibration in the consciousness *(spanda, camatkāra),* even as is the inner perception of pleasure and pain. The predominant note of aesthetic response, though, is wonder and delight, the delight of a marvelous enjoyment *(adbhutabhoga).* It is this logic that leads Abhinavagupta to conclude that *rasa* experience is, in the ultimate analysis, something private.

But, paradoxically, Abhinavagupta as well as the critics who followed him saw no conflict in maintaining that poetic emotions are the property at once of the poet and of his public, intersubjectively, that is, and that they can arise only from the public context of the poem. *Rasa* or the aesthetic relish is common to both the poet and the reader. The poet's initial apprehension of the aesthetic potentiality of his material may be called the seed of the *rasa* manifested in the work. It is only when the poet is filled with *rasa* that the work too will be suffused with it. That is to say, the poet will then be able to think up the right details and put them together in the right way. The same *rasa* will then be manifested in the poem and relished by the reader. But, in a way, both the poet and the reader are viewing the poetic situation in the same "aesthetic" light and having the same kind of perception—the poet while composing the poem and the reader while contemplating the finished work.[58] The character or the person of the play or poem cannot of course be said to have an "aesthetic" perception of the emotions he is undergoing. But, inasmuch as his experience is the nucleus of the poem or the poetic occasion (the poet puts himself into the experience of the character, and the reader too does the same in contemplating the poem), they are all bound together in a common matrix.[59] The assumption of such an affinity of nature is vital to any conception of emotive aesthetics. Since, thus, the whole poetic process is fraught with emotionality, and since the emotive element is what makes our experience of literature a valuable one, it would be wrong to abolish all affective reference, as the cognitive critics tend to do.

I have argued from the standpoint of the *rasa* theory that the values a poem communicates are emotive, not cognitive, and that the experience provided by them is, by common consent, held to be pleasurable. It is not of course the case that whatever values people perceive in a work are out there in the work as properties of an object, like the flatness of a table. It is, on the other hand, because an emotive situation is already freighted with value that people recognize the signs of value in a poetic presentation. In turn, of course, they see these values as factors in the object that account for their rapturous experience.[60] In any case, it seems absurd to say that feelings exist in the poem as objective qualities but that they cannot be experienced and shared as feelings or that literary works can be effective in specific ways but that they need not produce any effects in the minds of readers. For one thing, such a claim would fly in the face of overwhelming public testimony. The objection that the reader's response to a poem is variable, being something subjective, also need not be taken seriously. For, although reactions may vary in degrees of intensity, they appear to be the same in kind. It is not conceivable that someone who witnesses *King Lear* will react to it in any other way than that in which one normally reacts to a tragedy.

This argument does not perhaps set to rest the initial question, namely, the relevance of affective reference to critical discourse. The assertion that a play like *King Lear* arouses the tragic emotion, besides expressing it, plays no part in our criticism of the work as an adequate or inadequate presentation of the tragic situation. The structure of events, the characters' speech and behavior, the propriety of the language to the speaker and situation, and so on are matters that can be appraised only in terms of certain public norms, conventions, and usage. We do not judge the work by measuring the degree of emotion it has aroused in us or in others, as we do not have adequate means for that purpose. Even if it is granted that a literary work must arouse feelings because it expresses feelings and also that feelings have a way of spreading to others by the power of sympathy, it would be redundant for purposes of critical statement to say that the work arouses feelings because this idea is implied in the fact of the work being an expression of feelings, and it would not be critically significant since it does not provide the criterion by which the presented situation may be appraised.

However, it can be claimed for the *rasa* theorist that, in spite of his interest in the psychology of aesthetic response, he does not make critical judgment a matter of the reader having some private thrills. The public criteria are never lost sight of—so much so that the objectivity of the work itself as a verbal construct and of all discourse in connection with it is fully guaranteed.[61] Even Abhinavagupta, despite his transcendental vocabulary, is at no time seen to neglect logic or leave the objective work behind. While he speaks at length of *rasa* as aesthetic experience, he also draws a clear distinction between the "excitement" of the reader *(rasāveśa)* and the emotion objectified in the work and says that, because the response of a reader is not something fixed but contingent on his disposition, one should be guided by the verbal presentation of the emotion alone. The excitement of the reader is possible only through the *rasa* manifested in the work itself.[62] It is only the *rasa* objectified in the work that is fit for comment. It is assumed of course that poetry gives pleasure and that it exists for that purpose only. But pleasure as such, while it may help differentiate the fine arts from the useful arts—and this may be the whole point of Abhinavagupta's elaborations on aesthetic experience—does not furnish the criterion for critical evaluation. That is why both Plato and Aristotle, while they recognized pleasure, were careful to subordinate that consideration to the concern with the object of imitation.[63]

Abhinavagupta's excursions into the psychology of response must therefore be understood only as an attempt to describe and isolate the aesthetic state and to indicate why people consider it to be valuable, not as a groundwork for the criticism of literary works themselves. There is no suggestion in Abhinavagupta or in the critics who followed him that the aesthetic object is beyond analysis and accessible only to subjective contemplation. The whole body of Sanskrit criticism is, in fact, primarily devoted to problems of poetic semantics and to the setting up of rules and principles for judging works of literature. Critical interpretation in Sanskrit, too, is predominantly cognitive and addressed to the task of explicating poetic meanings. The Sanskrit critic hardly ever talks about his own experience but rather concentrates on the linguistic form, the concrete body of literature, and its efficacy in terms of its expressive function. Thus, the emphasis is predominantly objective and analytic. The concern with the psychology of response is at best secondary.

3

THE ESSENTIALITY OF THE EMOTIONS

The *rasa* theory asserts not simply that poetry expresses emotions but that the expression of emotions is the sole aim and the common denominator of all literary productions. The evocative purpose, it claims, is what differentiates literary discourse from other types of discourse. That poetry expresses feelings and communicates emotive values will be accepted by many. But the further claim that the emotive element is the only thing of importance in poetry and that it can satisfactorily account for all elements of value in it and for all types of literary writing will be seriously questioned. It was questioned by the critics of the Rhetorical (Alaṃkāra) school, who thought of poetry mainly in terms of its linguistic, structural features. But the advocates of *rasa* maintained that the belief that a poetic statement, of whatever kind, can be valued for anything but its emotive element is a chimera. For there is no poetry that has not a touch of emotion; behind every image or idea is the ghost of an emotion lurking. Again, emotion is not simply implicit in all poetic expression; it is the sole point of reference and measure for judging the efficacy of all its elements, such as diction, image, form, and style. *Rasa* is the shaping principle and inner essence *(ātman)* of poetic art.

The Problem of Definition

A theory that claims for the emotive principle a place of centrality in poetic discourse must of course consider the various elements of poetry and determine their relative importance. It must, in other words, define the nature of poetry in terms of its necessary and sufficient conditions. The problem of definition engaged the minds of the Sanskrit theorists in a most serious way since it was deemed to be of crucial importance for critical discourse. For, obviously, no critical discussion of literature is possible until we know the nature of the thing we are studying. Therefore, it was customary for every manual of poetics to begin with a chapter on the nature of literature and then to proceed to an analysis of its constituent elements. Moreover, poetics, in the Sanskrit, as in the Western classical, tradition, was understood as a scientific discipline *(śāstra)* rather than as an expression of taste or personal preferences. Any generalization about the nature of literature had to be strictly logical: it must extend to all instances of the type denoted by the term and must not include instances not covered by it. It must, in other words, avoid the faults of "too narrow" *(avyāpti)* and "too wide" *(ativyāpti)*. A formal definition *(lakṣaṇa)* of a term should isolate "the property which serves to distinguish the thing defined from all other things."[1]

But it was by no means the case that the Sanskrit critics arrived at such a rigorously logical definition of poetry. The task was obviously not an easy one even for these pundits who, with all their scholastic training, brought to their task the combined force of logic, grammar, and semantic analysis. Bharata, the first systematic writer, does not attempt a formal definition of poetry. His approach is descriptive rather than logical. He enumerates and analyzes various linguistic and formal features of dramatic poetry, such as diction, figures, metrical patterns, styles, and so forth. However, he does assert that *rasa* is the most vital element in poetry and that there can be no real poetry in the absence of *rasa*.[2] But the force of this assertion was lost on subsequent generations until the advent of the *dhvani* critics. The generally descriptive emphasis of Bharata's treatment seems to have set the pattern for a large majority of even post-*dhvani* critics, who, in their attempt to do justice to all the elements mentioned by Bharata, offered undiscriminating, blanket-term definitions that seek to accommodate virtually all the elements that are found in poetry. Typical of this kind is Hemacandra's syncretistic definition: "Poetry is word and meaning [together], that are free from faults, possessed of excellences [special qualities of sound and sense] and figures."[3] In this he follows Mammaṭa, who, in spite of his acceptance of the centrality of the *rasa-dhvani* principle, offers much the same definition, but with the proviso that poetry can sometimes be without figures.[4]

There was also another line of theorists who delighted in inventing master concepts like *vakrokti* ("curved" or "crooked" speech), *camatkāra* (poetic charm), and *aucitya* (propriety), by reference to which they sought to account for all known elements of poetic art.[5] Some others loosely employed terms like "special" *(viśiṣṭa)*, "agreeable" *(iṣṭa)*, and "charming" *(ramaṇīya)* in speaking of poetic meanings.[6] However, the critics of the Rhetorical school, beginning with Bhāmaha, also lent a certain focus to critical discussion through their attempt to discover the poetic differentia. Thus, the two major principles of definition to emerge from this school were (i) deviant expression *(vakrokti,* understood in a broad sense and as including the principle of figuration or *alaṃkāra),* which was first expounded by Bhāmaha and later developed into a master concept by Kuntaka, and (ii) style (or *rīti*), advocated by Vāmana. The *dhvani* critics, who propounded the theory of suggestion, shift the focus of discussion from the purely formal, structural emphasis of the previous schools and advance a novel theory of poetic semantics. But they also, paradoxically, uphold Bharata's doctrine of *rasa* and admit that as the ultimate term of reference and the defining principle.

Criteria of Definition

There were, in the main, four major schools of poetic criticism in Sanskrit: (i) the Alaṃkāra school (figurationists)—Kuntaka may be counted among them, in spite of his slightly different emphasis; (ii) the Rīti school (though confined to one man, Vāmana); (iii) the Dhvani school (of suggestion); and (iv) the Rasa school. The concept of *rasa,* propounded by Bharata, was, as I said above, developed and defended by the *dhvani* critics Ānandavardhana and Abhinavagupta. But it was not used by them as the sole principle of definition. It was subsumed under the larger concept of suggestion. It was the later critics Viśvanātha and Mahimabhaṭṭa who attempted a strict definition of poetry in terms of *rasa.* But the substance of their argument still came from the formulations of the *dhvani* exponents, who, in a sense, may also be referred to as the *rasa* theorists.

The first two schools, Alaṃkāra and Rīti, were, in spite of mutual differences, formalists in their approach to literature in that they believed that either deviant expression or formal structuring of one sort or another was the defining characteristic of poetry. The *dhvani* theorists, on the other hand, tried to distinguish literature by positing a special semantics of suggestion. The *rasa* theory seeks its principle of definition, not in any peculiarity of the linguistic medium, or in any special semantics of poetry, but in the kind of meaning that literature purports to communicate. It argues that the presentation of emotions is the proper object and domain of poetic discourse. This conclusion was implicit in Bharata but stated explicitly by Abhinavagupta and, in effect, also by Ānandavardhana.

Figuration, style, suggestion, and *rasa* were then the chief contenders in the debate pertaining to the nature of literature. There were, no doubt, other concepts that figured in critical discussions. I will look at some of them briefly, but only to dismiss them since they were not employed as instruments of definition.

Imagination was one such concept. The Sanskrit equivalent for this term is *pratibhā* (literally, poetic genius), and this faculty was distinguished from logical or analytic reasoning, called *prajñā*.[7] But, although nearly all critics paid homage to it, they never used it as a term of definition. It is important to note in this connection that the Sanskrit manuals make a clear distinction between the cause of poetic creation *(kāvya-hetu),* the "fruits" accruing from it *(kāvya-phala)* or the purpose served by it *(kāvya-prayojana),* and the nature of poetry *(kāvya-lakṣaṇa).* Significantly, *pratibhā* is mentioned as only one of the causes of poetry, together with training *(śikṣā)* and understanding of the world *(vyutpatti),* and not in the context of the definition of poetry. In fact, it may be safely concluded that Sanskrit poetics does not offer a systematic doctrine of the imagination; there is nothing in it to match the speculations of a Coleridge. But this, I think, is hardly a matter to be regretted because imagination is at best a dubious concept, and its usefulness for criticism has not been proved.[8]

Even as the Sanskrit critics do not try to define literature in terms of a special poetic faculty, they also do not define it in terms of its uses or good results or the purpose it serves in the system of human values. It is often stated, however, that the study of poetry brings both worldly goods and ultimate spiritual goods and contributes to the realization of the fourfold goals of man: *dharma* (righteous living), *artha* (worldly prosperity), *kāma* (worldly desire), and *mokṣa* (spiritual liberation). This statement is often made in apology to the logicians and the orthodox Vedic scholars, who said, "One should abandon the poetic talk."[9] Abhinavagupta rejects the view of poetry as an instrument of moral discipline or spiritual edification.[10] The *rasa* theory, which all critics accept implicitly, makes the experience of poetry an end in itself. Poetry has no utility value; it has to be valued purely for the aesthetic thrill it affords.

This is not of course to say that neither knowledge nor moral edification can be one of its aims. This is only to say that, whatever may have been the intent of the poet, it will be realized only in the form of delight, not in the form of a knowledge acquired, as something to be relished rather than as a belief we must subscribe to. Moreover, both aims, namely, pleasure and instruction or edification, may coexist in the reader's experience of an art object without a conflict being perceived between the two. For example, the Hindu epic *Rāmāyaṇa* is considered a holy scripture, but people read it equally for its poetic (human) interest.

That is to say that, although some people use the poem as an object of utility in the service of religion, it does not cease to be an artwork, a *rasa-kāvya,* and it is treated as such by the literary critics. Therefore, the Sanskrit critics separate the question of "fruits" from the consideration of the intrinsic properties of poetry, on which alone a true definition can be based. A true definition of poetry must also be inclusive enough to provide for the greatest possible variety of expression, regardless of whether it is intended as "play" (*krīḍā,* entertainment) or propaganda, whether it is encomium, wise saying, or moral exhortation.[11]

The Sanskrit critics also regard aesthetic experience as a unique sort of pleasure that only poetry can afford. They do not dismiss the "aesthetic emotion" as a "phantom state,"[12] although they say that it is only an extension of the ordinary psychic states of love, fear, sorrow, and so on freed from their limiting conditions of time, place, and person and therefore savored for its own sake. This is an important tenet of the *rasa* doctrine. However, the Sanskrit critics do not, as I stated in chapter 2, fall into the error of identifying poetry by the kind of experience it generates. To say that an aesthetic object yields a supernal joy is one thing and to define the object itself in terms of that effect quite another. I have stated that the main purpose of the Sanskrit critics was to analyze the poetic object rather than to dwell on its psychological effects. Understood in the light of this aim, *rasa* is the objective structure of meaning embodied in the poem, not purely the emotion generated by it.

In the West, "imitation" and "mimetic illusion" have long served as useful criteria for defining literature. In Sanskrit criticism, too, the notions of imitation and fictionality were entertained by many theorists before Abhinavagupta. Bharata spoke of drama as a mimetic reproduction *(anukaraṇa).* But this term was used largely in the context of the theater; it was nowhere offered as a definition of poetry as a verbal composition. A literary work is generally characterized in some such terms as "description" *(varṇanā)* or "depiction" or "exposition" of the emotions *(rasa-pratipādana)* rather than as a creation of semblance. In any case, as we shall see in chapter 9, Abhinavagupta rejects both the theory of drama as imitation and its implications of fictionality and representational illusion. Mimetic terms, such as "likeness making" *(sadṛśa-karaṇa),* "similitude" *(sādṛśya),* and "correspondent form" *(prati-rūpam, pratimā, pratikṛti),* are employed in Sanskrit treatises on art in the context of portrait painting and sculpture. The sacred images were, thought of, however, not as "likenesses" of any visible models but as symbolic representations of certain concepts, designed in accordance with canonical prescriptions.[13] Thus, in spite of the wide currency the term *anukaraṇa* had enjoyed in Sanskrit aesthetics, it can safely be concluded that mimesis was not a seminal principle in the Indian critical tradition, as it was in the Greek.[14]

There are, then, only four concepts that have been advanced as defining principles—figuration, style, suggestion, and *rasa*—whose claims we should now proceed to examine.

Poetry as Figurative Language

The pre-Dhvani school critics—Bhāmaha, Udbhaṭa, Daṇḍin, and Rudraṭa—were chiefly rhetoricians, interested in the analysis, definition, and classification of figurative types. Their basic analysis of poetic language was into sound or word form *(śabda)* and sense *(artha),* from which they derived the various categories of figures—phonetic and syntactic figures and figures of thought. Apart from the figurative types, they also analyzed special arrangements of phonemes, words, and sentences into stylistic structures or stereotypes. Certain collocations of phonemes, word compounds, and syntactic patterns were also supposed to possess special "qualities" *(guṇas),* such as sweetness, energy, clarity, and so forth, that were deemed to be aesthetically valuable. These qualities formed the basis for the classification of poetic styles into the graceful, the energetic, or mixed, or based on the practice of certain geographic regions, into Pāñcālī, Gauḍī, and so forth. All these elements, for them, constituted the formal body of poetry, as opposed to its thought content. The formal, linguistic features were, according to these critics, what lent charm to poetic expression; hence, they came to be known as poetic ornaments *(kāvyālaṃkāras).*[15] Thus, Daṇḍin defines the poetic body or content *(kāvya-śarīra)* as a sequence of words conveying a "desired" or agreeable meaning and the figures as the heighteners of its beauty.[16] Here, however, the implication is not that figures embellish the mere external form of poetry, as opposed to its inner spirit or soul *(ātman),* but that they are in fact an essential characteristic of the poetic mode—what makes poetry poetic.[17] The poetic body is constituted by sound and sense and rendered picturesque by figures; figuration is poetry's special mode of being. As such, it accounts for the whole body of what these critics call "poetic beauty." As Kuntaka explains, although when one speaks of poetry as embellished expression (or of language as the dress of thought) a distinction is implied between the meaning embellished and the embellishment, there is no real separation. The condition of being embellished is not something that is superadded to a preexistent nonpoetic content, but it is organically related to the way in which poetic utterance is conceived. Poeticity belongs to the undifferentiated totality of all the constituent elements of a composition. It is only for analytic purposes that one separates the two and speaks of the word and the sense as the embellished and the figurative manner as the embellisher *(alaṃkāra).*[18]

Implicit in all figuration is the principle of deviant expression. At the root of all figures is some element of exaggeration *(atiśayokti)* or "crooked" or oblique manner of speech *(vakrokti).* Thus, for Bhāmaha, the first writer in the rhetorical tradition, deviant expression is found in all poetic figures. "By this are poetic meanings defined."[19] Even the simplest figure, simile, involves the comparison of objects that are dissimilar with reference to place, time, or action.[20] Grammatical or phonetic regularity, as in chime, alliteration, and the like, too, is not characteristic of ordinary speech. Bhāmaha declares that all kinds of literature, both verse and prose, all types of styles, and all manner of presenting ideas or emotions "become important only if characterized by crookedness of speech."[21] You render speech interesting or arresting not by using plenty of superlatives and exclamations but only by cleverness in words and meanings.[22] Bhāmaha asks, " 'The sun has set, the moon shines, the birds are returning to their nests.' What sort of poetry is this? One calls this 'information.' "[23] Bhāmaha disregards the claims of "realistic portrayal" or naturalistic description *(svabhāvokti)* to be considered a figurative type, for a description of objects as they are in nature would indeed be dull and insipid without some element of surprise, some uncommon aspect, or some striking turn of expression to raise it above banality.[24]

The writers who followed Bhāmaha—Udbhaṭa, Daṇḍin, and Rudraṭa—adopted the general principles laid down by him and shared the same concern with figurative expression. However, they were willing to admit natural description to the status of a figure since even portraying an object according to its nature involves seeing it in an unusual light or an interesting perspective. Kuntaka, following Bhāmaha, rules out the case for natural description, understood as a matter-of-fact reporting of things as they are, but admits that such descriptions, although not deviant or striking in their form, can become heightened into poetry depending on the way the poet conceives and presents his subject.[25] By the same token, even descriptions of emotive conditions acquire a striking quality because they require an artful selection and development of the details of the theme.[26]

In Kuntaka, expressional deviation *(vakrokti)* is developed into a major doctrine comprehending all elements of poetic language. Kuntaka works out a detailed application of this concept to morphemes, to words and grammatical parts, to sentences, to particular topics, and finally, to larger compositions considered as wholes.[27] He tries to show that deviancy accounts for poetic charm in all these aspects of a poetic composition. He does not deal directly with figurative categories, their definition and classification, as the previous writers did, but subsumes the principle of figuration itself under the larger operations of deviant expression. Only an embellished or heightened form of expression deserves the designation of poetry.[28] But all heightening devices, including figures and stylistic (i.e., phonological and syntactical) features, are but the constituent elements of deviant speech—which is the common characteristic of all poetic ornaments and which is indeed synonymous with poetic activity.

Another concept that is implied in this approach to poetry through its formal-linguistic body and that runs concurrently with the notion of deviant expression is that of poetry as a special relation between, or a harmonious conjunction or "togetherness" *(sāhitya)* of, word and meaning. Bhāmaha, who was the first to propound this idea, emphasized the equal importance of the figures of sound and the figures of sense. Both sound and sense must contribute to the liveliness of poetic speech. "Word and meaning taken together constitute poetry."[29] Kuntaka understands this "togetherness" as a certain commensurateness *(saṃmitatva)* or tension *(paraspara-spardha)* between sound and sense. Neither a string of beautiful-sounding words nor a commonplace idea or a logical proposition will make for poetry.[30] It is only when both these are in conjunction and vie with each other that they generate any charm. A mere togetherness of word and sense—their innate relation—is not of course what is meant here since it is an indispensable condition of all intelligible speech. In no case can the word and its meaning afford to be divorced from each other. Therefore, this relation of word and meaning, in the poetic context, must be of a special sort: it lies in the mounted tension of the various features of sound and sense, "rendered striking by the operation of deviant expression *(vakratā)*."[31]

Poetry as Style

The figurationists no doubt considered the elements of style, such as structural features and style qualities, but they included all such elements in the general concept of figures or in the greater principle of expressional deviation. They gave greater relative importance to rhetorical figures than to style. In Vāmana, the first exponent of the doctrine of *rīti,* this position is reversed. Vāmana understands style as "a special ordonnance of words," the speciality consisting in the qualities, both of sound and of meaning, that particular collocations of phonemes, words, and larger syntactic units generate. The figures per se, both the phonetic and the lexical types, are subordinated to the principle of structuring. Poetry is defined by this principle; the figures are shown to be noninherent features and hence inessential, whereas the qualities located in style can contribute to poetic effect even without the help of figures.[32] Later critics of the Dhvani school take the cue from Vāmana and argue that figuration is neither a necessary nor a sufficient condition for a composition to be poetry. They also go a step further and assert that even compositional features, such as those discussed by Vāmana and the previous writers, are not indispensable for poetry. Moreover, the "qualities," which for Vāmana and others resided in verbal structures, are, in the view of the *dhvani* critics, affective properties located in emotive meanings, which the verbal structures acquire by association.[33]

The figurative poetic of the Alaṃkāra school seeks to provide a comprehensive principle for differentiating literary from nonliterary discourse by showing that a great many forms of expression and literary devices can be comprehended under figurative language. Vāmana's doctrine of style makes literary language a matter of structured expression and syntax. Neither theory of course ignores meaning in poetry. But poetic meaning itself is treated, not for its own intrinsic quality, but as an aspect of form. Poetry is primarily a mode of saying, a way of enforming ideas, rather than a kind of meaning or a type of discourse. In both theories, the focus of analysis rests heavily on the language of poetry, its formal body, not so much on its semantic content.

What we have during the pre–Dhvani school period is an endless proliferation of rhetorical and stylistic categories without any formulation of the one regulative principle by reference to which all elements of poetic language could be judged for their efficacy. The critics of the Dhvani school, Ānandavardhana and Abhinavagupta, give a new turn to the discussion of the problem of definition. The theory propounded by Ānandavardhana has come to be known as the theory of suggestion. But, as will become evident in what follows, it is a composite doctrine consisting of a theory of verbal function and a theory of a special poetic context, namely, *rasa,* which, by a sleight of hand, as it were, these critics manage to conflate into a single concept.

Poetry as Suggestion

The doctrine of *dhvani* seeks to identify poetry in terms of a special semantic function called implication or suggestion. It assumes that there is a third power of words or a third kind of meaning that is distinct from the two well-known verbal functions, namely, primary meaning and secondary or metaphorical meaning. Suggestion is a supernumerary meaning that comes into play when both the literal and the metaphorical functions have ceased their operation. But it flows from either literal or metaphorical meaning as a further implicative dimension—which may be an idea, a figure, or an emotive implication. Poetic figures, whether they involve metaphoric transference of one kind or another or explicit comparison (as in the simile), are still, according to *dhvani* theory, on the level of the expressed sense of words, whereas *dhvani* is essentially a technique of indirection.

A detailed examination of the implications of this theory will be reserved for chapter 6. What concerns us here is the validity of this concept as a principle of definition. The first question to be asked is, need all poetry necessarily arise from indirection or implication, however this function is defined? There is, for instance, a poetry of direct statement, of prophetic or visionary assertion (e.g., Wordsworth and Whitman) that cannot be called suggestive even by stretching that term. Emotive statements too can often be direct, and I shall argue that the evocation of emotions in poetry cannot be assigned to a special semantic function. There is also another kind of poetry, of "expressed" figures, according to the *dhvani* theorists, comprising the whole body of figurative expression, which is branded by them as inferior poetry. By excluding such poetry from the proper designation of poetry, the *dhvani* theory may be guilty of imposing an undue restriction on the scope of poetic expression and dealing with a special class of poetry rather than with poetry as such.

Second, is all poetry arising from *dhvani* good poetry? Ānandavardhana claims that all ideas, however trite and well worn, and all poetic figures suddenly spring to life at the magic touch of *dhvani*. The only way to test this claim is to look at his own examples. The following is one such example: "Only three types of men are eligible to harvest the gold-flowered earth—the brave men, the learned, and those who learn to serve." This statement is said to be a case of suggestion based on metaphor. The metaphorical expression "harvest the gold-flowered earth" indicates the idea of enjoying the fruits of the earth. But the intended praise of the three classes of people who are fit to enjoy the fruits of the earth is, instead of being stated explicitly, suggested through indirection. This may be a perfect example of *dhvani* in a strictly technical sense. But it is difficult to see in it all the secret charm that Abhinavagupta, in his commentary, attributes to it. He says that, because the intended meaning is concealed, it acquires a charm "like the cup-like breasts of a maiden."[34]

A certain polemic fervor would seem to vitiate the better judgment of the *dhvani* critics and make them blind to the real poetic merit of much fine writing. Not only do they tend to praise trivial lines on the ground that they contain an element of indirection (the texts are replete with such instances), but they equally tend to berate good poems because they are found wanting in indirection. Even supposing that there is a suggestive function of words distinct from their expressive function, must we discredit a fine simile or metaphor on the ground that it is based on the expressed sense of words? The real test of excellence of poetic figures is not covertness but their aptness and luminosity of conception and their power to objectify a feeling or idea. Again, if *rasa,* as I would argue, is to be eliminated from the scope of suggestion, the difference between *dhvani* and *alaṃkāra* (figuration) would be reduced to a difference in nomenclature. The *dhvani* critics do not show convincingly that a genuine distinction exists between suggestion and certain varieties of figurative expression. The specimens cited by them consist for the most part of forms of paradox, irony, condensed metaphor, and so forth, which the traditional writers would certainly regard as cases of oblique or deviant expression. No wonder, then, that the proponents of this theory themselves, in effect, give up the case for *dhvani* when they subject that concept to the jurisdiction of another, more central, concept, namely, *rasa,* and make that the overall subsuming principle of definition.

Poetry as Emotive Meaning

The *dhvani* theory fails to show that there is a special semantics of literature. Obviously, literature exploits all the resources of language—phonic, grammatical, and lexical—direct and oblique expression, and conventional and deviant features. The best definition of literature is perhaps contextual and one that takes into account the nature of the literary situation and the purpose and motivation of the sentences employed in it. It is easier to define the nature and type of a discourse by its context than by its linguistic form.[35] It is in these terms that the *rasa* theory conceives of the nature of literature. The purpose of literary discourse is, according to this theory, neither the statement of universal truths nor the prompting of men to action but "evocation." Bhaṭṭanāyaka, a staunch defender of the *rasa* doctrine as well as a critic of *dhvani,* distinguishes the poetic from other forms of literature, such as the Vedas, scientific, ethical, and historical texts, by its evocative aim *(bhāvakatva).* In poetry, both words and meanings directly contribute to the aim of *rasa*-evocation and are subordinated to that activity.[36]

Abhinavagupta agrees with Bhaṭṭanāyaka that the function of poetic language can be said to consist only in evocation.[37] Pleasure alone is the primary end of poetry; the instruction provided by it is but a remote aim.[38] In his commentary on Bharata, he states that drama, though a form of verbal knowledge, is distinct from the scriptures and scientific treatises, whose aim it is to instruct or to give information, because its mode and purpose are primarily presentational; in it, emotions are rendered immediately as objects of gustation.[39] Poetry too, he declares, is in this sense essentially enactment, although language is its sole medium and mode of presentation.[40] Bharata had stated that "no poetic meaning subsists without *rasa*."[41] According to his etymology, *bhāvas* (emotions in poetry) are so called because they bring into being (*bhāvayanti,* evoke) corresponding aesthetic moods.[42] They are an "instrument of causation" *(karaṇa-sādhanam).*[43] Therefore, Abhinavagupta concludes that "*rasa* is the fundamental aim and purport of poetry."[44] He never tires of reminding us that "there is no poetry that is devoid of *rasa*. . . . Poetry lives by *rasa* alone."[45] Ānandavardhana too says, "Where *rasa,* in its various forms, is not the subject matter of discourse there no manner of poetry is possible."[46]

Since the evocative function is thus a necessary condition of all language that deserves the designation of poetry, it follows that all elements found in poetry, such as ideas, images, figures, and structural features, are subservient to this function. This the *rasa* theorist proceeds to demonstrate. He argues that ideational elements have no independent interest in poetry except insofar as they are, in some way, connected to the speaker's feelings and attitudes. Poetry has no use for facts unless they are related to an emotive situation. The difference between history and poetry is that, in the former, facts are related for what they are worth, as information, whereas in the latter they are shown to be affecting someone's feelings. Abhinavagupta remarks that the mere relating of events does not constitute drama; it would be drama only when events are presented with a view to exhibiting the feeling qualities latent in them.[47] There is no poetic theme that is not infused with *rasa,* no object that does not become the cause of an emotion. This applies to descriptions of nonhuman or inanimate objects as well; they invariably become factors in the humanizing perception. There can be no purely objective description of insentient things.[48]

There can also be no poetry of thought as opposed to a poetry of feeling.[49] The profound eschatological reflections of Sir Thomas Browne, the serene nature meditations of Wordsworth, and the metaphysical discriminations of Wallace Stevens—all have a feeling content, however implicit, and become connected to the objects and expressions of some feeling or other. Stevens's "Thirteen Ways of Looking at a Blackbird" and "Anecdote of a Jar" are not, to the extent that they are poetry, merely motives for metaphor, or ideas of order, or analyses of metaphysica, but express the poet's sense of wonder at certain phenomena of perception, in spite of the popular view that the poet is interested simply in exploring the workings of the imaginative faculty for the sheer knowledge value of it.

Even as all themes and ideas become poetic when infused with *rasa,* all elements of language—figure, meter, rhyme, and all such verbal and phonological devices—must also derive their efficacy from a *rasa* context by contributing to the evocative function. They do not rest in themselves since they can be understood only through *rasa,* which is the final resting point of all poetic discourse.[50] In reply to the figurative argument, the *rasa* theorist maintains that figures are inessential and dispensable. Compositions possess abundant charm if they treat their themes in keeping with *rasa,* even though they may be devoid of any well-defined or striking figures.[51] Figurativeness cannot be employed as the differentia of poetry because of the faults of "too broad" and "too narrow": much nonpoetic discourse is figurative—the Vedas are full of figurative expressions—and some poetry is nonfigurative, for example, emotive statements and realistic descriptions. Ānandavardhana says that figures are extraneous in the sense that they are modes of patterning sounds and meanings or peculiarities of expression and hence pertain to the linguistic form, the "body" of poetry *(kāvya-śarīra),* not to its intrinsic nature *(kāvyātman),* namely, *rasa.*[52] However, they do function in association with emotive meanings when they are used appropriately. But, since they do not appear in invariable association with *rasa,* they should not form part of the definition of poetry.[53]

The same holds for style *(rīti),* understood as a particular disposition of words and syntactic units. The established view of the *rasa* theorist with regard to the status of style is that stylistic features—clever combinations of sounds, striking syntactic arrangements, and so forth—have no aesthetic value when they are cultivated without regard to the particularities of meaning.[54] Nor are they organically or invariably related to the meanings expressed by words. When there is a proper emotive context, however, such features perform an evocative function, although not in an invariable manner.[55] Moreover, there can be poetry even without any structural peculiarities. Thus, style too cannot serve as the differentia of poetry.

The view of poetic language outlined above is, paradoxically enough, a view advanced by the *dhvani* theorists themselves, who, by their theory of suggestion, were at the same time arguing for a special poetic semantics. The inconsistency of their position lies in the fact that, although they start out with a theory of poetic language, they end up by propounding a theory of poetic context. *Rasa,* being the proper aim of poetic discourse, is what provides a context for the functioning of the linguistic form. The delineation of the emotions depends not on any special linguistic operation or structuring but on there being an emotive situation consisting of certain causes that produce emotive attitudes in people, who register them in their behavior (speech and action). This situation, these critics themselves say repeatedly, is described through the literal function of words itself. Such descriptions may no doubt make the fullest use of figurative and other devices, but they are not dependent on any one of them. The *dhvani* critics argue, however, that the emotive import of the described situation is obtained through suggestion. But this latter point, as I shall show in chapter 6, is not convincingly made. At any rate, both Ānandavardhana and Abhinavagupta admit that suggestion only culminates in *rasa* because of the essential character of the latter.[56] If this is the case, then, it is *rasa,* not *dhvani,* that should be taken as the central, subsuming principle from which all other theories and explanations of poetry must derive their validity.

From a reading of the classic work *Dhvanyāloka* and the "Locana" commentary, one thus gets the impression that the emphasis of their authors is divided between suggestion and *rasa.* For, in defining the essential characteristic of poetry, they still stick to *dhvani* and incorporate that term in their definition. Later writers like Viśvanātha, in his *Sāhityadarpaṇa,* and Mahimabhaṭṭa, in his *Vyaktiviveka,* take strong exception to the definition of poetry in terms of suggestion. Viśvanātha objects that mere suggestiveness, indirection, or obliqueness cannot be the defining property of poetry since even riddles and the like would then have to be admitted to the rank of poetry. His own formal definition of poetry is "a composition whose essential characteristic is rasa."[57] If *rasa* is accepted as the necessary condition of poetry, then all other elements, such as figures and style, can take their proper place as its "causes of heightening," according to their function in an emotive context, and poetic blemishes *(doṣas)* can be understood as "detractors thereof."

Mahimabhaṭṭa does not accept suggestion as a verbal function at all—it is inferential meaning. Neither is *rasa,* according to him, a special type of poetry since all poetry is by definition *rasa* expression. Charming words and turns of expression, which is what suggestion finally amounts to, do not constitute poetry if they are devoid of *rasa.*[58] Therefore Mahimabhaṭṭa declares that "poetry is to be understood as the description of the causes and circumstances of emotions."[59] It is simply "the art of selecting and combining the elements of an emotive attitude or situation."[60] Ideas and formal features can aid in manifesting *rasa* only by being absorbed into its causes and expressions.[61] It is interesting to note that this is precisely what the *dhvani* theorists themselves seem to be saying in spite of their commitment to suggestion. Often it would seem that, when they are talking about *dhvani,* they actually mean *rasa.*

This argument of the *rasa* theorist that the emotive content alone is of primary importance in poetry and that language and style are subsidiary may be challenged on two grounds. First, it may be pointed out that certain compositional features, such as parallel and antithetical construction, rhythm, and style qualities (density, symmetry, and so on), and the figurative or indirect mode of expression possess an intrinsic interest regardless of emotive content and that such characteristics are in fact constitutive of the aesthetic character of a work. Second, the *rasa* doctrine cannot account for every type of literature either. There are, for instance, pure descriptions of mountains, rivers, and cataracts and interesting accounts of the behavior of monkeys, children, and so forth. It would be farfetched to try to show that some remote connection with *rasa* exists even in such cases. If *rasa* is such a pervasive element, then, why not accept it in such sentences as "There goes the cow," "The deer is running," and so on? Such, in fact, is the substance of Jagannātha's objection to the definition offered by Viśvanātha that poetry is essentially emotive discourse.[62]

The *rasa* theorist can answer these objections. To the point that formal features or figurative devices could be aesthetically significant in themselves, it may be replied that no one would use such devices—a deliberate metaphor or a turn of expression—pointlessly. All such expressions must have a motive and a context—either to secure emphasis, to clinch a point, to produce a reaction, or just to be funny. A strikingly metaphorical or alliterative speech, for instance, would be a madman's talk if employed without any contextual relevance. In poetry, the motive for employing them is to create a vivid presentational effect. It is from the emotive context that linguistic forms derive their force and come to be recognized as style. Style in poetry is largely a matter of contextual function.[63] Again, even such statements as "The deer is running" would, given an appropriate setting, be expressive of attitudes and feelings. When, for instance, observing the animal's suppleness and grace of movement, someone says, "Look, the deer is running!" the feeling could be wonder. The nature descriptions of Thomson, to give another instance, are not mere objective reports but suggest a mood, usually of sublime wonder. This would be true of even the slightest imagist lyric where nothing happens and no emotion is expressed. But even here there is an implicit attitude—wonder or some such feeling. Otherwise, the utterance would be pointless as a speech act. As Beardsley observes, a poem, as an illocutionary act, must contain three fundamental features —"an implicit dramatic speaker, a situation, the speaker's attitude toward that situation—how he purports to feel about it, his emotions, and reflective thoughts."[64]

It may therefore be allowed that emotiveness is a necessary condition of what we call poetic discourse. But does it constitute a sufficient condition since in life situations too we find plenty of emotional expression, even as we have suggestion, metaphor, irony, and so forth in everyday language? The *rasa* theory too might thus seem to suffer from the fault of "too wide," like the other theories. In replying to this objection, we may use Abhinavagupta's argument that *rasa* (in the sense of the aesthetic emotion) is not the same as life emotion but is a supramundane *(alaukika)* state, wholly confined to the experience of literature. In life, one normally "expresses" one's own emotions, or, if one is reporting about other people's emotions, it is only with a view to informing someone about them or to prompting him to act on them or react to them in a personal manner. In literature, on the other hand, the object is not to express personal emotions or to prompt people to action but to present a situation purely for its relish. In literature, moreover, the presented emotions are generalized and freed from all particularities of time, place, and person so that the reader will view them in a detached frame of mind.

Abhinavagupta emphasizes the nonpragmatic, nonutilitarian aspect of the aesthetic attitude. He says, "In witnessing a drama, a spectator will not have even a trace of the feeling that 'today I must do something useful.' In its place there is the feeling that 'I am going to enjoy a unique spectacle.' "[65] An aesthetic object has to be contemplated for no other reason than the pleasure it yields. The point of this argument is that the attitudes and expectations appropriate to a literary presentation are qualitatively different from those appropriate to an emotional situation in real life, and therefore the literary situation is not the same as the life situation.

Put in this way, the *rasa* theory would seem like the "aesthetic attitude" theory, familiar to Western criticism since Kant. But the trouble with this theory, as George Dickie has argued, is that the assumption of a special "aesthetic" attitude, which the spectator is supposed to bring to the object somehow, cannot help us to identify and reidentify a particular object as an aesthetic object. Since the aspect of an object depends on how it is regarded, the same object may become aesthetic on one occasion or to one person and nonaesthetic on another occasion or to another person.[66] But it would be odd to say that a poem or piece of music could change its identity according to the attitude adopted toward it. Moreover, the point that a disinterested attitude alone is the right attitude toward a given object cannot be proved except by showing that it is demanded by the nature of that object.

Modern institutional theories of literature, too, do not offer a satisfactory account of this literary phenomenon, for no convention exists to the effect that literary works should be read for their impersonal or universal significance alone or that the information offered by them is not something to act on. The atemporality and impersonality of poetry, its transcendence of the "spatial, temporal and personal deictics," rightly emphasized by Jonathan Culler, is not, as he thinks, a literary convention merely but, as I shall argue below and again in chapter 9, a semantic feature of the text that dictates that we apprehend the utterance differently than we do an empirical speech act.[67] Moreover, a thing does not, as John Ellis argues, become literature or an artwork simply because it is "used" as literature or artwork, even as it does not become so because we bring a certain kind of attention to it.[68] Nor is it the case that the status of an artwork is necessarily something arbitrarily conferred on an object by an institution.[69] If an object is of a certain kind—an artwork—and demands to be looked at in a certain way, its own nature must reveal that fact.

In its final implication, the *rasa* theory appeals neither to the aesthetic attitude nor to the institutional criterion but to the nature of literature itself as a type of discourse. When Abhinavagupta asserts that the aim of poetry is *rasa* evocation, he means that this aim is implicit in that form of discourse as its meaning. The noninformative, nonpractical, purely evocative or presentational aim of literature is not something that a community or convention dictates but an implicit feature of literary communication.

In demonstrating this point, Abhinavagupta draws on a line of reasoning employed by the *Mīmāṃsakas.* Arguing that the import of the Vedic texts is to prompt people to perform certain ritual acts, the *Mīmāṃsakas* urge that declarative statements or reports of what great people did, such as "Prajāpati cut out his fat and offered it to the fire," would be pointless, occurring in an injunctive context, unless they are taken as indirectly aiding the purpose of the injunctive texts through a praise of the actions being enjoined. That is to say that, in their final import, such statements too are injunctive, although they are in a declarative form; their purpose is to prompt people to action *(bhāvanā).* The qualified performer of the ritual gets the notion that he too should offer fat to the fire. By the same token, such literary statements as "Hara or Umā said so" must also prompt readers, not, however, to perform actions, but to contemplate the emotive significance implicit in them, because such statements do not make much sense as mere information.[70] Sentences such as "Othello murdered Desdemona," "Caesar was assassinated by the conspirators," and so on or the personal confessions or reflections of a Coleridge or a Wordsworth would have very little interest or relevance to the reader as statements about other people's experiences or actions. Nor do they contain explicit or implicit exhortations, warnings, and the like. Besides, an incident like Caesar's assassination, in the play by Shakespeare, is not merely reported as a historical fact but is made the nucleus of a whole complex of emotions, affecting other people's minds and their actions. The upshot of the matter is that it is the particular context of the literary presentation as a discourse type and its semantic exigencies that dictate to us the need to see it as a kind of prompting or evoking rather than as an informative discourse.

Another factor, mentioned by Abhinavagupta, that points to the evocatory aim of literature is that the very impersonality of the literary communication—the author is not speaking to the reader in person, nor is he addressing any matter that is of direct concern to the reader—rules out the possibility of the reader's interpreting the message of the work in a practical or personalized way. "Evocation" is not, however, to be understood in the sense of actually producing a mood in the mind of the reader, for this would mean judging the work in terms of the "affective fallacy." What is meant is that the purpose or illocutionary intent (force) of a literary work is to present or elaborate an attitudinal or emotional situation so that the presentation will call up the situation in the reader's mind in its fully imagined detail and will be recognized as the situation of a particular emotion.[71]

It is to be assumed, of course, that the work will induce in the sympathetic reader a delectable experience. But this experience can come only through the meanings of the poem, only when the reader recognizes the described situation as carrying an evocative force. "Evocation," or *bhāvanā,* as Bhaṭṭanāyaka conceived it, is a special potency assumed by the verbal presentation itself, and, as Abhinavagupta explains, it should be understood in the sense of "bringing about the perception" of *rasa* or, to put it differently, making the *rasa* available to perception.[72] It is in this sense that the *rasas* are said to be evoked by the poem. The poem may, then, be deemed to have discharged its function once it has delivered its meanings, whether it actually arouses the corresponding emotions in the mind of the reader or not. Such is also the *Mīmāṃsā* view of the prompting *(bhāvanā)* effected by the Veda. According to *Mīmāṃsā,* the injunctive verb in a sentence such as "One who is desirous of heaven should perform sacrifice" has the potency to go only as far as causing the cognition that an injunction is meant, regardless of what results or perlocutionary effects may issue from the injunction.[73]

I have defined literature by its nonpractical aim and its aim of delineating the emotions purely for evocative purposes. This is not to say that other aims, such as informing, exhorting, and so forth, are inconsistent with the aim of evoking. Often all these aims may coexist, as in the case of good journalistic reporting. Stephen Crane's accounts as a newspaper correspondent were often turned into little stories (e.g., "The Open Boat"), and most of Hemingway's Nick Adams stories originated as a war correspondent's accounts of actual events and impressions. Moreover, the literary quality of a work cannot be identified solely by the aim with which it was produced. Elizabeth Barrett Browning's poem "How Do I Love Thee" was intended as a personal communication to Robert Browning rather than as an objective presentation or dramatization of feeling. Many lyric poems that we know may have been of this sort. But these works cannot, on the score of their practical aim, be debarred from the designation of poetry since they would still be emotive presentations —portrayals of love or of some other affective situation—even if they were written with a practical intent. What makes a work literary is its presentational force: it must be a configuration of the conditions of an emotive situation in accordance with Bharata's formula, a configuration that will have the force of a portrayal or description.

The argument of this chapter has been that literature cannot be identified by linguistic or formal criteria and that the best definition of it would be one that is based on the type of discourse it purports to be, the nature of its message, and the purpose toward which it is directed. Many of the formal qualities and semantic functions (such as metaphor, suggestion, fictiveness, well formedness, and so forth) are neither necessary nor sufficient conditions of literariness. Some of them can be found outside literature, and they are also not possessed by all works of literature. Emotiveness too is no doubt found in nonliterary utterances. But I have argued that the emotiveness of literature differs from that of ordinary life in that a literary presentation, as a discourse type, aims at "evocation" rather than mere expressing or reporting of feelings and attitudes and that in that respect it is formally different from utterances in ordinary life situations. I have maintained further that evocation is the dominant aim of literary discourse and that the informative, didactic, or other aims, where they too are present, are incidental to that aim and do not constitute the defining conditions of literature.[74] Finally, the view, argued by the followers of Wittgenstein, that literary works can be interesting to us for many reasons and in many different ways and that it is therefore futile to attempt to define literature by a set of necessary and sufficient conditions must also be rejected.[75]

4

THE LOGIC OF THE EMOTIONS

I have been arguing that the theory of poetic emotions, as set forth by Bharata, is a viable general theory of poetry, capable of distinguishing the poetic from other types of discourse as well as of explaining all its elements and values. But much yet remains to be said about the exact manner in which emotions get expressed in poetry. The question has been posed whether there is any necessary or causal connection between the objects and the emotions they arouse and also whether there are any emotions at all apart from their criteria. If, as the eighteenth-century empiricist account of emotions supposed, the connection between the two is merely contingent, then it is possible for anything to give rise to any emotion and for anything to be the expression of any emotion.[1] We may "feel pity for stones and fear of capital letters."[2] Besides, the appeal to the inaccessible inner states, in the eighteenth-century theory, reduces the discourse concerning the emotions to a private language. The Wittgensteinian solution to the problem is to abolish the reference to inner processes and to limit discussion to the criteria, determined by context or convention, that would count as a description of those inner processes.

The Sanskrit critics too deny that a causal connection exists between objects and emotions or between emotions and their behavioral expressions. Objects need not arouse any emotions at all in a person. But when they do, though in no constant or necessary way, they can be called the "causes" *(vibhāvas)* of those emotions.[3] Besides, as we shall see below, an emotive situation is identified, not by a single condition, but by a number of conditions in conjunction. The appeal to the inner states is not altogether abolished, of course. But the focus of the critical discussion is on the criteria. A poem or drama has to exhibit the emotions according to the logic governing emotional expression. As Casey remarks, "Emotions too have their logic, and are subject to objective tests."[4] This is precisely the point of Bharata's *Rasa-Sūtra,* on which the whole doctrine of poetic emotions rests. The following exposition of the *Sūtra* will make it quite evident that the *rasa* theory is completely analytical in its treatment of the poetic emotions and offers us an intelligible vocabulary for describing and analyzing poetic structures.

The *Rasa-Sūtra:* Criteria and Typology

The doctrine of *rasa,* as originally formulated by Bharata in the sixth and seventh chapters of his *Nāṭyaśāstra,* rests on the following assumptions. (1) Emotions are manifested in poetry, as in life, by a combination of situational factors. (2) There is a specific number of emotions. (3) Some of the emotions are permanent, irreducible mental states, while others are fugitive and dependent. The permanent ones alone can be developed into aesthetic moods or *rasas.* (4) A poetic composition is an organization of various feeling tones, but it invariably subordinates the weaker tones to a dominant impression. (5) Feeling tones are brought together in a poem, not indiscriminately, but according to a logic of congruity and propriety.

I shall develop these points one by one.

The Formula for the Expression of Emotions

We should first go over Bharata's *Rasa-Sūtra* once again and analyze its implications: "Emotions in poetry come to be expressed through the conjunction of their causes and symptoms, and other ancillary feelings that accompany the emotions."[5] Bharata here stipulates four necessary conditions that must be present for an emotion to become manifested: (i) causes *(vibhāvas),* (ii) symptoms *(anubhāvas),* (iii) other (ancillary) feelings *(vyabhicārins),* and (iv) their conjunction *(saṃyoga).*

Causes. The causes of an emotion are those that generate or excite the emotion or are the occasion of that emotion. In Sanskrit, the cause is designated by the term *vibhāva*—a word synonymous with *kāraṇa, hetu, nimitta,* all of them meaning "cause." It is also called a *vibhāva* in the poetic or dramatic context because it causes the knowledge of an emotion through words, physical gestures, and involuntary psychic symptoms (sweating, trembling, and so forth) expressive of that emotion.[6] The "cause" is, again, of two kinds.

The first is the primary cause or the object of the emotion (intentional object, in modern terminology), which is defined as "that thing, resting on which, as its object, emotions like love are born."[7] The Sanskrit term for this is *ālaṃbana-vibhāva*. This may be a person, scene, object, or thought that excites a person's emotion and appears to him in a certain light or under a certain description. Emotions are invariably object directed, and, although they may lie dormant in our natures as potential forces or predispositions, it is only in the presence of their appropriate objects that they manifest themselves. It is not, however, the case that the mere presence of the object will necessarily excite an emotion in a person. It will not, unless the object is "intended" by that person as an object of his feeling and he is moved to think of it under a certain description.[8]

Second is the exciting cause *(uddīpana-vibhāva)*. The object of an emotion is the generative cause of that emotion because, although it is the object to which the emotion is directed, it is also the reason for that emotion.[9] That is to say that the emotion will not possibly arise in a person without the actual presence or thought of that object. But the object in itself is not sufficient for the emotion to develop unless the circumstances are also appropriate. For example, love between two young people grows into a full-blown passion when conditions, such as privacy, moonlight, a pleasant climate, and so forth, are present. So under the exciting causes are included all the attendant circumstances that enhance the feeling. In a poetic presentation, the exciting causes may be used as mood-building devices to reinforce the basic emotive tone of the poem or story. Familiar examples of these would be the "atmospheric" setting in Poe's "The Fall of the House of Usher" and the images of sterility, dryness, agony, and death in Eliot's *The Waste Land*. The exciting circumstances do not of course "cause" the emotion; emotion is caused by the object. They simply help the emotion to exhibit itself, and therefore they are called "causes" in a secondary sense.[10] One critic, however, goes so far as to say that, without them, "the generated emotion is as good as not born."[11]

Expressions and Symptoms. Emotional states will become objects of discourse only when they are expressed in an overt or visible way, in speech, action, or gesture. In the words of Charlton, "The idea of any emotion is . . . in general bound up with the idea of how it is manifested."[12] Hence, the conjunction of the symptoms with the causes is of the utmost importance in any discourse about the emotions. The Sanskrit word for behavioral expressions is *anubhāva*—which means etymologically "that which follows or ensues from the feeling (as its effect)." *Anubhāva* is that which "makes the feeling apprehensible."[13] The expressions—the words, actions, or gestures—are in one sense the effects of their emotions and appear after the emotions. But, from the point of view of the observer, they are the indicative signs of the emotions—

motions, changes in appearance, and actions that point to the emotions.[14] Through them, the emotions, which, being internal conditions, must otherwise remain unknown, are made known or objectified.

In poetry or in drama, these behavioral expressions are the only means of presenting the emotions—they are the subject matter of what in Sanskrit is called *abhinaya* (presentation or enactment).[15] *Abhinaya* is so called because the physical or verbal exhibition of the expressions leads the spectators or readers toward the emotions, of which they are the visible signs. As Abhinavagupta puts it, "Expressing the emotions is leading others toward a knowledge of those emotions. Hence they (shrugs, sidelong glances, knitting the eye-brows, and so forth) are at once expressions as well as the actions exhibited *(abhinayas)*."[16] Bharata shows how the various emotions are "caused" and how they must be exhibited on the stage. Grief is born out of bereavement by death of a dear one, loss of property, experiencing the sorrow of those who are near to you, and the like. These are its "causes." It is exhibited by shedding tears, wailing, weeping, turning pale, a hoarse voice, a sinking of the limbs, stretching or rolling on the ground, crying aloud, long and heavy breathing, trembling, numbness, loss of memory, going mad, becoming immobilized, becoming hysterical, dying, and so forth. These are its symptoms or expressions. Bharata specifies the conditions for the presentation of each one of the forty-nine emotions he lists. He defines a poetic emotion as a meaning that is brought about by its appropriate causes and apprehended by its expressions, consisting of speech and action.[17]

Of the physical expressions and gestures mentioned above, one can see that some—for example, shedding tears, change of color, and trembling—are bodily conditions that directly emanate from certain psychic states, whereas others—hitting, crushing, crying aloud, and so on—are gestures that are relatively more voluntary and capable of being controlled. In a sense, all of them are directly expressive of mental states in that they follow as effects from the inner feelings or appear in association with emotion-producing objects. Some gestures may of course be acquired in the course of social experience. Thumping, leaping, gnashing the teeth, crying, and the like are not always socially acquired gestures, as they are observed in gorillas, and babies start crying even before they pick up adult gestures.

The point here is that tears, trembling, and horripilation are not even gestures in the usual sense of the term any more than shivering and chattering of the teeth on a cold morning are. (One does not turn pale or faint at will.) They are, on the other hand, symptomatic reactions caused directly by certain psychic conditions and may be called emotion symptoms, as opposed to emotion expressions or emotional behavior, which are voluntary. These inner symptoms are called *sāttvikabhāvas,* or mental reactions, because they are directly produced by mental states. Bharata therefore treats them as a separate class, distinguishing them from verbal expression and bodily gestures, and lists eight of them: stupefaction or immobilization, perspiration, horripilation, change of voice, trembling, change of color, tears, and fainting. These reactions are not easy to exhibit on the stage; they can be accomplished only by an extreme concentration of the mind on the part of the actor so that he either brings himself actually to feel these mental states or successfully simulates them. Indeed, Bharata asks, how can they be enacted by someone who does not feel them?[18] These involuntary reactions are also called *bhāvas,* or mental states, and classified as such since they arise directly out of the inner states *(sattva);* but they are also a variety of "expressions and symptoms" since they appear as the outward signs of the mental states.[19]

Ancillary Feelings. When a feeling is being expressed or portrayed in a poem as a primary mood, other feelings that normally accompany it are called its ancillaries. No feeling, however basic, appears in its severest purity of form but attracts other emotions as well. Thus, if love-in-union is the emotion being treated, it will attract a host of other feelings—bashfulness, infatuation, agitation, eagerness, pride, cogitation, vacillation, gladness, and many others, except laziness due to lack of interest, ferocity, and revulsion, which are inimical to that state. Love-in-separation attracts self-deprecation, doubt, fatigue, jealousy, brooding, anxiety, drowsiness, dreaming, awakening, malady, mental derangement, fits, and so forth.

These ancillary feelings are called *vyabhicāri-bhāvas* or *saṃcārins* (transient or fleeting emotions) because they come and go at will in association with the principal emotions and help stabilize them. Without the reinforcement of the fleeting emotions, no emotion can be developed into an enduring mood. What we call a mood is a whole sequence of different feelings that, intermingling and interacting with one another, emerge as a single dominant strain or impression. Hence, poetic organization consists, not only in presenting emotions through their objects and expressions, but also in developing an emotion into a sustained mood by exhibiting an entire emotional sequence of alternating strands.

It is to be understood, however, that the "ancillary feelings" are not a necessary condition for expressing emotions, in life or in art. Emotions are manifested by their causes and effects. They are necessary only for prolonging and sustaining a mood over a length of time. They are only a collateral support to the emotion to be developed, a means to reinforcing and enhancing it. Emotions are caused by their objects, manifested by their expressions, and nourished by other ancillary feelings.[20]

It is of course possible, in a work of a short compass, such as a sonnet or haiku, to exhibit one single strand in all its intensity. For example, this brief anonymous lyric turns on a single feeling—the lover's intense pining for his beloved:

> Western wind, when wilt thou blow?
> The small rain down can rain,—
> Christ, if my love were in my arms
> And I in my bed again!

Or take Wordsworth's poem "A Slumber Did My Spirit Seal," in which a single emotion, namely, grief at the death of Lucy, is presented; or Keats's sonnet "On First Reading Chapman's Homer," which expresses the poet's wonderful sense of discovery, all the images consistently contributing to that feeling (wonder) alone, without any other intervening strains. Other examples are Tennyson's "Break, Break, Break," Blake's "The Tiger," and Hopkins' "The Windhover." A variety of emotional strands is not always necessary, then, for an emotion to be successfully presented in a poem. However, since Bharata was dealing primarily with drama, in which the interlocking of various strands is vital for the growth and elaboration of the theme, he stipulates the introduction of other emotions as well. Only when emotions are presented with their full paraphernalia of causes, effects, and concomitant feelings can they be sustained throughout the length of a drama.[21]

Their Conjunction. So far I have described the constituents of an emotive situation. For any situation to be described as emotive, there must first be an object that excites an emotion in someone and that that person becomes aware of under a certain description and directs his emotion at. Second, that person must, not merely feel the emotion, but express it in outward behavior. The ancillary feelings, as we have seen, are not a necessary condition for a situation to be emotive, only a factor in its development. Thus, the entire logic of emotional discourse seems to hinge on the objects and expressions.

But, as noted above, emotions, objects, and expressions are not bound to one another in any necessary or constant relation. None of the factors of the emotive situation are separately capable of manifesting *rasa* because they do not stand in any fixed relation to any one emotion; each, by itself, is common to more than one *rasa*. An object like a tiger may inspire heroism in one or wonder, fear, or wrath in another. Likewise, the same woman may be an object of love to a lover and an object of aversion to a monk. Thus, the objects are not exclusively attached to any particular emotion. Similarly, an outward expression, like tears, also belongs equally to grief, fear, and the erotic emotion. One sheds tears because of an eye disease or a death in the family, another in the ecstasy of sexual union. A girl who is in tears could have been peeling onions or grieved by the death of her lover. Bharata's analysis shows that each one of the psychic symptoms may be caused by a variety of mental or physical conditions.[22] The behavioral signs too stand in no invariable relation to any single emotion. The same holds for the ancillary emotions. For instance, anxiety may accompany love-in-separation as much as grief or fear.

This being the case, how can we deduce the emotions from their objects and expressions? It is in response to this question that Bharata stipulates a third condition, namely, the "conjunction" *(saṃyoga)* of the emotive factors. Abhinavagupta puts the case thus. The emotive causes and symptoms are in no fixed relation to the emotions singly, but "when the totality of conditions is given there is no inconstancy. Thus, where the death of a dear one is the circumstance, lamentation and tears are the behavioral expressions, brooding, dejection, and so on, are the other feelings, it cannot be anything but grief."[23] Emotion objects and emotion expressions are then "separately necessary conditions, and together a sufficient condition, for the operation of an emotion-concept," as a recent writer puts it.[24]

This is not, however, to say that all the conditions should always be present in a given presentation. Such a full layout of the situational factors can be expected only in a long composition in, for example, a drama, an epic, or a novel. In a short lyric, on the other hand, it often happens that only one or two of the factors are prominent and the others merely suggested, yet there is not obstruction to the manifestation of the *rasa*. Why, then, do our critics insist on the conjunction of all the elements? The explanation offered is that in such cases the other factors are supplied through implication, by the force of the context. In any event, all the necessary conditions must be assumed for a clear identification of the emotion involved. In most imagist- or haiku-type poetry, for example, in which only an object—a cat, a bird, or a wheelbarrow—is presented, the rest of the factors constituting the emotional complex, including the poet's own reactions to the object, the light in which he sees it, and so on, are to be elicited from the poem itself.

In the poem "Hunter," by Lorca, which follows, a brief vignette is given of four pigeons being shot by the hunter and falling to the ground, but no indication is given of the feeling aroused in the speaker by the scene:

Above the pine trees
four pigeons go through the air.

Four pigeons
fly and turn round.

They carry wounded
their four shadows.

Below the pine trees:
four pigeons lie on the earth.

In spite of the apparent neutrality of the tone, a sense of pity, perhaps mixed with horror, is strongly indicated. In Emily Dickinson's "After Great Pain a Formal Feeling Comes," the feeling of pain is identified by its effects on the nerves, the heart, and the feet, but the cause of pain is not given—one is left to infer what it might be. But because there are no grounds for making an inference, one has to understand that it is just any pain or pain in general, but one so acute that it numbs the senses. In Tennyson's ballad "Home They Brought the Warrior Dead," on the other hand, a complete situation is presented with its objects and expressions. When the body is brought home, the widowed woman's reactions are expressed first by motionlessness ("Yet she neither moved nor wept") and then by tears and lamentation, as the old nurse sets his child on her knee ("Like summer tempest came the tears— / 'Sweet my child, I live for thee' "). The absence of any accessory emotions does not, however, in this case, detract from the fullness of presentation. A complete emotive situation is rendered vividly in the short compass of three ballad stanzas.

As Abhinavagupta points out, however, it is only when the full paraphernalia of objects, expressions, and accessory feelings is present that the composition will be most effective.[25] For this reason, the dramatic presentation has been regarded as the best form of entertainment because, in it, a whole situation is elaborated with a picture-like vividness. In a written composition, such as a novel, however, this picturesqueness results from the verbal descriptions, and the appropriate actions have to be visualized. In a short lyric, even these descriptions are often absent, and therefore the imaginative reader will supply, in various ways, the proper background.[26]

There Are a Specific Number of Emotions. Bharata lists as many as forty-one mental states, each defined by its objects and expressions.[27] Of these, eight are called "basic or durable emotions" *(sthāyins)* since, in Bharata's view, only these can be given extended treatment and developed into full-fledged dramatic emotions. The other thirty-three can only play the role of accessories to the basic emotions. (I shall return to this point in the next section.) The eight "psychic symptoms," mentioned before, are also classed by Bharata as mental states, but, as their place and function is among the "expressions," they should be omitted from this list of mental states.

Basic Emotions. According to Bharata, the eight basic emotions are sexual love; comic laughter (ranging from an amused smile to a loud guffaw); grief, including self-pity and pity of others; rage; the heroic emotion; fear; revulsion; and wonder. Later writers sought to add other categories like quietude, filial love, love of god (religious emotion), and so forth to the list. (The question of the number of *rasas* is a hotly debated issue in Sanskrit criticism, and I shall have occasion to discuss it toward the end of this section.) The case for quietude being a distinct dramatic emotion came to be accepted after Abhinavagupta's eloquent plea on behalf of it. By "quietude" is understood a state of mental repose or serenity in which the mind is freed from all passions and perturbations and rests in itself, so to say. This is the condition that wise men and Yogis are known to enjoy.

It is objected that such a state of subsidence cannot be admitted to be a dramatic emotion because it cannot be presented in action, being a cessation of all activity and all agitations of the mind. A negative state or a state of neutrality (Yogic detachment) is hardly an emotion—a *bhāva*. Abhinavagupta rejects this line of argument and maintains that subsidence is not such a purely negative state but a positive experiential condition whose essence is inner joy. Besides, he points out, everything that can be experienced can be described and dramatized. It also cannot be objected that a state of subsidence, even if it can be presented, would not be dramatically interesting. For a drama that has subsidence for its theme would not present this state alone; it would also present other emotive conditions or crises of experience that produced this state: world-weariness, disenchantment, aspiration, quest, and so forth. Subsidence comes only as a climax to these preceding conditions. The movement from one condition to another can be adequately portrayed, and it can make for intense drama (e.g., the life of Buddha, which has been a popular theme with playwrights and choreographers).

Furthermore, although the state of subsidence is not, in itself, an expressive state, the very absence of expressive gesture, as in deep sleep and Yogic meditation, may be taken as a kind of gesture.[28] That subsidence can be treated as a poetic mood is also attested to by a poem like Andrew Marvell's "The Garden" and by much of the nature poetry of Wordsworth. Wordsworth is describing what the Sanskrit critics call the *śānta rasa* when, in his "Tintern Abbey," he speaks of "that blessed mood"

> In which the burthen of the mystery,
> In which the heavy and weary weight
> Of all this unintelligible world,
> Is lightened.

Accessory or Transient Emotions. The remaining thirty-three accessory emotions are discouragement (self-disparagement), debility (caused by both physical and mental conditions), apprehension (doubt, suspicion), envy, intoxication, weariness, indolence, depression, anxiety (worry), distraction, recollection (turning things over in the mind), contentment, shame, unsteadiness, jubilation, agitation, stupor, pride or arrogance, dejection, impatience (eagerness), sleep (drowsiness), amnesia, coma, awakening, indignation, dissimulation, ferocity, self-assurance (born of understanding), malaise, insanity, death (the state of mind accompanying death, or the "dying" experience), fright, and deliberation.

The following conclusions may be drawn from the elaborate typology of emotions that Bharata works out.

1. All the emotions, both stable and transient, are defined by their criteria, namely, their causes and expressions.[29] The distinction between the permanent and the transient emotions is central to the *rasa* doctrine and will be discussed more fully in the next section.

2. Some of the states listed by Bharata as mental states, such as debility, intoxication, sleep, and so on, are only physical conditions, and some of them may be caused by purely physical factors, for example, sleep by fatigue, disease, and so on. But what is meant here is not the physical conditions as such but the mental states they give rise to.[30]

3. The question may be asked whether Bharata's list of emotions is exhaustive enough to include all mental states, sensations, and attitudes known to man. It does not, for instance, provide for feelings of desire, say, the craving for a glass of beer on a hot day, or for honor, hatred, jealousy, suspense, and so on. This objection may be answered by pointing out that some of our words for mental states are multivalent and do not signify any specific feeling. "Desire" is such a word; it can take in almost any feeling. There is no such thing as desire per se. Desire for a glass of water is more accurately thirst, desire for food is hunger, desire for a woman is erotic love, and so on. Honor, hope, and hatred are not clearly defined psychological states. Hate may express itself as anger or

disgust, for example, "I hate his guts," "I hate drooling old men." Filial or fraternal love is again a composite term for a variety of feelings, each defined by its own objects and other circumstances.

Along these lines, there is a great deal of discussion in Sanskrit criticism as to whether the devotional sentiment *(bhakti)* can be admitted as a legitimate aesthetic emotion.[31] Theorists of the devotional schools argued that love of God was not only a distinct *rasa* but *rasa* par excellence and superior to the ordinary poetic emotions, which have their basis in man's earthly nature, are finite and transient, and cannot be said to produce supernal joy. And they tried to assign to it its own specific defining properties.

Abhinavagupta, in his disquisition on *śānta rasa,* denies a separate status to *bhakti* and to other sentiments like tenderness, filial feeling, and so forth as these only culminate in other mental states like love, pity, and the like. The devotional feeling cannot be an independent *rasa* as it has its substratum in *śānta* (quietude) or in one of the other basic emotions. Second, Abhinavagupta argues that the religious emotion, whatever its content, is still a psychic state and must be presented in poetry in terms of human responses, of joy and sorrow, pleasure and pain, not as something removed from man's psychic nature. An emotion, such as the love of Krishna or Jesus, may have a religious attitude for its subject matter, but it is still a human emotion and must evoke a human response. A difference in content does not constitute a difference in form and character. The love presented in a devotional poem may be one that is directed toward no man or woman, but toward God; yet it is realized as a human emotion, as though it were an entirely human context.

God relation as a theme does not call for a separate aesthetic. There is nothing specially "religious" about it in aesthetic terms. In poetry, all emotions and all motifs are invariably humanized and generalized; they are secularized, or sacralized, if you like. The distinction between "secular" and "sacred" ceases. Religious poetry is not then another kind of poetry but one of its many expressions. Moreover, what we call the religious emotion is not one single emotional attitude; rather it admits of a number of attitudes, depending on the circumstances. Thus, the devotional mystic can go through the whole gamut of emotions in relation to his god—from erotic love to fear. He pines for his god, enjoys union with him, laments his separation, suffers grief and despair over the fallen condition of his soul ("the dark night of the soul"), marvels at god's grandeur, is afraid of his wrath and disgusted with his own body and by his sensuous attachment to worldly things, and, finally, rests in god realization. For illustration, one may consider the poems of Edward Taylor, Donne, Herbert, Hopkins, the saint poets of India, and many others besides. It can therefore be concluded that there is no basic emotion called the devotional sentiment or love of God, with its own distinctive criteria.

4. Some of the categories into which Bharata divides the transient emotions seem, however, to overlap, their distinctions too subtle. For instance, discouragement, depression, and dejection are not clearly distinguished. All three are forms of mental travail and do not justify a separate classification distinct from grief, which is a basic emotion. What we call grief comprises them; indeed, there is no grief apart from them. Similarly, indignation and ferocity would be forms of wrath and apprehension and fright forms of fear.[32] However, these and other inaccuracies and redundancies in Bharata's classification do not seem to upset the validity of his crucial distinction between the primary and the transient emotions.

Durable and Transient Emotions

The distinction between basic or durable emotions and transient or fleeting emotions is perhaps Bharata's most original contribution to the aesthetic of emotions. This idea, which is practically unknown to Western criticism but for vague intimations of it in recent theory,[33] is the very cornerstone of the aesthetics of *rasa.* It accounts not only for the complex ways in which a poem can get organized but also for the sources of its unity, without which no aesthetic work can make a solid impression.

There are both psychological and aesthetic reasons for distinguishing between the two kinds of emotions. Bharata himself does not go deep into the logic of this distinction except to say that some mental states are more stable and powerful than others and, by their very nature, tend to dominate over them. Further, he states that the basic emotions alone can assert their identity even though they become mixed up with a welter of other feeling states.

Abhinavagupta, Bharata's commentator, however, attempts a psychological explanation. His argument is that the basic or primary emotions are so called because they are ever present in the mind as part of man's psychic heritage—as innate dispositions or impressions that lie in a latent or potential form and are awakened into action whenever appropriate objects present themselves. In this sense, they cannot be said to be "caused" by their objects inasmuch as the objects merely serve to bring them into an active state. The objects may be called their instrumental or efficient cause *(nimitta-kāraṇa)* rather than their inherent cause *(samavāya-kāraṇa).* It makes better sense to say that a man loves a woman because he has the sexual urge in him than to say that he feels the sexual urge because of the woman.[34] The transient emotions like agitation, shame, and indolence, on the other hand, appear only when their causes appear and disappear even as their causes disappear, without leaving any traces behind.[35]

However, distinguishing between the basic and the transient states on the basis of their being or not being permanent dispositions may be challenged. For one thing, it can be argued that the transient feelings are as much embedded in human nature as inherent traits as are the basic ones like love and revulsion.[36] Again, Abhinavagupta's further assertion that the basic emotions can exist in their forms even without their objects cannot be supported by his own logic concerning the emotions.[37] First, no emotion may be said to exist until it is felt, it will be felt only when the causes are present, and it can be named and identified as an emotion only when it is so exhibited by its objects and expressions. Again, if the basic emotions can exist without their causes and endure beyond them, why cannot the transient emotions? All feelings may be said to exist as potentialities that can be activated when suitable circumstances present themselves.

A more satisfactory reason adduced in support of this distinction is that transient emotions are not capable of existing by themselves; they are not meaningful without reference to one or another of the basic emotions. As Abhinavagupta states, "For that reason [i.e., since the transient emotions are not independent], when someone says, 'this man is wearied,' the question arises 'Why is he like that?' This indicates the contingent nature of that feeling. But when someone says, 'Rama is full of heroic fervor,' the question 'why' is not asked. In such cases, the only question that can be asked is whether the given objects and circumstances . . . are appropriate to the emotion [indicated]."[38] Similarly, when it is said that Romeo is in love with Juliet, no questions need be asked because this condition is sufficient unto itself and hence self-explanatory. The same logic applies to the other primary emotions.

The transient states, however, cannot find a resting point in their own nature or establish an independent context for themselves. Having no fixed identity or status, they move about with many different basic emotions, appearing and disappearing like bubbles and taking on the form and hue of the emotions they associate themselves with. A transient emotion is so called because it "goes astray in many different directions," with other emotions that are more powerful than itself.[39] Any given transient emotion is common to more than one state of mind. Thus, the feeling of agitation can appear in love, laughter, anger, revulsion, or wonder; debility and depression in grief, fear, and love-in-separation; and so on. The durable emotion is so called because it is an irreducible psychic stereotype that, although it attracts a variety of other feeling conditions and is fed by them, persists unchanged, giving its own stamp to them. To quote from the texts, "The emotion which is not swallowed up by other emotions whether friendly with it or unfriendly, which quickly dissolves the others into its own condition like the salt sea, which endures continuously in the mind, and which, in conjunction with other feelings and circumstances, attains to its fullest expression as rasa—that is the durable emotion."[40]

Since the transitory states cannot culminate in any particular mood by themselves, the durable emotions alone can be developed into aesthetic moods or *rasas*. That is, they alone can be sustained through a whole composition. The transitory states can exist only as accessories to one of the prime emotions, serving the purpose of intensification or contrast. Of course all mental states are volatile and pass away like bubbles even as they come into being. So the only way of stabilizing a prime emotion in poetry is to exhibit it again and again through its attendant conditions and accessories. The transient emotions cannot be stabilized even by repeated exhibition. As Jagannātha points out, the stability of the basic emotions is due to the fact that they can be sustained throughout an entire work by being manifested repeatedly.[41]

However, the basic emotion seldom appears in its severest purity of form but assimilates other major or minor emotions with which it has organic affinities. A major emotion can of course assimilate another major emotion, but only as its subsidiary. Thus, the erotic feeling, although it can be conceived to occur in its purity at least for a moment, soon gets mixed up with the feelings of wonder, laughter, and even grief (in love-in-separation) and with such transient feelings as eagerness, bashfulness, envy, jubilation, anxiety, distraction, and so forth. A transient emotion too can no doubt attract other transient emotions as its accessories. But it must necessarily get connected with all its train to some basic emotion, which then will become the dominant mood, subordinating both the transient emotion and its accessories.

The foregoing analysis shows (i) that the same transient emotion can go with more than one basic emotion, (ii) that a basic emotion can take a number of transient as well as other basic emotions as its accessories when it is being developed as a major theme, and (iii) that, even when it appears in the midst of a combination of other emotions, the basic emotion does not change its form but only proliferates, the other emotions lending it an effect of variegation.[42] Thus, when a basic emotion is nourished as a principal theme throughout a composition by being exhibited repeatedly with its full paraphernalia of objects, expressions, and accessories, it becomes a dominant or presiding emotion and is called a *rasa* or poetic mood. This is the substance of Bharata's *Rasa-Sūtra*.

The Poem as an Organization of Various Feeling Tones

Although, as we have seen, it is possible to structure a short poem on a single basic emotion in terms of the material conditions specific to that emotion, it is often necessary, for its intensification and prolongation, to introduce other connected emotions. When so supported by subordinate motifs, the basic emotion becomes stabilized and is able to extend itself through time. Therefore, Bharata emphasizes the introduction of various emotional strains by way of consolidating the main emotion. "Rasa-manifestation," he says, "is effected through the conjunction of many different emotions."[43] "There is no poem," he declares, "that consists of one emotion only. A poem gains in intensity through the clash of interacting emotions."[44] Abhinavagupta observes that, even in the treatment of love-in-union, poets often introduce lovers' quarrels and other elements of conflict in order to avoid the feeling of satiety. He quotes Vātsyāyana, who, in his *Kāmasūtra,* says that love often goes awry and thrives on conflict.[45]

It should be remembered, however, that, although a poem may be composed of many different emotions, only one of those emotions is to be established as its dominant theme. For a single unified discourse cannot contain two parallel tones or interests. This would undermine the unity of impression. When two or more primary emotions are introduced in a poem of some length and each one receives a degree of elaboration, which of them will become the ruling emotion of the poem will depend on how the poet treats his subject matter. But, if one emotional pattern is exhibited over and over again and is echoed and reechoed in all parts of the work, that pattern would then become the dominant theme and dictate the tone of the entire work. The conclusion of the work is also, of course, of the utmost importance for the final impression, for example, the happy ending in the Elizabethan and Jacobian tragicomedies and in *Śākuntala* of Kālidāsa. In any event, there is no incongruity in introducing other *rasas* into a poem in which one particular *rasa* alone is being developed since that single *rasa* will become the abiding emotion and the others its accessories.[46] The *rasa* chosen to be the dominant mood of the poem spreads itself as a pervasive quality of the work through all its parts, whereas the other major emotions, which are drawn into the work by the force of the situation, powerful as they may be, are limited to certain parts of the work and therefore cannot hurt the preeminence of the main *rasa*. In fact, they will aid its intensification as well as spread.[47]

That a poetic emotion, in a structure of some length, develops by incorporating other major and minor emotional strains may be illustrated by Hamlet's first soliloquy in act 1, scene 2: "O, that this too too solid flesh would melt. . . ." The prevailing mood of this piece is grief, but it also attracts other related feelings such as revulsion and anger. Hamlet's sense of being tainted by his mother's incest and his revulsion against "all the uses of this world" is expressed in lines 1–10. There is pity expressed for his dead father, anger at the thought of his mother's hasty marriage, and his own helplessness and muted anguish at the thought that his heart must break in silence. But these other, intervening feelings only serve to intensify Hamlet's tragic anguish and culminate in one dominant impression.

In a drama or narrative, or even in a long lyric, there is of course ample scope for the proliferation of the emotions. In a short lyric, on the other hand, in which a single event, idea, or image is usually the focus, the dominant tone consists of a single corresponding mood, revealed through an interlocking of details pertinent to that mood alone. However, even within the limited scope of a short poem, it is possible to achieve a degree of complexity, as often happens in Shakespeare's sonnets. Sonnet 29 is, for instance, structured on a "reversal" of thought, as many other sonnets of Shakespeare's are. It begins on a note of dejection and self-disparagement: "When in disgrace with Fortune and men's eyes, / I all alone beweep my out-cast state." In the last five lines, however, the mood is resolved into one of intense joy and sweetness, which prevails as the final tone of the poem:

> Haply, I think on thee,—and then my state
> Like to the lark at the break of day arising
> From sullen earth, sings hymns at heaven's gate.

There is such a complete reversal of mood here that the previous condition is totally set aside and swallowed up in the quality of the present moment. This is obviously due to the order in which the feelings are stated. Joy, being the final note, automatically becomes the dominant tone as well.[48]

The Art of Combining the Emotions

If, as we have seen, a poetic composition, of at least some length, develops through an interaction of two or more emotional strains, it follows that poetic construction must depend on artfully combining the emotions according to their natural affinities. For emotions can be friendly toward or opposed to each other. Any given emotion does not go with all other emotions in a promiscuous way but follows a certain logic, a code of behavior, not imposed by extraneous conditions, but intrinsic to its nature.

This point may be illustrated by means of a musical analogy. In Indian music, in a *rāga* (a melodic structure consisting of some specific notes), there is the keynote (which is most characteristic of that *rāga*), called the *vādi* (sonant), some notes that are "consonant" with that note, called the *saṃvādi,* and other notes that are "dissonant" with it and that are introduced for contrast, called the *vivādi.* There may, again, be some others that follow the sonant and the consonant, and these are called *anuvādi.*[49]

In terms of this analogy, we have, in a poetic structure, a basic emotion that is developed as the dominant or major tone and on which the poem rests, other emotions congruent with the basic emotion that come in as its accessories and that may be called the minor tones, and yet others consonant with the minor tones that may be called subtones. A given emotion can sometimes consort with emotions opposed to its own nature, but only under certain conditions; these may be called the discordant tones. The Sanskrit critics work out a detailed classification of "concordant" and "discordant" emotions and lay down guidelines for the combination of emotions within a single composition.

Concordant and Discordant Emotions. It is common knowledge that some mental states are mutually incompatible with each other and cannot coexist whereas others can consort well together at all times. Thus, one cannot be both attracted and repelled by the same object at once or feel pity and rage toward the same person, or pity and fear, or love and fear. On the other hand, the sense of wonder or the comic can cohabit with erotic love, heroism with fury, fear with disgust, and so on. While this is true, we must be able to specify the precise conditions under which emotions are found to be congruent or incongruent with each other. For, sometimes, emotions can come together and collide with each other, in the same situation, without regard for natural affinities, for example, love, pity, and rage in the murder scene in *Othello.* Even opposite emotions can cease to be opposite under certain conditions; for example, jealousy in an erotic context need not always be destructive of love but may actually aid it. A distinction should also be made between the emotion expressed by one person and the reaction it produces in someone else. Thus, heroism in the warrior will produce wonder in his friends and dread in his enemies. Wrath in a person may inspire dread in some and wrath in others.

In determining mutual opposition between emotions within a poem, we must therefore take the following factors into consideration: (i) whether the contradictory emotions appear in the same locus (person) or in different loci; (ii) whether they appear in a locus at the same point in time and in the same circumstances or at different times and in different circumstances; (iii) whether they appear in the same locus successively or with other intervening emotions; (iv) whether they are caused by the same object or by different objects; (v) whether they are treated as being equally powerful, or whether one of them is subordinated; (vi) and, finally, whether the opposition is between two basic emotions, between two transient ones, or between a basic emotion and a transient emotion.

Opposition between emotions is defined as the inability of two emotions, caused by the same object, to coexist in the same substratum at the same time and, consequently, the obstruction of one by the other, that is, one knowledge obstructing the other.[50] The sense of obstruction occurs when one emotion is repelled by another emotion. For example, the knowledge that X loves Y does not permit the knowledge that the one abhors the other. This is a natural incompatibility between these two basic emotions—love and disgust. Similarly, two transient emotions too can be naturally opposed: for example, contentment and anxiety, eagerness and deliberation, elation and depression. There can also be a natural enmity between a basic emotion and a transient emotion—between heroic feeling and depression, grief and elation, fear and elation, the comic spirit and apprehension or anxiety, and so forth.

However, natural incompatibility is not the sole reason for the opposition between emotions. The opposition will occur only when there is a direct confrontation between incompatible emotions. That is, first, the emotions must arise in connection with the same object—caused by that object and directed at it. Romeo's love for Juliet is not opposed by his hostility toward her family, the Capulets. As Ānandavardhana explains, "Real opposition results only when a single cause gives rise simultaneously to two opposite effects, not when two mutually opposed causes contribute toward the production of a single effect."[51] This type of opposition may be termed "opposition due to the object being the same."

Second, the opposite emotions must reside in the same person—this is "opposition due to the locus being the same." Heroism in Caesar will not be opposed by fear in the Pompeians. The mere presence of two discordant emotions within a composition need not necessarily result in conflict. For example, the comic element in a Shakespearean tragedy does not undermine the tragic sentiment because it appears in a different substratum and is directed at a different object.

Third, the emotions must occur in quick succession: love and hate, pity and fear, wonder and revulsion (inspired by the same object), occurring alternately will destroy each other. This is "opposition due to rival emotions occurring without interval." But, when these emotions are separated by intervals of time that allow for other circumstances to warrant the emergence of an opposite emotion, there will be no confrontation. Othello's initial passion for Desdemona is not contradicted by his jealous rage at the end.

Fourth, the contending emotions must be of equal strength, for, if one of them is more dominant, it will soon subdue its opponent and establish its own tone. This may be called "opposition due to the rival emotions being equally important." Pity and wrath, for example, could alternate for a while until one finally yields to the other. The contention in Othello's mind, in the murder scene, between two equally powerful emotions —pity and rage—is resolved by the final prevalence of rage over pity. However, in such cases, it is always the "negative" emotions—wrath, fear, disgust, and the comic spirit—that tend to prevail over their opponents. Thus, a combination of love and disgust, of equal force, would result in disgust. Love, appearing together with fear, will be extinguished by fear, the heroic by fear, wonder by rage, pathos by the comic, and so on. In any case, of course, opposition can happen only to an emotion that is treated as the principal meaning of the text *(vākyārthībhūta),* namely, to the basic emotion that is stabilized as the *rasa*. Further, it is possible only within a single context of meaning and in a sentence with a univocal meaning. In polysemous cases, there can be no opposition since the sentence conveys two different meanings and should be treated as two different sentences *(vākyabheda)*.[52]

As a general rule, opposition between emotions is removed (i) by locating the conflicting emotions in different substrata, (ii) by directing them to two different objects, (iii) by subordinating one of them, (iv) by introducing another emotion that is friendly to both to mediate between the opposites, and (v) by not overdisplaying the emotion that is opposed to the dominant emotion of the poem (e.g., comic episodes, when introduced in a tragedy, should not receive extended treatment). Tables 1, 2, and 3 show the mutual relations between the *rasas* and the means by which opposition between them is eliminated.

The rules outlined above are only the broad directions set down by our critics. There may be many other ways of handling the treatment of emotions and controlling the tone of the poem. In any case, the prime concern of the poet should be to ensure that only one unified tone prevails throughout a composition and that all other tones and subtones are subordinated to the principal mood, according to their natural affinities. In terms of the *rasa* doctrine, a poem is a hierarchical structure in which different themes and motifs are arranged in an order of greater and lesser limbs or parts *(aṅgas),* each according to its importance and rights of precedence, and all parts are focalized and made to contribute to one dominant impression. Aesthetic unity can be described only as the functional cooperation of all parts in the interests of a unified whole.

These principles, propounded by the *rasa* theorists, are not merely arbitrary rules of composition; they have a psychological validity. In a

Table I
Concordant and Discordant Emotions

Basic Emotions	Concordant Emotions	Discordant Emotions
Erotic love	Heroism, the comic, wonder, fury (demoniacal love, not normal)	Disgust, tragic grief,[a] fear, fury (in normal cases), quietude (subsidence)
The comic	Erotic love, rage	Grief, fear
Grief	Fear	Rage, the erotic, the comic, the heroic
Rage	Disgust, the heroic, the comic	Wonder, fear, grief, the erotic, quietude
The heroic	Wonder, rage, the erotic	Fear, disgust, grief, quietude
Fear	Grief, disgust	Rage, wonder, quietude, the heroic, the comic
Disgust	Fear	Wonder, the erotic, the heroic
Wonder	The erotic, the heroic	Fury, disgust, fear, grief
Quietude[b]	Wonder	Fury, fear, disgust, grief, the erotic, the heroic

[a]Depression, despair, distraction, etc., which go into the tragic sentiment, appear in love-in-separation. But tragic grief itself is incongruous with its tone.

[b]No emotion in its turbulent form can coexist with this mood.

poem, in which there is an organization of diverse emotional strains and impulses, there is no place for two contradictory mental states. The nature of our mental apprehension is such that the quality of one moment is lost in the contemplation of a succeeding moment. So it is not possible for a variety of impressions that are qualitatively different to subsist simultaneously in a single moment of apprehension. Of course, no poem, however long or short, unless it is of the purest imagist type, consists of a single moment of perception. But our experience with long poems, plays, and novels has shown us that, although a series of qualitatively different moments are necessarily involved in any such construction, it is still possible for a given quality to prolong and spread itself in time and emerge as a dominant impression, coloring our entire percep-

Table 2
Synaesthesis, or the Mixing of Discordant Emotions

Based on the Substratum	Based on the Object	Based on the Moment of Apprehension
1. By placing the opposite emotions in different sub-strata, the opposition is removed, e.g., heroism in the protagonist and fear in the antagonist. 2. When two opposites are located in the same character, one is subordinated to the other: pity and rage in Othello.	By directing the opposite emotions on different objects.	1. Opposition between two emotions is removed by interposing a third, which is friendly to both. 2. By introducing interven-ing circumstances between the rise of the one and the rise of the other—circumstances that would warrant a change of attitude in the character toward an object.

Table 3
What Happens When Opposites Are Combined without Regard for Propriety?

1. Love + disgust = disgust.
   Love + fear = fear.
   Love + rage = rage.
   Love + pathos = pathos.
2. The comic + pathos = comic.
   The comic + fear = fear.
   The comic + rage = rage.
3. Pathos + rage = rage.
4. Rage + wonder = rage.
   Rage + fear = fear.
5. The heroic + fear = fear.
   The heroic + disgust = disgust.
6. Fear + any other emotion, friendly or unfriendly = fear
7. Disgust + wonder = disgust.
8. Wonder + pathos = pathos.
9. Quietude + any other emotion would nullify that emotion.

tion of the work. The mixture of diverse emotional tones does not produce a new compound, in which the ingredients preserve their distinctive flavor, or an altogether new synthesis different from its ingredients. It is always the stronger element that asserts itself. Therefore, the concept of *rasa* requires that there be a single dominant emotion. It rules out the possibility of a "cocktail" of emotions in which the mixture produces a new compound relish.[53]

A surprisingly close parallel in Western criticism to this theory of emotional unity can be seen in the work of the eighteenth-century Scottish critic Kames.[54] Kames distinguishes between "concordant emotions," which mix intimately, and "discordant emotions," which refuse incorporation or mixture. Two emotions are said to be similar when they produce the same tone of mind. Kames is most emphatic in stating that the mind cannot fundamentally take on opposite tones. Dissimilar emotions may succeed each other with rapidity, but they cannot exist simultaneously. Opposite emotions arising from connected causes and directed toward the same object, such as love for a mistress and resentment of her infidelity, do not admit any sort of union. They can only govern alternately until one obtains ascendence. If the two emotions are unequal in force, the stronger will extinguish the weaker after a conflict. Dissimilar emotions proceeding from causes that are unconnected also cannot be felt except in succession (e.g., good and bad news arriving at the same time—the birth of a son and the loss of your house by fire).

In every case, Kames declares, regard must be shown, in treating the emotions, for their congruity and propriety. Kames remarks on the very skillful manner in which the opposite passions of love and jealousy are reconciled by Shakespeare in the murder scene of *Othello*. He does not, however, work out a detailed typology of emotions in the manner of Bharata, nor does he distinguish between basic and transitory states. Some of the emotions mentioned by him are also not clearly defined psychological states. Thus, honor, hope, and grandeur or sublimity cannot be regarded as independent mental states. For instance, the case for sublimity being a distinct emotional tone is not made out, for, in terms of the *rasa* theory, the term "sublimity" serves indifferently for the heroic, the tragic, the wonderful, and the serene. There is the epic-heroic sublimity of the *Iliad,* the tragic sublimity of *Oedipus Rex,* the "wonderful" sublimity of the eighteenth-century poetry of natural description, and the more serene sublimity of Wordsworth's nature mysticism. Some of Kames' categories, like despair and dejection, also overlap.

The Modern Aesthetic of Irony. Such a theory of poetic unity will have important consequences for modern ideas of irony, tension, synaesthesis, and tragicomedy. The prevalent belief today, in the wake of Eliot, Richards, and the rest, seems to be that emotive tones can be combined indiscriminately and that such a combination is valuable for its inclusiveness. Richards builds the notion of irony as a copresence of opposite tones into an aesthetic doctrine. Synaesthesis, according to him, is a state of unmitigated tension between equally opposed impulses that refuse suppression or sublimation.[55] The *rasa* theory, as noted earlier, no doubt provides for ample variety and complexity in the organization of feelings within a poem. It even makes it possible for heterogeneous impulses to be incorporated within a single poem according to certain principles of decorum. But what it most emphatically denies is that it is possible to unite in any real sense totally contradictory feeling tones and that, even if they could be juxtaposed, they could remain in a state of continued tension without resolving themselves into a dominant impression. Often, in fact, it can be seen that even in the supposed cases of irony there is an implicit conformity to the decorum of the emotions outlined above.

For instance, tragedy, for Richards, provides the ideal model for an inclusive structure, which, in effect, is an ironic structure because of its attraction of the opposite impulses of pity and terror. But, while pity and terror are not exactly opposite impulses in terms of our doctrine of emotions, pity and levity or derisive laughter are. Richards' reason for considering them as opposites is that "pity is the impulse to approach, and terror the impulse to retreat."[56] Although, in this sense, pity and fear are like heat and cold, an opposition will not occur between them until there is a direct confrontation, in the sense that I defined above. That is, they must appear with equal force, in the same person, toward the same object, and at the same time. This never happens in any tragedy, Greek or Shakespearean. Although, as Aristotle said, most tragedies are wrought out of both pity and fear, pity alone is the essential element of tragedy and its dominent tone; fear, wherever it enters, is subordinated to it as its accessory. If fear were treated as the principal theme, it would become a horror drama, like the Gothic romance. Even if both pity and fear were treated with equal emphasis, fear would still swallow up pity and become the principal theme.

Richards is of course concerned with the structure of the reader's response, even as Aristotle has the spectator's experience in mind when he talks about the catharsis of the emotions. For Richards, the aesthetic poise is in our response, not in the structure of the stimulating object—a hypothesis that would no doubt defeat the very labor of criticism. Even then one must ask whether it is natural for the reader to feel attraction and repulsion for the same person of the drama either simultaneously or successively. It would, however, be natural for him to feel pity for Othello and repulsion for Iago. This being the case, no "reconciliation of the opposites" is involved in tragedy because, in the first place, there has been no direct confrontation between them.

Again, the "opposites" listed in Coleridge's famous definition of imagination as "the balance or reconciliation of opposite or discordant qualities"—sameness and difference, the general and the concrete, the individual and the representative, the idea and the image, emotion and order, and so on—are no opposites at all within the meaning of our theory of poetic unity or of the term "irony" as defined by Richards.[57] Much less are they all logical opposites. At any rate, it is doubtful whether Coleridge himself would have cared for a poetry written according to the "ironic" prescription. For, in the same sentence, he speaks of "unity of effect" and of "modifying a series of thoughts by some one predominant thought or feeling"—a lesson that his modern interpreters seem to have ignored. No Romantic would have liked to combine levity and seriousness, for instance. Witness Coleridge's own discomfiture with the comic scenes in Shakespeare's tragedies. On this point, the Indian theory would not of course support him, as we saw earlier. But, in any case, it seems paradoxical that Richards should try to derive a theory of irony from the Romantics, and even more paradoxical that he should use a Romantic concept to berate Romantic poetry, as when he says that Wordsworth's "Tintern Abbey" is not itself a good instance of imaginative poetry.[58] Equally ironical is his rejection of Greek tragedy as "pseudo-tragedy."[59]

At any rate, the *rasa* theory argues that aesthetic poise results, not from an unresolved tension of feeling tones, but from their resolution into a single tone. Sometimes, though, a poem may cultivate "an unresolved conflict with the intent of displaying its unresolvedness."[60] But it would be wrong to say that the state of unresolvedness results in a dubious or contradictory tone. For example, Hamlet's irresolution in the third soliloquy ("To be or not to be"), considered as an assertion pattern, continues unresolved even to the end of that passage. But his crisis of irresolution itself appears in no uncertain light. It is an expression of the tragic burden that weighs on his mind. Similarly, although an unresolvable conflict is the theme of Eliot's "The Love Song of J. Alfred Prufrock," the resultant tone of the whole is one of melancholy or restrained plaintiveness. In *The Waste Land* too, in which the ironically juxtaposed serious, half-serious, and satiric voices merge into the single anguished voice of the Tiresias figure, the dominant tone is that of tragic anguish.[61] No work may thus remain inconclusive in terms of its tone, however intransigent its theme may be.

The *rasa* theory also sees no harm in the intense cultivation of a single channel of interest, as in Greek tragedy or the Romantic lyric. But of course even a relatively simple organization will naturally present the whole "complex" of the emotion, its rhythms and tensions, and it will incorporate a variety of other tones congruent with it. Again, intensity of meaning in poetry is to be judged not always by the number of emotions incorporated—although a complex organization may have its advantages —but sometimes by the clarity and force of the emotions presented, be they one or many. It is not necessarily judged by its "secondary and tertiary co-implications" either, as Richards argues, but equally by the luminosity of the single evocative sense or image.[62]

Most cases of irony, then, are not ironic in the sense that they reconcile opposite tones. They may include contradictory elements, although not without regard to unity of tone—without proper subordination, that is. The Greek as well as the Elizabethan tragedies conform to this aim. A play like *Romeo and Juliet,* as Robert Penn Warren argues, may be free from "purity of effect" (the ironist's bugbear) because of its inclusion of various strands of interest.[63] But it most certainly maintains "unity of effect" in spite of the wit and realism of some of its scenes because the emotions are managed exactly right.

For instance, the bawdy jests of Mercutio happen outside the wall of Juliet's garden, not within the garden itself, and they do not happen simultaneously with the love scenes, but at another time and in another clime and context. There is no juxtaposition between them and the poetry of the balcony scene. The lovers themselves have no share in them, so the balcony scene itself remains pure romance and pure poetry. Warren argues, however, that even this scene escapes the condition of pure poetry because Juliet, who distrusts "pure" poems, deliberately, as it were, mars the purity of the moment by a rigorously logical metaphor —that of the "inconstant moon": "She injects the impurity of an intellectual style into the lover's pure poem."

Warren is no doubt right in attacking the kind of facile, sentimental poetry that does not "prove" itself, that does not, in other words, firmly establish the logic of its emotions. However, the supposed opposition between the "intellectual style" and the "pure poem" does not exist. For the intellectual quality of the metaphor in question mixes well with the tone of the lovers' dialogue. Thus, neither within the balcony scene nor outside it is there any real confrontation of opposites; "installing Mercutio in the shrubbery" does nobody any harm, and it also does not produce the impurity that Warren wishes so devoutly.

A poem, we have admitted, is a complex of various tones and subtones, and *Romeo and Juliet* has many of these, ranging from love to tragic grief. But this would not justify the introduction of irrelevant or destructive associations, which is what Warren seems to mean by ironic or impure poetry. In the final analysis, though, Warren does seem to concede the case for "unity of effect," as when he describes a poem as "a dramatic structure, a movement through action towards rest, through complication towards simplicity of effect." It is precisely this rest, born of ultimate resolution, of which the *rasa* theorist is speaking.

The alleged opposition between thought and emotion, wit and passion, and the belief that a union of the two will produce the desired tension or complexity is another misconception that has reigned supreme in modern criticism. It can be maintained, from the standpoint of the *rasa* theory, first, that the operations of the intellect—logic, ratiocination, casuistry

—are not necessarily inimical to emotional expression. In fact, a good deal of intellection or ratiocination enters into certain types of emotive discourse, and it is especially appropriate to amorous as well as devotional casuistry, as borne out by the practice of Shakespeare and the metaphysical poets as well as of the Sanskrit, Persian, and Urdu poets. The comic spirit too is not inconsistent with such sentiments as love and wrath, and it goes particularly well with love in the courtship phase *(pūrva-rāga)*.

Second, poetic expression is coextensive with intelligent discourse and often takes the form of assertions, denials, questions, explanations, and so on. It uses all the structures of logical reasoning, sometimes in perverted ways, although poetry is not, as a rule, mere pseudo-logic. A good number of figurative structures, of which poetry makes constant use, are based on logic and reasoning. For example, some of the most impassioned passages in Shakespeare and Milton, expressions of grief and the like, are also tough-minded reasonings: consider Shakespeare's sonnets 94 and 120 or Samson's cry of despair in *Samson Agonistes* (lines 80–105) beginning "O dark, dark, dark, amid the blaze of noon." But it would be wrong to conclude from this that thought or reasoning is opposed to feeling and therefore sets up an ironic contrast. Thought in poetry does not exhibit itself as a separate mental activity; much less does it modify feeling. It is itself a mode of feeling. Eliot himself would agree that thought is merely the subject matter of feeling or, alternatively, a mode of expressing feeling.[64]

The belief that the tragic and the comic can be intermixed, not as in the Elizabethan double plots, but in a way in which there is a complete interpenetration and balance of the two elements, underlies the modern conception of tragicomedy (also called "black comedy").[65] In the purely tragic, or in the purely comic, unity of tone is possible. But the tragicomic is characterized by "split tones" or "split moods." The effective copresence of pathos and comedy, sharpening each other, produces a new irony.

While this is a widely held belief, it is not clearly demonstrated by the actual practice of playwrights. Even in the tragicomedies of Sean O'Casey, a staunch advocate of this genre, the purity of their final tragic impression remains unaffected by the mixture of wit and laughter (e.g., *Juno and the Paycock* and *The Plough and the Stars*). The case of the absurd drama also does not show conclusively that tragedy and comedy can be so blended as to produce a unique and single emotion, a split mood that is at once tragic and comic. The situation of complete stalemate treated in *Waiting for Godot,* characterized by Beckett as a tragicomedy, may be tragic in its metaphysical significance, but the tone of its treatment is comic throughout because the characters themselves appear to take their plight in that light. Pinter's *The Birthday Party* is, however, different: there, as Pinter himself explained, the situation is at first funny but then becomes no longer funny: "The horror of the human situation rises to the surface."[66]

For anything to be tragic, the subject (the sufferer himself or another person affected by his suffering) must register pathos; the tragic sense is necessarily self-directed. For a play to be comic, the subject need not, however, feel comic himself or recognize that he is the cause of laughter. But comic laughter can also be, and often is, self-conscious. The characters in many absurd plays do not seem aware that they are behaving absurdly. Ionesco's *The New Tenant* is a case in point. The new tenant not only designs his whole absurd situation but is perfectly happy and contented with it.

5

MODES OF MEANING: METAPHOR

Verbal Functions and the Question of Supernumerary Meanings

The two well-known functions of language recognized by nearly all schools of Indian philosophy and noticed in the Vedic language by the ancient exegetes Jaimini and Śabara were primary meaning *(abhidhā),* based on established usage, and metaphorical or secondary meaning, also called indication *(lakṣaṇā, guṇavāda).* But, as noted in chapter 3, the *dhvani* theorists, in their anxiety to differentiate poetic meaning from conventional meaning—the language of the scriptures and scientific treatises—claimed that there was a third potency of language or a third kind of meaning, called suggestion or implication *(vyañjanā),* that was characteristic of the poetic use of language. They had to fight a long philosophical duel with the traditionalists, who maintained that the secondary function was quite sufficient to account for all meanings that the denotative capacity of words could not explain and, hence, that there was no need to postulate an additional semantic function. The *dhvani* critics also had to meet the argument of the rhetoricians (the school of *alaṃkāra*) that suggestion was none other than figurative language and so could be subsumed under it. In fact, the theory of *dhvani* was advanced as a rival to the figurative poetic of the rhetoricians, who had dominated the early phase of Sanskrit criticism.

The idea of an additional or unstated tertiary meaning, postulated by the *dhvani* theory *(dhvanir nāma arthāntaram),* raises some semantic problems. When can a sentence be said to convey a meaning other than what is expressly stated by its words? It also involves a consideration of what is broadly called "metaphoric" or "secondary" meaning (I shall use these terms interchangeably). Therefore, before we can examine the implications of the *dhvani* theory, we should understand the nature of primary and secondary functions according to the Indian theory of meaning.

Primary Meaning

Despite individual doctrinal differences, most language philosophers of India agree that the primary meaning of a word is what has been assigned to the verbal sign as its meaning by common usage or convention in the form, "From this word, this meaning is understood." In the language of the texts, "Primary meaning is what is directly signified by the word."[1] A word conveys a particular meaning only when the convention with regard to its meaning is grasped; without such a comprehension, the word does not become an expressive sign.[2] What is called the primary significative capacity of the word is the relation subsisting between the sign and the meaning signified by it *(signifié)*. The meaning of a sentence is made up of individual word meanings and their mutual relation, which, in turn, is determined by three factors.

Syntactic Expectancy or Incompleteness. Syntactic expectancy *(ākāṅkṣā)* is the mutual need of the meanings of words for each other to make up a unified sentence meaning, for example, "Bring the cow." Words that do not need each other syntactically cannot constitute a sentence, for example, "cow, horse, man, elephant." A sentence may be said to be complete when it is syntactically complete and can be explained without the help of other words. However, sometimes even syntactically complete sentences may remain logically or psychologically incomplete and may therefore require other words or sentences to complete their sense: for example, "Bring the cow" may give rise to the question "Which cow?" and require the specification "The white one." In such cases, the scope of the term "expectancy" will have to be extended to relations between the sentences of a text and to meanings inferred from the context as well.[3] This condition is most important for the explanation of meaning since it has a bearing on the determination of what constitutes completeness of a sentence and on the further question of when a sentence may give rise to a related meaning.

Phonetic Contiguity. Words must be uttered together in succession so that their relation becomes apparent to the hearer. "Devadatta," "bring," "the horse," uttered at long intervals of time will not be seen as a connected utterance. Phonetic contiguity *(saṃnidhi)* is no doubt a normal feature of human utterances, but not a necessary condition for words to get related syntactically. Syntactic expectancy is what relates the words into a meaningful structure.

Logical Compatibility or Consistency. The words of a sentence must have competence for mutual connection. They should be so related that their combination will produce a knowledge that is compatible with our experience. Logical consistency *(yogyatā)* is not, however, a necessary condition of verbal comprehension—even from a sentence like "He wets with fire" some sort of understanding does result, and a metaphoric use of that sentence is also conceivable. But it is required for the validity of that meaning. It is also an important criterion for determining secondary meanings, for a sentence, as we shall see, does not invite a secondary interpretation unless its literal sense is in some way logically incompatible.

Secondary Meaning

Primary or literal meaning has been defined as that meaning that flows directly from the form of words as signs or, more precisely, from words in their sentence context. It is directly conventional and is grasped immediately as the word is pronounced. But secondary meaning is not so apprehended; it is arrived at as if with some effort—through interpretation by means of other words in the context.[4] In its primary capacity, the expressive word conveys its meaning without any obstruction or intervention *(nirantarārtha-niṣṭha).* The secondary meaning is got indirectly from the meaning of the word or words, not via the relation of the signifier and the signified. It is "indicated" *(lakṣya)* owing to the intervention of the primary meaning. First, we understand the primary meaning of the word; then, when that meaning is found unsuitable in the context, we construe a second meaning and transfer it to something related to the primary meaning. This metaphoric function may be defined as a certain superimposed or extended activity of the word, located in the intermediate sense *(sāntarārtha-niṣṭha).*[5] To put it differently, metaphorical meaning is an unstated meaning arising out of some relation to the stated (literal) meaning.[6]

While most critics agree that there is a secondary function of words and that words do sometimes give rise to unstated meanings, there are many conflicting views as to its precise mode of operation and the conditions under which secondary meanings are generated. The questions that are raised in this connection center round the following issues: (i) whether there is any one condition or a combination of conditions that generates the second meaning in all cases; (ii) whether the secondary meaning is generated by a single word or phrase or by the whole sentence; and (iii) whether the second meaning can be said to arise out of the word at all, inasmuch as it is not related to the word directly, but only indirectly through the primary meaning conveyed by the word.

The Conditions of Secondary Meaning

Incompatibility of Primary Meaning. A crucial question concerning secondary meaning is, When can a sentence be said to generate a meaning that is not stated by its words? The most plausible and generally accepted answer to this is, Only when there is an impasse in construction or a breakdown of its logical sense *(mukhyārtha-bādha).* When the literal meaning of a sentence is not vitiated in any sense, there will be no need for a metaphoric meaning. One does not think of a second meaning (except of course in the case of pun words, which carry double meanings as part of their denotation); neither will one have the motivation to look for another meaning or another possible construction. A writer on logic explains, "A sentence does not seek another sense than the literal when it is satisfactory by reason of the fitness of the connection among the literal meanings of its component words. But when the connection fails it is made up by a meaning topically hinted at by any of the words."[7]

Thus, in the stock example "The village is on the Ganges"—which, in Sanskrit, is not a dead metaphor, unlike "Stratford-upon-Avon"—there is a syntactic incongruity *(anvayānupapatti)* because the grammatical parts of the sentence do not connect according to rules. Consequently, there is an obstruction to the sense. It is not possible for a village to stand *on* the stream of a river. The word "Ganges" has its primary signification in the sense of "the stream of the Ganges" and not in anything else, either connected with it or not connected with it. But, as this sense has broken down, we invoke a second sense connected with it—"on the bank of the Ganges"—to explain away the difficulty, for sentences must at all costs be made sense of. Again, in "Devadatta is a lion," though there is no obstruction to the syntactic sense, there is obstruction to the logic of the statement because of the imputed identity relation *(abhedānvaya)* between the two terms of the metaphor, "Devadatta" and "lion." A faded metaphor *(nirūdha-lakṣaṇā)* has of course the sanction of usage and is not noticed as a deviant expression. But all intentional metaphors *(prayojanavatī lakṣaṇā),* such as the above, require an explanation in terms of an extended meaning.

But is semantic or logical incongruity always necessary for a metaphorical use? The sentence "Protect the curds from crows" is not obstructed in any way. But it would be if the speaker meant to say "from all animals that might eat the curds." Hence, some logicians argued that it is not incongruity of the sentence meaning that should be taken as the condition of secondary meaning but incompatibility with the speaker's intended meaning *(tātparyānupapatti)*. Secondary meaning is the meaning "intended" by the speaker.[8]

The objection to this view is that, in the present example, the word "crows" can be taken as being analogous for all animals that might rob the curds—the crows being but one instance—and the secondary meaning explained without resorting to the speaker's intention. That the purport of the sentence is that the curds should be protected from all such creatures can be gathered from the context of the utterance itself. Therefore, some, including the Mīmāṃsakas of the Bhāṭṭa school, favor the view that "incompatibility of the literal sense with the purported sense" is the condition of secondary meaning. Here the word "purport" (or *tātparya*) is a contentious term. Whereas the logicians use it in the sense of the speaker's intended meaning, others understand it as the final contextual meaning or "utterance meaning." Thus, secondary meaning could also result when there is an incompatibility between the syntactic meaning and utterance meaning.

The sentence about protecting the curds, although it is not linguistically anomalous, is still incongruous when the nature of the utterance is taken into acount. No one would ask to have his curds protected from the crows merely, if his concern was the safety of the curds. In this case, then, we can tell right away that there is an extension of meaning involved. But sometimes we would not be able to tell from the utterance itself that it has been used metaphorically until we have ascertained the entire speech context, including the nonlinguistic setting. Thus, "There go the men with umbrellas" could be a literal use if all the men in the group were holding umbrellas. But, if the speaker was referring to them collectively as umbrella bearers since some of them were holding umbrellas, it would be a case of secondary or extended meaning. To take a modern example, "He lives in a glass house" would be literal use if the person referred to actually lives in a glass house. But, if it is the case that he lives in a brick or stone house, it would be a case of metaphor. Similarly, "Sally is a pig" is literal use if Sally is the name of a pig but metaphorical if it is the name of a girl. These examples show that the same sentence could be literal in one context and metaphorical in another. Therefore, the Bhāṭṭa Mīmāṃsakas, among others, insist that it is not incongruity within the sentence but incongruity or inapplicability of any kind that constitutes the germ of secondary signification *(lakṣaṇā-bīja)* and its recognizable mark.[9]

It should be noted, however, that the incompatibility we have been speaking of must be of the kind that can be removed or explained away by some means. It must, in other words, be only apparent, not real. This, in the language of *mīmāṃsā,* is called apparent inconsistency or apparent failure of meaning *(anyathā anupapatti).* A metaphorical statement is false on the surface only—that is, when it is taken literally—but true when it is forced, through construal, into conformity with literal norms or with a set of truth conditions. Genuine contradictions like "He wets with fire," "the son of a barren woman," and "John has a hairy bald head," inconceivable combinations like "the rabbit's horns" and "sky flower," and lies cannot be explained away through interpretation; they can only be admitted as such and the case dismissed. A false statement bears only a literal interpretation. No doubt, even contradictions and nonsensical expressions, like "Saturday is in bed," "Green ideas sleep furiously," "Quadruplicity drinks procrastination," and so forth, can be made sense of by inventing a metaphorical context for them. But then, the contradiction would only be of the apparent kind, not the real. At any rate, the single criterion for any metaphorical interpretation is the apparent inconsistency of literal meaning.

Relation to the Primary Meaning. Incongruity of primary meaning is a necessary condition of metaphor only in the sense that it starts the inquiry by providing the reason for another explanation of the sentence. It is the cause *(hetu)* of the secondary explanation, but it does not complete the process of explanation and deliver the unstated second meaning.[10] For that we need another force, which is "relation to the primary meaning" *(mukhyārtha-saṃbandha.)* I said at the outset that metaphorical meaning comes out of the literal meaning of words, as a deduction from it, and not directly from the verbal signs themselves. But, for a proper explanation of the sentence, the second meaning that we invoke must in some way be related to and arise out of the words actually used. For a sentence cannot say one thing and mean a completely unrelated thing. "Give offerings to fire" cannot mean "Eat dog meat."[11] Similarly, "a village *on* the Ganges" cannot signify a village "*on the bank of* the Ganges" for want of a convention in that regard. Thus, "relation to the primary meaning" is the ground of secondary meaning, its underlying rationale, while "incongruity of primary meaning" is its condition precedent.

The grammarian Nāgeśa offers the following definition: "The term 'secondary meaning' is applied to the understanding which is preceded by the knowledge of an obstruction to the sentence meaning, and which results from the recollection of a relation to the meaning understood through the primary significative power of the word."[12] Thus, from the sentence "The village is on the Ganges" one understands that the village is stationed on the stream of the river. Then one sees the impossibility of that meaning. After that, one examines the question of what the speaker might have meant by the sentence. Then one tries to construe the sense of "bank" from the word "Ganges" on the basis of some accepted relation to that river.[13]

This relation between the stated and the unstated meanings can be of various kinds, and their enumeration varies from writer to writer—resemblance, inherence, contrariety, association, and so forth.[14] But, for convenience, we may adopt Kumārila's classification of these relations into *(a)* those based on similarity (called *gauṇī vṛtti,* or qualitative transfer, which would cover all expressions based on the figure metaphor) and *(b)* relations other than similarity, such as cause-effect, part-whole, genus-species, container-contained, adjunct-subject, contrariety or opposition, and so on.[15]

However, the mere relatedness to the primary meaning cannot be the definition of secondary meaning, for it cannot by itself produce the secondary meaning without the prior cognition of "obstruction to the literal meaning."[16] One does not import a second meaning simply because it is related to the primary meaning. One does so only in answer to an impediment to the first meaning and to remove that impediment.[17] Obstruction to the primary meaning is then the sole cause of secondary meaning, while the criterion for determining it is relation to the primary meaning.

The Motive for Metaphor. While these two conditions seem sufficient for explaining the metaphoric process, some critics, especially the followers of the *dhvani* theory, would like to add "the motive for secondary use" *(prayojana)* as a condition of secondary meaning.[18] All intentional metaphors must presuppose a special purpose for their use, for no one would deviate from normal or matter-of-fact usage without some compelling reason. This purpose could be either to convey an idea in an indirect manner or to secure a special emphasis. One may sometimes resort to a condensed expression for the sake of economy of effort *(lāghavaṃ lakṣaṇā).* For instance, instead of having to give a long list of animals and birds from which the curds are to be protected, one could simply say "Protect the curds from the crows." According to the *dhvani* critics, the motive for the expression "the village on the Ganges" could be to suggest, through indirection, the ideas of coolness and sanctity associated with the Ganges. Hence this purpose, which prompted the speaker to use a metaphoric expression, also enters into the explication of the sentence as a separate condition.

Objections could be taken to this view from the general standpoint of *mīmāṃsā* and logic. The question to be asked is whether what is called purpose is the cause *(hetu)* of the secondary function or its final result or purport *(phalitārtha)*. That the speaker wanted to accomplish his meaning in a way distinct from the direct mode of speech and that he had a special motive for choosing the metaphorical mode was of course the reason for the use of the metaphorical expression *(pravṛtti-nimitta)*, but only in the order of conception, not in the order of our understanding. The motive is what prompted his expression, but it is not needed for our understanding of the secondary meaning. That is, the knowledge that the speaker's purport, in the Ganges example, is to suggest the notion of the coolness and sanctity of the place is not required for removing the initial obstacle to the literal meaning and for the understanding that "a village *on* the Ganges" ought to mean "a village *on the bank of* the Ganges." If, on the other hand, the motive for the metaphorical expression is taken as the purport of the sentence, then, obviously, it should come at the end of the whole process of construction as its ultimate result *(parama-tātparya)*, not as its condition precedent. Such being the case, it is difficult to admit the motive element as one of the root causes of secondary meaning.

The Nature of Metaphorical Transfer. All definitions are agreed on the point that secondary meaning is an unstated meaning deduced from the stated, primary meaning on the basis of some relation, actual or imagined *(āhārya)*, between the two. It is also recognized that, unless this relation is located in the stated meaning and is indicated by it, it will not become available at all. Unless the word "Ganges" suggested the related sense of "bank," we could not progress in our explanation from step 1, "incongruity of primary meaning," to step 2, "relation to the primary meaning." Therefore, the stated primary meaning itself must bring about the knowledge—or recollection, to be more precise—of the unstated secondary meaning. In other words, the relation based on the stated meaning causes the understanding of the unstated meaning.[19]

Two questions are in order here. Is the second meaning, deduced from the primary meaning, something necessary and definite and something that invariably follows from the first meaning? In the example we have been discussing, the stream and the bank are of course related through inherence, as part and whole, or through proximity. But there are other things also associated with the river, such as fish, boats, and crocodiles. How, then, does one recollect the sense of the "bank?" This question is answered by saying that, while there may be many other ideas also associated with the river, the only relevant factor in the context of the sentence would be something that will serve as a substratum for the village to stand on, and this consideration will be the criterion for arriving at the sense of the bank. The context of the sentence will itself dictate the choice of the relevant feature.

There is the second question of what happens to the primary meaning once the secondary meaning is established on the basis of some relation to it. Does the metaphoric word surrender part or all of its meaning to the word or words substituted? Evidently, there cannot be a complete cancellation of the literal meaning in the metaphorical process. For our analysis of secondary function has revealed that secondary meaning must grow out of the literal meaning, not independently of it, and that it must be explicable in terms of it. As Kumārila observes, the word can, in no event, give up its meaning, nor can another meaning appear without some basis.[20] If the primary meaning were completely abandoned, there would be no secondary meaning since there would be nothing to serve as a ground of relation between the two.[21]

We must therefore conclude that secondary meaning involves rejection of only part of the primary meaning of the metaphoric word and retention of part of it. Thus, even in the example "A village on the Ganges," in which "Ganges" comes to mean "the bank of the Ganges," the original sense of the word "Ganges" is not completely abandoned—the extreme proximity of the location of the village to the river is what is preserved of that meaning. The village stands not merely on the ground mass *identified as* the bank of the Ganges but on the ground mass *distinguished* by its proximity to the stream of the river. What is rejected is the idea of the village being stationed on the river itself.

In secondary meaning of the type involving similitude between two terms (as in the figure metaphor)—for example, "Devadatta is a lion"—there is also selection from a set of features (predicates) pertaining to the class "lion" and cancellation of the rest. The second condition of secondary meaning, namely, "relation to the primary meaning," calls for a relation only in respect of some properties that are common to both the primary and the secondary referents, not of all properties. Predicate selection is determined by the context. Thus, in the example given above, the word "lion" conveys to us a complex of properties, such as animality, ferocity, carnivorousness, portliness, courageousness, and so forth. Every entity is in fact such a bundle of properties, some defining and necessary, some "nonnecessary," in terms of Beardsley's analysis.[22] Of these, we select only one or two features that may most suitably be applied to Devadatta, such as portliness or lionheartedness, and reject the rest, for it is only in those terms that a man may be spoken of as a lion, even figuratively.

Although rejection of some aspects of the original meaning is common to all metaphoric expression, the indication of another meaning on the basis of a connection with some other aspects of it is implied in all secondary operation.[23] Secondary meaning implies obstruction to the primary meaning. But the primary meaning is retained in the understanding, however indirectly. What, however, causes the breakdown of the primary meaning is the inclusion of all the features pertaining to the primary referent, as in speaking of Devadatta as a lion or of the stream of the Ganges as the ground on which the village is located.

In the ironic type of sentence, the import of the proposition is completely contrary to its surface meaning, so it may not seem to fit the description given above of the secondary process. In the example "Go, eat poison," addressed by a well-wisher to a friend going to eat at the house of the foe of the family, the command to eat poison is completely set aside and its very opposite understood from the sentence: "Do not eat poison; eating at his house is like eating poison." But even this type is regarded as secondary meaning, of the kind based on contrariety *(viparīta-lakṣaṇā),* since it has all the formal and logical features of secondary meaning. First, there is the obstruction to the literal sense—the injunction to eat poison and its incompatibility with the character of the speaker, who is not normally expected to issue such an injunction. As for the second condition, the very opposition between the two senses, between the injunction (literal sense) and the prohibition (the purported secondary sense), may be taken to constitute a relation, on the basis of which the final import is reached. That is, the enjoined eating of the poison is construed as the "counterpositive" of the prohibition not to eat poison.[24]

Metaphor and Simile. Judged by the criteria discussed above, it appears that the figure simile cannot be admitted to the class of expressions we have called secondary or metaphorical meaning. The difference between a simile and the figure metaphor is not merely a formal difference—similarity in the simile is verbally stated by means of the comparison signs "like," "as," "similar to," and so forth—but a logical difference. The real test of metaphor is that, in it, nondifference is predicated of the subject *(viṣaya)* and the modifier *(viṣayin).* In "Devadatta is a lion," the complete nature of the lion is superimposed on Devadatta, which is what causes the impediment to the primary sense. In a simile, on the other hand, only similarity is asserted. All similarity statements of course imply a basic difference between the objects compared. The essence of a simile is that, in it, the similarity is associated with difference, whereas in metaphor there is only nondifference. But, as a simile is constructed in the form of a statement of similarity in difference, there is no obstruction to the literal meaning and no secondary operation.[25]

It may be argued that, even in the form of an explicit simile-like comparison, for example, "Devadatta is (courageous) like a lion," there is an obstruction to the literal meaning: Devadatta and the lion cannot be courageous in the same sense; they do not behave in the same way, and therefore such similes are also metaphorical in their implication. But it must be admitted that, even in comparisons of this kind, there must be some actual ground, a perceived resemblance between the two objects, something in the behavior of the man, in the example given above, to suggest a resemblance to the behavior of the lion. Otherwise, one would not think of a lion in connection with a courageous man. Anything can be compared to anything if a certain resemblance is found between them—lovers to a pair of compasses, and so on. Hence, the comparison can be taken literally.

Whether the Word or the Sentence Is the Focus of Secondary Meaning

Another issue that relates to the discussion of secondary meaning in the Sanskrit texts is whether the word or the sentence is the locus of the metaphorical change, whether secondary meaning is produced at the level of the single word or phrase or at the level of the whole statement. The answer to this question is attempted differently by different schools of thought. For the followers of Bhāṭṭa *mīmāṃsā* and for the logicians, who believed in the semantics of the word *(abhihitānvaya-vāda),* words, separately, have meanings in themselves, but they give a connected meaning when put together in a sentence owing to their mutual syntactic need. Sentence meaning is the meaning of words that are syntactically connected *(saṃsargo vākyārthaḥ).* For the followers of the Prābhākara school, on the other hand, while words do have core meanings, they express not isolated meanings but only syntactically connected meanings *(anvitābhidhāna).* Thus, in the sentence "Chaitra cooks," the word "Chaitra" means not the isolated person called Chaitra but Chaitra as the agent or subject of the activity of cooking, and the verb word "cooks" means the activity of cooking, which has Chaitra for its agent. Both schools accept secondary signification as a distinct verbal function. But, according to the former school, it is the word or phrase that takes the metaphorical meaning. For the latter school, however, since words function only in interaction with the other words of the sentence, metaphoric meaning is generated by the whole sentence, by the interaction of all its parts. In the examples "The village is on the Ganges" and "Devadatta is a lion," it is not merely the words "Ganges" and "lion" that are obstructed in their primary sense but the predication as a whole.[26]

The upholder of the first view (of the word-focused metaphor) might grant that the entire sentence meaning is necessary for determining that the literal meaning is incongruous. But he would insist that the metaphorical transposition or displacement of meaning takes place in a single word or phrase of the sentence, not in the whole sentence. It is the word "Ganges" or "lion" that suffers the semantic change and hints at an extended meaning, while the other words of the sentence preserve their natural signification. It is that word alone that is substituted by another, more suitable word. In "The clouds are crying" and "The branches are fighting with one another," the focus of the metaphor is the verb. Thus, it is always possible to isolate the word or words that take the substitution from the rest of the sentence. One might therefore say that, in a metaphorical sentence, the incompatibility of a single word or phrase with the rest of the sentence establishes a need *(ākāṇkṣā)* on the part of that segment of the sentence for some unuttered word (or meaning) that has to be supplied to fulfill that need. When all the words of the sentence are used metaphorically, no comprehension results.[27]

While one can thus argue effectively for secondary meaning being focused in the word in the case of straightforward metaphor, in which both terms of the metaphor—the subject and the modifier—are placed on a common footing *(sāmānādhikaraṇya),* it is not so easy to isolate a single focus word in instances of secondary usage involving contrariety *(vyadhikaraṇya).* In the ironic statement "Eat poison," which implies "Don't eat in his house," the whole sentence is obstructed in its literal meaning, and the implied secondary meaning is got by transforming the whole sentence into something like "Food in his house is poison, so do not eat in his house." In any case, not all ironic statements involve the whole sentence. Almost any metaphor can be used ironically, as when Devadatta is called "a lion on the battlefield" and what is meant is that he is a chicken or when a stupid person is spoken of as "a teacher of the gods" (Bṛhaspati). In such instances, the force of the metaphor is centered on the single word or phrase, and, by substituting that part alone, that is, "chicken" for "lion" and "the opposite of the teacher of gods" for "a teacher of gods," we can derive the secondary meaning.

The whole discussion as to whether the word or the whole sentence is the locus of the secondary meaning is perhaps purely academic and inspired by the doctrinal differences of the rival schools. Between the two views, however, the one that emphasizes the dynamics of the whole sentence would seem to be nearer the truth since secondary meaning results from the pressure of the whole predicated meaning, not merely from the deviation of a single word from normal uses. But the other approach from the angle of the word also has a point in that, when the second meaning is arrived at from the sentence as a whole, the single word or phrase takes on the burden of the change.

Is Secondary Meaning Verbal Meaning at All?

We have seen that secondary meaning is derived, not directly from the word, but indirectly, via the meaning of the word. That is to say that it is "deduced" through reasoning on the meaning of the word, not "signified" by the word. But here the question arises as to whether a meaning deduced from another meaning can legitimately be said to issue from the word at all. The knowledge derived from words has for its source the verbal signs themselves, and no other source. For most philosophical schools, verbal knowledge is distinct, both in content and form, from deductive reasoning and direct perception.[28]

This being the case, it may be questioned whether the secondary meaning can be assigned to the capacity of the words themselves. Objections based on this consideration have taken two forms: the old grammarians argue that all verbal meaning is primary meaning and that there is no secondary meaning, and the critic Mahimabhaṭṭa holds that all extended or implied meaning is inferred meaning and not strictly that of the words.

For the grammarians, all verbal usage is of the primary kind, carried out by the expressive capacity of the words *(śakti).* Words have endless potentialities and are capable of conveying all sorts of meanings *(sarve sarvārthāḥ),* according to their use. Pāṇini did not recognize metaphorical meaning as a distinct linguistic function. According to him and his commentators, instances of extended use could be explained by the regular rules of grammar without the necessity for assuming a second function of words.[29] According to Patañjali, commentator on Pāṇini, the meaning of a word is all that is conveyed by the word.[30] Later grammarians too were of the view that a verbal relation is possible only between the word and its meaning and not between that meaning and another meaning.[31] In the "Ganges" example, for instance, it is asked whether the word "Ganges" conveys the indicated second sense of "bank" with or without the medium of another word. If it is without the medium of another word, then the first word should always convey that other sense "bank." If it is through the medium of another word (the word "bank"), then why is the first word ("Ganges") necessary to get to the second meaning ("bank")?[32] On this view, then, secondary meaning, which is the final purport of the sentence, is but an extension of the primary operation itself. From the point of the initial understanding of the expressed meaning until the final understanding of the purported meaning, it is only one extended activity of the word *(dīrgha-dīrgha-vyāpāra),* like that of an arrow that, in one stroke, performs many actions, such as piercing, splitting, and so forth.[33]

For Bhartṛhari, the grammarian, word meanings have no reality except in connected sentences. All meaning occurs at the sentence level, not, however, as a concatenation of separately existing word meanings, but as one indivisible whole, called *vākya-sphoṭa,* that strikes the hearer in a single moment of understanding. Arguing from this standpoint, Bhartṛhari says that it is meaningless to discuss the various functions of words, such as primary and secondary. Even in cases in which the surface meaning of the sentence is obstructed and requires another meaning for its explanation, the final meaning alone should be taken as the "operative" meaning of the sentence.[34] This final meaning is derived not from any competency of the words themselves but from the context. In the example "A village on the Ganges," there is neither the abandonment of the uttered word "Ganges" nor the supplying of the unuttered word "bank." The uttered word cannot bring the unuttered word to mind because its function is to convey its own meaning. It cannot also take us to the unuttered meaning because there is no relation between the two. For the same reason, the meaning of the uttered word cannot lead to the unuttered word. If, again, the meaning of the uttered word were to lead to an unuttered meaning, it would be a case of inference, not verbal knowledge. For all verbal knowledge must proceed from the word. Therefore, Bhartṛhari concludes that the sentence itself, with the help of the context, causes the knowledge of any other meaning required to complete it, as in the case of elliptical sentences like "Door! Door!" or, to remove the incongruity, as in the case of metaphorical statements. But this process is purely mental, although prompted by words, since we mentally supply the required meaning without the intervention of another word.[35]

Mahimabhaṭṭa, in his polemical work *Vyaktiviveka,* also voices similar objections against the theory of many meaning functions.[36] An advocate of the "one word, one meaning" view, he argues that words have only one power: the denotation of their conventionally assigned meanings. A word, as a sign, is not capable of diverse operations and cannot extend to another meaning in respect of which there is no convention. Neither can it surrender its own meaning. It seems to convey different meanings only because of differences in the conditions of its use *(samagrīvaicitryāt).* Thus, what is claimed to be another meaning of the word is only another use of the same word. In places where a second meaning is implied, owing to the breakdown of the denoted meaning, it is only reasonable to assume that the function belongs only to the meaning, not to the word. For, if verbal activity is to be assumed even where there is no convention, then all words would, under some given conditions, give rise to another meaning in the manner that they express their own meanings. Thus, when one meaning gives rise to another meaning, secondary or tertiary, it is no longer a verbal operation but inference. In metaphorical statements, the conditions that give rise to another interpretation, namely, the unacceptability of the first meaning and the contextual factors, serve as a logical sign for the inference of the second meaning.

But it may still be maintained, against these objections, that there is a secondary function of words and that it is distinct from their primary denotative activity. The very fact that in metaphoric constructions the literal meaning breaks down argues for secondary meaning being a distinctive function. When a speaker equates two entirely different or incompatible things and speaks of them as one (metaphor), or equates the part and the whole (synecdoche) or the container with the contained (metonymy), or states a particular and implies a whole class of objects (as in "Protect the curds from the crows"), or says one thing and means the opposite (irony), he cannot be said to be using words in their normal signification. The grammarian's argument that any word can convey any meaning according to the conditions of its use is certainly an extreme view and one that is apt to upset the whole convention of linguistic usage. Bhartṛhari may be right in his monistic view that the ultimate meaning of a sentence *(vākyārtha-sphoṭa)* is its sole meaning, for the sentence will rest there and not in the intermediary meanings. But that does not warrant the conclusion that there are no intermediary meanings or meaning stages or any separate functions that account for these stages. If all meanings are one kind of meaning only (in the night all cows are black), there will be no scope for analysis and discrminiation.

The objection that secondary meaning cannot be derived from words since it is not directly related to the words may be answered by saying that an indirect relation to the word is also a legitimate verbal relation since verbal understanding does result from it. Granted that the relation between the word "Ganges" and the sense of "bank" is a mediated relation, through what is related to the primary meaning of "Ganges." But it is still a verbal relation because the secondary sense is based on the word actually used, namely, "Ganges." This word is needed for the second meaning, and therefore it is, in a sense, the expresser of the second meaning. Therefore Śabara, the commentator on the *Mīmāṃsā Sūtras* of Jaimini, poses the question, "How is it possible that a word denoting one meaning should have signification in another meaning?" and says, "It is by conveying its own meaning."[37] Words have their innate capacity to convey other meanings—associated meanings and connotations—

through the medium of their primary meanings. These extended meanings must still be deemed to come within the purview of the words since they are obtained through the agency of the words. Hence, the secondary function is called the "tail-end of Denotation" *(abhidhā-puccha).*[38]

The other objection that the movement from one meaning to another meaning is a matter of inference and not direct verbal activity also cannot be sustained. Although both secondary meaning and inference imply deriving one idea from another, there are important formal differences between the two activities. First, secondary meaning involves incompatibility between two given ideas, for example, Sam, being human, cannot be called a pig. But there is no such contradiction in inferring fire from smoke; there is only the recollection of their invariable connection. Second, the motives in respect of the two operations are different: in the case of inference, it is the desire to infer the unknown fact from the known fact *(sisādhayiṣā),* whereas, in the case of secondary meaning, it is the desire to remove the incongruity between two terms. Third, whereas invariable concomitance *(vyāpti)* is the ground of inference—the presence of smoke must always and necessarily lead to the inference of fire—it cannot be claimed that there is such a necessary connection between the primary and the secondary meanings. Secondary meaning is obtained from the contextual factors, which may vary from case to case and which do not fix the metaphorically affected word in any definite meaning. "Fire," in "The boy is fire," could in one case suggest "brilliance," and in another "hot temperedness."

Metaphor and Symbol. Sanskrit criticism has no concept of a symbolic meaning apart from the well-known functions of primary, secondary, and suggested meanings. So if there is a special semantic activity called "symbolic expression," it must come under either secondary meaning or suggestion. The question whether there is a suggestive function as distinct from the secondary will be decided in chapter 6. For the present, our problem is, Is symbolic meaning a secondary function of language, and is it governed by the conditions we have stipulated for secondary meaning?

While the term "symbol" may have many different senses, there are mainly two senses in which it is often understood in Western criticism, especially in the literary context. First, a symbol may be understood as an object or image, verbally presented, that embodies or signifies a complex of feeling and thought and that is "an outward sign of an inward state."[39] This definition comes close to Eliot's conception of "objective correlative" as "a set of objects, a situation, a chain of events which shall be the formula" of a given emotion "such that when the external facts . . . are given, the emotion is immediately evoked."[40] An object or event may be called an "outward sign" or "formula" of an inner state in the sense that it manifests or objectifies the inner state or, put another way, it points to an emotion as its objective sign. It is through such signs, as we have seen in chapter 4, that we are able to identify the emotions. Such signs are either the objects of the emotion or its exciting causes. Melville's "white whale," in *Moby Dick,* acquires a great deal of emotional significance by being the object of emotion to several characters, but chiefly to Ahab. Hawthorne's "scarlet letter," too, gathers its meaning and emotive power by being an object of different emotions to different persons—pride, shame, loneliness, anguish, and so on. But the theme of the novel is not the scarlet letter, in the way that the white whale is the theme of *Moby Dick,* but the sin of adultery and its repercussions. As the significance of the scarlet letter is due to its association with Hester's adultery and other circumstances, it is rather an accessory to the main emotional theme and an exciting cause than the primary object of the emotions expressed by the characters. But, understood as objective signs, these images cannot be called symbols—if by symbol is meant a sign that "stands for" some other, separately existing object or idea. The whale or the scarlet letter does not stand for the emotions it arouses in people; it simply arouses these emotions in people.

The white whale and the scarlet letter may, however, serve another function. They may also have a metaphorical significance—the white whale may stand for the ambiguity of reality, immanent evil, and so forth and the scarlet letter for the "burning brand" of sin. But this is the second sense of "symbol" that we should consider. In this sense, a symbol is "an analogy for something unstated," "an embodied or immanent analogy."[41] In other words, it is a concealed or hermetic metaphor in which the other half of the metaphor, namely, the subject or tenor, is suppressed and only the modifier (vehicle) is given. This, in Sanskrit rhetoric, is called metaphor by suppression *(sādhyavasāna-lakṣaṇā),* which is a variety of secondary signification. The definition of this type runs as follows: "When the subject of superimposition *(viṣaya)* is so presented that it is swallowed up by the object superimposed *(viṣayin),* thereby being suppressed or concealed, it would be secondary signification by suppression."[42] Thus, when a human carrier is called a bull, in the form "The porter is a bull," we have a regular metaphor. But, when, referring to the porter, one says "This bull here," or when Churchill referred to Mussolini as "this utensil," or when Christ is referred to as "the Lion of Judea," we have metaphor by suppression. The "star" image in Whitman's "When Lilacs Last in Dooryard Bloom'd" invites an application to something outside itself and radiates a significance not directly expressed by its own words. It works as a hidden analogy to the dead hero. Yeats's "image out of Spiritus Mundi" ("The Second Coming") is another such example.

A symbol cannot of course be explicated without seeing what it symbolizes or refers to. But what is symbolized—the missing term or symbolic referent—can, as in the above examples, usually be obtained from the context of the poem. It is equally necessary that the literal meaning should be incompatible or defective in some way for a symbolic interpretation to be warranted—reality is not a white whale nor President Lincoln a fallen star. When a symbolic statement is not vitiated in any way, and when the context does not provide a clue as to the meaning symbolized, we cannot even recognize a thing as symbol. A symbol can thus be seen as a species of metaphor. The process involved in interpreting it is basically that of a metaphor, although its structure is not that of a metaphor.

The Vedic language too provides many examples of symbolic usage. But the exegetes classify all such expressions under the general category of metaphoric speech. For example, the sacrificial bull is described as having four horns, three feet, two heads, seven hands, and so forth. Its heart is the sacrificial post, its chest the sacrificial altar. Similarly, the cosmic person, Puruṣa, is described as having the sun and the moon for his eyes. The symbolism of such expressions is explained as a certain mode of figurative description in which an abstract conception, such as the sacrifice or the cosmos, is given a bodily form following a similarity in some respect between the two terms *(śarīratvena rūpaṇam)*.[43] It is not necessary of course that the symbolized object should be an abstract concept; it can also be a state of mind or mood *(un état d'âme)*—horror, ennui, *gouffre,* or some other intangible feeling—but pictured in terms of an image, which then becomes a metaphor for that state of mind, for example, Rimbaud's "drunken boat," Mallarmé's "swan."

The account given above of secondary meaning or the principle of metaphor, in its broadest sense, would seem comprehensive enough to cover all cases in which an implicit meaning is involved in addition to what the words of a sentence state explicitly. Some recent theorists have, however, doubted that we can have any comprehensive rule for all figurative constructions. But our analysis has shown that the conditions governing secondary meaning, namely, incompatibility of the primary meaning and relation to the primary meaning, apply equally to cases of metaphor, irony, synecdoche, and metonymy, which are the major tropes. Paradox and oxymoron, too, are, like irony, basically forms of secondary meaning based on contrariety. Exaggeration (the figure hyperbole) must also be considered a species of metaphoric speech since the same test of literal falsity applies to it. If a statement were literally true, we would not even call it an exaggeration.

The case of allegory and myth, however, seems different. In allegory, two meanings exist together as parallel strands, without the first meaning being modified or canceled out. Again, since in an allegorical statement the second meaning is not logically demanded, the text itself must contain an explicit indication of its presence. Otherwise, we would not notice it. Mythical statements, too, must be distinguished from figurative discourse. The actions of anthropomorphic deities, for instance, are not always amenable to metaphoric construal as they do not suggest adequate conceptual terms or equivalents into which they can be translated. Statements about them should perhaps be taken at face value, as assertions about another way of experiencing or conceiving of reality.[44]

The Indian theory of metaphor may thus be seen to be in substantial accord with the view defended by Beardsley in recent times.[45] The notion of semantic or logical anomaly seems to be essential for the understanding of metaphoric speech. But this anomaly, as noted above, must be of the apparent kind and explainable through another interpretation. The second, metaphorical, interpretation is what validates the judgment expressed by the sentence. Again, semantic anomaly can be defined, ultimately, only as a violation of the truth conditions applicable in a given context of use, not merely as a violation of the linguistic norms or standard usage—although some cases of metaphor may be recognized by this test. Thus, a statement can be metaphorical in its purport even when its surface syntax and semantics are normal. However, as the Mīmāṃsakas argue, it is not necessary for recognizing a metaphor by its purport to ascertain the speaker's intention. The context of utterance alone is sufficient for the purpose. The Indian theory of purport *(tātparya)* provides for illocutionary considerations without actually appealing to "intention."[46] At any rate, the central and inescapable issue in dealing with metaphor is the relevance of the question of truth. We can judge a text to be metaphorical only by applying the calculus of truth functions to it. This is the requirement of *yogyatā,* or logical compatibility, emphasized by the Indian theorists.

It has been argued by some recent theorists, against Beardsley's theory of metaphor, (i) that no general theory of metaphor is possible and that there is no single test for metaphor or "no simple recognition signs for detecting metaphors"[47] (ii) that there is no well-marked distinction between literal and metaphoric usage; and (iii) that metaphor is not concerned with any truth claims but that it is a certain "game with language."[48] Ted Cohen objects that "literal falsity" cannot serve as a test for recognizing metaphors because some statements can be "twice-true," that is, true both literally and metaphorically.[49] But this objection may be met by saying that sentences such as "Christ was a carpenter" (Cohen's example) and "Moscow is a cold city" cannot be used both literally and metaphorically in any single instance of speech act. (This, in *Mīmāṃsā,* is called the maxim of nonsimultaneity of literal and metaphorical senses.)[50] If, in a given instance, what is being said is that Christ was a carpenter in some metaphorical sense, any reference to his being a carpenter's son would be pointless. The context of the sentence may be supposed to fix the word in one or the other meaning. Although, considered in isolation, the statement is true both literally and metaphorically, a metaphorical use of it will necessarily set aside the literal meaning as being unsuitable in the context. Conversely, if the literal meaning is appropriate in the context, it will render any metaphorical interpretation unnecessary. Thus, the test of inappropriateness *(anupapatti)* may be seen to be operative even in such examples.

Metaphor, as Margolis argues, may be a game in which we play by deliberately "deforming" things. But even for playing a game we need a logical apparatus, and that, in the case of metaphor, can only be the criterion of logical or semantic inconsistency. In the Donne example (which Margolis discusses) "I dye / As often as from thee I goe," for instance, the "deformation" of the sense of "dye" is made possible only by the logical absurdity of a man dying so very often.[51] This example also demonstrates the fact that words do have their primary meanings, fixed by usage, from which a metaphorical use may be said to be a deviation. This is the basic presupposition of most Indian theories of meaning. It is also clear from the foregoing discussion that sometimes words and sentences are not used in their literal sense and that the distinction between literal and metaphorical is an undeniable fact of our linguistic practice. Therefore, notwithstanding arguments to the contrary, it seems reasonable to assume that something like an established use and an extension of it can be distinguished and that criteria can be set up for the explanation of each mode.[52]

6

SUGGESTION

The Basis of Suggestion

Since suggestion has been claimed to be an entirely distinct kind of verbal operation, not comprehended by the primary and metaphorical functions, it has to be shown what its basis is and how precisely it differs from the established modes of speech. Basically, of course, there are only these two uses of language. If there is to be a third kind of meaning, it has to be brought forth by these very uses of language. As a verbal mode, suggestion must depend on either primary meaning or secondary meaning. Accordingly, suggestion is classified into two broad divisions: (i) that which is based on secondary meaning *(laksaṇā-mūla)* and (ii) that which is based on primary meaning *(abhidhā-mūla)*. In the first type, the expressed meaning is "not intended or meant to be conveyed" *(avivakṣita-vācya)*. That is, either it is completely set aside *(atyanta-tiraskṛta)*, as in most cases of metaphor, for example, "Like a mirror *blinded* by breath, the moon now does not glow" (in which the primary sense of "blinded" is inapplicable to "mirror"), or it is shifted or used with a slightly different emphasis *(arthāṇtara-saṃkramita)*, for example, "Dirty clothes are not clothes" or "I am not Prince Hamlet" (Eliot, "Prufrock"), where only certain connotations of the predicate words (the second "clothes" and "Prince Hamlet") are emphasized and their designation is set aside because of its inapplicability. In the second type, that based on primary meaning, the expressed sense is intended, but it subserves a further implied sense, such as implications arising out of literal statements. This type is called *vivakṣita-anyapara-vācya*.

Under the first type may be included all kinds of metaphorical expressions that, in addition to their metaphorical sense, also convey an implied sense or connotational meanings that are not required for resolving their incongruity on the literal level. The traditional figurative categories, including metaphor, are treated by the *dhvani* theorists as a case of expressed meaning. (This point will be explained later.) All such figures could, however, in the *dhvani* view, become suggestive if they also contain another implicit or "embedded" figure or if a figure is merely hinted at instead of being formulated explicitly. Coming under the second type, namely, suggestion based on primary meaning, are *(a)* paronomastic expressions, which convey two or more meanings as part of their primary signification but which can become suggestive when they point to an implied comparison or contrast; *(b)* implications, which, due to contextual pressure, flow out of sentences that are not logically vitiated; and *(c)* emotive statements, which describe an emotive situation in literal language. Emotive meanings can also, no doubt, be expressed in metaphorical language. But the basic facts of an emotive situation are often stated in literal language, and the *dhvani* theorist claims that there is suggestion even in such cases. We shall see in what sense such statements can be said to be suggestive.

Suggested meanings, whether derived from the primary or the secondary function of language, are again divided into three major categories: (i) suggestion of an idea *(vastu-dhvani),* (ii) suggestion of a figure *(alaṃkāra-dhvani),* and (iii) suggestion of a *rasa* or emotive meaning *(rasa-dhvani).* Another classification of *dhvani,* from a different point of view, is into (i) that which is based on the word *(śabda-śakti-mūla)* and (ii) that which is based on meaning *(artha-śakti-mūla).* In the first variety, the actual word used is vital for the suggestion of another meaning, and it cannot be substituted by its synonym, as is the case with paronomastic expressions or as in cases in which the connotations of a word are lost by substitution. In the second variety, suggestion is brought out by meanings alone, which can be expressed in other terms as well.

There are innumerable other divisions and subdivisions of *dhvani*—literally scores—criss-crossing one another. But they are not important for our discussion of the general theory. The chart below provides a simplified and rationalized classification of the major *dhvani* types.

Secondary Meaning versus Suggestion

Secondary meaning is no doubt an unstated meaning, and there seems to be no harm in accepting it as a suggestive function. But, for the *dhvani* theorists, this is not the case. Suggestion, according to them, does not occur at the level of metaphorical meaning; it is distinct from the meta-

- Suggestion
  - Based on Secondary Meaning
    - Suggestion of an idea
    - Suggestion of a figure
  - Based on Primary Meaning
    - Paronomastic expressions with embedded figures
    - Implications from literal statements (idea or figure)
    - Emotive meanings

phorical function. But how is this distinction demonstrated? Their argument is that there is a suggestion that arises out of the secondary sense and that is presupposed by it, namely, the motive element or the purpose *(prayojana)* for which a speaker has resorted to a metaphorical expression. Thus, in the example about the village "on the Ganges," the motive could be to praise the sanctity and coolness of the location. If this was the speaker's motive, then the literal form "The village is *on the bank of* the Ganges" would not secure this special kind of meaning or emphasis desired.[1] Now, the associations of coolness and sanctity are not carried by the land mass alongside the river but by the stream itself. Therefore they must arise out of the word "Ganges." Thus, we admit secondary meaning in "the bank of the Ganges" to remove the incongruity of the utterance and a tertiary meaning or suggestion in the associated meanings conveyed by the word "Ganges."

By analyzing this paradigm case (discussed in all texts), we arrive at the following three stages of meaning. (1) The word "Ganges" takes us to the sense of "stream" by the direct relation of word to meaning. (2) The sense of "stream" takes us to its related meaning of "the bank of the stream" by an indirect relation of one meaning to another meaning. (3) The second meaning "the bank of the stream" suggests the third meaning of "sanctity" and so forth, associated with the river, by another removed relation of the first meaning to the third meaning, in which the bank is recognized as distinguished by the properties belonging to the Ganges. It is at this final stage that the suggestive function enters. Abhinavagupta lays down the rules of suggestion as follows: "A further (unstated) meaning, relationship to the primary meaning, and inadequacy of the conventional meaning—these are the regulative principles of the suggestive function."[2]

Now it is claimed that this motive element (the coolness and the sanctity of the place and the praise implicit in it), which is the final purport of the sentence and the reason for the secondary use, is neither a denotative nor a metaphorical function but another, implicative function of the metaphorically affected word *(lākṣaṇika-śabda)* itself, that is, "Ganges," in the present example. If the purported idea of sanctity and coolness is to be got from the sentence, it is argued, it can be in only one of the following ways.

1. The word "Ganges" itself should directly denote that meaning. But this cannot be since there is no convention *(samaya)* to that effect. This word only denotes the stream of the river. So it is not the primary meaning.

2. That meaning should be derived from the secondary meaning of the word "Ganges," namely, "the bank." But this too is not possible, first, because, obviously, the properties of sanctity and the rest belong to the Ganges by inherence and are not directly related to the bank in the way that the bank is related to the Ganges. That is to say, the bank is not holy by itself; it is holy because the Ganges is holy. Second, the sense of "the bank" is not obstructed in any way so that it could, in turn, give rise to another secondary meaning; it is perfectly compatible with the idea of the location of the village. Third, there is also no further purpose served by making the purported idea of sanctity and coolness the object of another secondary operation. That is, the sense of "the bank" could yield the further notion of sanctity only if it cannot be explained in any other way. But the purpose for which that sense is brought in is already explained by its suitability for being the location of the village. Fourth, it is not also necessary, for resolving the incongruity of the statement, to import the notion of sanctity and coolness. Thus, none of the conditions of secondary meaning is fulfilled.

3. It is not also possible that the same word "Ganges" could, after delivering the sense of "bank" through one secondary operation, convey the sense of sanctity and coolness through another secondary operation, for it has exhausted its function in delivering the first secondary meaning.

4. We cannot also conflate the secondary meaning "bank" with the purported idea of "sanctity" and admit secondary function in "the bank of the Ganges *as qualified* by sanctity," for the object of the apprehended secondary meaning is "the bank of the Ganges," not "sanctity," which is the resultant *(phalāṃśa)* of that knowledge. The resultant or fruit of knowledge must be distinct from its object.[3] Again, if the bank is taken as qualified by the said properties, then the speciality of the use of the expression "a village *on* the Ganges" would remain unexplained, for, if these properties were possessed by the bank, why would anybody resort to that expression instead of the more normal "a village on the *bank* of the Ganges"? Therefore, in its final import, the bank is understood as having the qualities of the Ganges, by association with the Ganges, in the

form "The village is situated on the holy bank of the Ganges," thus implying praise of the site of the village.[4]

5. Finally, the suggested notion of sanctity must be supposed to be derived from "Ganges" itself because no other word in the sentence is capable of conveying it. Further, in conveying that notion, the word "Ganges" is not obstructed in its primary sense as it was in giving rise to the secondary sense of "bank." No part of its original signification is canceled, for the sense of the Ganges being a stream is fully required for carrying the associations of sanctity and so forth.[5]

The primary sense of "Ganges," then, discharges two functions at once: it conveys the sense of "bank," which is related to its core meaning "stream" by proximity or inherence, and it further suggests the qualities of sanctity and so on, which are associated with the object denoted by that word. These associational meanings may be said to flow out of that word via its meaning or alongside it.

Here one might object that, since these associated meanings cannot be obtained from the word "Ganges" directly through its primary activity or from the indicated secondary meaning, they are not got through the activity of words at all but through some other kind of knowledge, such as inference. Verbal meaning is, by definition, "what is not obtained from another source of knowledge" *(ananyalabhyaḥ śabdārthaḥ).* But the *dhvani* theorist replies that these associated meanings cannot be "inferred" because there is no necessary connection between the denoted object and the qualities suggested. That is, everything connected with the Ganges is not holy and pleasant since there may be skulls on its banks and corpses floating on its stream. But this is not to say that the word in question is incapable of conveying that meaning, for that meaning is brought about only by the activity of that word. There is no other source for that knowledge except that word. As Mammaṭa says, "Inasmuch as the meaning that suggests another meaning is itself cognizable by means of the word, the word is helpful in the suggestion of that [other] meaning."[6] That is to say that anything cognized through any other means of knowledge cannot be called verbal suggestion. Therefore, the *dhvani* theorist concludes that the motive for secondary use is cognizable only through the word actually used and that the function of that word in conveying that meaning is none other than suggestion.[7]

A supernumerary meaning is normally invoked only when the literal meaning is blocked. But, as the *dhvani* theorist shows, the word "Ganges" is not blocked in giving rise to the suggestion of sanctity and so forth. How then is it possible for that word to generate the suggested meaning? To this the *dhvani* critic replies that, after the cognition of the secondary sense, namely, "bank," there still remains the question of a purpose for the use of the expression "on the Ganges," where only the "bank" is meant, and that there is, in this regard, a need or expectancy *(ākāṅkṣā)* to be fulfilled since the meaning of the utterance is not complete without the element of purpose. So one construes this purpose from the context of the utterance. But, when this purpose is so obtained, it is still on the basis of the word actually used ("Ganges"), and therefore the word alone can be said to be the source of that meaning, by virtue of another activity called suggestion.[8]

What the *dhvani* theorist is trying to say, through all this tortuous reasoning, is that what, in modern terminology, we call "connotational meanings" are not metaphorical meanings but meanings derived from the primary designation of words as additional meanings, which the words themselves throw up by virtue of their own potency. They are not due to any metaphorical process; rather, the metaphor is explained or effected by means of them. That is, without invoking the idea of the holiness of the Ganges, in the present example, we cannot explain why we have a structure like "a village on the Ganges." Again, in the regular metaphor "Devadatta is a lion," we cannot effect the metaphorical interpretation "Devadatta is courageous like a lion" without the notion of courageousness, connoted by the word "lion." Such connotations provide the ground of relation to the primary meaning of the metaphorical term and help us make the metaphorical connection. Hence, the *dhvani* theorist argues that this connotative function is a tertiary activity of words, distinct as it is from both primary and secondary signification.

Most words do of course convey a wide range of connotations or associated meanings—the dangerousness or mysteriousness of the sea, the forlornness of the widow, the erotic or mystical qualities associated with the jasmine or the rose, the malevolence of "whiteness" in Melville's *Moby Dick,* and so on. But these are purely adventitious meanings—some constant but incidental (e.g., the dangerousness of the sea), some nonpermanent and incidental (the comfort and cosiness connoted by "home"), and others purely arbitrary (the malevolence of the sea, the symbolism of the rose). They depend entirely on two factors: certain incidental or imputed characteristics of the object denoted and the context of use.[9]

This being the case, are we justified in bringing such meanings within the proper scope of the meanings of words? The answer to this question will depend on how one chooses to define the limits of the "meaning" of a word. We find diverse views on the subject among the ancient Indian thinkers: that an object term, noun or verb, expresses only the universal or defining properties of the objects or actions named, not all the attributes present in them, although they too are understood in a general way; that all forms and qualities belonging to the object denoted must be deemed to be signified by that word; that part of the meaning of a word is its principal meaning and the rest is incidental; that an object in the world has all kinds of potentialities but that the word becomes associated with one of the things inherent in the object and is said to be expressive of it; and so on.[10]

In any case, we may take it that a general term can only "designate" some fairly central, defining characteristics of the object denoted, what Beardsley calls its "necessary properties," due to the presence of which the word is applied to the object.[11] Every object in the world carries a host of attributes, and every action is a series of motions and processes. No single word can express all the attributes present in the thing. Some of these will form the principal meaning of the word, and the rest will be merely incidental. These incidental or "attendant" properties may be said to be "connoted" by the word. But, since these incidental meanings too are contained within the potential meaning of the word, it can be argued that they fall within the range of its expressive power.

However, two points are in order here. First, while the *dhvani* theorist may be right in arguing that the connotative function is distinct from the metaphorical and needed for the determination of the metaphorical meaning the metaphorical process or at least one condition required for that process, namely, obstruction to the primary meaning, is equally necessary for the connotations to come into play. Turning to the Ganges example again, without the element of incompatibility in the statement about a village "on the Ganges," we would not be alerted to the presence of the connotations of coolness and sanctity in the word "Ganges," on the basis of which we determine the purpose of the statement. Similarly, the connotations of courageousness and majesty associated with the lion, in the example "Devadatta is a lion," are activated only because of the metaphoric use of the word "lion." In fact, it may be seen that many cases of connotation are cases of metaphorical meaning. The term "bread," for instance, has been used in a variety of contexts and so may be called highly connotative. But, when we examine some actual instances, it will turn out that the term is being used as a regular metaphor. In the sentences cited by Beardsley as instances of word connotation—"This is the bread of life," "Cast your bread upon the waters," "I do like a little butter to my bread"—the term "bread" is being used metaphorically.[12]

The second point to be noted is that connotational meanings cannot be brought out by the independent power of the word itself in isolation but are entirely dependent on its context of use. In other words, since they are not the core meanings of the word actually used and cannot be conveyed by it, they must be brought to light by other words or meanings in the context. Thus, the word "Ganges" cannot connote the sense of holiness unless some other word or sentence in the context, or something in the nonverbal situation, has pointed to that sense, even when it is granted that a quality such as holiness is one of its associated commonplaces. For that word or object does not always carry that association. In "There are crocodiles in the Ganges" or "My boy got drowned in the Ganges," there is no connotation of holiness. In fact, Ānandavardhana recognizes that suggested meanings are adventitious and entirely context dependent. Primary signification, he says, results from the fixed nature of the word, established by convention; it is understood in invariable association with the word. Suggestion, on the other hand, is variable because it is determined by extraneous conditions, and, without a knowledge of these conditions, it must remain unapprehended.[13]

If, thus, suggested meaning is got through the expressive power of some other word or words in the context, then it cannot be the function of the suggestive word itself. It would be unjust to attribute to a word the function performed by another word. I will not press this point since, in a sense, as the foregoing discussion has shown, that word (e.g., "Ganges" in the example discussed) is still the source of the suggested or connoted meaning. However, as the so-called suggestive function is largely a contextual function, would it be right to call it a third kind of semantic activity? No doubt, words interact with one another when used in a connected discourse, and sometimes they generate unstated meanings and meaning connections. Implication is involved wherever meanings have to be supplied or connections established in order to remove an apparent inconsistency or to complete the sense of an utterance. But all this is due to contextual action; it is not something that is produced by any single word or sentence by itself.

Contextual action is all embracing and is often needed for determining even primary meanings. "Context" is defined in the *mīmāṃsā* texts as "the mutual requirement of one sentence for another."[14] Often sentences remain logically or psychologically incomplete in their sense even though they are syntactically complete. The expectancy *(ākāṅkṣā)* of a sentence extends both backward and forward, and it is only by linking it with another sentence that has gone before or that follows it, in a connected discourse, that we complete its sense.[15] All meaning is in fact contextual. So what point is gained by assigning it to a special verbal activity called suggestion? It is probably for this reason that the Mīmāṃsakas do not consider contextual implication as a separate verbal function, although, in their exegeses, they constantly appeal to unstated meanings and motives. The logicians too object that it is cumbersome to assume a third verbal function to explain the element of purpose in metaphor since the connotations of words, as in the Ganges example, can be obtained by a mental reflection on the meanings of words, together with the contextual factors. Thus, the secondary function itself can account for the motive element.[16]

Moreover, the *dhvani* argument leads to another embarrassment. Since all suggested meaning is contextual meaning, it should follow that all contextual meaning is suggested meaning. But, at this rate, the protagonists of *dhvani* will have to admit that implications of the most prosaic and trivial sort, such as those in the Vedic sentences and the much-labored "a village on the Ganges," are also instances of poetic suggestion.[17] They do in fact realize this difficulty. But the solution they offer is unconvincing and circular. They argue that, although all cases of secondary meaning involve a suggestive element in respect of the motive element, they are not all instances of poetic suggestion because they lack the element of beauty.[18] It is no doubt recognized by them that beauty in poetry consists of *rasa* evocation. But, in saying this, one is only abandoning the case for suggestion.

Suggestion and the Figurative Principle

It is important for the *dhvani* position to argue that implied meanings of any sort are distinct from metaphorical meaning as *dhvani* has to be shown to be a third function of words. Suggestion of one sort—that based on word connotations—is of course involved in the metaphorical process and coexists with it. But it is not of the form of metaphor because it is not generated by the basic conditions required for metaphor.

This position leads the *dhvani* theorist to deny secondary function even in patently ironic instances, in which the statement implies the opposite of what it says on the surface. The following is cited by them as an illustration of a type of suggestion in which one idea gives rise to another idea—in this case, the expressed meaning has the form of an injunction, whereas a prohibition is really what is meant: "Now, you holy man, you can freely wander about these precincts, as that dog [which used to scare you] has been killed by the furious lion dwelling in the thick woods on the banks of the Godavari."[19] These words are spoken by a woman who does not like the intrusion of a certain monk into the garden by the river, which she has been using as a meeting place. The holy man is already inhibited in his movements by his fear of the dog, so the mention of a lion roaming the woods is hardly likely to encourage him to visit those precincts. Evidently, then, the statement contains an implicit prohibition even though it has the form of an invitation.

The *dhvani* critic argues that this prohibitory sense is not due to secondary function because the statement is not obstructed in any way in its primary meaning. So what causes the apprehension of the contrary sense must be suggestion.[20] But this is incomprehensible because the statement contains a glaring contradiction, and the implied prohibition becomes possible only because of the incongruity between the timidity of the holy man and the ferocity of the lion.[21] An obvious point that the *dhvani* critic misses here is that, had the statement not been inconsistent in some sense, there would have been no need for the suggested meaning either, for, as long as a sentence makes sense on the literal level, it would not warrant recourse to another meaning, whether secondary or tertiary.

A host of other examples are discussed in the texts to buttress the argument that suggestion can arise even without the rejection of the ostensible meaning. The following verse is cited as an example of the kind of suggestion in which the expressed meaning is intended but an implied meaning is also brought out by the power of that expressed meaning: "Of what name is this young parrot and on which mountain peak, and for how long, did he perform penance, O young maiden, as a reward for which he is pecking at this plum, red like your lip?" In its implication, this is a eulogy addressed to a lady by an impassioned lover, who communicates to her his secret desire in an artful manner. What is suggested is a parallel between the action of the parrot and that of the would-be lover—the speaker wishes he were in the position of the parrot, in relation to the maiden's lips. This meaning, it is argued, flows directly from the expressed meaning of the sentence; there is no secondary meaning here because the literal meaning that "the lucky parrot is pecking at the plum that is red like your lip" is intact.[22]

On closer examination, however, this statement turns out to be a variety of figurative expression called "eulogizing the irrelevant" *(aprastuta-praśaṃsā),* in which a description of the irrelevant or noncontextual subject points to the relevant and contextual. Here, the description of the parrot is the noncontextual meaning—the lover cannot simply be saying "What a lucky guy the parrot must be to be pecking at the plum!" Such a remark would be rather pointless in the lover's context. This consideration, together with other telltale signs, such as the absurdity of a parrot performing a penance and the likening of the plum to the lady's lips (which would also have been pointless without an amorous intent on the part of the speaker), leads to the suggestion of a parallel between the explicit subject (the parrot) and the implicit subject (the would-be lover), the latter being the contextual or relevant meaning. Thus, even in this case, there is obstruction to the surface meaning, on the basis of which we arrive at the implied contextual meaning—the parallel of the lover savoring the maiden's lips. It can thus be shown that the examples given by these critics to demonstate that one meaning can imply another, concealed meaning even without the operation of secondary meaning are in fact cases of straightforward secondary meaning. The implied meaning in them is made possible by some obstruction to the literal meaning *(anupapatti)*.

Secondary meaning, as noted in chapter 5, is involved in the major figures of thought (or lexical figures), such as metaphor, metonymy, irony, and so forth. (Others like simile, the rhetorical figures like apostrophe, personification, and zeugma, and phonetic and syntactic figures are the obvious exceptions.) But, consistently with his stated position, the *dhvani* theorist argues that such figures are not cases of suggestion; they belong rather to the category of expressed meaning since secondary meaning itself has its basis in expressed meaning.[23] The point of his argument is as follows. First, insofar as these figures are based on secondary function and involve some incompatibility, the secondary meaning that they demand is required for resolving that incompatibility; hence, it is not another meaning of that statement. Nor is it obtained through indirection. Suggestion, we recall, must be an additional meaning, and it must be obtained indirectly from the expressed meaning through implication.

Second, the suggestive function, it is asserted, cannot be subsumed under figurative expression even when a figure contains an implicit meaning. For figures, by the very nature of their function, serve only to embellish the expressed idea; for example, a metaphor is only an ornamental way of stating a literal fact or idea, and the implied idea is in every way subordinated to it. In a suggestive statement, on the other hand, the suggested sense alone is of primary importance. As Ānandavardhana says, "Only those instances are to be regarded as pure suggestion without any admixture, where both word and meaning are employed solely with a view to bringing out an implied sense."[24] When, for example, Wordsworth says of the city of London, "This City now doth, like a garment, wear / The beauty of the morning" (sonnet "Composed upon Westminister Bridge"), the suggested comparison of the personified city to a lady wearing a beautiful garment is merely incidental, serving to ornament the expressed meaning of the statement that the city looks beautiful in the morning.

Figurative expression can, however, become suggestive when, "by the power of meaning, one figure hints at another in the form of resonance."[25] Many figures, no doubt, quite naturally suggest another figure in this way. For instance, simile, metaphor, or hyperbole are implied in most figures. When the poet says, "I wonder whether it is a face or the moon, whether they are eyes or blue lotuses," and so on, the figure is a type of doubt *(saṃdeha)*. The speaker cannot decide which, of two similar things, is which—face or the moon? But it also implies the presence of a metaphor and a hyperbole—the speaker is implicitly identifying the face with the moon, the eyes with lotuses, and so on or, in effect, speaking of the luster of the face and the eyes hyperbolically.

In the *dhvani* view, however, this would still be an "expressed" figure because the idea itself is explicitly formulated in the form of doubt and culminates in that form; the embedded figures are not the focus of the statement. The following verse exemplifies the type of "suggested" figure in which the main focus of the discourse is the suggested element: "O long-and-tremulous eyed one! While your face is smiling and the quarters are filled with the lustre of your beauty, this ocean does not swell in agitation, even a little. From this I should think that it is surely no more than a mass of dull matter."[26] This statement is based on a "suggested metaphor." The luster of the lady's smiling face filling the quarters and the idea that it ought to cause tides in the ocean is made possible only on the basis of the suggested metaphorical identification between the lady's face and the full moon. The whole statement is also framed within a hyperbole. But this figure is expressed in so many words. The implied metaphor is thus the main point of the poem. To give an example from English poetry, in the line by Pope "Or stain her honour, or her new brocade" ("The Rape of the Lock"), which is, grammatically, an instance of zeugma, the implied antithesis or anticlimax may be taken to be the focus.

Many figures of speech discussed by the Sanskrit rhetoricians do imply an element of suggestion—an oblique reference or a periphrastic way of saying. A figure can occur in a suggested form also, and, when it does, it does not cease to be a figure. No one has placed such an injunction. Whether it is an idea that is implied or another figure, it is still a figure. Since, thus, suggestion is a pervasive element in figuration, one might argue that there is no need to posit a new theory of poetic language. This, in essence, is the objection raised by the critics of the traditional school, the figurationists.[27] But it can be argued from the standpoint of *dhvani* that the fact that some figures involve suggestion does not entail that suggestion itself is not a distinct principle. Besides, the term "figuration" does not designate a specific mode of semantic operation. Rather, it stands for any type of specially structured expression—phonetic or semantic—that is picturesque, striking, or deviant. At any rate, the principle of suggestion is not covered by figuration.

While this point of the *dhvani* theorist may be allowed, it should still be questioned whether he is justified in denying the poetic efficacy of all figures that are not suggestive in the limited sense defined by him. He has argued that a simple figure like simile, based on primary meaning, or metaphor, based on secondary function, is not properly a case of suggestion and hence is to be regarded as an inferior mode of expression. But even a plain simile or metaphor could be poetically effective—suggestion or no suggestion. No one has placed an injunction against it. Besides, as these critics themselves admit, is not all language, direct or indirect, literal or figurative, charged with *rasa* in the context of poetry? It seems that the *dhvani* theorist makes the scope of poetic language unnecessarily restrictive in his anxiety to show that suggestion is different from all other modes of expression.

Primary Meaning and Suggestion

The *dhvani* theorist has argued so far that, although the suggestive function is presupposed in all secondary function as its motive element, it is not defined by that function, nor is it coterminous with it. The secondary meaning is really a replacement for the primary meaning and, in a sense, an extension of it.[28] The suggestiveness implied in metaphorical expression is also no doubt rooted in the primary sense because, in radiating a second, implied sense, the primary sense is not nullified (in suggesting the idea of sanctity, the word "Ganges" does not shed its primary sense of stream). But it is not at the same time identical with primary meaning as it is determined largely by certain extraneous conditions, such as the context.[29] But I have argued that one basic condition for another meaning to arise out of a word or sentence is for that expression to become obstructed in some way. I have argued further that the connotations of words often involve this condition and that the contextual action that calls forth the connotations need not be assigned to a special semantic function since it is a pervasive feature of all verbal meaning. The *dhvani* examples actually demonstrate that metaphorical function is involved wherever another idea or figure is implied by a metaphorical statement.

Now we must examine the *dhvani* theorist's other contention that there is a suggestion flowing out of sentences that are not vitiated in their primary meaning. Such a suggestion can arise only in two kinds of situations: (i) when a sentence conveys a second meaning because of double meaning or homonymous words or (ii) when the sentence meaning is incomplete logically or psychologically and demands the supplying of another meaning to complete it.

Homonymous Words

Supernumerary meanings can be readily admitted in the case of homonymous words *(nānārtha-śabdas),* for, obviously, when a word has two or more senses, all of them can be entertained simultaneously without loss to any one of them. The figure paronomasia (*śleṣa,* or coalescence) is defined as an expression in which different senses coalesce in the same phonetic form.[30] Thus, if multiplicity of meanings is taken as the criterion of suggestion, then even common puns—which are no doubt a rich source of ambiguity in poetic language—should be eligible for that title. The objection to this is that all the different meanings of a pun word are conveyed directly by the word itself by virtue of its capacity to denote many ideas at once. The power of signification of that word extends to all its senses equally, and all those senses must be supposed to be equally important. Such being the case, all the senses must be regarded as the primary meanings of that word. Neither can multiple meaning of this type be considered "indirect" or "implied" meaning since it proceeds directly from the word without the intervention of the meaning. Therefore, according to the *dhvani* theory, the figure paronomasia is to be regarded as an "expressed" figure.

However, there can still be a suggestion based on homonymous words when a further meaning, other than the meanings directly conveyed by the pun word, is hinted at owing to the power of those very meanings, that is, when that expression points to another figure, such as a simile, metaphor, or paradox. A paronomastic expression conveys two (or more) meanings, of which one may be contextual *(prākaraṇika)* and the other noncontextual *(aprākaraṇika),* or both contextual. But, when the context of the sentence points, without explicit mention, to a relation, such as similitude or opposition, between the two meanings, we have a properly suggestive figure. This view is summed up by Mammaṭa as follows: "When a word, having several meanings, has the range of its expression restricted by 'connection' and such other conditions [i.e., the contextual factors], if there appears the cognition of a meaning other than the directly expressed, that function which brings about this cognition is suggestion."[31]

This statement presupposes a theory of meaning, which we must first consider before we can understand the exact mode of operation of homonymous words. A general semantic principle accepted by all Indian schools is monosemy or unity of meaning. There is the *mīmāṃsā* rule that a sentence should be directed toward a single idea or purpose. The same sentence cannot deliver many different meanings in the same instance of use. A homonymous word can be said to have many senses and convey all of them at once only in its lexical form, not in a sentence context. Not all its senses can be found together in any particular instance of use.[32] Hence, when a sentence is composed of a word with multiple meanings, all but one of its meanings will have to be set aside and the word fixed in one single meaning. This meaning will be the purported or "contextual" meaning and the others "noncontextual" or unwanted meanings.

The established rule followed by the Vedic exegetes as well as others in determining the exact meaning of an ambiguous or equivocal expression is the consideration of what are called the "contextual factors" *(prakaraṇādi)*—also known as "restrictive principles" *(abhidhā-niyāmakas)*. These are many: (1) the purpose to be served *(artha)*, (2) the subject matter under discussion *(prakaraṇa*, or context), (3) an indication from another place in the discourse *(liṅga)*, (4) propriety *(aucitya)*, (5) reference to the place *(deśa)* and (6) to the time *(kāla)* of an event, (7) the association that is known to exist between two things *(saṃyoga)* (8) or their opposition *(virodhitā)*, (9) the proximity of another word *(saṃnidhi)*, (10) accent *(svara)*, (11) grammatical gender *(vyakti)*, and (12) gesture *(abhinaya)*. Broadly speaking, these factors consist of *(a)* the grammatical means, such as gender, parts of speech, and flexional endings, *(b)* the verbal context provided by other words in the sentence or in other sentences given in a text, and *(c)* the situational context, such as gesture and other nonverbal circumstances.[33]

The point that the contextual factors normally restrict the meaning of a homonymous word to a single sense by precluding all other, irrelevant meanings may be illustrated by the following lines from Shakespeare's sonnet 83, discussed by Empson:[34]

> I never saw that you did painting need,
> And therefore to your fair no painting set;
> I found, or thought I found, you did exceed,
> The barren tender of a poet's debt. . . .

Here, the word "tender" has at least three senses, pointed out by Empson: "offered payment of what is due," "tender regard," and "person who tends (looks after)." Corresponding to the three senses, the sentence could mean (i) "I found you exceeded the worthless offer a poet could make in payment of the debt he owes you (the debt of compliments due to a lover or patron)"; (ii) "I found you exceeded (your tenderness toward me exceeded) the barren tenderness I owed you as your poet, hired to praise you"; and (iii) "I found that you exceeded (taking 'exceed' as an intransitive verb), i.e., surpassed, what I, your poet, have been commissioned to bring you by way of praise, and I *found* that I was a barren 'tend-er' of a poet's debt (second object of 'I found')." The various meanings of the statement do not agree among themselves, as Empson admits, and the syntax of the line and the verbal context clearly point to the first interpretation as the strongest and render the other meanings irrelevant. However, Empson argues that it is hard to keep these "incipient" double meanings out of one's mind, and their presence certainly serves to present "a complicated state of mind in the author" by including the whole ambiguity in it.[35] But this point is inadmissible. The poem no doubt presents a complicated state of mind, not, however, by virtue of the ambiguity of its meaning, but by virtue of the feeling being so complex. Moreover, as the Mīmāṃsaka would argue, when only one sense—that which is the most relevant—is sufficient for the purpose, why invite a second and a third meaning as well?

It must of course be recognized that, when the meaning of a homonymous word is restricted by the context to a single consistent meaning, the other meanings are not prevented from entering into the cognition of the reader, for the word is capable of all these meanings and continues to exert its power even after the context has pegged it down to one particular meaning. If the knowledge of the context should prevent the recollection of the noncontextual meanings, then how could we even set aside the other meanings as not being the meanings supported by the context?[36] What the contextual factors do is not to obstruct the recollection of the unwanted meanings but to limit the word to the sense required. As Bhartṛhari says, even when unintended meanings are present, only the operative meaning (the meaning that led to the use of the word in question) should be accepted.[37]

It is not, however, always the case that a homonymous word is restricted to only one of its senses. Some or all of its senses may be simultaneously operative. In fact, all deliberate puns are like this, for, if a pun were meant to convey only one sense, it would not be a pun. The word "tender," in the Shakespeare example, does not operate as a pun as the other senses are ruled out by the context. So also the expression "out of joint" in the line from *Hamlet* that the time is "out of joint," and so on. A word can be said to be a deliberate pun if more than one of its senses can be shown to suit the context or be required by it. This would be the case only when one of the following conditions is satisfied: first, when two senses are presented, either one would equally serve the purpose of a given statement; second, when both senses are relevant and go to make up a single sense by reinforcing the idea in question; and, third, when both meanings are contextual and relevant because an implicit comparison or contrast between the two is purported by the sentence.

The following lines from Chaucer's *Troilus and Creseyde* (2.752), also discussed by Empson, will illustrate the first condition:[38]

> Right yong, and stand unteyed in lusty lese
> Withouten jalousye or swich debaat.

III
Suggestion

Of the several senses of the word "lese" pointed out by Empson, we may consider two: the sense of an open land or meadow and the sense of a net or noose. These senses suggest two alternative interpretations of the sentence: (i) "I am free and unentangled by any sort of restraints, like a colt on an open pasture" (metaphor), and (ii) "I am not entangled in the net of desire." The first interpretation seems to be the more straightforward of the two because, in the context of the passage, Creseyde is thinking of the loss of freedom that might result from her taking a husband: "Shal noon housbonde seyn to me 'chek mat.' " However, "Withouten jalousye" may support the second interpretation. In any case, since Creseyde's loss of freedom is what is in question, whether due to external restraints or to her own native passions, either one of the meanings will fit the context, or both equally.

The following words of Lear (*King Lear,* 1.4.320), which Empson quotes as an example of his second type of ambiguity (where two or more meanings are resolved into one), illustrate our second condition:

> Blasts and fogs upon thee.
> The untented woundings of a father's curse
> Pierce every sense about thee.

Here, as Empson remarks, the wounds may be the cause of the curse uttered by the father against his child (Goneril) or the effect of the curse uttered against the father by the child. Both meanings are relevant and factual, mutually support each other, and, in Empson's words, "make up one single-minded curse."[39]

In the following couplet from Pope (*The Dunciad,* 4.201–202), a comparison is based on the two meanings of a double meaning word:

> Where Bentley late tempestuous wont to sport
> In troubled waters, but now sleeps in Port.

Here "Port" means both a seaport and port wine, and it is used in both senses. Several verbal functions or levels of operation are active here. The surface meaning is contradicted by the facts of the case—Bentley is not a sailor, and Clare Hall is no harbor. So we construe another, metaphoric sense on the basis of the pun word "Port": Bentley, who used to sport in some, metaphorical, "troubled waters" (in some political or other upheavals), now drowns himself in wine. But the very fact that a double-meaning word has been used and that it yields two parallel meanings, one applicable to the literal statement and the other to its metaphorical counterpart, requires that they be related in some way. Otherwise, no point would be seen in the use of a pun word. This consideration prompts us to assume a comparison between the two ideas. Bentley's present condition of drowning in wine is likened, by implication, to the resting in port of a heroic sailor after a tempestuous career on the high seas. As Empson explains, "This placid afterdinner drink is like having reached a harbour."[40] This comparison has the effect of mock heroically elevating the subject of the statement, namely, Bentley.

The implications of this example may be analyzed as follows, in terms of the *dhvani* theory. The metaphorical meaning that Bentley is not sleeping in any harbor, but is only drunk with wine may be taken as the "contextual meaning"—the meaning that is required by the context owing to the incompatibility of the literal meaning—and the idea of Bentley being like a sailor resting in the harbor (which is the third meaning) may be taken as the "noncontextual" or "superfluous" meaning, not strictly required for fixing either the metaphorical sense of Bentley "sporting in troubled waters" or the relevant sense of "Port." Both these senses are determined by the context, by the fact that certain truth conditions have been violated—Clare Hall is not a harbor, and so forth. The suggested third meaning may thus be said to flow out of the predication of the statement after the context has fixed the problematic words in their relevant sense. In this sense, it is an additional or superfluous meaning. Here, the *dhvani* theorist would make two claims. First, he argues that the implied comparison between Bentley and the reckless adventurer-sailor is a third, suggestive dimension, unaccounted for by both the secondary function—which yields only the metaphorical meaning (that Bentley is only drunk with port)—and the primary function, which yields the meaning that he is sleeping in the harbor. Second, he argues that the implied comparison cannot be arrived at through the operation of the context. The capacity of the context extends only as far as limiting a double-meaning word to one single "purported" meaning. The context has no control over the surplus of extra meanings flowing from it. Hence, the suggested comparison between Bentley and the sailor is a further meaning that flows out of the contextually determined meaning.

But his point is not justly argued. It is quite arbitrary to limit contextual action in this way. It may be asked how even the implied comparison based on the two meanings of the homonymous word would be possible even through the power of suggestion if the contextual factors were disregarded. If such determining conditions as the context of the utterance, the presence of the other words in the text, and so forth are not to be respected, neither could the suggested meaning be fixed with certainty.[41] It is not also true to say that the suggested similitude between the two ideas (the contextual and the noncontextual) is present only as a gratuitous meaning not required by the logic of the statement. For we could not have a secondary interpretation of "troubled waters," in the present example, or the sense of "Port" as "wine" alone without the related idea of similitude between Bentley and the sailor. There is the maxim that, when, in a sentence, a double-meaning word is active in both its senses, the two senses cannot be taken as two unrelated meanings; they have to be connected in some way. For a man cannot be supposed to present an unwanted meaning that is in no way related to what he is trying to say. This the *dhvani* critics themselves recognize.[42] Therefore, we assume, on the strength of the context, a relation of similitude, as in the Pope example, or contrast between the contextual and the noncontextual meanings. In other words, we say that the purpose served by the pun is to set up a comparison or contrast between the first and second ideas.

Besides, it may be argued that, since this implied comparison or contrast is obtained neither directly from what the words signify nor from the metaphorical meaning, it can be got through a further reasoning based on the primary meanings of the words themselves, together with the contextual factors, without having to postulate a special verbal function for that purpose. Such reasoning is required for determining the meaning of even simple utterances. All contextual construction, that is, establishing connections among words, relating them to the larger setting of the discourse, and so on, is of this nature and requires the invoking of much that is not stated by words. If all this is to be given the designation of suggestion, then we are quarreling only about labels. Moreover, if suggestion is to be accepted in all such reasoning processes, it would be something ubiquitous, a common feature of most verbal discourse, and nothing peculiar to poetry.

Suggestion and Purport

Another contention of the *dhvani* theorist is that suggestion arises out of the primary meaning of a sentence as a "superfluous" meaning only after the words of the sentence, by virtue of their mutual syntactic connection, have delivered their "purported" meaning. Hence, it is not to be confused with what is called the "purport" *(tātparya)* of the sentence. But this term is a tricky one, and it has been the subject of a great deal of controversy in Sanskrit criticism. Whether "purport" is a separate semantic function or not—some people argued that it was—it is still a crucial factor in determining the meaning of sentences. At least three senses of this term may be distinguished: (1) the meaning "intended" by the speaker (a view entertained by the logicians but rejected by many); (2) the syntactically unified meaning of the sentence resulting from the mutual connection of its parts *(saṃsarga);* and (3) the meaning established by the words of the sentence, in its context, as its complete and internally consistent sense, or "utterance meaning" as opposed to "sentence meaning."

The last sense, which is the generally accepted sense, poses the question of what it is for a meaning to be complete and how far the expectancy *(ākāṅkṣā)* of a sentence can be said to extend in order to deliver a complete meaning. Much, in this context, will depend on the delimitation of the scope of the term "expectancy." For the Mīmāṃsakas, expectancy is not mere syntactic incompleteness but logical and psychological incompleteness also. The potency of a sentence reaches as far as its logic carries it. For instance, all injunctions presuppose three dependent elements: an end to be achieved *(sādhya),* the means of achieving it *(sādhana),* and the manner of performance *(itikartavyatā).* Injunctive sentences that lack any one of these elements must be taken to be elliptical for the elements not included. In the Vedic sentence "One who is desirous of heaven should perform fire sacrifice," the end to be realized is "heaven," the means is "fire sacrifice," but the mode of performance is not given. Therefore, it has to be supplied from another text laying down the necessary accessory details connected with the enjoined act: "One should offer a libation of curds," and so forth.

Even in ordinary examples like "There are crocodiles in the river," the sentence meaning does not make a complete sense—it does not state the purpose for which the assertion is made. The missing element has to be supplied from other parts of the text in which the statement occurs or from the context of utterance. Purport, thus, comprehends all external things that are needed for our understanding of the full import of the sentence. Therefore, the advocates of purport *(tātparya-vādins)* argue that "whatever the words of a sentence are directed toward is the meaning of the sentence."[43] On this view, then, all implications arising out of sentences, even when their literal meanings are unobstructed, could be brought under purport, and there would be no need to postulate a suggestive function. Purport itself can account for all unstated meanings, for it is not necessarily confined to the words actually used in the sentence.

The *dhvani* critics would, however, like to limit purport to the sentence meaning, to just what is got from the words in their syntactic connection, and admit a further, suggestive activity when the sentence that is syntactically complete points to another meaning not required for the completion of its own meaning.[44] The power of purport is exhausted when it delivers the sentence meaning. The *dhvani* critics do, of course, recognize metaphorical meaning as a separate function. It comes into play when the sentence meaning is obstructed. But suggestion of the type based on primary meaning can occur only when the sentence is not incongruous and delivers a consistent and syntactically complete meaning.[45] This position is summed up by the following: "Where a sentence, not being settled in its own meaning and not being complete, reaches out for the meaning toward which it is directed, that other meaning should be regarded as the proper scope of its purport. But where it is both complete and settled in its meaning and it also leads on to another meaning, there it is only the activity of suggestion."[46]

The same logic leads the *dhvani* critic to deny suggestiveness in elliptical or holophrastic constructions, for example, "Door! Door!" "Fire!" and in implications of the sort involved in "the remainder of the sentence" *(vākyaśeṣa),* for example, "There are crocodiles in the river." A sentence may be incomplete in two ways: it may be syntactically incomplete, as in elliptical expressions, or logically or psychologically incomplete, as in "There are crocodiles in the river," which may mean "So it is dangerous to bathe in that river." But such instances would not be a case of suggestion, according to *dhvani* theory, because, when a meaning is supplied to complete an incomplete sentence, it is not another meaning of that sentence but only what is required to make sense of it. Logical implications or "entailment," presuppositions, and so forth, too, cannot be called suggested meaning. For example, my saying that "the cat is on the mat" implies that I believe that it is on the mat and entails that "the mat is under the cat"; "the former is running" entails that "the latter is not running"; "Devadatta cooks" presupposes that he knows how to cook; and so on.

Thus, every statement implies, presupposes, or entails other statements. All such cases cannot be suggestion because they are not needed even for the completion of the sense. Nor are they strictly verbal meaning. Every word or sentence sets in motion a whole train of ideas or associations, and it would be absurd to include all of them within the range of meaning of the words actually used.[47] As Bhartṛhari says, a sentence should be taken to be complete if it posseses a minimum consistency and has no expectancy outside itself.[48] This view would be supported by most schools, including the Mīmāṃsakas of the Bhāṭṭa school and the logicians. The Mīmāṃsakas would insist, however, that the "sentence meaning" would sometimes extend beyond its syntactic limits and require for its completion meanings imported from the context as well.

In the *dhvani* view, suggestion can, however, occur in examples like "The sun has set," in which the purport extends only to the declaration that the sun has set. But the same sentence, it is claimed, can convey a wealth of suggested meanings in different contexts: an artisan to his fellow worker, "We'll stop work now"; a shopkeeper to his servants, "Now pack up the merchandise and go home"; a lady's maid to her lady going to her assignation, "Now it is time to start"; and so on. Whereas literal meaning is definite and constant (it is the same in all situations), suggested meaning is indefinite, depending as it does on the speaker, the person addressed, and the situation.[49]

This argument of the *dhvani* critic is, however, completely fallacious and inconsistent with his own premise. First, a sentence of this type is not even a complete utterance (although it is a complete locution) in the absence of any indication as to its illocutionary purpose, which only a context can provide for it. When this purpose is supplied, it would be only an "implicit conclusion" drawn from the sentence. Since it is imported for the purpose of completing the sense of the sentence, it can be regarded only as its purport or as "the remainder of the sentence." Bhartṛhari would argue that the implied meaning in such cases is in fact the operative meaning, for, as he asserts, the meaning of a sentence is not simply what its syntactic form reveals but the entire speech act. Thus, "Let us go. Look at the sun" is actually a reference to the time of the day, though the sentence says something about the sun.[50] Second, in claiming that a sentence of this type is capable of suggesting an indefinite number of meanings, the *dhvani* critic is forgetting that it could not mean ten different things in the same context. In the first place, no one would remark on the sun without some purpose or context. But, when a context is given, it is always something definite.

What we said of homonymous words is true of this case also. Neither a word nor a sentence can mean all its senses in any given instance of use. The *dhvani* critic is taking the sentence in isolation, as a grammatical paradigm, and attributing to it a virtue it does not actually possess—a highly questionable procedure. Finally, if meanings function so integrally, according to their contexts of use, the *dhvani* critic's attempt to limit the purport of a sentence to its grammatical sense merely, to "what comes out of the words actually present"[51] (here he follows the *nyāya* view of *tātparya*), and to invoke another, transcendent power called suggestion to account for what is only its most legitimate meaning sounds like a strange piece of casuistry. In the words of the commentator Dhanika, "Purport is not something that is weighed on the scales. No one has fixed a limit to it—that it reaches a point of rest with such and such a meaning. For the activity of purport extends as far as it takes to accomplish the purpose for which a statement is made."[52]

If thus the meaning of a sentence is taken as its final drift or utterance meaning, many types of implication, which for the *dhvani* theorist are due to suggestion, would come under purport. It is noteworthy, therefore, that some exponents of *dhvani* have expressed the view that even purport is suggested meaning and synonymous with it.[53] But, then, if all purported meaning is suggestion, even ordinary sentences, such as those cited above, would have to be designated as suggestion. Here, again, the *dhvani* critic may answer that not every kind of purported meaning is suggestion but only that which is evocative of some charming idea.[54] But how can this quality of charm or *camatkāra* (poetic thrill) be defined except in terms of *rasa?*

Suggestion and Emotive Meaning

The next argument of the *dhvani* theory is that in emotive statements there is a suggestive power flowing from the unimpeded, stated meaning. Emotive meaning represents yet another type of suggestion based on the primary function—the suggestiveness of homonymous words and implications of literal statements are the other types—and it is called *rasa-dhvani,* or evocation, or simply "emotive meaning." Now we should inquire whether the concept of *dhvani,* as defined by its exponents, can be rightly applied to *rasa* (emotive) expression or, more specifically, whether there is a sense in which emotive meaning may be said to be a special kind of activity of words, characterized as *dhvani,* or suggestion. It is argued by the protagonists of this theory (i) that *rasa* is a supernumerary meaning, distinct, although flowing, from the primary capacity of words; (ii) that it is indirectly arrived at by not being stated by its own name; and (iii) that in conveying the emotive sense the primary meaning subordinates itself to the implied emotive sense.

Emotions are no doubt presented in language directly by the expressive power of words that describe the objects and other circumstances of the emotive situation. Hence, they are said to be manifested by the primary function of words. A few examples will demonstrate this point. Consider Ophelia's description of Hamlet's enigmatic, yet deeply pathetic, behavior in act 2, scene 1. Lord Hamlet, she says to her father, "with his doublet all unbraced," and looking pale like a ghost, "comes before me." "He took me by the wrist, and held me hard," and then he "falls to such perusal of my face / As 'a would draw it." At last

> He raised a sigh so piteous and profound
> As it did seem to shatter all his bulk,
> And end his being.

Here, it is Hamlet's behavioral expressions that are described in a completely literal manner. His inner condition—pity, doubt, or distrust—is inferred from his actions. Or consider Wordsworth's portrayal of Michael's state of mind after the tragic desertion of his son Luke. The brokenhearted old shepherd spends long hours sitting alone and brooding by the sheepfold: "many and many a day he thither went, / And never lifted up a single stone." Again, the basic emotive conditions are rendered in plain, ordinary language. But can we say, then, that the emotions too, like their objects and expressions, are directly denoted by their words?

The *dhvani* critics argue that the sentence describing the objective circumstances of the emotion does not name the emotion *(rasa)* itself. An emotion cannot be evoked by the simple mention of its name. The word "pity" does not arouse pity either in the speaker or in the hearer. Even where such words are used, for example, the word "piteous" in the passage from *Hamlet* quoted above, the evocative force, if any, of such words is due only to the situational factors in terms of which the emotion is manifested. The explicit naming of the emotions in such instances would then have to be regarded as a superfluity or, at best, as a reiteration of what is already fully realized by the objective factors described.

If the emotion can be expressed by its own name, then it should remain unapprehended when the name is not mentioned, as in this heart rending cry of David: "O my son Absalom, my son, my son Absalom! Would God I had died for thee, O Absalom, my son, my son!" (2 Sam. 18.33). It is quite easy to recognize this as some sort of wail. But the feeling itself is not named. If emotion could be exhibited by the mere mention of its name, it should be possible to apprehend it even when the circumstances are not described. But this is obviously not the case. Lines like "I grieved for Buonaparté, with a vain / And an unthinking grief!" (Wordsworth, "1801") or "I loved her with a love that is more than love" (Poe, "Annabel Lee") do not properly exhibit either grief or love. They only give a name and designation to those emotions, but no local habitation.

If sometimes emotion names like "pity" seem to carry an evocative force (i.e., express the feeling of the speaker), it is due only to the fact that the context has supplied the necessary details that would make the use of such words expressive, in the sense that the speaker uses them to utter his feelings. For example, when Othello, being incited by Iago into a mad fit of jealousy, decides to put an end to Desdemona, he thinks of her gentleness and sweetness and of the pity of having to kill her: "But yet the pity of it, Iago! O Iago, the pity of it, Iago!" Here the word "pity" itself becomes an expression of Othello's sense of pity because that feeling has already been exhibited by other words in the context. It can thus be shown by positive and negative instances that emotions can be expressed only through the description of their conditions and in no case directly by the words naming them. There can be no apprehension of the emotive quality in a poem solely by the force of the words denoting the emotions.[55]

What, then, is the relation between the emotions and the language that must be supposed to express them? In other words, by what specific function of language is it that emotions get expressed in poetry? The *rasas* are not the subject matter of words directly since they are not stated by the words themselves. The sentence describing the objective circumstances of the emotion reaches only as far as that meaning and cannot deliver the emotion itself. The *Sāhityadarpaṇa* puts the case thus: "Rasa is not a matter of conventional meaning because the representation of the objects and expressions through the literal sense of words is not of the same form as the emotion conveyed."[56] Nor are the objects and expressions the same as the *rasa* presented; the *rasa* is something presented through their medium.[57]

Hence, it is urged that the *rasa* is got through the operation of suggestion, indirectly, not being conveyed by the words actually used. It constitutes "another meaning," transcending the literal meaning of the sentence describing the emotive situation. Since the sentence meaning does not rest in itself, it goes on to suggest the appropriate emotion. It does not, however, cancel itself in the process but, like a lamp illuminating a jar, reveals the other meaning. The implied emotive meaning follows in the wake of, and is understood along with, the literal meaning.[58] Hence, this variety of suggestion is classed as "suggestion brought about by the power of the expressed meaning." Again, since the suggested emotive meaning is held to be something outside the sentence meaning, it cannot be equated with the purport of the sentence; purport is limited to the sentence meaning.

A clarification of the term *rasa* or "emotive meaning" will be necessary at this point. When our critics say that *rasa* is not the sentence meaning but something that is got through its medium, they are evidently not referring to the emotion aroused in the reader or to the delectation resulting from the contemplation of the sentence meaning *(rasāsvāda)*. On the contrary, their whole attempt has been to show that *rasa-dhvani* (emotive suggestion) is a semantic function and a specific activity of words *(śabda-vyāpāra)*. They are also not saying that there is an "emotive purport" of language that is independent of "cognitive purport"—that is to say, that emotive meaning exists apart from the sense of words, from what the words designate or connote.[59] Such an argument would be incongruous because all meanings that come out of words must be part of their sense or cognitive content. Otherwise, they could not be obtained from the words at all.

Emotive meaning is, then, understood by the *dhvani* critics as an implication flowing from the literal meaning of the statement describing the emotive situation as its "cognitive import."[60] As noted in chapter 2, Abhinavagupta rejects the view that there is anything like an emotional apprehension that is not also a cognitive process, for that which is not cognized cannot be apprehended even emotionally. The same argument holds for feelings in words. One perceives feelings in words because words carry information about them in terms of the objects causing the feelings and the outward expressions, both verbal and gestural. Thus, it is quite clear that "emotive language" functions only through the meanings that the words convey, not independently of them.

Yet the question of how words acquire their emotive force remains to be settled. This question is in fact posed by the distinction the *dhvani* theory makes between the statement describing the emotive conditions and the feeling signified by it. Since the signified feeling is not directly reported by the words of the statement, it may be asked how it can be said to enter the words at all. The *dhvani* theorist's answer is that the emotive force of words is derived from their meanings, that is, from the objects denoted by them. To quote Ānandavardhana, "The rasas are suggested by the force of the meanings of words."[61]

That is to say that, given a set of objects, certain attitudes result, and the words that describe these objects and attitudes seem to take on a certain emotive force themselves. A word, such as "snake" or "lizard," may produce intense emotional reactions because most people hate snakes and lizards, not because there is anything in the word itself that causes these reactions. As Abhinavagupta comments, "Therefore the apprehension of rasa is only from the objects and other circumstances [of the emotive situation]. And when these objects and their concomitants, being presented by some choice words, become the cause of aesthetic rapture, this same power [of the objects] is lent to the words themselves."[62] Here, it is to be understood that the "choiceness" or speciality of words, mentioned in the quotation, can itself be defined in terms of the context in which the words appear, that is, by their suitability for clearly naming the objects or portraying the situation. So we cannot also accept a special emotive vocabulary that alone may be said to deliver the emotions. Just about any language can do the job given the right context.

It will no doubt be urged that there are evidently words that, having been used constantly in emotive contexts, have acquired more or less permanent emotive connotations, positive or negative.[63] But, even so, it should be pointed out that such words cannot be the carriers of emotive meanings without regard to the context of predication. A word carries an emotive force because that force is predicated of it. In other words, it is used in a context in which certain qualities are predicated of the objects denoted by that word, and the persons affected by those qualities respond to them in a certain way. As Abhinavagupta explains, if words like "garland" and "sandal" come to have an erotic appeal, it is because of the senses they convey in erotic contexts. It cannot be claimed that the same appeal will be carried over into other, nonerotic contexts. A clinical use of these very words is quite conceivable.

No word can therefore be said to be emotively neutral or charged in itself, nor can it be said that it has a more complex structure than some ordinary words. For example, the word "house," which in ordinary contexts is neutral, carries an emotional aura in uses like "The Fall of the House of Usher," "The House of the Dead," "The House of the Seven Gables," and so forth. Its emotive force depends entirely on how that object is presented. If sometimes some words are found to be more evocative than others, it is due to their previous association with "evocative" contexts. The very word "girl" sounds like music to many ears because of what it represents generally in our talk about girls. At any rate, as Ānandavardhana states, the speciality or uniqueness perceived in such words is none other than their power of conveying meanings related to the *rasas*.[64]

It is through such reasoning that the *dhvani* critic reaches the conclusion that the *rasas* are conveyed as verbal meanings. But, since these meanings are not literally stated by the sentences in which they occur, they are suggested, as implications arising out of the literal sense, and, hence, they constitute another meaning of those very sentences.

This claim needs to be examined more closely than is done in the traditional commentaries. If, as our critics argue, there is this implied emotive sense within the statement describing the situational factors, it must be asked what its precise nature is and what it amounts to. An example discussed in the *dhvani* texts in support of this argument is a verse from Kālidāsa's *Kumārasaṃbhava* (4.4). The divine sage Āṅgīrasa has come to the king of the Himālayas with the proposal that the king's daughter Pārvatī should be given in marriage to Śiva. The verse reads, "As the divine sage spoke these words, Pārvatī [sitting] by her father's side, with her face bent, counted the petals of a toy-lotus." Commenting on this, our critics say that the description of Pārvatī's gestures reveals another meaning, namely, her bashfulness (which is one of the feelings accessory to the erotic *rasa*) "even without the activity of words."[65] The suggested "other" sense turns out to be simply the notion of bashfulness as distinct from the conditions of that feeling. But, since for the *dhvani* theorist the mere cognition of the emotive conditions does not constitute cognizing the emotion, the emotion, or, strictly, the notion of the emotion, must be a separate cognition and, consequently, a separate sense. This is what, it seems, he calls *rasa* or the emotive sense.

It should be noted, however, that this sense is not a sense accompanying the emotion actually felt (by the character in the example given above or by the reader) and on which the emotion is dependent. The emotion is dependent on the literal sense (that Pārvatī sat with her head bent and so forth) and is produced by it. Empson seems to believe that there is an emotive sense of words in an emotive context. This is consistent with his view that emotions are not necessarily "in the words," in that the emotiveness of a word cannot operate independently of its sense—a view accepted by the *dhvani* theorist. Empson says, "Emotions which are in the words will normally evoke Senses that correspond to them" (except in swear words, intensifiers, and so on).[66]

On this view, a sentence, such as "The Queen, my lord, is dead" (*Macbeth,* 5.5; my example), which is an existence assertion, according to Empson's types, conveys sense A, which is that the queen of Scotland is dead. Further, it arouses emotion B! (B Shriek), which in turn calls up sense B corresponding to the emotion B! However, Empson's point that there is a separate sense relevant to the emotion is not clearly demonstrated. This "sense corresponding to the emotion" (sense B) is not related to sense A, and it also cannot come out of emotion B! because that emotion is not a verbal meaning but rather the perlocutionary effect of sense A, if it is supposed to occur in the hearer (Macbeth, in the present case). The messenger who brings the tidings to the king must have no doubt intended his utterance to carry affective force—he knows he is conveying dreadful news that is bound to deal a death blow to the already distraught mind of Macbeth. But this does not involve a difference in meaning. For the message, whether it has emotive force or not, is just that the queen is dead. If it affects the king in a certain way, as it does in the drama, it is purely a matter of his having certain attitudes and feelings toward the queen. These attitudes and feelings, when they are exhibited, are conveyed by other sentences in the context, not by the same sentence. Thus, Empson's sense B does not seem to have a locus and a definition.

The *dhvani* critic might seem to stand on a firmer ground when he attaches the emotive sense, not to the emotion aroused by the sentence, but to its literal sense (Empson's sense A) as its implication. But this implication, if implication it can be called, seems to be no more than the concept of the emotion, which merely serves to identify a set of conditions as being the signs of a particular emotion. If this is all that is meant, then the whole endeavor to show that emotive meaning is a suggested meaning is puerile. There are, however, more serious objections to the *dhvani* position to be considered.

1. The logician maintains that the so-called suggested meaning is in essence an inference from the primary meaning, in which the stated meaning functions as a logical sign *(liṅga)* in relation to the unstated

meaning. Hence "the apprehension of the suggested meaning is no other than the activity involved in drawing an inference from the sign."[67] There is no need to postulate a suggestive function since the knowledge of concomitance *(vyāptijñāna)* itself can deliver the implied meaning. In the example about Pārvatī, the bashfulness of the young maiden may be inferred on the basis of the invariable association existing between her gestures and the feelings they normally signify.

Mahimabhaṭṭa, a powerful opponent of the *dhvani* theory, also argues with the logicians that emotive suggestion is no other than deductive reasoning. According to him, emotions are inferred from their criteria—a view held by Śaṅkuka before him. The task of the poet is only to present the conditions that should serve as the signs of the emotion, which invariably lead to the manifestation of that emotion. Here, the *dhvani* critic objects that emotive suggestion is not of the same nature as logical inference because there is no invariable relation between the objective signs and the emotions that are supposed to be inferred from them—Pārvatī's gestures need not always mean bashfulness.

To this it may be replied that, unless a definite and determinable relation existed between the two meanings involved (the meaning representing the emotive conditions and that representing the emotion itself), even suggestion would not become possible. For nothing unconnected can be understood from the sentence. The *dhvani* theorist himself recognizes that, when the totality of the situation is given, there would be no uncertainty in identifying the emotion. A second objection to the inference theory is that no aesthetic relish can be expected to result from a mere inference of emotive meanings. In reply to this, one may say that this relish is in the very nature of the things inferred. The power to affect the mind or its absence has nothing to do with the mere fact of a thing being inferred. This is why a woman can cause intense excitement even though she may only be an object of inference.[68] The inference of fire from smoke can cause alarm if the fire happens in my own house, but, if it happens in somebody else's house, I would view it more neutrally.

2. Having reviewed the argument from the standpoint of the logician, it can be argued from the standpoint of the *mīmāṃsā* theory of purport, outlined above, that emotive meanings, though admittedly not stated by the sentence, are still the meanings of the sentence because they are understood from the sentence and are required for making a complete sense of it. In the example cited above—"Pārvatī sat with her head bent" and so on—the total intention of the statement is not fulfilled until the meaning relating to Pārvatī's emotions is also delivered. Pārvatī's gestures are meaningful in the context only as the behavioral expressions of her maidenly feelings, and, therefore, the implied emotion is logically

part of the meaning of the sentence. Every sentence, whether poetic, scriptural, or ordinary, is directed toward a purpose. In fact, as the Mīmāṃsakas say, the meaning of a sentence is the purpose for which it is uttered *(vākyasyārthaḥ prayojanam).* Poetic sentences have no other purpose for being than to evoke the *rasas* through the presentation of the conditions associated with them. Since the sentence presenting the emotive conditions is employed for the purpose of conveying the *rasa,* the *rasa* itself is the meaning of the sentence.[69] The expressive power of the sentence itself can fulfill the purpose for which the sentence is intended by attracting the *rasa* corresponding to the particular situation or set of conditions that the sentence is expounding. What the *dhvani* theorist has glorified as suggestion is only the primary capacity of the sentence.[70]

By the same token, the unstated emotive sense cannot also be legitimately called "another" sense *(arthāntara)* of the sentence describing the emotive signs. That Pārvatī is a bit embarrassed by the talk of her marriage is the proper meaning of the statement describing her reactions. The sentence describing the emotive situation is incomplete without its emotive import, and, hence, the latter meaning cannot be another meaning of that sentence. It is, in terms of the *mīmāṃsā* theory, more appropriately regarded as a case of "the remainder of the sentence" *(vākyaśeṣa)* than as another meaning. It would therefore be more convincing to say that the unstated emotive sense is the purport or final meaning of the utterance and that the power of giving rise to it belongs to the context rather than to any special verbal function. It may well be that it occurs at the ultimate stage in the apprehension of the total meaning, the sentence meaning being the penultimate stage—which we might separate for purposes of analysis (although the sequence is not noticed). But this is not sufficient reason for saying that it is a distinct verbal function. We may therefore conclude with Indurājā, in his commentary on Udbhaṭa, that "in the presentation of the rasas there is no supernumerary meaning involved," although we do not accept his view that *rasa* expression too is but a type of figuration (called *rasavadādi).*[71]

3. The *dhvani* critics also set great store by the fact that emotions cannot be expressed by naming them directly. This fact is adduced by them in support of the argument that emotive expression is achieved through indirection, which is the essence of beauty in poetry. Of course they are right in demanding that emotions be rendered properly in fully dramatized detail, in accordance with Bharata's *Rasa Sūtra*. But their claim that this method (of presenting emotions in concrete terms) is a method of indirection is open to criticism because there is no indirection involved in dramatizing the emotions through their objects and expressions. This is the only way in which an emotion can be presented at all. Again, what

point is gained by abstracting the emotions from their objective signs, which are their inalienable conditions, and then assigning them a separate semantic activity? Emotions, it is recognized, are produced by a set of conditions, and a causal relation *(kārya-kāraṇa-bhāva)* between the two has been accepted by the *dhvani* critics themselves.[72]

Granted, the conditions producing the emotions are not of the same form as, and logically identical with, the emotions that they give rise to because of the cause-and-effect relation subsisting between the two. But in what sense can an effect be said to be "suggested," rather than "produced" or "manifested," by its causes? In a sense, of course, all emotional expression, verbal or gestural, is necessarily indirect. An angry man, for instance, would not express his anger by saying "I am angry, I am angry." He would rather show it, in some other words or in action. But nothing is gained by calling this suggestion.

One notices in the *dhvani* argument a certain awkwardness of maneuver. The term "suggestion," within the meaning given here, is perhaps more justly applied to cases involving secondary meaning—contrary implications or secondary coimplications that modify the literal sense of the sentence. *Rasa* expression, on the other hand, involves no peculiarity of meaning. It can of course sometimes appear intermixed with figurative language *(alaṃkāra-saṃkīrṇa)*. But even there, basically, the *rasa* is manifested by the emotive factors described, and the figures simply aid the description. In its purest form, it need not depend on any secondary implication, oblique reference, or indirection, its power being derived solely from the objects and expressions described. When, for example, describing the grief of the newly widowed young wife Ratī, whose husband Madana, the love god, has been burned to ash by Śiva's wrath, Kālidāsa says, "She wept, with her hair dishevelled, and her breasts soiled with dust from lying prostrate on the ground,"[73] there is no way of reporting the reactions of this character other than by naming them in their own words. This is pointed out by the *dhvani* critics themselves.[74]

4. The third principle of the *dhvani* doctrine is "subordination" *(upasarjanī-bhāva),* by which is meant that a word or its sense subordinates itself in giving rise to another meaning.[75] This principle is involved in all secondary meaning function, where the literal meaning either completely negates itself or renounces part of itself in order to convey another, more consistent, meaning. But this seems to fit *rasa* expression rather badly. It makes no sense to say that the objects and expressions "subordinate" themselves to bring forth the implied emotion.

To sum up the above objections, the concept of "emotive suggestion" *(rasa-dhvani)* seems to me to conceal a trap. The attempt of the *dhvani* critics to assimilate Bharata's *rasa* formula into their special theory of poetic language does not come off too well. Granted that suggestion exists, it can be applied to emotive expression only by stretching the point. The notion of "another meaning," which is the defining property of *dhvani,* was probably applied by these critics to *rasa* only in a loosely extended sense. But, then, one cannot mount a serious theory of meaning on such grounds. Perhaps one reason why the language philosophers—Bhartṛhari, the Mīmāṃsakas, and the logicians—do not talk about emotive meaning is that emotiveness is not a function of the language itself but a superimposition, a "form of life," rather than a verbal mode. It may be no more than a coloration that words take on in emotive contexts, that is, by denoting objects that affect people emotionally. But this coloration is a quality of the context, not a verbal property, much less a verbal function. This the *dhvani* critics themselves have shown.[76]

Other Elements of Suggestion

In their anxiety to show that poetic suggestion is a distinct expressive mode, the *dhvani* theorists have argued not only that it is different from both primary meaning and secondary meaning—it is a third potency of language that is based on them—but also that suggestiveness is present in musical sounds and in physical gestures such as shrugs and sidelong glances. Suggestiveness is a far more extensive activity and comprehends nonverbal as well as verbal modes of expression. Ānandavardhana says that there is suggestion of the emotive type "in words, which carry meanings, as well as in musical sounds, which convey no meanings, and in gestures, which are not even sounds."[77] This statement might seem to conflict with his basic assumption that *dhvani* is a semantic function. But of course what Ānandavardhana is saying is that suggestion also extends to nonverbal expression—which does not militate against its being a function of the words too, although, evidently, it does not help his argument for suggestion being a verbal function.

However, there may be an objection to music and gesture being "suggestive" in the sense defined above. A case may perhaps be made for the suggestiveness of nonrepresentational painting. Thus, a clear and powerful streak of white across the heavy, thick black of the canvas can suggest the beam of a searchlight cutting across the night sky. As Beardsley explains, "A design suggests a natural object if it has some notable and quite distinctive characteristic—shape or color—in common with that object, but does not have enough in common with that object to represent it."[78] But how can a musical composition "suggest" anything since it does not mean or signify anything? It is not even a "sign" of something and has no referential relation to anything outside itself, consisting, as it does, solely of a progression of harmonies, rhythms, and modulations.[79] What our critics mean by saying that an emotion can be "suggested" by the sounds of music is, evidently, that emotion is "aroused" by them. But a musical note does not arouse an emotion because it means or refers to that emotion; if it does, it is only as an "object" of that emotion. That is to say, it causes some responses in sensitive listeners, even as a snake might cause trembling in me. But these affective responses cannot be called the meaning, much less "another meaning" (which is what would make it suggestion), of the objects that produced those responses. These objects are not semantic or meaning-bearing signs of the emotions but rather their causes—only signs have meanings.

The case of physical gestures is, however, different. Facial expressions, body postures and movements, hand gestures or the conventional *mudrās* of Indian dance, and even involuntary expressions like blushing, turning pale, and so on—these, I have argued, are "expressive" modes (unlike music) and the "logical signs" of the mental states with which they are associated. As logical signs they may be said to have meaning. But what do they suggest if by "suggest" we mean "convey another meaning in addition to their own"? A sign can signify its own meaning, not another. For example, the red traffic light or the stop sign on the road means "stop." It has no other meaning. It may be argued that, while the meaning of a gesture may not be "another meaning," it is still not directly conveyed by the gesture, and so it is suggestion. When a girl looks at a boy with sidelong glances, her feeling—amorousness, normally—is not "expressed" by her glances but indirectly conveyed. But this is casuistry. That feeling, anyway, can be expressed only by means of some such gesture. That the feeling itself is, at least logically, distinct from the feeling behavior may be granted. But it is difficult to see how any indirection of the sort that the *dhvani* theorist has in mind is involved in this. If a gesture, as a logical sign, is indirect expression, then every inference from a sign (the known fact) to the object (the unknown fact) must be held to be suggestion. But this will not be congenial to our theorist.

Often, in Western criticism, verbal suggestiveness is understood as diffuseness of meaning, shadowy portraiture, or lack of specificity of referential content, which is a feature of expression associated with Romantic-Symbolist poetry. For the Symbolists, "suggestion" or "indirection" signified a mode of presenting a theme or mood by a single, self-contained image or by images in series, not by direct statement, description, or narration. In accordance with a musical conception of poetry, the Symbolists also chose words more for their emotional aura or "atmospheric" quality than for the concreteness of their designation. They aimed at "spiritualizing" the word by purging it of all intellectual content and concrete reference. (Whether they succeeded in this is another matter.) In opposition to this is the view of Pound and the Imagists, which insists on clarity of image, precision, and concreteness. One remembers in this connection Hulme's and Pound's attack on the Romantic aesthetic. The presupposition of the Symbolist theory is that words in poetry, at least of the suggestive kind, do not convey ideas or images in clear outline but render them translucent, taking them through an atmospheric medium, as it were, and throwing on them an emotional coloring. Words serve merely as centers of semantic radiation. They dissolve into tone, and their sense is subordinated to their sound.

The *dhvani* theorists call a type of suggestion "resonance" *(anuraṇana),* and they also discuss the evocative function of word sounds and phonemes *(varṇa)* in special contexts. But they do not express the view that words can be effective in poetry by their sound structure alone or that they could convey "shadowy" meanings. What they mean by "resonance" is that a word can sometimes suggest more than one meaning in a given context, as it happens when a double-meaning word suggests a noncontextual meaning, or that one meaning can give rise to another related meaning. Again, when they say that the suggestive function of words is indefinite, they mean to say that it is indefinite only in relation to its conventionally fixed meaning, that is, variable according to the context of use, not that any meaning could be indefinite in terms of its reference.

Indefiniteness of reference could be said to result, not from verbal meanings themselves, for words always convey precise meanings in their contexts, but from the quality of the things—images or ideas that they refer to, from the "blurred edges" of the concepts themselves. Thus, we have the images of the Romantic landscape—"hamlets brown and dim-discovered spires," "far-foamed sands," and so forth—or the images of the Symbolists and Surrealists, drawn from the psychic or subliminal realms of consciousness, for example, Rimbaud's "the drunken boat." When objects are suffused with or toned to a subjective mood, they seem to appear without sharpness of outline. But this is in the nature of the mood expressed, not in the meanings themselves. It may be that emotions, being often complex, cannot be sufficiently grasped and analyzed or communicated in words. Nearly all language dealing with inner phenomena is handicapped in this way.

That all experience was beyond words and could only be hinted at by them through "faint clews and indirections" (Whitman's phrase) was at any rate the belief of the Romantics. Even so, every emotive state, however complex, and the image that is used to objectify it must have a clear center because it arises from a definite set of causes and circumstances, which are always concrete and specific. An emotion can be complex or ambivalent, but its perception is always clear—it must be ambivalence of a certain form or description. A vague emotion, like "nameless fear," is a pseudo-emotion. Given its conditions and their description, an emotion should always be analyzable in terms of its structure, according to the logic I outlined in chapter 4. The language, too, that presents the emotive objects and attitudes (however complex) is necessarily definite and precise inasmuch as it describes the outward phenomena, not the inner states themselves directly. In any case, there can be no indefiniteness of referential content. Hence, the common notion of the elusiveness of feeling tones in language is based on a misconception regarding words and how they come to convey emotive meanings.

While the Symbolist aim of diffuseness and the effect of mystery in images results in a kind of suggestiveness, the opposite method of the Imagist, of presenting a physical object in brief, but sharp, outline, achieves a different kind of indirection, an "accurate mystery" of the image "born out of the very precision of details" (Rene Taupin's phrase). The Imagist too, like his Symbolist counterpart, avoids direct statement and comment and presents the object in a stark, impersonal tone. But even an imagist poem is never meant to be a simple record of visual impressions. It too presents, as economically as possible, a state of mind, a mood, or a reaction to an external observation. The important point about this method is that it does not name or describe the feeling evoked by the object. Whereas in the Symbolist poem a vaguely defined emotion, whose causes are not specified, is objectified by means of a metaphoric image, in which the other term of the metaphor is suppressed, in an imagist poem, the object of the emotion is presented, and the attitudes and expressions, which that object evokes, are suppressed. Or, in a long poem composed on Imagist lines, a series of objects, a "constellation of particulars," is given, and their conceptual links are suppressed (Pound's method). The dynamics of the juxtaposition is itself supposed to reveal the meaning through indirection. This kind of suggestion does not, like the Indian *dhvani,* involve a supernumerary meaning; it is essentially what Otto Jesperson called "impression by suppression."[80]

The same principle of suppression also underlies the Symbolist method of constructing a poem. Although, unlike the Imagist, the Symbolist starts off with a subjective mood rather than with objects and seeks the objects with which to formulate it, he follows the same technique of grouping symbols together without supplying their thought connections. In the Symbolist method, the image presented functions as a metaphor for a mental state, and the symbolizing is a way of expressing an attitude *(anubhāva)* toward an object or situation *(vibhāva),* which is left unstated. In the Imagist method, the image presented functions as the object or situation, and the attitude evoked by that object or situation is left unstated. But, in either case, whether a single image or symbol is presented or several images or symbols in juxtaposition, the suggestion consists in the leaving of one of the factors of the emotive situation (objects or expressions) unstated.

As I showed in chapter 4, there could of course be a complete apprehension of the total emotive situation even when one of the two essential factors is given. When the objects alone are given, the responses are elicited from the context, and vice versa. The former method may be called "Imagist," and latter "Symbolist." But either way it can be called the method of indirection, or "suggestion by suppression," or partial omission. This method underlies the technique of the haiku, the Imagist poem, or of the narrative style of Hemingway, especially in his short stories. The method consists in the bare mentioning of significant details in the belief that they can speak for themselves, without the need for lyrical elaboration on their affective quality. Thus, in the Chinese poem "The Jewel Stairs' Grievance," commented on by Pound, the emotion is to be inferred from the described details: jewel stairs, therefore a palace; gauze stockings, therefore a court lady; and so on.[81] One may regard this as a case of *rasa-dhvani* (emotive suggestion) because the lady "utters no direct reproach."

Whether one should call this "suggested" or "inferred" meaning may be largely a quarrel about terminology. But is the implied or inferred emotion in this poem another meaning of the sentence describing the situational factors? No, because the utterance of the lady becomes meaningful only as an expression of her emotion. What is not given (the submerged part of the iceberg) is not another meaning of the poem. That the lady is grieving the tardiness of her lover in keeping their tryst is required for the completion of the sentence. Hence, it may be regarded as a case of *vākyaśeṣa,* or "the remainder of the speech," or purport *(tātparya).* But this, for the *dhvani* critic, would not be suggestion. Again, in such instances, suggestion may also be regarded as a case of inference, as the logicians would argue. Inference, evidently, plays a great part in poetic, as in ordinary, meaning. So suggested meaning may be equated with inferred meaning. As Beardsley observes, "What a sentence suggests, then, is what we can infer that the speaker probably believes, beyond what it states."[82] But the important distinction is, as Ānandavardhana reminds us, that all cases of inference are not cases of poetic suggestion.[83] The mere presence of inference will not result in *rasa.* Inferred meanings can indicate emotive attitudes in the speaker only when there is a context for them, that is, only when they are described as having emotive significance for the speaker.

Suggestion, in the way the *dhvani* critics define the term, runs into considerable difficulty because it is quite restrictive in its scope. It eliminates from the purview of poetic language what many people would consider its most common feature, namely, the language of metaphor, and it also eliminates the common varieties of multiple meaning and implications of the logical kind. Some Western authorities like Beardsley have defined the term to include all implicit or unstated meaning, that is, all elements of what the Indian theorists have treated as secondary meaning plus all elements covered by the term "purport," such as elliptical meaning, connotation, and so forth. Beardsley says, "What a sentence suggests I shall call its *secondary sentence meaning.*"[84] "Suggestion," understood in this way, inclusively, seems to cover most of the elements that we associate with poetic language. But does it bring out its differentia since what we call "suggestion" is equally "operative in all our ordinary speech," as Beardsley himself recognizes,[85] and also since there can be much poetry, such as objective descriptions of nature and pure emotive utterances, that contain neither metaphorical language nor any implied meaning?

It is also admitted by the Indian theorists that suggestion, even in their own limited sense, is characteristic of ordinary discourse. Hence, we cannot conclude with the *dhvani* critics that it is the "soul of poesy" *(kāvyātman)* or with Beardsley that literature is a "discourse with important implicit meaning" or "secondary levels of meaning."[86] As an objector to the *dhvani* concept said, suggestion is at best "as aspect of poetic discourse, not what defines its nature."[87] Therefore, the *dhvani* critics themselves finally veer round to the view that it is *rasa,* rather than *dhvani,* that is the defining essence of poetry.

The *dhvani* critics have, no doubt, rendered a great service by giving the concept of suggestion a firm semantic footing and by removing the imprecision that often vitiates our discourse about it. With their logical and psychological acumen, they bring immense clarification to our understanding of the ways of language in poetry. But it is doubtful whether they succeed in making out a foolproof case for poetic language being a specialized function. Their final contribution is, however, to the doctrine of *rasa* and to the theory of poetic semantics that derives from it.

7

STYLE AND MEANING

Figuration and Style

As noted earlier, the explanation of the difference between standard language and poetic language had been the central aim of Sanskrit poetics since the beginning of theoretical speculations in ancient India. Two main attitudes toward poetic language became polarized in the critical discussions that appeared roughly between the seventh and the eleventh centuries. Critics of the early, rhetorical tradition were concerned with the analysis and classification of figurative structures, and they assumed that "figuration" *(alaṃkāra)* was the essential element of poetic speech or poetic form and coextensive with it. Poetic usage was deviant expression *(vakrokti)* and involved either an unusual ordering of the sound features of words, in terms of the figures of the word *(śabdālaṃkāras)* such as alliteration, assonance, and chime (graphic forms were classified as figures of the word form), or a configuration of ideas or semantic elements in terms of the various figures of sense or lexical figures *(arthālaṃkāras)* such as simile, metaphor, and irony. What differentiated poetry from ordinary language and raised it above banality was the manipulation of sounds and meanings to produce striking effects.

However, the attempt of the Rhetorical school to bring under the rubric of figurative expression every conceivable poetic element, including the delineation of the emotions *(rasavat)* and even naturalistic description of objects and scenes *(svabhāvokti),* tended to rob the term of its definition and made it a convenient coverall for the infinite modes of poetic speech. This was a period of rhetorical chaos, for it produced an endless proliferation of figures and overlapping categories. (By the sixteenth century, there were as many as 125 figures, with further over-subtilized distinctions between eighteen varieties of metaphor, thirty-three of simile, and so on.) At the next stage in the development of Indian poetics appeared the theory of style *(rīti),* which thought of arrangement and patterning, rather than figuration, as the basic principle of poetry. Style was defined as a special disposition or structuring of words, both in their phonological and grammatical aspects. Styles were classified, on the basis of these variables, as graceful, striking, or mixed, or according to their geographic regions. There was no conception of period style or any notion of personal style (style as the signature of its author).

This was still a "deviant" view of poetic language and assumed a basic difference between the structure of poetic language and that of standard language. Neither the theory of style nor its predecessor, the Figurative school, offered an inclusive concept of poetic expression, its nature and mode of functioning. Their entire emphasis was on the elaboration of descriptive categories. These early theorists, no doubt, showed a faint awareness of the futility involved in their approach—they knew that formal modes were infinite and impossible to enumerate,[1] and they could not even be shown to be significant without some regulative principle, by reference to which their efficacy could be measured. This principle, these critics seem to have assumed, rather circularly, was no other than deviancy or peculiarity of expression, which lends beauty and novelty to poetic language.

It was in the work of the Dhvani school, however, that something like a unified theory of poetic language emerged and the relation between style and meaning came to be defined with greater accuracy. The *dhvani* critics rejected the exclusive emphasis on figuration and style. They gave the emotive content *(rasa)* the central place in their scheme and tried to derive the language from it. Poetic meaning is essentially emotive meaning, and the style of expression, too, could be considered only in conjunction with it and as serving an evocative function in relation to it. Style has no independent existence of its own in literature, apart from its function; it does not constitute a separate excitement. Style, being a formal (as opposed to semantic) function, is determined by and contingent on a style-creating context of meaning.

Sanskrit criticism does not have a single term to express all that is implied by "style" in Western critical parlance, which includes both the structural (phonological, morphological, and syntactic) and semantic (lexical) features of language. The only two terms that would cover the traditional sense of "style" as the manner of writing, as opposed to matter are *alaṃkāra* and *rīti*. Of these, the former is the more comprehensive as it includes both the structural and the semantic features of language use within its twofold classification of figures of sound and figures of sense. The figures of sound would cover all varieties of patterning, of phonic elements, at both the phonemic *(varṇa)* and the morphemic-syntactic level *(pada* and *vākya),* while the figures of sense would account for the patterned or deviant expression of the semantic or logical content of words and sentences. Some figures of sense, such as metaphor and irony, are of course based not on patterning of any kind—on recurrence or equivalence—but on semantic change. But if style is understood as deviation from literal norms, then metaphorical or secondary uses of language must also be considered style since they involve another mode of expression than the ordinary. Phonetic and grammatical patterning of any sort, including meter, is not a normal feature of everday speech and may be considered a deviant feature and stylistic.

In a sense, the concerns of both rhetoric, taken in its broader sense as the study of verbal devices employed in poetic or public speech, and stylistics seem to be the same. Both disciplines are concerned with structured expression, and both assume that a degree of deviancy is implied in all organized, as opposed to casual, speech. The rhetoricians are of course interested equally in the formal and semantic aspects of language. Some present-day stylisticians, who derive their methodology from descriptive linguistics, would, on the other hand, confine their study to the structural features of a text—its phonology and grammar—and exclude the contextually generated, extralinguistic matters of meaning, which do not easily lend themselves to formal description. Accordingly, semantic tropes and images, which are the traditional tools of rhetorical criticism, are considered to be mentalistic categories that cannot be investigated in terms of linguistic analysis; they have no formal regularities that could be analyzed. The figures of sound, like alliteration, rhyme, anaphora, and syntactic parallelism, as well as metrical features, on the other hand, fall directly within the purview of phonology and grammar.

Yet, in terms of the definition of style as deviation, even the lexical figures ought to count as stylistic devices, for, as deviant or foregrounded features of a text, they can be observed and classified, not directly of course as linguistic structures, but, indirectly as features derived from linguistic data. Many theorists of style today, including those who follow the methods of analysis of structural linguistics, would also therefore admit lexical aspects in their consideration of poetic style.[2] Rhetorical analysis is thus stylistic analysis, although its scope is somewhat narrower than that of the latter. The traditional Indian rhetoricians too, like their Western counterparts, were concerned with the formal aspects of poetic utterances.

That the figurationists were mainly interested in stylistic analysis is nowhere more evident than in the work of Kuntaka. In fact, the theory of poetic figures is developed by Kuntaka into a major stylistic argument. But Kuntaka's conception of stylistic form is much more comprehensive than that of the older rhetoricians as it includes, not only the well-known figurative types, but all other verbal devices—phonemic, morphological, and syntactic—that do not fall under the figurative categories and all semantic functions, such as secondary and suggestive, under the rubric of what he calls deviant expression *(vakrokti),* which he equates with poetic discourse. Kuntaka is concerned, not only with patterned features, but also with those unpatterned or nonrecurrent structures, such as phonemes, grammatical parts, words, and sentences, considered in isolation, that may acquire stylistic significance by virtue of some deviancy or speciality they involve.

Kuntaka defines deviant speech as "a unique way of saying," as opposed to the well-known modes of discourse.[3] This deviancy, according to him, characterizes both the sound structures of words, in poetry, and their meanings and may be classified into six major types: deviancy (i) in the arrangement of phonemes; (ii) in the use of stem and root (synonyms, modifiers, compound words, gender, verb, etc.); (iii) in the use of the terminal part of a word, both nominal and verbal (case, number, person, tense, voice, particles, and indeclinables); (iv) in the sentence, which, again, is of manifold types; (v) in the topic; and (vi) in a whole composition. Of these, some of the varieties and subvarieties pertain to the formal structure of language and others to its semantic content—that is, they relate to nonordinary ways of presenting ideas.

Deviancy of the first type consists in arranging phonemes in a way that is opposed to the standard modes of speech and covers such devices as various kinds of alliteration and chime. Deviancy of the second and third types has to do mainly with some special or peculiar uses of morphemes and words and their grammatical structures and relations. It also includes the choice of diction (epithets, synonyms, and so on). Kuntaka gives close attention to phonetic, grammatical, and lexical aspects of style and shows by illustrations how in each case the stylistic effect of a given sentence depends on a deviant or uncommon use of a linguistic form.

There is also the deviancy extending to larger units, on the level of the sentence, of a group of sentences forming a unified topic of discourse, and of whole compositions—all of which have reference to the larger context of meaning, the themes presented, and so forth. Under the fourth type, deviancy in the sentence, Kuntaka includes all poetic figures and all forms of concealed expression. Here Kuntaka argues that poetic deviancy is not necessarily confined to particular forms of language use but also extends to the way things are presented *(vastuvakratā)*. Even naturalistic description and the delineation of emotions imply some strikingness or picturesqueness of presentation. An object, for instance, is seen in a new light and presented in a language that is most appropriate to it. Naturalistic description is not the presentation of a bare fact but presenting it under an unusual aspect. To objects, whose nature is fixed for all time, the poet gives new forms. The expression of emotions, too, is a form of deviancy, although it may not be linguistically deviant, because it stresses the uniqueness of the object to which the emotion is directed.

The fifth type of deviancy, namely, deviancy in the topic, relates to the art of devising episodes or incidents in such a manner that they give the maximum consistency to the total plot of the story or drama. The sixth type, deviancy in an entire composition, consists in an original or novel treatment of a well-known theme. In matters of plot construction, thus, Kuntaka emphasizes the importance of novelty, originality, and inventiveness.

It may be seen from this brief outline that Kuntaka's conception of literary style covers the entire spectrum of literary expression, including its semantic content. Unlike modern stylistics, it takes into account, not merely the formal structures or microstructures, but all foregrounded features of literary expression, including the macrostructures such as the construction of fables, the interlacing of episodes, and so forth. In this, it is close to the methods of the Russian Formalists and the proponents of the Prague school, who take a broader view of the scope of literary style than the descriptive linguist.[4] Their concept of poetic technique as deviation from norm, as "deautomatization" or "defamiliarization," embraces not only the formal (phonetic and grammatical) structuring of language but semantic relations as well, and it covers both metaphorical and nonmetaphorical designations. Defamiliarization is found "almost everywhere form is found."[5] Everything seen and presented out of its normal context is poetic form. Objective portrayal of emotive and other subjects and thematic organization both involve some kind of deautomatization, even when they do not involve any deviation in terms of linguistic structure.

In many respects, however, Kuntaka's theory of expressional deviation may be considered an extension of the basic premises of the old Rhetorical school. Both Kuntaka and the older rhetoricians rest their argument on two assumptions. First, the literariness of literature can be best identified by the way it expresses thought rather than by any special characteristics of the thought itself. Literature is a particular mode of expression or language use rather than a mode of thinking or perception, and its differentia must be located in the "form" of its expression, not in the quality of its content. Figuration, understood broadly as a deviant mode of expression, is what describes the specific "form" of literature. Kuntaka differs from the traditional rhetoricians in some details, though, and he also extends the concept of figuration to features of language and meaning that are not formally marked off from ordinary modes.

Second, "form" in poetry *(bhaṅgībhaṇiti)* is something over and above the word form *(śabda)* and its sense *(artha)*. Poetry is no doubt both word and sense together *(sāhitya)*—the word, the phonetic form, cannot be separated from the sense it carries—but so is all verbal expression. Therefore, in poetry, both word and meaning stand in need of an additional something called ornamentation *(alaṃkaraṇa)* in order to distinguish poetry from ordinary discourse. The word and the meaning together constitute the body of poetry or its gross form *(kāvya-śarīra)*, and ornament (understood as technique or poetic form) is its special mode of existence *(kāvyātman)*. In the words of Kuntaka, "Poetry consists in being ornamented; what is ornamented is word and sense; deviant expression is the ornament."[6] The designation of poetic form as ornament might suggest that it is something extraneous and detachable. But this is not what is meant, for this "form" we are speaking of is the specific differentia of the poetic use of language and, hence, inseparable from what is called poetic expression.

The Concept of Rīti

Yet another concept of style that flowed out of the deviant conception of poetry is *rīti*, which is roughly translated as "style." The word means, etymologically, "the way or manner (of saying)." Even from the time of the earliest theorist, Bhāmaha, Sanskrit critics treated types of literary style, which are based on particular word collocations or collocations of phonetic and syntactic features, as a distinct element of poetic expression that is not comprehended by the principle of figuration. Styles were classified into Vaidarbhī, Gauḍī, Pāñcālī, and so forth, according to the geographic regions in which they happened to be most in vogue. But each type was defined strictly in terms of the particular combination of phonetic or syntactic features that it represented. Thus, the Vaidarbhī style contains no compounds and employs voiced consonants; it demands compactness, symmetry, evenness of syllable structure, and so forth. The Gauḍī abounds in compounds, high-sounding words, alliteration, and what is known as bombast or verbosity. The Pāñcālī employs middling compounds and so forth.

Styles were also classified as natural, ornate, and mixed, or graceful, striking, and mixed, on the basis of the frequency of certain phonetic and syntactic variables. It was realized of course that such classifications were purely arbitrary and futile since there could be any number of style types and any given set of stylistic features could occur in an infinite variety of combinations. As Daṇḍin remarks, "The ways of speech are infinite and their differences very subtle, and they vary with the character of each writer; and it is impossible to enumerate them all."[7] We can only describe and give labels to certain extreme types of composition, such as the ornate style, the grand style, and so on. Hence, no sanctity need be attached to the conventional classification of styles by the Sanskrit critics (or by the Western critics, for that matter) into three or four. What is more important is the concept of style itself, as they define it, and their analysis of the elements that go into it.

Style is defined by Vāmana as "a special disposition of vocables" *(viśiṣṭā-padaracanā),* meaning thereby a structuring or arrangement of phonetic and syntactic units. While, in a broad sense, even the structuring of phonemes, words, and phrases may be regarded as a type of figuration and a way of embellishing the poetic language, it is not wholly covered by the figurative principle, particularly by the figures of sound. For, whereas alliteration, both consonant and vowel alliteration, rhyme, and the like involve a repetition of identical phonetic or grammatical units, *rīti,* or style, according to Vāmana's definition, need not necessarily involve any such repetition. The use of compounded or uncompounded constructions or of certain phonemes—labials, sibilants, aspirated or unaspirated consonants or consonant clusters, and so forth—in a sentence or a group of sentences requires no repetition of identical sound units. Although alliterating phonemes and rhyming words may sometimes feature in a stylistic arrangement, it is rather on the basis of the prominence of particular sound collocations that a stylistic type is determined. The principle of phonetic figures is repetition; that of style is frequency or prominence. The figures of sense, as a general category, are distinguished from formal features by the fact that, while the latter are the special characteristics of a specific diction—a specific choice of word sounds and their collocation—the former, like simile and metaphor, may reside in any kind of diction; they are common to all styles of poetry and exist everywhere.[8] Thus, this distinction between figurative expression and style is central to the theory propounded by Vāmana. It is implicit in Daṇḍin, but it is firmly stated by Vāmana, although both writers speak of style as an *alaṃkāra,* not in the narrow sense of figure, but as an element of poetic beauty.

Style, understood as a manipulation and structuring of verbal forms—

phonemes, words, phrases, and syntactic units—into sound patterns may be further defined in terms of certain qualities, like energy, symmetry, clarity, sweetness, and so forth, that are stylistic properties or properties of composition *(bandha-guṇas)*. A distinction is made between "stylistic features," consisting of phonemes *(varṇa)*, words *(pada)*, and their combination into sound patterns, on the one hand, and "stylistic qualities" or tone qualities, on the other, which characterize these formal features. These qualities, deemed to be aesthetically valuable, provide the criterion for differentiating one stylistic type from another. In Vāmana's words, "The speciality of style is to be defined by its quality."[9] Each style type is a particular combination of qualities, and the qualities are realized in varying degrees in various style types. Thus, the Vaidarbhī style is characterized by a combination of all qualities, the Gauḍī by energy and brightness, and the Pāñcālī by sweetness and delicacy.

Traditionally, ten such qualities are enumerated, although the definitions of some of them vary from writer to writer.[10] These, according to Vāmana, are as follows: (i) energy *(ojas)*, consisting of compactness of syllabic structure, cohesion or bond density *(bandha-gaurava)*, and employing consonant clusters like *ṇḍ, ñj, rṇ, ṇṭ,* and *ṅg*, compound structures, and so forth; (ii) clarity *(prasāda)*, or looseness of syllabic structure; (iii) coalescence *(śleṣa)*, or smoothness resulting from the joining together of words; (iv) homogeneity *(samatā)*, or evenness of stylistic manner throughout a composition; (v) symmetry *(samādhi)*, or balance of ascending and descending rhythm (i.e., long syllables balanced by short syllables); (vi) sweetness *(mādhurya)*, consisting in the use of distinct, uncompounded words and in the absence of conjunct consonants; (vii) delicacy or tenderness *(saukumārya)*, resulting from the avoidance of harsh consonants and clusters; (viii) liveliness *(udāratā)*, consisting in the arrangement of words with gradually lengthening syllables and in various kinds of alliterating and rhyming structures; (ix) explicitness of words *(arthavyakti)*, resulting from the avoidance of ungrammatical or obscure words, double-meaning words, and so forth; and (x) luminosity *(kānti)*, consisting of polished words and elegant turns of expression.

Although style is defined by Vāmana primarily as having to do with the structuring of words, its application is not believed to be limited to the sounds alone; stylistic features belong, by extension, to meanings as well.[11] Therefore, Vāmana sets up a distinct class of ten qualities of meaning *(artha-guṇas)* corresponding to the ten qualities of sound or word form *(śabda)*. He uses the same set of labels to describe the various features of meaning, such as boldness of conception, pregnant statement, logical congruity, agreeableness of meaning, vividness of presentation, and so forth. Some of these qualities of sense also, in fact, involve figurative or periphrastic ways of expressing meanings.

Vāmana asserts that poetic beauty is to be judged only in terms of style, as constituted by the qualities of sound and sense. Style is the soul of poesy *(ritir ātmā kāvyasya).*[12] Vāmana's stylistic argument hinges on the distinction he makes between figuration and style. Style, he says, is a constant feature of poetic language and its defining characteristic, whereas figures are merely additional graces and hence nonessential.[13] Style itself is of course defined by the qualities of sound and sense, so the final distinction is between qualities and figures.

The *dhvani* critics support the view that figures are nonessential. But they deny that even style is essential for poetry, for, just as there can be poetry without any distinct figures, there can also be poetry without a marked style. Neither phonetic nor syntactic patterning is essential for poetry. The *dhvani* critics understand by *rīti,* or style, no more than "an arrangement or structuring of words—of phonemes, words, and compounds."[14] They do not also recognize the idea of a typology of styles—ornate, graceful, and so forth—because style types are only particular formations made up of specific features and their qualities and can be defined only in those terms.[15] Besides, infinite combinations and variations of stylistic features are possible. Each poem sets up its own system of regularities and equivalences. All that the analyst can do is to discover the pattern in each particular case. What is more important is that he should be able to show how a given structure harmonizes with the meaning expressed.

The *dhvani* critic rejects the assumption of Vāmana that structural features can by themselves become aesthetically valuable, without regard to meaning.[16] For Vāmana, as for the figurationists, meaning was not a criterion or determinant of style but simply part of style, a way of foregrounding the content through lexical choice, deployment of ideas, expressional deviation, and so forth. He did not pause to examine why formal or semantic patterning ought to be considered valuable in poetry or how it can even be a poetic differentia since nonpoetic, noncasual, or formal speech too sometimes exhibits a degree of patterning or arrangement, for example, Bacon's essays, sermons, orations, and so on. In any case, the advocates of style, like the figurationists before them, were not concerned with ultimate aesthetic criteria; they were interested only in enumerating the formal properties of poetic language. The Dhvani school's concern is, on the other hand, with the larger issue of the status of style in poetic discourse and with how formal features are related to poetic meanings. It is in their criticism that a proper account of poetic style is attempted.

The Meaning and Scope of the Term "Style"

As was noted in the foregoing pages, the central concern of both the figurationists and the proponents of *rīti* was with the form and manner of poetic expression rather than with its content. For both, this "form" had to be in some way conspicuous, deviant, or "special" *(viśiṣṭa)* to distinguish it from ordinary language. Conspicuousness was to be achieved either by highlighting the structural (phonological/syntactic) elements of language through patterning or by lexical or semantic deviation (consisting of some "twist" or straining of the logic of thought, called *vakrokti,* or "crooked expression"). Thus, what these critics conceived of as "poetic form" applied to the whole "linguistic body" of poetic utterance, as distinguished from its "content of thought." "Poetic form" is thus "style" or *manner* of expression *(bhangī-bhaṇiti,* in Kuntaka's language).

Kuntaka, no doubt, extends the concept of form to include thematics, even as the Russian Formalists do. But we may argue against such inclusion on the ground that constructing a plot according to the laws of necessity or probability, deploying a theme through a selection of relevant details, and so forth cannot be considered the style of a composition, for there is no other way of telling a story than by presenting the temporal and causal relations of the events narrated. Even where a breaking or disarrangement of the natural, real-life sequence of things is involved, for example, beginning in medias res, presenting an effect and working backward to its causes, and so on, there is no deviation from the normal modes of thought, for, in reporting an event, we normally proceed from the present moment to its antecedents, from the effect to its causes. When ideas or thought processes are naturally (i.e., by virtue of their own *gestalten*) "formed" in a certain way, it cannot be called "style" in the sense of "a special manner of presenting ideas." Similarly, presenting an emotive situation through a literal description of its objects and expressions or portraying natural objects in realistic language also cannot be regarded as style. Vāmana bases his theory of style on the general principle of patterning rather than on semantic deviation.

The second noteworthy point about both the figurationist and the stylistic arguments is that what is called the "formal body" of poetry also includes the "structure" of the meaning embodied, as distinct from the meaning or logical content *(artha)* itself. In other words, structuring the meaning in a conspicuous way or presenting it through a mode of speech that is different from casual talk is a way of "enforming" it, even though it may not exhibit any extraordinary or deviant use of the linguistic form itself. Thus, presenting an idea through a striking simile, metaphor, or some other figure would be a way of giving that idea a formal body, and it too will function as a foregrounding device. The implication of this is that all secondary or nonliteral modes of predication, including the "suggestion" of the *dhvani* theory, fall under the formal aspects of the poetic language. As noted in chapter 5, most figurative structures involve the secondary function. As for the figures based on the primary function, such as simile, they too can be classed as formal devices since they serve to highlight the idea being expressed. What, then, we call style is the totality of the verbal form plus the semantic mode or the mode of expressing meanings, considered as a formal choice or device, to which the Sanskrit critics give the designation "poetic form."

According to the *dhvani* argument, no doubt, suggestion is not merely a formal feature but something essential to the nature of poetic expression. But, whatever the *dhvani* theorists may say, the implicative mode or the method of indirection, whereby meanings are implied rather than stated explicitly, is still a manner of expression and distinguishable from the matter expressed, and in that sense it ought to be considered an aspect of the formal body of poetry. Such a recognition is in fact implied in the *dhvani* critic's argument. Meaning, he says, is of two kinds: the expressed and the implied. But meaning, as such, does not deserve the designation of poetry, for ordinary speech and Vedic scriptures too have meaning. Therefore, there must be some speciality in the mode of conveying meanings, that speciality is suggestion, and suggestion is the soul of poetry.[17] When meanings can be conveyed directly and literally, the choice of an indirect or implicative mode of expression would be only another manner of saying the same thing and a stylistic alternative to the literal mode. In applying the principle of suggestion to literary examples, the *dhvani* critics constantly oppose the suggestive manner to the literal meanings of the passages to show how another semantic mode is in operation there. It thus turns out that even suggestion, which they claim to be the essence of poetic speech, is, like the metaphorical mode, but an aspect of the poetic form rather than of poetic meaning. It too is a way of saying and a peculiar or striking mode of speech, even as figuration is, according to the older critics.

We have seen that all types of suggestion, except the emotive type and the type in which meaning is left incomplete, actually involve the secondary function and may be subsumed under that. I have also argued that there is no suggestion, in the sense defined by the *dhvani* theorists, in emotive statements. Emotive meanings are conveyed by the primary functions of words. Thus, the *dhvani* theory, in its quintessential elements, is a theory of poetic form or style that says that the form of expression, rather than the content of thought, is what distinguishes poetic speech.

Paradoxically, the *dhvani* critics are also committed to the doctrine of *rasa,* which holds that emotive meanings, rather than the style of language, are of prime importance in poetic expression and ought to receive first consideration. They realize that the basic meanings of an emotive situation, the objects and expressions, are delivered through the primary expressive power of words. Emotive meanings are essentially literal meanings, and they constitute the content of the poetic utterance. It is only when considered in conjunction with these that figures and all other formal devices, including *rīti* (phonetic and syntactic structuring), become significant as style. It is not that they have no place or function in poetry, for they do serve a "suggestive" or "evocative" function in relation to those meanings. Particular sound structures, syntactic arrangements, and figurative modes are seen to intensify the *rasa* in hand; they are "the causes of intensification of rasa" *(rasotkarṣa-hetavaḥ).*[18] Abhinavagupta states that, in the final analysis, even suggestion must subserve the end of *rasa* by heightening the emotive force of the meanings. Suggestion too, then, is a formal device, like metaphor, alliteration, and so forth and, in that sense, an embellishment of poetic speech *(alaṃkāra),* not a necessary or invariable condition.[19] The earlier critics had, on the other hand, maintained that formal embellishments (call them figures or style) were an inalienable part of the poetic mode of speech and its defining characteristic.

However, both the figurationists and the *dhvani* critics are in agreement regarding the general nature of the poetic form and the elements that go into its composition. There is, first of all, the word form or the phonetic structure *(śabda),* and then there is the sense that it carries *(artha).* Together they constitute the body or the physical structure of language. What we call style is a third element that is superimposed on the word and its meaning (the linguistic form): it is the manner of using words to convey meanings. Every use of language is no doubt a manner of using words, but in poetry it has to be something different. It must be an unusual way of handling the linguistic medium—its sounds, its grammar, and its logic. But, since all words possess a form and must be meaning bearers, what may be called the stylistic form of words, as opposed to their linguistic form, is neither their phonetico-grammatical structure nor their basic semantic function but an additional quality that their linguistic form acquires, or rather a function it performs, in some instances of language use. The implication of this is that words become stylistic not in their primary role of conveying meanings but only when there is some speciality attaching to their use. The poetic use of language is thus a unique way of employing words (and their meanings).

Here, the figurationists would insist that poetic language is distinguished by its having a "style," in the wider sense of the word, whereas the *dhvani* theorist would say that figures and style (*rīti,* the latter term understood narrowly as phonetic and syntactic structuring) do not serve to define it, for some poetry at least could occur without them. But *rasa-dhvani* (by which they really mean "emotive meaning"), which need not always have a distinct linguistic form, must be present invariably in order for an utterance to be called poetic speech. But, either way, the style of language, when it can be distinguished as such, serves an ornamental function in relation to its formal body (consisting of the word form and its meaning). A linguistic form, then, becomes a stylistic feature when it functions as an ornament to its meanings by virtue of its sound structure or its semantic mode.

The view of style that can be elicited from the general discussions in the Sanskrit critical texts of the nature and place of language in poetry is thus one of style as ornament. This view has the following implications. First is an implication that I have already touched on, that style in language is a special manner of employing word forms and meanings and distinct from both. Style is not just linguistic form or its meaning but a special function that a linguistic form performs in relation to its meaning. Hence, the term "style" is applied more properly to the "formal" aspects of language (which would include both structural features and semantic modes—metaphorical, suggestive, and so forth—regarded as formal choices or devices) than to its "meaning-expressing" function. Two implications follow from this first point and need to be substantiated: (i) style is not linguistic form per se, not just any language use, but one that performs a special function; and (ii) style is not a "meaning-expressing" function.

Style Is Not Linguistic Form Per Se

One broad definition of style, given from the point of view of modern British linguistics, reads: "The kind of language use which is the result of a combination of context, medium of utterance and human beings who participate in the language activity of any situation."[20] The fault with this is that it is a definition, not only of style as normally understood, but of all verbal meaning in general. If "style" is understood in this way, simply as any kind of language use, then every linguistic form will be a case of style because every use of language (including parking signs) has some kind of style. Such a view will result only in a completely futile quantification and tabulation of all the items of a given text.

Richard Ohmann's definition, in the light of transformational-generative grammar, of style as a choice from among the transformational alternatives (different expressions) of the same proposition also cannot help us identify something as style.[21] It can account for the formal difference between two passages having the same meaning. But it cannot explain what it is that makes a particular choice of language stylistic.

A more satisfactory definition may be attempted along the lines suggested by Enkvist.[22] For a linguistic form to be recognized as style, it must possess a "style marker"; it must, in other words, be marked off in some way from normal discourse, judged by linguistic or contextual norms. Thus, all figurative devices and secondary use of language would be a case of deviation from literal norms. "Please pass the sodium chloride," rather than "Please pass the salt," said in the dining room situation, would be stylistically marked because "sodium chloride" does not belong in that kind of register. The speaker is probably trying to be funny. In this case, it is the contrast with the contextual norm rather than any linguistic deviancy, that marks the locution as stylistic. Some items of a text can, however, be stylistically neutral, either structurally considered or when they are matched against literal or contextual norms.

Style Is Not a "Meaning-Expressing" Function

I have argued that only the formal aspects of language rather than its meanings, should be regarded as constituting style. Style is a function of words in their formal relation, not in their basic semantic operation as meaning bearers.[23] This is not to say, however, that semantic structures and relations, like metaphor, irony, and so forth, should fall outside of the scope of style altogether. For, in addition to their meaning-expressing function, they also have a noticeable formal structure and, as particular stylistic choices, a formal function, namely, that of reinforcing meaning. They make a difference in form without making a difference in meaning. The implication of this is that a metaphoric, ironic, or implicative expression is substantially the same as its literal counterpart but formally different.

The generally accepted view of the Indian philosophers as well as of Western critics is that a metaphor is explicable in terms of its literal meaning; it must in fact be capable of being translated into literal terms in order that its form may be recognized as metaphorical.[24] If this is so, then, the difference between "The ship ploughed the waves" and "The ship sailed the waves as the plough ploughs the ground" cannot be a difference in substantive semantic characterization. It is not being suggested of course that the metaphorical can be reduced to the nonmetaphorical since there is the difference of form that is stylistically significant. What the metaphor loses when paraphrased is no part of its substantive meaning but a stylistic effect. The choice of a metaphorical manner of speaking would then be a stylistic choice and a stylistic alternative to the literal mode because the same message or thought content could be expressed in more explicit terms.

However, a clarification is necessary here. There is of course a semantic difference between a sentence in the metaphorical form ("Richard is a lion") and its literal counterpart ("Richard is brave like a lion"). Obviously, they are not the same kind of predication either in form or in meaning, and their truth conditions also differ. This has been stated in chapter 5. But, when it is considered that the purport or ultimate meaning of the metaphorical statement, when reexpressed in literal terms, is substantially the same as its "ostensible" or syntactic meaning, the difference between the two predications would reduce to a mere formal difference. By saying that Richard is a lion, one could mean only that he is brave like a lion.

For purposes of this discussion, therefore, the term "meaning" should be taken as comprehending the final contextual meaning or purport *(tātparya)* and that meaning considered to be the same in substance as the sentence meaning but different in form. When Beardsley says that "only differences in form that make for differences in meaning can count as stylistic differences" and that texts that differ in style cannot be synonymous, he is, if I understand him correctly, thinking of the difference between the literal sentence meaning and its implied or secondary meaning and showing that there is both a formal and a semantic difference.[25] This is of course right, regarded from one angle. But it seems important to maintain that stylistic differences can hold only between synonymous utterances because, if two expressions differed in meaning as well as in linguistic form, then there would be no question of a comparison between them. Each form would only be discharging its proper meaning-expressing function, so much so that there would be nothing that could be called style as distinct from meaning.

The "purport" of an utterance, which I have taken as my point of reference, is not, however, to be equated with its "illocutionary" meaning. In the sense that I understand that term, purport is the final logical meaning in which the sentence rests—as in the metaphorical examples. An illocutionary act is often something that is performed by means of this final meaning, although sometimes it may coincide with it. Thus, in the metaphorical instance "Richard is a lion," meaning "Richard is brave," the illocutionary act of "praising" is implied. In the ironic expression "A swell guy!" (when the man is a bum), the illocutionary force of "mocking" or "ridiculing" may be implied. In the sentence "There is a bull behind you," in which the primary meaning is intact, the warning "Watch out!" is implied. But in this case, the implied warning is the purport of the utterance (for without the implied warning the assertion would be incomplete) as well as its illocutionary meaning. In the example discussed by Beardsley—"I came, I saw, I conquered," which is ostensibly an assertion—there is also a substructure, a subordinate illocutionary action, namely, that the speaker (Caesar) is "boasting" of his achievement (if acts like "boasting" and "joking" can be considered illocutionary types).[26] This last meaning may be taken as the purport of the utterance because, evidently, Caesar could not have been simply making an assertion about his coming, seeing, and conquering—that would be stating an obvious fact and hence pointless.

However, while, as Beardsley argues, the presence of an implicit meaning, even in nonmetaphorical uses, may be admitted as a stylistic feature in virtue of its formal identity, it does not appear that an implicit illocutionary meaning is always a condition of style. Not all stylistically different expressions need have implied illocutionary meanings. For example, between the sentences "She has the most beautiful black hair" and "She has raven hair" there is a stylistic difference because of the metaphor in the second sentence but no difference in illocutionary force—both sentences are "praise" of the woman. The metaphor, in this case, depends neither on the illocutionary force of the statement nor on any contextual juxtaposition to become a style marker. It is recognized as a metaphor by its own deviant logical structure. Moreover, if illocutionary force is taken as the determinant of style, then grammatically deviant uses like "he danced his did" (Cummings) and "a grief ago" (Dylan Thomas) could not be recognized as stylistic features because the difference between their ostensible form and the form of their literal paraphrase may not make a clear difference in their illocutionary force.

The connotations of words may, in some cases, affect the illocutionary act potential of an utterance. Thus, in the example cited earlier, "Pass the salt"/"Pass the sodium chloride," or in Beardsley's example "Go home"/"Return to your abode," the connotations of the two sets of words "salt"/"sodium chloride" and "home"/"abode" are different because the words of each set individually belong to different registers or semantic fields.[27] They also change the illocutionary force of the utterances from a simple request or command to making the same speech act in a jocular manner (which may be a subordinate illocutionary action). They may also be said to produce a stylistic difference, judged by contextual norms. But the same matter can be viewed in another way, and it can be argued that the difference between "home" and "abode" and between "salt" and "sodium chloride" is not a substantive semantic difference. To deny that these words have roughly the same meaning is to deny that any two words can be synonymous at all. The hearer of these sentences will get the same message in either case, although he will see a difference in tone—which, in effect, is another, subordinate illocutionary action—in the utterance employing "abode" or "sodium chloride." On this ground, one could argue that the stylistic difference between the two utterances is due to their having roughly the same meaning but different forms.

These comments may be applied to the following poetic example:

So *wore* the night; the East was gray,
White the broad-faced hemlock flowers

In these lines from Browning's "Serenade at the Villa" (my emphasis), the substantive meaning, including the emotive tone, of "So wore the night" would remain the same even if the poet said "So the night passed slowly and tediously"—which is the dictionary meaning of "wore." The reader would get the same information about the speaker's emotional attitude. What the line loses by substitution is an effect of implicativeness. The word "wore" conveys the sense of exhaustion and attrition without spelling it out in so many words. The difference is slight, but it is formally, that is, stylistically, significant.

In summary, meaning expression cannot be a function of style, for that function belongs to words by their nature as signs. To say that a linguistic form is stylistic in the very role in which it expresses meaning is to deny that it has anything like style. Other implications of the ornamental view of style, which I shall be illustrating in their proper places in the chapter, are as follows. First, since style is not a meaning-expressing function, it cannot be a vital function but some other, "superfluous" function. This can only be that of "heightening," "reinforcing," or "embellishing" the meaning. Literature is not simply a type of language use but a type of meaning (emotive meaning or *rasa,* as I have argued). It is not defined by its stylistic form. Since essential literary meanings are conveyed by words in their meaning-expressing capacity, the meaning-heightening function can only be something superadded to meaning. Second, some literary examples are stylistically neutral. That is to say that they are effective even without stylistic reinforcement.

Implied in the above are three other theoretical assumptions about language. First, words have stable (core) meanings—a view held by the Mīmāṃsakas and the logicians, as opposed to the view of some grammarians that word meanings are an unreal abstraction except on the level of analysis and that the indivisible sentence is the primary unit of meaning. Second, two expressions can have the same meaning though they differ in form—the synonymy postulate. Synonymy, at the sentence level, is, however, to be understood as sameness, not merely of syntactic or locutionary meaning, but of the final meaning of the utterance or purport (explicit or implied).

Third, another assumption that is of relevance to our general discussion of style and language is the dualism of sound and sense, the sign and the *signifié*. This is a fundamental axiom of the Indian philosophy of grammar in the Pāṇinian tradition.[28] The verbal sign is conceived of as a union of two logically distinct entities: the audible (phonetic-grammatical) form, called *śabda,* and the inaudible, mentally perceived sense or object-content, called *artha*. It is by assuming such a duality that all linguistic analysis is made possible: for example, we are able to speak of synonymous and homonymous expressions in language, and we are able to judge the success or failure of a language use. Moreover, unless we consider sound and sense, form and content, and style and meaning as separable terms, we cannot possibly judge the felicity or otherwise of a linguistic expression. To differentiate style from meaning and to judge the appropriateness of the one to the other is required by the very nature of critical discourse. Without such a differentiation, in fact, the critical mind will be paralyzed. On the organicist view of the identity of form and content, there would not be anything like style or anything like critical judgment. The concept of *sāhitya*—of literature as the mutual viability or commensurateness of sound and meaning—is also dependent on this distinction. Hence, the Sanskrit critics take the duality of sound and sense as axiomatic all through their theorizing about language and literature.

Style and Emotion

I have stated before that, in terms of the *rasa* doctrine, emotions are expressed in poetry by their objects and situations, not by virtue of any special power inhering in words. Emotiveness is not a function of verbal meaning. The implication of this for our theory of style is that there is no organic or necessary connection between the emotion and its verbal expression. This view follows logically from the general view of language accepted by many philosophical schools in India, including the Mīmāṃsakas, the logicians, and the grammarians. These schools rejected the "picture theory" of language. Meaning is not of the same form as the word and does not share a common locus with it *(sāmānādhikaraṇya),* nor is the word similar to its referent.[29] Again, where a word exists, the object denoted by it does not necessarily exist, for example, historical persons and fictitious entities like unicorns and the horns of a hare, of which, no doubt, the words do cause cognition.[30] Bhartṛhari also argued that words cannot express the essential nature of objects, external or internal, and that they have but an imputed relation with the things that they stand for.[31]

The literary critics too entertained no illusions about language being an incarnation of thought. The *rasa* theorist would agree with Wittgenstein when he says that the verbal expression of pain does not describe the natural expression of pain but takes its place.[32] Pain words cannot hook onto pain directly but only become associated in consciousness with pain through their connections with natural expressions of pain, such as winces and moans.[33] In other words, emotive words act merely as arbitrary signs of emotive behavior, and this is how they refer to emotions. This is precisely the point of Abhinavagupta's statement, quoted before: "Therefore, the apprehension of rasa is only from the objects and expressions. And when these objects, etc., being presented in some choice words, become the causes of aesthetic rapture, this same power [of the objects] is lent to the words themselves."[34]

It follows from this view of language and the emotions that words have no settled power of evoking emotions, in that any words or any style of expression can deliver that meaning. As linguistic forms have no inherent relation to ideas or emotions, they are variable, and they stand substitution. Any given meaning, whether poetic or ordinary, can be expressed in countless numbers of forms, depending on how the speaker has cognized a certain thing and wishes to present it. Hence, the *dhvani* critics declare that style, understood as the linguistic form, is, first, inconstant, contingent on its context of use, or variable in relation to the ideas or emotions to be expressed. Second, it is indeterminate: that is, a given style feature can go with more than one emotion and produce more than one effect. Conversely, a given emotion can also be expressed in a variety of stylistic modes. Third, again, stylistic forms are infinite. Not only are stylistic devices polyvalent, but they are also endless. The number of options, transformational and lexical, available for the expression of a given meaning are endless. Therefore, it would be quite futile to attempt to set up paradigms for all of them.

Let me illustrate the first two points. The particular collocation of phonetic and lexical features that characterizes the grand style—iambic rhythm, epithets, extended similes, invocations, and so forth—seems to go well with the epic-heroic emotions. But we cannot argue from this that the epic emotion demands this form of expression and this alone. Nor can we say that the epic emotion is the reason for the use of the grand style or that the grand style is the reason for calling the emotion epic since the grand style can be used for expressing such entirely opposite emotions as the heroic and the mock-heroic, for example, Pope's translation of Homer and his mock-heroic satires and Homer's *Iliad* and his mock-epic *Margites*. We cannot deduce one from the other. On the basis of stylistic analysis alone, we should not be able to tell the *Iliad* from the *Dunciad*. All this points to the primacy of meaning in any stylistic consideration, for it is meaning that gives style its linguistic warranty. Without a properly evocative context, that is, the basic emotive meanings, a style feature cannot perform its function as style. In what follows, I shall look, in some detail, at the phonological and lexical aspects of style by way of further substantiating the concept of style outlined above.

The Sounds of Language

The question whether the sound properties of words are in any way related to meaning, whether they affect meaning at all, and how they affect meaning is a stylistic consideration. The view that words, in their own form, are organically related to their meanings and could express or reveal the nature of things or that sentence forms correspond to thought forms has been held by many since the time of Socrates and Plato and has reappeared in modern dress in the aesthetic of Susanne Langer, in the "Fido"-Fido theory of meaning, and so on. All such theories ultimately derive from a mimetic view of language (the Bow-Wow theory).[35] Few language theorists today would perhaps seriously maintain that there is a necessary connection between the forms of words and their meanings.[36] The sound properties of words cannot have any bearing on their meanings in that they neither alter the meanings nor, for that matter, influence the emotive qualities of the things that words, as phonetic configurations, refer to. A rose by any other name would smell as sweet. The point is too obvious to need elaboration.

But the crucial question for the analyst of literary style is, If, thus, no intrinsic connections exist between the sounds of words and their meanings, how can we account for the sense of sound-meaning harmony, which is a very real aspect of poetic language? Therefore, Hymes argues that the nexus between sound and language is not quite so arbitrary as it is often made out to be but a phenomenon to be reckoned with.[37] He tries to demonstrate, by his analysis of a number of English sonnets, that there is a congruence between sounds and meanings that can be objectively analyzed. For instance, in Wordsworth's sonnet "Westminister Bridge," Hymes argues that there are certain "summative" words—"air" and "still"—and certain dominant phonemes (/e r/ in "air," and /l s t/ and /i/ in "still") that express the theme of the poem and that there is a correspondence between the two.

There may be something arbitrary in ranking one or two words as summative words and also in picking on a few phonemes as the dominant phonemes of a whole poem. In any case, even if it is shown that the dominant sounds and the summative words do coincide in the poem, how is the idea of congruence of sound and meaning established since, as Hymes himself admits, there may be no universal or original relation between sound features and the ideas or feelings expressed by words?[38] If this much is granted, then the sounds can be no more than a fancied "reverberation of the thought."[39] Undeniably, though, the sounds do play a role by seeming to reinforce and support the meaning.[40] I shall argue below, however, that even this kind of relation is variable: that is, a given sound structure need not always be associated with the same meaning.

All attempts to show that the sounds of words are somehow relevant to criticism start on the assumption that words, in their formal shapes or physiognomy, are an imitation of the structure of meanings. Evidently, Hymes believes in this since he opens his paper with a quotation from Langer.[41] In onomatopoeic instances, of course, the link between sound and sense is more apparent. In "pop," "buzz," "hiss," "cuckoo," and so on, what the words designate coincides with their sound structures. The connection is physical and in the same material medium, so one may say that the sound of the word is an imitation or "presentational equivalent" of its meaning.[42] But, where the meaning of a word is not its sound, there cannot be any such equivalence. For instance, the sound of "never more" in Poe's "The Raven" has, in spite of its seeming congruence with the meaning, nothing in common with the speaker's sense of desolation and loss.

The syntax of language is also a phonological aspect of style since it affects the sounds of words. Most stylistic analyses assume a correspondence between syntax and the structure of meaning. The assumption that syntax mimes the "form of thought" is the basis of Donald Davie's book on poetic syntax.[43] It should be noted, however, that a given syntactic structure cannot by itself be a sure indication of an emotive import. To cite an example discussed by G. N. Leech, "I kissed thee ere I killed thee" *(Othello)* exhibits a high degree of syntagmatic correspondence between its two segments, the principal clause and the subordinate clause —identity of structure (subject + verb + object), identity of pronouns in the same case ("I" and "thee"), identical morpheme (/ed/) in equivalent syntactic positions, plus the initial phonemic correspondence (alliteration and assonance) of "kissed" and "killed" reinforcing the syntactic pattern.[44] But a degree of regularity can be observed in casual utterances as well, such as in "He found his key and opened the door," also cited by

Leech, or in jingles and nursery rhymes. Obviously, in the *Othello* example, the stylistic effect is due to the ironic contrast between kissing and killing, not to the syntactic patterning or the phonemic recurrences. Substantially the same emotive effect may be gained by virtue of the contrast implied between the two meanings even if one said "I loved you once, but now I had to kill you," or something to that effect.

The following sentence from Bacon has both a parallel syntax and semantic foregrounding: "Some books are to be tasted, others to be swallowed, some few to be chewed and digested" ("Of Study"). The syntax reinforces the distinctions made between books of various kinds, although the focus is on the semantically deviant words "tasted," "swallowed," "chewed," and so forth. But neither feature is an indication that an emotive meaning is involved. The style, conspicuous as it is, lends the statements only a certain pointedness and balance, and also perhaps a witty quality, that characterize some types of formal discourse, including sermons, orations, and so forth.[45] Other features of syntax, such as inversion and series, may also perform a stylistic function in some contexts.[46] But it would be wrong to assume that they become significant regardless of meanings. For example, in the line "Puffs, Powders, Patches, Bibles, Billet-doux" from Pope, it is the insertion of a disparate lexical item ("Bibles") that makes the syntax stylistically significant, the implied antithesis changing the tone of the utterance from that of a mere inventory to one of good-natured mockery, such as is employed in talking about "the vanities of the fair sex" (Pope's stated purpose).

The illustrations given above have brought out three points concerning the function of sounds in literary style. (1) Since sound structures are not directly expressive of meanings and do not affect meanings, they can play only an evocative or heightening role in literary expression. (2) Their function is detemined by the semantic context in which they occur and is dependent on it. (3) Therefore, their connection to emotive meanings is purely incidental, something that is imputed to them or carried over to them from the meanings themselves, as a resonance or reverberation. This is substantially the position that the *dhvani* critics take with regard to the sounds of language. In terms of the *dhvani* theory, a meaning can be both "the suggestor" *(vyañjaka)* and "the suggested" *(vyaṅgya)*—the former when it gives rise to another, implied meaning and the latter when it is itself that implied meaning. But a word, in its phonetico-grammatical form, can only be a suggestor, never the suggested.[47] That is to say, since it has no meaning-expressing function, it can serve only an evocative purpose. Evocativeness, in this case, is necessarily an affective function since it has no bearing on the meanings expressed by words. Thus, on this level, phonemes, words, grammatical parts, sentences, and collocations of words and sentences can all become suggestive in their phonic form alone, without having to express any meaning.[48]

Illustrating the evocativeness of phonemes the text says, "The palatal /ś/ and the retroflex /ṣ/, in conjunction with /r/, and a frequent use of the retroflex /ḍ/ are opposed to the erotic rasa. Hence these phonemes are not evocative of rasa. But these very sounds become evocative when placed in the context of Revulsion and the like. Therefore phonemes too can be infused with rasa."[49] But the question is asked, As phonemes are not by themselves meaningful, how can they be suggestive? Abhinavagupta explains, "Even in types of suggestion where the resonance of the word is the source of evocation, it is only by the power of the sense conveyed that the suggestive function is realized. The power of the sound is merely an incidental aid."[50] Again, he says that, while the evocative power is felt in all parts of a sentence, the description of the emotive objects and expressions in conjunction is "the very life of rasa evocation."[51] The classic statement of the Dhvani position is, however, contained in the following statement, which I have already quoted in part:

> Although the full realization of the objects, expressions, and ancillary feelings [constituting the emotive situation] is the condition for aesthetic enjoyment, still those objects, etc. become like that [relishable, that is] when they are presented in words whose sound structures are in some special way harmonious. This is known from one's own experience. For this reason, even phonemes, of a soft or harsh nature, become a contributory factor in aesthetic relish, even though they are only sounds grasped by the ear and have no relation to the meanings conveyed at the time of their being heard. . . . The rasas are not manifested by the phonemes only—it has been stated over and over again that rasa-expression is only through the conjunction of the objects, etc. Although phonemes are grasped by the ear alone, their effect does indeed extend to rasa-evocation, like the nonverbal sounds of vocal music, and like the rhythmic syllables, the beat [of the hand, to keep time], and imitative sounds such as *ghra,* employed in playing the percussion instruments. . . . Therefore, the apprehension of rasa is only from the presented objects, etc. And, when those objects and the rest, being presented in some special choice of words, become the causes of aesthetic rapture, the same power [of the objects] is lent to the sounds themselves.[52]

This passage brings out emphatically many of the points I have made before: that neither the individual sounds of words nor their collocations have any direct emotive import, the power of evoking emotions residing in the objective conditions described (in the meanings, that is) but that they do seem active in *rasa* evocation as contributory causes and that, as such, they can act only as suggestors *(vyañjakas)* of emotions owing to their association with emotive meanings and contamination by them. The sounds of words are thus parasitic on the sense conveyed, meanings and meaning associations simply coloring the sound impressions. The analogy from vocal music and drumming brings out the point that, while the sounds of words do contribute to the emotive effects of the verbal presentation, they do not define the emotiveness itself.

As regards the role of syntax, the *dhvani* critics follow the same line of argument. Modes of construction *(saṃghaṭanā),* they say, are not directly or independently evocative of the emotion. Nor is there any fixed relation between emotive meanings and modes of construction. As the text puts it, "Qualities (emotional properties like sweetness, energy, and so on) are seen to have a fixed scope (that is, they belong to the nature of the emotions). But there is no such conformity in respect of style of construction. Long compounds are found in compositions treating erotic love, and uncompounded constructions in wrath and the like."[53] The Sanskrit examples discussed by the critics show that, while what may be called a vigorous style consisting of a collocation of harsh syllables like /ś/, /ṣ/, /r/, /ḍ/, and /ṭ/, and aspirated consonants, or compound constructions, may be found suitable for expressing heroism, fury, disgust, and the like, the converse is not true. These very sentiments can be expressed equally effectively in soft syllables and in uncompounded syntax. A compound construction or a collocation of harsh consonants may also be seen to consort well with certain types of erotic expression, although that emotion would seem to call for a more melodious and graceful structure. Other kinds of patterning, such as parallel or antithetical construction, repetition, and so forth, some of which are included under the figures of sound, also stand in the same relation to meaning, and they are by no means indispensable for *rasa* expression.

The point that emerges from these observations is that structural characteristics are variable and contingent on the context of meaning for becoming stylistically significant. They are also not sure indications of the structure or quality of a meaning. For A. A. Hill, a structural analyst, however, the formal regularities of a text take precedence over its meaning. He says that "it is form which gives meaning and not meaning which gives form."[54] His procedure is to work from the linguistic characteristics to the semantic structure of a poem, the assumption being that formal considerations are logically prior to the fixing of meaning. The meaning of a text is no doubt decided on the basis of its grammar and syntax—its linguistic form. But it is difficult to see how it can be said to depend on the stylistic features of the text—formal symmetries and so forth—that Hill is talking about. Hill's method of deriving meaning from purely linguistic criteria sometimes also leaves out important considerations of the context and logic of a given text.

For instance, in keeping with his definition of style as any patterned expression, Hill declares that the sentence "John is a fox, Mary is a cat, William is a rat" is stylistically significant—for him even adventitious alliterations and jingles are poetry. He says, "The stylistic structure is meaningful and takes precedence over the merely linguistic structure and the linguistic meaning."[55] I should argue, however, that the parallel syntax in the example would not even be stylistic if John, Mary, and William were the names of household pets; it would then be a mere enumeration. If, on the other hand, they were names of persons, the meaning of the utterance would be radically different and would have to be understood metaphorically. But, in that case, it would be the metaphor that would be stylistically prominent, not so much the structural symmetry. It is thus clear that, while the "linguistic structure," understood as the grammatical form of a sentence, determines the structure of its meaning, the "stylistic structure" can be determined only after the meaning has been established. A more sensible approach than the one followed by the linguistic stylisticians would therefore be, first, to ascertain the logic of the discourse from its ostensible linguistic form and, then, to analyze those features of its language that are marked in some way and that may be of significance to its meaning. The resultant "style" of the text will then have received its proper justification.[56]

The Lexical Aspects of Style

So far we have considered the phonic forms of language that may be called stylistic because they contribute in some way to the meanings of a text. Under the lexical aspects may be included all those linguistic forms that have a reference to the meanings of words, as opposed to their phonetic forms. Thus, features of language use, including particular grammatical forms and vocabulary items, may be brought under this head. Although such features appeal to meaning and are meaningful units, they may be considered stylistic, not in their meaning-bearing role, but in the respect in which they, in their forms, contribute something to the effect of the meaning. In their analyses of poetic samples, the *dhvani* critics examine all such features—vocabulary items, morphemic units like case and conjugational terminations, prepositions, conjunctions, tenses, number, gender, primary and secondary affixes, compounds, and so forth. They also show how they can all become evocative in appropriate contexts. Figurative uses of language too are included among evocative devices.

As an example of a lexical item becoming stylistically significant, consider the conjunction "and" in "many and many a day he thither went, / And never lifted up a single stone" (from Wordsworth's "Michael"). Here, "and" has the implication that, for a man who was as heartbroken as Michael was, it was but natural that he should not lift up a single stone. Figures of sense, like simile, metaphor, and irony, may also be treated as stylistic devices of content or devices of semantic foregrounding. All these can of course be studied purely as structural features, but the *dhvani* critics insist that they cannot be of literary interest if they are not employed in the aid of *rasa*. Where *rasa* is not present, they merely result in a certain peculiarity of expression. Figures are not, by themselves, vehicles of emotive values but become so when they are employed specifically for that purpose. It is the emotive context that gives them stylistic value.

This is not, however, to say that figures are completely extraneous to poetry. They are extraneous only in the sense that they are not a necessary condition of poetry. But where they are present they could aid *rasa* evocation and thus become an integral part of the expression. Emotional themes are often expressed in the language of metaphor. Therefore, Ānandavardhara declares that figures like metaphor are "not extraneous to the delineation of the rasas."[57] An apt simile or metaphor can lend stylistic support to a message that is intrinsically interesting as an emotional expression, as in these lines from Yeats: "An aged man is but a paltry thing, / A tattered coat upon a stick . . ." ("Sailing to Byzantium").

Although emotive expression may often take a figurative form, it need not always be in that form. According to the *dhvani* critics, suggestion of the *rasa* type can occur in two forms: pure and mixed with figures *(śuddha* and *alaṃkāra-saṃkīrṇa)*.[58] The following verse in Sanskrit is cited as an illustration of the type that occurs without any figures: "He whom you followed even into the forest with feigned anger, with tearful and piteous eyes, though stopped lovingly by mother—that very husband of yours, O sweet, still lives with a heart of adamant, even when he is parted from you, and even though he sees the quarters darkened by the new rain-bearing clouds.[59] These are the words of Rama, who is lamenting his separation from his wife, who has been abducted by the demon king Rāvaṇa. The mood is love-in-separation. The statement conveys with remarkable fullness the hero's grief through a bare description of the emotive conditions, so much so that it may be said to be stylistically neutral.

That a conspicuous style is not indispensable for effective literary expression may also be illustrated by a passage from the *Iliad,* where Hector has fallen at the hands of Achilles and his body is badly mutilated and defiled and tied to Achilles's chariot and dragged along. Hector's mother, Homer says, "tore her hair, and plucking the bright veil from her head cast it away with a loud and bitter cry of grief." The old king "grovelled in the dung." As for Andromache, "The world went black as night before Andromache's eyes. She lost her senses and fell backward to the ground."[60] This passage is wholly inconspicuous in respect of style (but for the trite simile). There are no grammatical equivalences, no sound linkages, and no special structuring devices. But what makes it literature is the quality and nature of its meaning. What one may call the "effect" of the presentation is delivered by the meanings conveyed, not by its linguistic form, which may be changed, the meanings translated into another language. The artistry of such writing consists in selecting and deploying the appropriate details pertaining to the situation and presenting them in an accurate selection of language. But this is not a matter of style at all, in the sense defined by me.

The Graphological Aspects of Style

Some recent writers on stylistics would like to include graphological and typographic devices as well among the elements of style, in addition to phonological, grammatical, and lexical features. Since most literature nowadays comes to us in the written medium, the look of the words on the printed page and the manner in which a writer has chosen to transcribe the vocal sounds of his language in writing could be of significance to the style of a composition. Thus, a poem is realized not only in its phonic substance but in its "graphic substance" as well.[61] Poets have been known to use graphological and typographic devices to give "visual support" to the meanings conveyed. These devices are exploited with great skill in journalism and advertising. e. e. cummings is the foremost among modern poets basing their poetry almost exclusively on grammatical and typographic subversions.

The use of graphological devices was known to the Sanskrit poets also. There was a class of figures called "pictorial figures" *(citra)* comprising various kinds of word play—anagrams, puzzles, riddles, and also graphic figures. A graphic figure—of which there were several varieties—is defined as an arrangement or patterning of the letters of words into interesting shapes of objects. The syllables of verses were arranged in imitation of objects, such as a sword, a wheel, a bow, a plough, an arrow, a lotus, a pestle, a lance, and so forth. The principle underlying these figures is of course different from that involved in a stylistic use of visual forms to support and reinforce the meanings of the words, as in some instances, both classical and modern.

In the Sanskrit picture poetry, however, the visual pattern need not have any bearing on the meaning of the verse. A verse may be in praise of a king and its form that of a lotus. So it cannot be said that the form reinforces the meaning in any way. It is there simply as an extraneous ornament, a superaddition, to the meaning, very much like the typographic arrangement of a poem on the printed page, where the arrangement has no grammatical, metrical, or rhythmic significance. The closest analogy is perhaps "concrete poetry," in which the visual design is believed somehow to provide an extra dimension to the meaning, without being in any way related to the meaning. The basic assumption in concrete poetry seems to be that it is possible to extend verbal meanings into a spatial dimension.

But, stylistic as all such devices may be, in a manner of speaking, they cannot be called verbal style since they belong to a different medium and are completely outside the field of operation of either the linguistic form of words or their meanings. The visual support that graphological forms are said to lend to the meanings must be considered extraneous to the nature of the word and its meaning. Verbal meanings do not need any visual support. The visual shape of words on the page ought not count toward their meaning because words exist primarily as sounds *(śabda),* not as pictures *(citra).* Literature has its mode of existence solely as verbal sounds. Therefore, the *dhvani* critics, rightly I think, do not consider such writing poetry at all. Trick writing or "picture poetry" *(citrakāvya),* as it was called, came to acquire a pejorative sense and was consigned to the lowest regions of poetic limbo.

To sum up, the main thrust of the theory of style advanced in this chapter is that style in literature functions only in relation to meaning, and, as such, it is contingent on meaning. This meaning, which in literature is *rasa* or the mood depicted, is what makes a linguistic form stylistically functional. It follows from this that meaning is logically prior to style, for, unless the meaning is first determined, there can be no determination of how functional a linguistic item is with reference to that meaning.[62] Critical procedure necessarily involves the deciding of meaning in terms of language and the language (as style) again in terms of meaning.

As meaning is all-important for style analysis and is the first consideration, the criteria for style analysis are semantic and contextual, not merely formal.[63] A noncontextualized formal item cannot be said to function as style.

I have stated that stylistic devices are polyvalent and that the connection between style and meaning is not an organic connection but one that is purely associational. Hence, in judging stylistic appropriateness, we have no more solid ground for our statements than to say that, given the kind of meaning, the form seems to go well with it—it seems to support the meaning—although this may not be the only way of stating the meaning.[64] This is especially the case with the phonological features of style.

I have argued that stylistic difference can obtain only between synonymous utterances; two linguistic forms are different in style when they have the same meaning. This necessarily involves the related notion of paraphrasability. Sameness of meaning is no other than the paraphrasability of the referential content of words.[65] Now, of course, only the semantic features of style can be explicated and restated in other words. The sound texture of style—the elusive emotive properties of sounds and syntax—can be neither paraphrased nor translated into another language. The phonetic and grammatical traits of a text can also be distinguished by their formal regularities and so forth without depending on meanings for their determination. But semantic features become style markers only in the respect in which they are different from their paraphrasable meaning. This difference is however, not a difference in substantive semantic characterization but a formal difference.[66]

If style, as I have argued, is definable as a special, reinforcing function that a linguistic form performs in certain types of contexts, then the conclusion is inescapable that it is an ornament. For, as I have tried to demonstrate, the essential meanings of literature can sometimes be expressed without the appurtenances of style. Moreover, to say that style as a poetic ornament is dispensable and detachable is not to say that it has no place in literature. Where it is present, it does serve a valuable aesthetic function.

Literature cannot also be identified as a type of language use with its own characteristic style, as some other types of discourse, such as legal, technical, and the like, can be. It employs all kinds of registers and all types of styles.

Finally, the concept of style as ornament is nothing new or aberrant but has a respectable ancestry not only in Sanskrit criticism but in the Western tradition as well. Informed readers will readily see that it was a pervasive belief right from Aristotle through the Renaissance to the eighteenth century. The organic conception of style originated in nineteenth-century Romanticism and has been developed into a mystique in our own century.

8

THE LOGIC OF INTERPRETATION

In the foregoing chapters, I have already touched on various principles involved in construing the meanings of texts, such as unity of meaning, the purposiveness of human discourse, the contextual factors that help to determine the precise meanings of words and sentences, and some of the methods employed in arriving at the drift of human utterances. Underlying the various theories of meaning discussed is also the implicit assumption that verbal meanings are explicable purely in terms of the linguistic system in which they operate and with the help of the well-known principles of reasoning and that they do not depend for their comprehension on such extraneous factors as the person who authored the text and the person who interprets it. In this chapter, I shall deal, more systematically, with the problems of interpretation, in the light of what the Indian philosophers, especially those of the Mīmāṃsā school, have had to say about them.

The Scope of the Term "Interpretation"

The precise meaning of the English word "interpretation" is perhaps not easy to fix since a number of different activities, such as explication, elucidation, description, and so on, that are involved in what we call the explanation of meaning are indiscriminately called by that name.[1] To "interpret" a text, as I understand that term, is to "construe," to "give a coherent account of" its overall meaning or purport, including those meanings that are only implied and have to be deduced from its linguistic data. Interpretation is thus a more comprehensive process than any of the other activities mentioned above, although it presuppposes all of them. Explication statements, however, may often be interpretive since they involve an interpretive judgment and require the taking of certain decisions with regard to the total meaning of the text.

The word in Sanskrit that comes closest to this general sense is *mīmāṃsā,* which literally means "investigation" or "inquiry." The word "exegesis" may also be taken as a near equivalent. The Mīmāṃsakas were a school of exegetes who were concerned with the correct determination of the meanings of the Vedic texts and with the settlement of dubious or problematic passages in them. Their method included not only the fixing of the meanings of particular words—verbs, names of sacrifices, and so forth—but primarily also the larger task of determining the import of sentences in the light of the overall purpose or intent of the Vedic texts. *Mīmāṃsā* is known as the science of sentences *(vākya-śāstra),* as opposed to grammar, which is the science of words *(pada-śāstra).* Therefore, the term "interpretation" will be taken by me to comprehend all that is implied in the *mīmāṃsā* method of exegesis, namely, the whole process of reasoning involved in construing the meaning of a text. The distinction made by Hirsch between the "meaning" embodied in a text as a determinate structure and the "significance" some people attach to it, as a value they see in it, and consequently between "interpretation" and "evaluation," will also be useful in delimiting the scope of interpretation.[2] I shall briefly touch on the problem of evaluation in chapter 10.

Presuppositions of the Indian Theory of Interpretation

The *mīmāṃsā* principles of interpretation were derived from a long tradition of Vedic exegesis and were codified for the first time by Jaimini (ca. 200 B.C.) in his book of aphorisms called *Mīmāṃsā-Sūtras.* This exegetical tradition produced what may be called a science of interpretation with a body of rules that could be applied to any linguistic text, scriptural or nonscriptural. The grammarians too made their separate contributions to the theory of meaning. The aphorisms of Pāṇini, with the commentaries of Patañjali and Kayyaṭa, provided the basic rules for linguistic analysis and were referred to constantly as a primary source of authority. But interpretation itself was held to be a separate discipline. The knowledge of grammar certainly helps in the understanding of syntactic meaning. But all deeper investigation of the larger, contextually derived meanings of a text must depend on exegetical discussion. Interpretation, thus, is not to be confused with the study of language, for it has its own canons of logic.[3] These canons, as formulated by Jaimini and his commentators, became the groundwork for subsequent philosophical debates. They also influenced the traditional attitudes of Indian critics toward literary texts and their interpretation. Although literary theory in India developed as a separate discipline from the linguistic sciences, such as phonetics, grammar, etymology, and exegesis, and sometimes also as a rival school with its own distinctive contributions to linguistic speculations, it conformed in the main to the precepts, terminology, and methods of analysis established by the language philosophers.

There were of course a bewildering variety of theories, and even the exegetes were divided into rival schools. But there was general agreement on some of the fundamental questions concerning language. According to Jaimini, the three major axioms of interpretation were (i) the autonomy of verbal meaning, (ii) its impersonality, and (iii) unity of meaning. The first axiom relates to the inherent capacity of the verbal sign to convey meanings and its independence of any external authority or of corroboration by another source of knowledge. The second relates to the impersonal character of verbal knowledge and its independence of any personal author who could give words their significative capacity, or "intend" their meanings. The third relates to the univocity of all verbal meanings, without which the capacity of words to act as signs would be upset and human discourse itself would be undermined.

While the principle of unity of meaning was accepted by all schools, opinion was sharply divided, especially between the Mīmāṃsakas and the logicians, on the question of semantic autonomy and impersonality and the problem of intention that they involve. The logicians, who had a stake in maintaining that the Vedas had a personal creator (god) and that all verbal knowledge was authoritative only insofar as it was the testimony of a trustworthy person, hotly contested the *mīmāṃsā* premise. However, the view that prevailed in practical interpretation, both of literary and of philosophical texts, was the one established by the Mīmāṃsā school.

The Vedic exegetes who developed the science of interpretation were, no doubt, dogmatists who believed in the absolute authority and infallibility of the Vedic word. But their observations about the nature of language and the procedures they set up for the interpretation of verbal texts were seen to possess a general validity for all types of discourse. Although they claimed a special status of infallibility for the words of the Scriptures, they admitted that the validity ascribed to the Vedic word was in no way different from that demanded of ordinary discourse. The language of the Vedas was the same as that of common parlance and subject to the same conventions and canons of logic as the other; otherwise, we would not even comprehend the Vedas. Jaimini declares, "But there is no difference in the signification of (Vedic) sentences."[4] Not only is the verbal usage in the Veda the same as ordinary usage, but the things spoken of in it are also the same as those of worldly discourse.[5] Śabara states that Vedic usage must derive its sanction from worldly usage; worldly usage is the only authority as far as words and meanings are concerned.[6] This is obviously true of statements in literature too, as in other types of discourse. However different they may sometimes look, literary statements are subject to the same rules of interpretation as ordinary statements and to the same validity tests. There is no special grammar for poetry. The literary critics, much as they sought to differentiate poetic from ordinary discourse, proceeded on this assumption with regard to literary texts.

The Autonomy of Verbal Meaning

The belief in the autonomy of verbal meanings is fundamental to the *mīmāṃsā* theory of interpretation. The aphorism of Jaimini (1.1.5) affirms the independent and self-explanatory character of the verbal symbol. Whether the word-meaning relation is an artificially created convention, as the Indian logicians argued, or something uncreated and primordially given, as the Mīmāṃsakas maintained, the expressiveness of a word must be accepted as belonging to it as an inherent potency—when the word is cognized, what is denoted by it is also cognized. Without such an assumption, no verbal usage would be possible.[7] The word-meaning relation is also invariable and constant in the sense that the word continues to exist in its own form even though articulated by different men with variations of pitch, tone, volume, and so on and is recognized as being the same in all cases. (Like Saussure, the Indian theorists valorize *langue,* or the impersonal apparatus of language, as opposed to *parole,* the particularities of individual utterances.)

The word-meaning relation must be assumed to have existed prior to the uttering of the word, and it may be supposed to exist even if the word is not uttered. This is described as a "stream-like continuity," which characterizes all linguistic usage.[8] This is not to deny that the meanings of words can change from era to era. But the meanings of the words given in a text, such as the Veda, are themselves not variable, having been irrevocably fixed in their forms. These meanings, it is claimed by the Mīmāṃsakas, can be correctly interpreted by persons who are conversant with that usage. At any rate, subsequent changes of meaning do not affect the fixity of the symbols once they have been used in a text. Diachronic problems are problems that one encounters in the process of acquiring the knowledge of a language; they are not problems of interpretation. All interpretation presupposes proficiency in the language of the text to be interpreted. Whether it is Chaucer, hieroglyphics, or Sanskrit, the problem is the same—that of deciphering the language code in question. But, once this knowledge is assumed, the rules and procedures of interpretation are the same for all kinds of texts. In this sense, all interpretation is synchronic.

Words are an independent source of knowledge. They are also self-revealing because they do not require for their meaningfulness any person or any other means of knowledge, such as sense perception or inference.[9] What causes verbal understanding is the knowledge of the meanings of words. Verbal knowledge is distinct from sense perception because words present only concepts or images, not the things themselves as apprehended by the senses.[10] Again, whereas sense perception can reveal to us only things existing at the present time, words can cause knowledge of things that are past, present, and future and of things that are subtle, hidden, or remote.[11] Deity, heaven, moral duty, and nonexistent objects like "hare's horn" can be revealed through the words that describe them. Verbal knowledge is also not inferential knowledge because it is got directly from words, not "inferred" from them.[12]

The Impersonality of the Word

Following from the notion of verbal autonomy is the idea of impersonality. If the verbal sign is capable of signifying its meaning by its own potency, it does not depend on any human or divine agent to give it its meaning. The Mīmāṃsakas of course believed that the word was not created by anybody but had been there from the beginning of things. But, even on the logicians's view that the verbal convention was created by the will of God, or by human will, as in the case of proper names and technical words, it does not appear that it depends on the will of any particular speaker for its signification once a convention has been created. The individual speaker does not will or determine the meaning of a word because he has not created the convention; rather, he draws on the convention. This, in the ultimate analysis, is what is meant by saying that verbal meaning is impersonal and independent of any human agency. Kumārila explains that, in regard to its own signification, the word, scriptural or other, is independent of the speaker.[13]

The logicians, however, put forward other arguments for the personal derivation of verbal meanings and of their validity. Apart from the question of how the word-meaning relation was created, they contend that, since meanings are conveyed by sentences and not by isolated words, the combination of words into an orderly arrangement can only be effected by the will of an agent.[14] Like the intentionalists in the West, they set great store by the willed character of all speech acts. "Personal derivation" they define as the act of being composed by the free will of a person.[15] An utterance has meaning because the speaker has desired to cause a certain understanding through the medium of words. The validity of verbal statements is due to the trustworthy character of the speaker, not to the intrinsic nature of the statement itself.[16] In the case of scriptural statements, the assumed reliability of the divine author is itself evidence of its validity. But this is a dogmatic assertion. For the reliability of the speaker, even if he is the Almighty God, cannot be sufficient proof of the truthfulness of a statement. How would you know that the speaker is reliable without some other corroborating evidence of his reliability?[17]

According to some Mīmāṃsakas (the followers of Prabhākara), ordinary human statements are necessarily unreliable since they proceed from a personal speaker and are subject to error and suspicion.[18] Only the Vedas, which were not believed to be the work of a personal author, human or divine, were free from defects. But, as the Mīmāṃsakas of the rival school of Kumārila Bhaṭṭa point out, there cannot be any such differentiation between scriptural and human utterances, for the conditions of validity are the same in both. They must both be deemed valid unless they are invalidated by other proofs.[19] Moreover, the argument in terms of authorial reliability fails to see that meaningfulness and truthfulness are two separate inquiries. Even contradictory statements like "Fire is born out of water" do not fail to convey meaning, although they have no truth value. The truth or falsity of statements has no bearing on their meaningfulness.[20]

At any rate, the general assumption of the Mīmāṃsakas that the Vedas are impersonal leads them to an exclusive reliance on the texts of the Vedas themselves. As a commentator puts it, "In the absence of a person who can be presumed to have composed the Vedas, the verbal injunctions contained in them must be taken to be conveyed by the words themselves."[21] The theory of impersonality allowed the Mīmāṃsakas to formulate a consistent theory of language without any reference to the author at all and committed them to a totally objective interpretation of linguistic texts. As a linguistic text is a self-sufficient structure capable of delivering its own meaning, any reference to an author or a reader is extraneous to its interpretation. Neither term plays any significant part in the hermeneutic act. The meaning of a sentence is determined not by a particular person using a particular set of words but by a long convention associated with words.

As the scholiast Śabara points out, it cannot, for instance, be said that "the idea present in the mind of the speaker is different from what is expressed by his words."[22] Conversely, one also cannot say that the meaning of a sentence is different from what the hearer understands from it. If, then, what the speaker has intended and what the reader understands are one and the same thing, and if both are located in the word itself, both the speaker and the hearer become an unnecessary burden. The *Mīmāṃsā* position with regard to the autonomy of the word is supported by the grammarian, who also accepts the innate potency of the word to express meanings. For the grammarian, naturally, the word is all in all. He declares, "We are those who go by the (unquestionable) authority of the word. For us, what the word says, that is authority."[23]

But it might seem that this position of the Mīmāṃsakas is rather dogmatically asserted than properly reasoned out. For what the words say is often not so straightforward as is made out by these philosophers. Granted that meanings are language bound and subject to the controls exerted by it. But, even so, neither the implications of verbal meanings nor their genre traits (the kinds of meanings they are) are given; the interpreter has to construe both.[24] Besides, meanings are not objective entities; they have their being in the consciousness of men who "will" them. Only intelligent beings can be said to possess the expressive power. When one speaks of the "potency of words," one is only extending to words what really belongs to the human expresser of meanings. In banishing the author from his discourse and investing the word itself with the expressive potency, the Mīmāṃsaka is reifying what is essentially a form of consciousness. It can be shown, in fact, that the advocate of verbal autonomy cannot altogether dispense with intentionalist vocabulary. Human intentions are constantly appealed to in all interpretation. Speech acts are intentional behavior and can be interpreted only in terms of motives and intentions. Terms like "purport" and "intent" can be justified only with reference to a speaker and what he purports or intends to say. Even the so-called contextual factors have an inevitable reference to the speaker and what he says or implies. Thus there seems to be no escape from the idea of human agency, however anxious the Mīmāṃsaka may be to do away with it.

But this predicament, the Mīmāṃsaka shows, is more apparent than real. The Mīmāṃsaka does not deny that language necessarily implies a communicative situation—a speaker and a person spoken to, an encoder and a decoder. Nor does he assert that words somehow exist outside human intelligence. Verbal signs serve a pragmatic purpose in human intercourse. All speech is purposive. But, when he argues for the impersonality of the word, what he means is that verbal usage does not depend on, is not determined by, the will of any particular user or interpreter. When someone utters a word, he does not create it; the utterance serves only to manifest the existing word. The word continues to exist in its own form and within its own range of meanings through shifting uses, however inventive the user may be. What the speaker wants to say and what words he should choose are no doubt a matter of his will. But the rules of the language game, in terms of which his will is actualized, are not bound by his will. "Not even a thousand scriptures can make, of a *ghaṭa* (pot), a *paṭa* (a piece of cloth)."[25]

In all textual interpretation, we no doubt posit a speaker and set him against a background of discourse. We say that, because the speaker is such and such and this is the context of his words, he must have meant this, and so on. As Hirsch says, the text has to "represent *somebody's* meaning."[26] But by granting this we are not committing ourselves to the personalist position because this "somebody" is not a real somebody but "anybody"—what Wimsatt and Beardsley called the "dramatic speaker" to whom we impute the thoughts and attitudes of the text.[27] He is no more than a logical dummy that we set up in order to make sense of the text as human expression. This is another sense in which a linguistic text can be said to be impersonal. When the person of the text is no one in particular, he ceases to be "personal" in any significant sense of that term.

As for the objection that, in speaking of the "intent" of a text, we are actually appealing to the speaker's intention, there is an extended discussion of the meaning of the term *vivakṣā* (the wish of a speaker to express a certain meaning) in the *mīmāṃsā* texts.[28] In reading the Vedic texts, the Mīmāṃsaka appeals constantly to implications and unstated meanings, sometimes even at the expense of rejecting direct assertions, on the ground that such is or is not the "intent" of the Veda. But this, the opponent argues, is inadmissible because implications cannot be generated and direct assertions cannot be rejected except with reference to the speaker's intention. In ordinary utterances alone is there a possibility for rejecting a meaning resulting from a direct assertion as not being the one intended by the speaker, for the speaker could say, "This is not what I meant." But, since in the Veda there is no speaker, on the Mīmāṃsaka's own showing, and since the word actually employed is the sole means of knowledge, whatever it says must be accepted as authoritative *(pramāṇa)*.

In reply to this, Kumārila explains that, when one speaks of the "intent" of the Vedic sentence, no actual wish or intention of a speaker is meant. The intent of a text is to be understood simply as what may be accepted as its meaning on the basis of the logic of that discourse. We attribute intention figuratively even to inanimate things, as in the usage "The river bank wishes to fall down" (an expression in Sanskrit). In the Veda, the word itself is the speaker; the injunctive word alone does the impelling: "Just as in the case of personal assertions [in a live situation, that is] it is the person speaking that is the impeller [who, by his injunctions, impels someone toward an action], so in the case of Vedic sentences the impelling is done by the injunctive potency of the word. In the Veda, it is the injunctive word that takes the place of the impeller, and the potency of the injunctive word that of the wish of the impeller."[29]

Three points emerge from the statement just quoted. First, the Vedic sentences are capable of expressing their meanings by virtue of their own potency. Second, the term "intention" is applied to such meanings only figuratively on the analogy of ordinary human situations, in which there are speakers who express their intentions and purposes in actual speech. In the case of the Veda, these purposes and needs are determined entirely by the words of the text. Third, there is also a difference to be observed between the ordinary speech situation and that of the Vedic text. Whereas, in actual communication contexts, the speaker perhaps figures more prominently as he is addressing himself to a live audience, in a text such as the Veda the word itself becomes the speaker and the source of intelligence radiating its own meanings.

But this is said only metaphorically as no particular speaker is present in our consciousness when we read the words of an impersonal or anonymous text. Strictly speaking, of course, intentions and purposes cannot be attributed to words; only persons could have them. What is meant by saying that "the injunctive word takes the place of the impeller" is that whoever may be giving the injunction—god or man—is a fictional construct, albeit logically necessary, and must be present as a presupposition of all meaning. But the meaning and authority of the injunction is understood from the injunctive word only, regardless of who issued the injunction—the red light or the stop sign is a common example. What is true of the Vedas is true of all other kinds of texts. They are meaningful regardless of who composed them. This being the case, the author himself becomes as functionless as "the dugs hanging down the neck of a male goat" *(ajagalastana)*—to use an expression in Sanskrit. As for the interpreter, the fact that he merely construes the meanings presupposes the prior existence of those meanings as objective and sharable entities. Construction is always of a previously existing meaning.

A lot has been said, in recent criticism, about the "implied author," and it is claimed that he has a distinctive presence even in an objective form of presentation (drama or novel).[30] But, on the *mīmāṃsā* view, the implied author, even in a lyrical poem, in which the author may be supposed to be speaking in his own voice, would simply be the dramatic speaker, with no reference to the author in his own person. We understand the poem directly by construing its meaning. Any conclusions that we may draw about the poet's stance would simply be those that are drawn from the meanings of the poem (and attributed to the poet) and often a paraphrase or explication of the poem. Even in ironic works (Swift's "A Modest Proposal," "An Argument against Abolishing Christianity," and *Gulliver's Travels* are the patent examples), the author is present merely as another speaker—narrator/speaker—over and above the character/speaker, who presents a point of view. But even he has no existence apart from the meaning of the text. For this ironic point of view is not recognized as any particular person's point of view but as the final meaning of the text in question. To put it differently, our sense of how the work was intended to be taken is simply our sense of how it may be construed—of what can be taken as an acceptable meaning, as Kumārila has pointed out.

Intentionality. The *mīmāṃsā* theory of impersonality does not, then, seek to abolish the notion of the speaker from the speech act. What, however, it asserts is that the putative intention of the speaker may be set aside as a needless assumption. Now it may be urged that, while this argument speaks to the question of authorial intention or what the author actually intended his work to be, it does not abolish the notion of "intentionality" itself—the notion of human utterances having to be intended in order to be meaningful. Many exponents of speech act theory would therefore like to reinstate "intention" in some form or other, as a reaction against the purely objective approach advocated by Wimsatt and Beardsley and by the linguisticians as well.[31] An utterance performs an illocutionary act because the speaker has intended it.[32] An illocutionary act, such as a request, can be performed felicitously if and only if the speaker "takes responsibility" for the satisfaction of certain conditions.[33]

Here, it should be asked how the speaker's "taking responsibility" for these conditions or constitutive rules can be the condition precedent of the hearer's understanding of the illocutionary meaning of an utterance. How, too, is the understanding of the speaker's illocutionary "intention" different from the understanding of the illocutionary "force" of the utterance? The speech act theorist does no doubt admit that meaning is rule governed.[34] But, if that is the case, it will be quite useless to appeal to intentions in speech acts since these intentions are achieved simply by the hearer's understanding of the meaning of the utterance. In fixing the illocutionary force of a sentence, the hearer decides that the speaker's utterance should count as illocutionary type x since conditions y ought to mean x in context c. The common expression that such and such is the "intention" of an utterance is another way of saying that such and such is its "meaning."

By the same token, it cannot be necessary for our understanding of the nature or force of a literary work, such as *Don Quixote,* to find out with what intention its author presented it. A. J. Close argues that our finding works like *Don Quixote* funny "is normally dependent on our prior recognition that they are intended as such."[35] But this is evidently to put the semantic cart before the horse. For one thing, we would not read *Don Quixote* as a parody if it is not, and does not mean, a parody, even though it was intended as a parody. Second, even granting that our reading the work as a parody "logically" implies that it must have been intended as such, such a recognition comes only after we have interpreted the work as a parody: it is a parody and therefore it must have been intended as a parody, not the other way round. In any case, our recognizing the intentionality of the work plays no part in the interpretation of its meaning. We should therefore conclude that what Close calls "recovering the intention" of the work is simply achieving an "acceptable" interpretation by means of the criteria we normally apply in interpretation—verbal meanings, context, usage, and so forth. Once again, it appears that "intention" is indistinguishable from "meaning."[36]

The whole issue of intentionality, as seen by the Indian philosophers, turns on these very questions: (i) whether intention is a separable and independently identifiable term, distinct from meaning, and (ii) whether the knowledge of the speaker's intention is a necessary precondition *(hetu)* for verbal comprehension. While for the Bhāṭṭa Mīmāṃsakas intention is not a factor in verbal understanding, for the Mīmāṃsakas of the Prābhākara school and for the logicians the meaning of a sentence, especially in ambiguous cases, cannot be determined without a decisive knowledge of the speaker's intention *(tātparya-niścaya).* As I mentioned earlier, for the followers of Prābhākara the scriptural sentences alone are independently meaningful and a reliable source of knowledge, whereas human utterances are meaningful only as they lead to the inference of the speaker's intention. The hearer understands the meaning of an utterance only after inferring that the speaker has put the words together in a faultless and significant manner to convey his intended meaning. Hence, there can be no determination of its purport without reference to the speaker's intention.

The logicians too take a similar stand. They define intention as the desire of the speaker to convey a certain meaning *(vaktur icchā tātparyam).* They do not, however, understand it as a mental aim merely, the notion actually present in the mind of the speaker, but rather in the sense of intentionality, which, they maintain, is a logical precondition for understanding verbal meanings. Verbal understanding takes the form, This is the meaning intended by the speaker. The determination of the speaker's intention with regard to the meanings of words and their connections in a sentence is the cause of verbal comprehension. Only through the medium of the speaker's intention to convey a connected meaning is the sentence meaning apprehended. Where there is no clear sense of such intention, utterances will be liable to fanciful interpretations.[37] Even in ordinary sentences like "Bring the pot," the hearer grasps the purport of the sentence in the form that the speaker has uttered the sentence with the desire of causing the comprehension in the hearer that a pot is to be brought, and the knowledge of this intention is the cause of verbal cognition in the hearer. "Purport" is to be defined as that which is uttered or put together by the speaker with the desire of causing the knowledge of it.[38] It is this desire of the speaker that fixes the meaning of the word "pot" in that sense. When there is a doubt whether that word has been used in the sense of a "pot" or metaphorically in the sense of "a piece of cloth," the determination of the speaker's intention is the cause of verbal comprehension.[39]

Some logicians of the old school define secondary meaning as "the purport of the speaker to convey another, non-primary meaning" or "another meaning related to the primary meaning that is uttered with the intention of causing the knowledge of such a meaning."[40] In expressions like "A village on the Ganges," in which the literal meaning is obstructed, it is only after ascertaining that the speaker's intention is to use the word "Ganges" in the extended sense of "bank" that the hearer understands the meaning of the sentence. Otherwise, the word "village" might come to mean "fish." In polysemous instances, again, where more than one meaning is conveyed by the words, it is the speaker's intention that decides the particular sense in which the words are to be taken. For example, on hearing a sentence like "Bring *saindhava*" (in which the Sanskrit word means both "salt" and "a horse") or "There is Hari" (in which "Hari" means the sun, fire, the moon, Indra, and so forth), all the meanings of the homonymous word are grasped. One does not know from the sentence alone in what particular sense the speaker has used the word.

It may be argued of course that the contextual factors (in the first example, the man is eating at the table, not dressed for a ride) decide the meaning of such expressions because it is through them that the speaker's intention is reached and the word restricted to one desired sense. What is called the speaker's purport is already contained in the contextual factors. Therefore, it is to them that the status of being the cause of verbal cognition *(kāraṇatva)* must be accorded. But the logicians reply that the contextual factors cannot disambiguate the meanings of such words. The only factor that determines the denotative function of a word is the hearer's ability to recognize its significative capacity. When the many meanings of a pun word are well known, they will all be recollected anyway, even without the aid of the contextual factors; if they are not well known, they will not be recollected even though there is a context for them. Moreover, the contextual factors are many and variable, so the speaker's intention fixes the context of an utterance and gives words their specific meanings. Context, however, indicates the intention of the speaker and acts as a logical sign in relation to it.[41] Verbal understanding results from connected meanings only when aided by the knowledge of the speaker's intention. Contextual factors cause verbal cognition only indirectly by revealing the intended meaning of the speaker.[42] Hence, it is the knowledge of the speaker's intention, not the knowledge of the context, that should be accepted as the immediate cause of verbal comprehension.

The Bhāṭṭa Mīmāṃsakas and the Vedāntins deny both that intentionality is the cause of verbal comprehension and that it is distinct from meaning. First, if by speaker's intention is meant the psychological datum, it cannot be known except by way of meaning.[43] Again, what is to be done in the case of works of unknown authorship, such as the Vedas, where any attempt to ascertain the author's intention would be a futile venture? If, on the other hand, intention is understood, not as the desire of the speaker to convey a certain meaning, but as the "intentionality" of a statement—its being an intentional act—then it is not distinct from meaning. As such it has no independent operation *(vṛtti)* in verbal comprehension, nor is it by itself the cause of verbal comprehension. Granted that the purport of a sentence is what is intended by the speaker, but intention itself has to be ascertained only after ascertaining the purport of a sentence, with the aid of context, the syntactic connection of words, and so on.[44]

The logicians have argued that contextual factors help only indirectly in verbal understanding by revealing the speaker's intention. Following a well-known maxim in Sanskrit that says, "When a thing is what it is by reason of something else, why speak of it as the cause of that something?" the Bhāṭṭa Mīmāṃsakas show that this line of argument is clearly circular. When the knowledge of the speaker's intention is itself made possible by the meaning of the sentence, as revealed by the totality of the linguistic and contextual setting, and is constituted by that meaning, why speak of it at all as the cause of the meaning?[45] Moreover, meanings are directly signified by words, not inferred from the speaker's intention. It is the intention that is inferred from the meaning. So how can there be an inference of meaning from that which in turn has to be inferred?

Replying to the followers of Prābhākara, the Bhāṭṭa Mīmāṃsakas assert that neither the intention nor the reliability of the speaker can be established before understanding the meaning of the sentence.[46] Second, the purport of a statement is easy to understand even without the inference of the speaker's intention because, "Are not words capable of expressing their own sense?"[47] The meanings of physical gestures and actions may not sometimes be so apparent. But words carry their meanings on their face, as it were, whether someone intended them or not. I have argued that language, as a source of knowledge, is self-luminous. The fact that meanings are intended by the determining will of a speaker does not take away from the independent ability *(śakti)* of words to signify meanings. A lamp may have been lit by Devadatta, but its ability to give light is its own. As the Vedāntins point out, words repeated by a parrot or Vedic hymns chanted by an illiterate brahmin (computer sentences, for a modern example) do yield meanings even though they are not intended. To this the logicians may reply that they were still intended by their original authors—by god, who composed the scriptures, or by the parrot trainer, as the case may be.[48] But this argument does not answer our initial objection that the identification of the authorial intention is not a necessary precondition of verbal comprehension.

Again, with regard to the argument of the logicians that the context of a sentence is something determined by the speaker's intention, it must be pointed out that context is something that all speakers act in and does not depend on the will of any particular speaker. Both word meanings and sentence structures follow a time-honored convention and belong to a public context of discourse. Hence, the purport of a sentence is what the words mean in a context; the intention of the speaker is at best a remote cause, not an immediate cause of its comprehension. The Vedāntins reject the logician's definition of "purport" as "consisting in being uttered with the desire of causing a particular cognition." Purport is simply "the competency of the sentence to generate a particular cognition." The sentence "There is a pot in the house" is competent to generate precisely that kind of cognition, not the cognition of there being a "cloth." "And the *definiens* of the competency to generate the said cognition alone is verbal potency *(śakti)*."[49]

The logicians seem to disregard the efficiency of language as a medium of communication when they place even word meanings and word relations at the mercy of the speaker's intention. Surely, in the example "Bring the pot," the word "pot" *(ghaṭa)* could not mean "a piece of cloth" *(paṭa)* even if the speaker intended it to do so. If it did mean "a piece of cloth" in some metaphorical usage, that meaning would be supplied by the words themselves and their apparent relations without our having to invoke a separate condition called intention. Similarly, in the homonymous example "Bring *saindhava,*" as far as the hearer is concerned the purport of the utterance is conveyed by the context (the speaker is eating) and by the meanings conventionally assigned to the word *saindhava* (which can mean only "salt" or "a horse," or perhaps also "an inhabitant of Sindhu" in some contexts, but not many more things). I am not denying that speech is an intentional or purposive action or that every composition in words must have an author. I am only questioning whether there is anything like "authorial intention" separate from the meanings of words and whether the determination of that intention is the cause of verbal cognition. The term *tātparya,* or intention, must then be understood simply as the purport of the sentence. I further assert that the purport of a written text can be adequately ascertained by means of the indications *(liṅga)* contained within the text itself, or, in ordinary speech situations, by means of the context of utterance, because, once the speaker's intention is expressed, the task is of verbal construction only.[50]

The literary critics, too, do not recognize authorial intention as a separate condition of meaning. The intention of a statement is simply the syntactic relation between the words or the total contextual meaning. In practical criticism, they proceed on the assumption that a literary text, even like the scriptural text, is impersonal. They admit, no doubt, that poetic language, especially of the suggestive type, where an unexpressed meaning is also implied, depends on the poet's intention to produce some special effects in that it does not necessarily conform to any existing conventions in respect of linguistic usage. But they also distinguish between intention, which can be inferred from the words, and meaning, which is the object of that intention and which is signified by the words. One infers from the words that a certain idea is the object of the speaker's intention. But the inferred intention itself does not constitute the meanings of the words. The meanings of words are not "inferred" from words; they are due to the significative capacity of the words themselves. Even implied or suggested meanings, as we have seen, are deduced from the meanings of the words themselves, not via the intention of the speaker. Thus, the notion that a certain idea has been "intended" has no direct bearing on the explanation of meaning.[51] Accordingly, the Sanskrit critics understand the task of interpretation to be one of analysis and explication of what is strictly given in the literary text. Hardly ever do they, in their commentaries, refer to the author, except by way of identifying a work.

The main premise of the Mīmāṃsakas, that verbal meanings are impersonal and autonomous and that one need not go beyond the words to elicit their meanings, and the various rules of interpretation devised by them have been the accepted mode of procedure for all traditional branches of learning in India, for example, jurisprudence, philosophy, and literary criticism. It is of course recognized in all quarters that words are tricky instruments and cause difficulties of interpretation since their meanings assume a bewildering variety of forms. In any case, we have only the words to go by for the determination of what is meant. As Bhartṛhari declares, "The word alone is the binding factor because it has its capacity fixed [in connected utterances, that is]."[52]

Unity of Meaning

The third axiom that is fundamental to the *mīmāṃsā* science of interpretation is unity of meaning. Unity of meaning is to be assumed of all human discourse, whether in a sentence or in an extended composition. This concept is widely accepted in all branches of inquiry in India, and even the literary critics, who had a stake in maintaining the value of polysemy, especially of poetic suggestion, had to recognize this principle.

The *mīmāṃsā* theory of monosemy is based on the realization that indefiniteness destroys linguistic discourse as it cuts at the very root of the convention of verbal signs. Signs will cease to signify if they lack definition, and there will be no fixity for Vedic injunctions, whereas injunctions are best conveyed within the meaning of a unified utterance.[53] A unified utterance is one that presupposes a single consistent motive or purpose; it represents an integral idea. Unity of purpose is also what defines a sentence, according to *mīmāṃsā:* "A sentence is 'one sentence' by reason of the singleness of its purpose, such that when the words are separated they are found to be wanting (i.e., incapable of effecting the purpose)."[54] When the sentences are equally independent of one another or express two distinct purposes, they should be treated as syntactically distinct.[55] It is the commonness of purpose *(prayojanaikya)* that binds the words together into a single sentence, not mere syntactic expectancy or one verb word, as the grammarians thought.[56]

Unity of meaning is of two kinds: the unity of a sentence *(padaikavākyatā)* and the unity of a sequence of sentences *(vākyaikavākyatā)*. Different words with different meanings make up a unified sentence meaning, and different sentences are similarly focused on a unified sense in a sequence of more than one sentence or in an entire composition. The criterion for determining the unity of a larger text is again commonness of purpose. This criterion is constantly applied by the Mīmāṃsakas in determining the comprehensive intent of the Vedic texts.

Sentence Types and Unity of Discourse. A most important aspect of the *mīmāṃsā* theory of discourse is the concept of sentence types. The Vedic texts, like any other texts, naturally contain different types of sentences, analyzed by grammarians: declarative, imperative, commendatory, and so forth. Since, for the Mīmāṃsaka, unity of purpose, both at the sentence level and at the level of a whole text, was a primary prerequisite of meaning, the problem was to reduce the different sentence types to a unity. This he does by subordinating them to one central type, which, then, would be the "dominant mode" of that discourse.[57] On this basis, he decides that, in its overall purport, the Veda is an "injunctive discourse" dealing with *dharma* (*dharma* is simply what is enjoined) rather than a reference discourse.[58] Its aim is not to convey information regarding the nature of already accomplished things *(siddha)* but to prompt people *(bhāvanā)* to things that are yet to be accomplished *(sādhya),* to certain ritual acts, that is.

Here, the problem for the interpreter is how best to account for the presence of the many noninjunctive passages, which have no direct bearing on the actions enjoined but which certainly are an integral part of the Veda. They must somehow be connected to the principal part of the text. Otherwise, they would incur the charge of pointlessness *(ānarthakya-doṣa).*[59] Therefore, the Mīmāṃsaka tries to show that, although such passages are not syntactically connected with the injunctive texts, they become meaningful when taken in conjunction with the principal statements. Jaimini declares, "But they are taken as forming a single sentence with the injunctive passages, and as such they could be authoritative as eulogizing the particular injunctions."[60] The noninjunctive texts share a common object with the injunctive texts—they prompt the reader toward the performance of the enjoined actions, indirectly, by praising their excellence.

Although the two types of texts are syntactically distinct and express two distinct ideas, they yet have a mutual need *(ākāṅkṣā)* for each other. Take for an example, the following passage from the Veda: "One desiring prosperity should sacrifice the animal *śveta* to Vāyu; Vāyu is the swiftest deity." The statement about Vāyu (the wind god) is a mere description and does not indicate any action to be performed or anything connected with action. But it becomes significant when construed as forming one sentence with the injunction *(vākyaikavākyatayā).* What is implied by the description is a commendation of the sacrifice offered to Vāyu: a sacrifice offered to a swift deity always accomplishes the result quickly. In the same manner, the *mantras* (hymns in praise of gods), lyrical passages, and so forth also serve the purpose of commending the actions enjoined. Deprecatory passages serve the purpose of creating an aversion in the mind of the sacrificer to what is prohibited.

The noninjunctive passages in the Veda are divided into three types: metaphorical statements *(guṇavādas),* reiterations of already known truths *(anuvādas)* (e.g., "Fire is an antidote against cold"), and statements of past events *(bhūtārthavādas)* (e.g., "Indra raised the thunderbolt against Vṛtra"). Since these types of sentences serve no visible purpose in their own meanings, they are taken as implying praise or deprecation of matters enjoined or prohibited. Such statements are called *arthavādas,* or declarative or commendatory texts. An *arthavāda* is defined as "what is meant for the purpose of an injunction" *(vidhiśeṣa).* Thus, all parts of the Vedic text are shown to be included in the verbal prompting that is the sole purport of the Veda.[61]

The *mīmāṃsā* doctrine of *arthavādas* offers a most valuable hermeneutical principle that can be applied to all types of discourse, scriptural or nonscriptural. As I argued in chapter 3, the aim of a literary text is not injunction, instruction, or the assertion of universal truths but evocation, which is also a kind of verbal prompting. As such, a literary text too imposes on its sentences a total unity of discourse. If evocation is the end of literature, all types of sentences employed in it, including commands, requests, wishes, commendations, and descriptions, must be considered to be subordinate to that unitary end and contributing to it. That is to say that, when such sentences occur in a literary context, they are invariably related to the evocatory aim and understood as expressing specific moods on the part of their speakers, indirectly also prompting the reader toward the moods so expressed. As a commentator explains, "Even as in a scientific text all the parts lead to a connected meaning, in poetry, the rasas, such as love, are the final import of the sentence."[62]

Thus, nature descriptions in poetry, as in the descriptive tradition of eighteenth-century English poetry, do not terminate in being merely objective reportings about sights and scenes—such reportings would be pointless and to no purpose. They also prompt us to contemplate how wonderful the described scenes are. Even in pure imagist verse or haiku, where only a scene or object is presented in the briefest outline and no predication is made about its emotional significance, a state of mind or an emotional complex is usually implied, and the presentation makes sense only as an evocation of some sort. Similarly, assertions of general truths in the poetic context, for example, "They also serve who only stand and wait," "The paths of glory lead but to the grave," and so on, or philosophical assertions like "Our birth is but a sleep and a forgetting" do not merely persuade us into a belief in their validity; rather, they serve to reveal the speaker's mood. Prayers ("Avenge O Lord thy slaughtered saints"), imprecations ("Ruin seize thee, ruthless king"), and exhortations ("Say not the struggle not availeth") are, however, illocutionary acts that are directly expressive of emotions and attitudes and should be taken as expressions of anger, enthusiasm, and so forth on the part of the speakers, according to their contexts. In a longer composition, such as a play or novel, the sentences descriptive of the emotive situation would constitute its principal meaning, and all other types would be *arthavādas* in relation to them. Poetry is thus a kind of verbal prompting *(śābdī bhāvanā);* it prompts us to contemplate and relive certain ordinary human experiences.

The Problem of Multiple Meaning. The principle of unity of meaning is rigorously applied by the Mīmāṃsakas to all cases of multiple meaning. They were no doubt fully aware that there is no fixity about either words or sentences. A word occurring at different places may bear different meanings, and it may be used in its literal or in a secondary sense. The same is the case with sentences. But they insist that it is manifestly wrong to take a word or sentence used in one and the same place as conveying two different meanings. They disapprove of multiplicity of meanings even in the case of synonyms. Jaimini declares that it is improper that the same meaning should be carried by many different words.[63] Commenting on this, Kumārila says that, since names are used for referring to objects, it is unnecessary to have more than one name for an object.[64] Synonymity is accepted in cases in which there is a long-established usage connecting words with their meanings (e.g., *hastaḥ, karaḥ, pāṇiḥ,* all meaning "a hand").

A more serious problem is that of polysemous words and sentences that convey many meanings at once. According to the Mīmāṃsaka, it is also not right to attribute several meanings to one word.[65] One of the Mīmāṃsā maxims is "nonassumption of multiplicity of senses" *(anekārthatva-akalpanā).* A word, uttered once, will exert its meaning only once. That is to say, it will not convey a second meaning in the same effort.[66] The same goes for the sentence. Śabara declares, "One sentence can have only one meaning, so that no one thing can be taken as connected with two things at one and the same time."[67] The Mīmāṃsakas protest against plurivalence in human discourse because a man cannot be supposed to be saying two unconnected things at the same time. As Kumārila puts it, when a man's purpose is served by only one meaning, a second and a third meaning would be quite useless for him.

A major problem of interpretation arises here. How can one explain away the many meanings of a polysemous word or sentence? To solve this problem, the Mīmāṃsakas devised an elaborate set of rules called *nyāyas* (axioms of construction), by means of which all ambiguities due to multiple meanings or shifts in meaning can be settled and both words and sentences fixed in a single suitable meaning. The following are the most important among them.

1. The most important of these maxims, the principle of "bar" *(bādha)* or "exclusion" is applied in judging the relative weight of two texts or propositions or of two meanings of a single word or proposition. The application of this principle is one of the means of reconciling conflicting texts or conflicting considerations (which are capable of being reconciled). There are very many types of "exclusion," literally scores, discussed in the *mīmāṃsā* texts.[68] The following are a few that are relevant to the question of unity of meaning. (i) That which has multiple meanings is barred by that which has a single meaning; that which is denoted by many words is barred by that which is denoted by one word.[69] That is to say that, of two related words occurring in a text, if one of them has many meanings and the other a single meaning, the former is excluded by the latter, and both words are taken in a single sense, that is, in the sense of the latter word. (ii) That which is secondary is barred by that which is principal.[70] This is the principle of subordination *(guṇa-pradhāna-bhāva)*. For instance, the many meanings of a word cannot exist as parallel or coordinate meanings. One of them must be taken as the principal and the others subordinated to it, as in some way qualifying the principal meaning. (iii) A manifest sense bars a sense got through implication. The primary sense bars the secondary sense.[71] (iv) An ellipsis filled up by an expression that occurs in the text excludes one that is imported from outside the text.[72] (v) The etymological sense of a word is excluded by its conventional sense.[73]

2. Another important axiom is that of nonsimultaneity *(ayaugapadya)* of many meanings because of mutual repugnance. For instance, a word cannot be employed in both its literal and its metaphorical senses at the same time. For, when the metaphorical sense is invoked, the literal sense is nullified.[74] Again, the same word can convey more than one meaning only one after another, not simultaneously, in the same instance of use, that is. Not all the meanings of a double- or multiple-meaning word can be operative at once or be equally important. As Bhartṛhari says, "Simultaneity is avoided and the word established in one meaning due to [the contextual factors such as] purpose, situation, or association with other words."[75] As we have seen in chapter 6, where some or all of the senses of a homonymous word are entertained, the various senses are forced into relation as subject and modifier, or they become fused into a single meaning. Many Sanskrit writers on rhetoric agree that the figure paronomasia has no separate scope of its own; it invariably attracts some other figure like metaphor. At any rate, what we have in paronomasia is

not a dubiety of unconnected meanings but a coalescence in which the interaction between ideas and images produces a unitary sense.

This, as noted before, was also the substantial position of the *dhvani* theorist on the question of multivocity of meanings. The *dhvani* critic claims that the suggested sense is inconstant *(aniyata)* because it has no well-settled form like the conventional relation of word to meaning but is conditioned by other adventitious circumstances like the context. But he admits that "it is indefinite in its lexical form, not in its essential suggestive function."[76] Even suggested meaning must be one and precise. If it were completely indefinite, it would be futile to examine it since each reader could interpret it according to his whim. Moreover, as the *dhvani* critics themselves point out, the literal meaning, which gives rise to another, unexpressed sense, becomes necessarily subordinated to the other meanings, or is nullified by it altogether, so that the univocity of the sentence is preserved.[77] A linguistic text is not the legendary cow of paradise *(kāmadhenu),* which you could milk at will and endlessly.[78] It is necessarily both limited and precise in its meanings.

3. A third important axiom is that of apparent inconsistency *(anyathā anupapatti* or *arthāpatti),* by which all secondary interpretations of meanings, extensions, supplying the ellipses, and so forth are justified. Kumārila states, "It is only by Apparent Inconsistency that we infer the potentiality of all things. . . . We infer an unperceived potentiality in a certain word only when we find that the meaning cannot be explained in any other way."[79] The words of a text must be construed in their natural and ordinary meanings unless such a construction leads to an absurdity or the context or object of the statement requires a different construction. The Mīmāṃsaka insists that metaphorical interpretation should be resorted to only when it is absolutely necessary, not by needlessly setting aside the direct meaning.[80] We have seen the operation of this principle in secondary meaning as well as in much suggested meaning. Although the *dhvani* critics claim that poetic suggestion is not subject to the principle of apparent inconsistency, it is actually due to its operation that an implied meaning arises from the surface meaning of a sentence.

4. By far the most important and inclusive principle of construction in the *mīmāṃsā* tradition is the maxim of precedence or supercession, that the meanings directly asserted and got through literal construction are more authoritative than those construed by other, indirect means, such as the context. "Construction by context," where it becomes necessary, must receive its sanction from the direct assertions contained in the text.[81]

5. Another maxim is that of the remainder of the passage *(vākyaśeṣa).* The Indian theorists are most emphatic in declaring that meanings can-

not be left undefined and that all ambiguities and doubtful constructions must be resolved through explanation. Patañjali declares, "The correct meaning of a word is to be determined by explanation [in case of doubt], but doubtfulness ought not to result in lack of definition."[82] This maxim, as stated by Jaimini, says, "In all doubtful cases, a definite conclusion can be arrived at with the help of the rest of the passage or text."[83]

6. The maxim of meaninglessness or futility *(ānarthakya)* requires that no part of a text may be rendered useless or nugatory. Every word or sentence of a text must be assumed to have been written with some purpose in view.

7. A related maxim is presumption against contradiction *(sāmañjasya).* It states that contradictions within a text are not to be presumed where it is possible to reconcile them. The method of figurative interpretation *(guṇavāda)* is one important way in which contradictions may be reconciled.

Indicative Marks. Since the Mīmāṃsakas believe that the meaning of a text can be objectively ascertained from the evidence provided by the text itself, they list six more principles of explication called *liṅgas,* or marks indicative of the purport of a passage. These are (i) consistency of meaning between the opening and the conclusion of a passage or topic; (ii) repetition or reiteration of the main theme; (iii) the introduction of a new idea; (iv) the end in view; (v) corroborative or commendatory remarks, as distinguished from the main theme; and (vi) arguments in support of the main theme.[84]

Determinacy and Interpretive Certainty

Rules of Interpretation: Their Admissibility

With such an impressive armory of interpretive rules and procedures as those outlined above to rely on, it might be expected that the meanings of a text can be interpreted with certainty and all doubtful cases resolved. However, from the intentionalist point of view, there could be no canons of construction, first, because no possible set of rules can give us an insight into the author's verbal intentions. The norms and guides for construing a text must therefore be evolved by reconstructing the author's aims and attitudes.[85] I have already, in effect, answered this objection. Second, it is objected that, because every rule has an exception, an implicit proviso, it is not really a rule.[86] But this does not stand to reason. Although many rules have a limitation attached to them, a few are fundamental to human reasoning and do not have an exception. Such are the maxim of meaninglessness and the related axiom of presumption against contradiction, the principle of the remainder of the passage *(noscitur a sociis),* the maxim that the express mention of one thing implies the exclusion of another *(expressio unius est exclusio alterius),* and the maxim that direct expression precludes implication *(expressum facit cessare tacitum).* Some of the other rules have limitations attached to them. But, since the conditions of application of the rules are precise and specific, there ought to be no difficulty in their application. It has also been questioned whether there is a common set of canons appropriate for all types of texts—literary, legal, philosophic, and so forth. But, as we have seen, the *mīmāṃsā* theorist assumes no difference between scriptural and secular language. It follows from this that there can be no separate sets of rules for different types of discourse. The only canons that apply in all cases are those of ordinary language.

Context as a Determinant of Meaning

Many of the *mīmāṃsā* maxims depend quite heavily on contextual factors—both verbal and situational. I have stated that context is all important for interpreting verbal meanings. Context, as I have defined it, is whatever is required for making a full and coherent sense of a statement. But it is, in a way, what the words themselves express immediately and demand for their completion, or for their intelligibility, if they are obstructed in their literal meaning. In ordinary speech situations, no doubt, utterances are often taken in conjunction with their nonlinguistic contexts. But, in a written text, obviously, all that is required for the understanding of its meaning must be supposed to be given in the text itself, as its verbal context, consisting of the words that precede and follow and their implied connections with the passage in question.

The Mīmāṃsaka recognizes of course that context is not something that is directly stated by the words of the text; it has to be construed from the stated meanings through a process of reasoning. But this does not justify Hirsch's conclusion that all interpretation is a "probability judgment."[87] A sentence such as "My car ran out of gas" (Hirsch's example) can no doubt hold out an array of possibilities (even as the sentence "The sun has set," discussed before, can) when considered in abstraction. (The *dhvani* critics too, we recall, adopted this line of argument.) But, when a context is supplied to it, which has necessarily to be a particular context, there can be no variability. Hence, Hirsch seems to be wrong in assuming that "context" is not "a fixed given, but something that can just be as variable as the word at issue."[88] The integralist position maintained by the Mīmāṃsakas would not favor any consideration of meaning in isolationist terms. Meaning is to be understood as the sign situation in its entirety.

The Limits of Contextualization

Some of the contextual factors, as we have noted, no doubt take us outside the text, especially in the case of live utterances. But even these "situational" factors, which enable us to reconstruct the immediate setting of the communicative act, must be taken as part of the meaning of the text because they are needed for its completion or justification. Hence, the autonomy of the text as a structure of meanings is not affected by its context dependence.

The structuralists and the semioticians would, however, like to extend the context of a literary work beyond its textual limits to cover the larger communicative and cultural processes, continuities, and correspondences. A verbal text is seen by them both as a semiological and sociological fact. It is wholly dependent on its background of conventions, codes, and cultural assumptions and can be understood "only within the context of a system of enabling conventions" that constitute it and give it its meaning and identity.[89] Meaning itself is produced through the operations of reading, according to certain shared, preexisting categories or "codes," rather than contained in the text. No doubt, no linguistic text is self-referential; it requires a knowledge of the world that is represented as its meaning. Meaning, as understood by the Indian theorists, is a relation subsisting between the sign and what it signifies and thus involves a reference to what lies outside the sign *(bāhyārtha)*.

But the structuralist concept of "intertextuality" demands much more than a referential relation between the text and the world. For the structuralist, no doubt, the social reality or the interpersonal world of ordinary discourse itself is a "text." But this is not all that is meant. "Intertextuality" further implies that a literary text cannot be understood except by relating it to other literary texts that are within a given system. As literature itself forms a system with its own conventions and expectations, each text is constituted by a network of relations; it is a plurality of other texts. So literary competence involves knowledge of these wider areas that extend beyond the text. Culler says, "It is . . . only too clear that knowledge of a language and a certain experience of the world do not suffice to make someone a perceptive and competent reader."[90]

Granted that the reader does not approach the text with a tabula rasa. But the question still is whether these larger extensions of the text can be admitted as part of its verbal meaning and whether they are required for the interpretation of those meanings. Sometimes, no doubt, one needs a special set of facts to explain a highly allusive work, such as *The Waste Land,* or a work that uses another text as its basis. But, surely, not all works are of this nature. In order to understand the basic meanings of, say, a Shakespearean drama, a novel by Hardy, or a poem by Wordsworth or Coleridge, one need not seek outside information from other texts, cultural codes, and so forth or place the work in a network of relations. All that these works appeal to and require of the reader is a capacity for understanding and a knowledge of the world of ordinary experience, which is largely uncodified and perhaps uncodifiable and which can be supposed to be at the disposal of every mature reader. Also, most generally, except where the text is of an esoteric sort, the only codes needed for interpretation are the norms of rationality and acceptability. But these are not, as Culler thinks, "conventions" in any significant sense; they are rather implicit in the way we reason about things, in life or in literature. Moreover, we do not need any special literary competence to be able to recognize the significance of a poem or novel, its thematic unity, and so forth. As Reichert observes, "anyone who can read can read literature."[91]

It will of course be urged that for interpreting a text it is necessary to identify the type of meaning or generic class it represents and that this knowledge can come from the reader's acquaintance with other literary texts. A correct reading of *Don Quixote* as a parody of chivalric romance or of "The Rape of the Lock" as mock-heroic would require the prior notion of what a chivalric romance or epic is. But I should argue that fundamental generic notions, such as tragic, comic, heroic, and so forth (which are implied in the theory of emotions we have examined), are universal concepts and part of the common human heritage, not confined to any particular language culture or, for that matter, to literature at all. Even a child can enjoy a "marvelous" tale without knowing about the marvelous as a literary genre. Any adult reader can identify *Don Quixote* as a parody of exaggerated or crazy notions of heroic or romantic behavior without the knowledge of the literary conventions surrounding the text; that the book is a parody is anyway writ large on every page.[92]

It thus seems reasonable to assert that, to interpret and appreciate a single literary text, one need not go so far as to relate it to the whole universe of literature, to the vast network of textuality, and look at literature itself "as a system within a larger system of human culture."[93] To do so would be to stretch the meaning of context to absurd limits, and it would not be interpreting the text any more but interpreting the world. Meaning, as the structuralists contend, is no doubt system bound. But that system is defined by the linguistic structure, its grammar, and setting, in short, by whatever is immediately required for a successful interpretation of the verbal signs; it does not include "the totality of the existing states of affairs" in the world (Wittgenstein's phrase). Structuralism, even Frye's archetypalism (e.g., Tom Sawyer's adventures in the cave are a displaced version of the dragon-killing myth; Hamlet's leaping into Ophelia's grave is an instance of the classic descent into the underworld),[94] leads us away from the proximate concerns of the text as an artifact and from its dramatic center into needless distances and abstractions.

This is not of course to deny the value of scholarly information and of cultural-historical studies. This is only to say that, while such studies may enrich our appreciation and bring corroboration to our reading, or perhaps, where necessary, establish a text for interpretation, they cannot be a substitute for interpretation, nor do they add to or alter the meaning of the text. The interpreted meaning of the text is not deduced from such sources.

Criteria of Verification

An intentionalist like Hirsch is led by his logic to argue that the well-known criteria of verification, such as coherence, cannot be decisive in adjudicating between rival interpretations of a text. Since no one can be certain about the author's meanings, there can be no coherent interpretation of a text. In principle, no doubt, there can be only one correct interpretation. But this would be the one that best accords with the author's meanings. Reconstructing the author's typical stance involves admitting extratextual evidence in support of an interpretive hypothesis. It also implies that any such hypothesis can be only provisional since the uncovering of some new data might require a different construction of the poet's stance. Thus, there can be no finality about any construction of a text's meaning.[95]

This logic has been applied by Hirsch to Wordsworth's poem "A Slumber Did My Spirit Seal," and the conclusion reached that, of the two interpretations offered by Brooks and Bateson, each one permitted equally by internal evidence, Bateson's is the more probable because it is grounded on a consideration of the author's typical attitudes. But, from the standpoint maintained in this book, it can be seen that the poem makes complete sense in terms of its linguistic evidence and that, since its meaning is wholly contained within the text, no other information is needed for its interpretation and none is also likely to turn up to upset our present construction of its meaning, as long as it satisfies the criterion of coherence or consistency. By applying the rules of interpretation discussed above, it can be shown that Brooks' reading of the poem is the correct one and gives a coherent account of all its features.

For one thing, it would be gratuitous to suppose, as Bateson does, that there is any suggestion of pantheistic thought in the last two lines of the poem: "Rolled round in earth's diurnal course, / With rocks, and stones, and trees." For, if an affirmative thought that the girl has become part of the sublime processes of nature is what is implied, it would be a straight contradiction of the preceding line: "No motion has she now, no force, no life; / She neither hears nor sees." There is not also sufficient warrant for reading pantheistic implications into "rolled round" or into "trees." In other contexts, the word "trees" might connote life, but here it appears in a series with inert objects—rocks and stones. We should therefore take these words at their face value, for to import any other meaning into the poem would be a violation of the rule of literal construction—that no word should be taken in an implied sense unless its literal meaning leads to a manifest absurdity. Explicit meanings, we have seen, are more authoritative than implicit meanings.

Moreover, the fact that Wordsworth's typical attitudes were pantheistic does not necessitate this poem's being pantheistic also—this Hirsch himself admits.[96] So why raise the issue of the poet's attitudes at all? Thus, when all the facts of the poem are considered, Brooks' conclusion that the poem expresses inconsolable grief would seem justified. The changed condition of Lucy from a vivacious little girl to an object among other objects is what inspires the speaker's grief, and the grief is inconsolable because there is no other, hope-inspiring thought. The tone of elegiac mourning is sustained all through.

Historicity versus Determinacy

The Sanskrit critics do not deal directly with the question of historicity; they, like their counterparts in the Western classical tradition, do not even seem aware of it as a specific problem of interpretation. But they would, consistently with their theory of meaning, reject the view of the modern hermeneuticians that meanings are historically bound and that the historicity of a text or of its interpreter determines its meanings. On the *mīmāṃsā* premise that verbal meanings are self-explanatory and that once a text, such as the Veda, is given a certain shape and structure it stands immutably fixed in its own form, a competent reader, conversant with its language, should be able to recover the text as an object without having to resort to any sources of knowledge that are external to it. All that is required for verbal comprehension, even of past works, is a knowledge of the word as sign—not any special perspective or a "fusion of horizons."[97] This is especially the case with literary works, whose appeal is not to any past mode of consciousness but to a universally shared experience of the emotions.

Thus, a Shakespearean drama, say, *Julius Caesar,* can be understood by all those who know the language, without any reference to the Elizabethan or Roman world picture. That is to say that whatever world picture is presented in the play is contained in it only as its meaning and has to be elicited from the words of the text, not from books of history, and that, although the play may be dealing with a life that has the characteristic flavor of the Elizabethan or Roman world, the experiential frame in which it is embedded and the moods it evokes have no reference to an alien mode of thinking and feeling. Thus, all circumstances described in it, including those that are specifically historical, function as an objective, situational frame for the emotions evoked. It is in this sense that all art is said to be contemporary.

Meaning, Response, and Indeterminacy

The classical notion of the text as a system of internal dependences, self-contained and self-explanatory, is attacked also by a school of theorists who follow the phenomenological approach.[98] These critics would like to include the reader's response to a literary work, as well as the history of its reception, in the case of a past work, as an inseparable part of the interpretive act. A literary work is there, no doubt, only to be realized. But it is difficult to see how the actions involved in responding to a text can properly be said to form part of the meaning of the text. The meaning of a text is clearly what the words say, not the perlocutionary effects they produce on a reader or generations of readers. These may vary from person to person and from age to age. These critics assert in fact that meanings are not only variable but indeterminate. A text is potentially capable of different realizations; different readers will realize it differently, and the same reader will realize it differently at different times according to changes in his perspective. Hence, the text is also inexhaustible. There is the "unexpressed reality" of the text that is realized in the imagination of the reader.

Even the simplest statements are of course capable of opening out unexpressed imaginative horizons in any fertile mind. There may be depths of meaning embedded in it that remain beneath the surface of words like the submerged part of an iceberg. Meanings spread inward in the reader's mind to the full range of their significance, and, as the Chinese saying goes, "The sound stops short; the sense flows on." But these "metatextual" actualizations can hardly be brought under the head of verbal meanings because they neither flow from the words of the text directly, or indirectly from their meanings as secondary implications, nor are they needed for the completion of the meanings of the text. Besides, if they too were to be regarded as part of verbal meaning, there would be no restriction on the scope of words, and a sentence may never come to a stop. One would also be guilty of confusing verbal understanding with the long train of mental reflections and psychological associations that invariably follow that understanding. But these, most Indian philosophers insist, are two distinct operations.

Unity of Meaning and Unity of Interpretation

The *mīmāṃsā* theory of meaning, for which I have been arguing in this chapter, not only grounds textual meaning on a solidly objective foundation by making it an utterly formed and finished thing but also, consistently with its position, rules out multiplicity of interpretive choices and explanatory models and the disputes that arise in consequence. If a linguistic text, as a determinate structure of meaning, exhibits "unity of meaning," it must require "unity of interpretation" as well. But many influential critics and critical schools of our time have converged to argue against univocity and closure, advocating flexibility in critical judgment and an open-textured pluralism.

The anticlosural tendency is quite evident in both structuralist-semiotic and poststructuralist thought (in spite of its anti-intentionalist and impersonalist stance) and follows from its conception of meaning. The text having been displaced as an identifiable structure and as a source of meaning by the reading process, which "produces," rather than "construes," meanings through various procedures of code reorganization, the door is wide open for plurality and endlessness of reference. For Barthes, as for Eco, the discovery of structures is an infinite process—a continual structuration, infinite semiosis.[99] Meaning is a play of language, an endless play of signification. The same thought is echoed in deconstructive criticism too, although it is directed toward the goal of dismantling structures. The dialectic self-reversal of meaning, which should go on endlessly until it reaches a point of no return, leads to a critical inability to conclude, to undecidability and indeterminacy. On such a view, obviously, there is nothing left for a text to be.[100] The pursuit of signs becomes an end in itself, yielding its own peculiar thrill or titillation, as in Barthes. Against such views, we can only reiterate our position that it is impossible to read or criticize a work without appealing to its identity, integrity, and stability as an object. Any reading must be anchored in a determinate text. Completeness and certainty of meaning are a logical and psychological necessity.

At any rate, deconstructive readings do not show convincingly that the texts they analyze are the kind of things that they are made out to be, namely, self-subverting structures. Barbara Johnson's reading of Melville's *Billy Budd* is a case in point.[101] Her argument, in the main, concerns the interpretation of the central incident in the story, namely, that in denying Claggart's foul accusation of duplicity with a blow Billy unwittingly kills him. Johnson says that Billy's very act of denial proves the truth of Claggart's accusation, thus undermining the assumption of Billy's innocence that the text promotes. But this can only be a misinterpretation, for Billy's outraged reaction to Claggart's malicious charge can hardly be a demonstration of the "truth" of that charge for the simple reason that Billy is not guilty of it in the first place, as evinced by the text. Billy can be shown to be guilty only through perverted readings, by imputing to him unconscious motivations, and the like.

Admittedly, there are a host of ironies and ambiguities in the story, as there are in the other works of Melville. But it can be shown that they contribute to its unity, to its profoundly tragic tone. They are the very conditions of tragedy in Melville. Johnson's essay reveals the characteristic deconstructionist distortions, namely, importing meanings into the text, grafting onto it a set of prefabricated models and categories, and thus turning the language of the text into a metalanguage: for example, the opposition between Billy and Claggart is said to be an opposition, not between good and evil, but between two conceptions of language, or two contradictory models of signification, or two types of reading—Billy is the literalist, Claggart the ironic reader, Captain Vere the judicious reader, and so on. The focus is no longer on the human drama that the story enacts but on the allegory of a text describing its own signifying processes.

Equally unconvincing are Paul de Man's discussions of the rhetorical question as a deconstructive model and as an illustration of his theory that it is impossible to choose between literal and figural meaning. For example, in Archie Bunker's question "What's the difference?" or in Yeats' famous line "How can we know the dancer from the dance?" (from "Among School Children"), the same grammatical model, according to de Man, engenders two meanings that are mutually incompatible—one figural (which assumes that a question is not really being asked) and the other literal (which treats the question at its face value). Says de Man, "it is impossible to decide by grammatical or other linguistic devices which of the two meanings . . . prevails."[102]

But it is possible to show, by closely examining the context of each example, that a question is not being asked at all and that the literal meaning is simply canceled out by the figurative. In Yeats' poem, a straightforward reading of the last stanza, in which the line occurs, suggests the following interpretation. Labor becomes blossoming or dancing where the body is not bruised to pleasure the soul. But neither the spontaneous blossoming of the chestnut tree nor the ecstacy of the dancing body betrays the labor of growth or movement. To be able to tell the difference between the blossom and the bole, the dance and the dancing body, would be focusing only on the labor involved without the pleasure that that labor engenders. Thus, the poet is not asking to know but denying the difference assumed by the question.

Reader-oriented theories, such as those of Norman Holland and Stanley Fish, have also, in different ways, tried to displace the focus on the text as an object and center it on the reader's experience, whereas for the phenomenologist reading is an interaction between the textual object and individual consciousness.[103] For Holland, reading is a form of self-re-creation or self-replication—a view that must lead to complete subjectivism. For Fish, on the other hand, the text is an event that "happens to, and with the participation of, the reader" rather than a thing in itself. It is constituted by the reader's interpretive experience. Reading is, accordingly, "an analysis of the developing responses of the reader" as he follows the succession of words in the text.[104] The objectivist does not of course deny that meaning is an event in the communicative process and depends on a mind to read it and elicit it from the verbal structure. But, inasmuch as the verbal structure itself is the source of meaning and the reader does not generate the meaning, Fish's charting of "the reader's developing response" may be more accurately described as the charting of "the structure of developing meaning" in the text.

The theory of "aspect seeing" or "seeing as," advocated by the followers of Wittgenstein, assumes that the same text may be seen under a variety of aspects, on the analogy of a picture that can be seen now as a duck and now as a rabbit. But the fallacy of applying the visual analogy to verbal meanings is that, whereas perceptual objects may change their aspect according to the conditions of perception, words never change their aspect. They are not guided by the angle of vision of the interpreter. As signs, they carry their interpretation on the face. There can be "thirteen ways of looking at a blackbird," but there can be only one way of reading the poem of that title by Wallace Stevens. The theory of "seeing as" makes interpretation a way of "fancying" verbal meanings, not an act of understanding and analyzing them. According to it, it would appear that one could read any sort of meaning into a work and view it now as a tragedy and now as a romance or a grotesque farce, according to the fertility of one's imagination.[105]

Margolis rightly points out that interpretation is not aspect seeing in Wittgenstein's sense but has to do with evidence and justification. But he reaches the conclusion that there could be several competing, nonconvergent, and seemingly incompatible, but "plausible," interpretations of the same work, based on different categories or models of explanation.[106] The end result of all such arguments is to discount the objectivity and self-explanatory nature of the work. Morris Weitz too exaggerates the problem of critical divergences, which to him are inherent in the very nature of critical discourse.[107] However, a close examination of the issues in *Hamlet* criticism, listed by Weitz, will reveal that there is a remarkable degree of agreement on the essential nature of *Hamlet* as a drama of tragic grief. Critical quarrels over the play, where they are genuine quarrels, do not pertain to its essential features, but to peripheral issues.

For instance, no conflict is apparent between the view that the play is a revenge tragedy and the view that it is a ritual drama. Disputes need not arise on descriptive issues if all the data of the text are carefully sifted and collated. Questions like "Is Hamlet mad?" and "Is he melancholy?" can be settled by textual evidence. The text itself contains the clarification of terms like "mad" and "melancholy." Reichert agrees that there can be, in principle, an exclusively correct interpretation of a work.[108] But he thinks that even descriptive statements relating to the factual properties of the text are explanatory hypotheses involving complicated reasoning about the data.[109] In every work, there will be at least some factual matters, and direct statements pertaining to them, whose meanings do not have to be drawn out through any elaborate hypothesizing. Such, for instance, are the facts relating to the basic plot of *Hamlet*. Even interpretive statements ought to yield univocal solutions to problems that are based on verifiable data.

There is perhaps greater scope for disagreement on evaluative issues. But even here consensus is possible if only the right criteria are applied and the right reasons given. Critical dissensions are often due to the fact that critics tend to neglect the essentials and pitch on the nonessential properties of what they conceive to be a good work of art. If, for instance, they rest their arguments on what Weitz calls the "unchallengeable" criteria of value and ask, Does *Hamlet* fulfill the essential criteria of a tragedy? Does it exhibit unity of tone? Is its treatment of character and action a just representation of human experience? and so forth, they are more likely to come up with mutually agreeable answers. But if their questions are based on nonessential criteria like the unities, decorum, conformity to certain assumed moral standards, and so forth, there is bound to be disagreement.[110] Although evaluations, by their very nature, are not true or false statements about the properties of a work, still they can be supported by objective reasons, that is, by descriptive and interpretive statements, about which agreement is possible.[111]

To sum up, the logic of interpretation outlined in this chapter flows from the basic postulates of the *mīmāṃsā* theory of meaning. Semantic autonomy, impersonality, and unity of meaning are the three pillars on which the *mīmāṃsā* theory rests. *Mīmāṃsā* maintains that a linguistic text is sufficient unto itself as a bearer of meaning and can speak for itself without external aid. No doubt, all meaning is context bound. But this dependence of verbal meanings on context should not be construed as a limitation on textual autonomy, for context is what the words of the text themselves presuppose as a condition of meaning. Similarly, the fact that a text refers to an outside world does not also constitute a limitation on its autonomy. Meaning is external reference. But how far the context of a text should extend and what extensions of meaning should be admitted as those that fall strictly within the bounds of verbal meaning are matters that can be decided only by reference to the purpose of the discourse in hand.

On the contentious question of impersonality versus intentionality, no doubt, the Sanskrit theory reflects the same oppositions that one finds in the Western critical tradition. Even as the intentionalists in the West do, the Indian logicians sought to save the role of the divine or human will in verbal communication. However, it is the nonintentionalist argument that has prevailed in the traditional Indian approach to linguistic texts, and its influence is evident in the theory and practice of the literary critics as well. The typical attitude of the literary commentator is summed up in these words of Mallinātha: "All this is being commented upon by me only by way of explicating the meanings of the text. I say nothing that is not in the text and not warranted by it."[112]

The third axiom states that a word is necessarily univocal in any single instance of use. Only a unified meaning can make for the determinacy of a text. Multiple meanings should be forced into unity through elimination, assimilation, or subordination. Unity of meaning naturally demands unity of interpretation. All apparent contradictions within a text are to be reconciled in the interests of unity and consistency, and ambiguities and doubtful constructions too must be resolved through explanation. At no cost can meanings be left indefinite. Divergencies in interpretation too must be settled through discussion, for the assumption that there can be as many interpretations as there are interpreters will destroy the fixity and stability of the verbal sign. It is of course fully recognized that there will be disputes in the construction of meanings, given the complex ways in which words behave, and that there will be errors of linguistic perception. But these can be settled in all cases only by a further examination of the text, not by appealing to a misplaced attitude of tolerance.[113]

Finally, the exegesis of verbal meanings is as rigorous a science as any other (e.g., logic) and follows certain well-defined rules of construction. These rules make it possible for the interpreter to ascertain the meanings of a text, which is "an utterly formed thing once and for all, for one and all."[114] Criticism is not, after ali, an arena for contending idioms and world hypotheses, and we are not here

as on a darkling plain
Swept with confused alarms of struggle and flight,
Where ignorant armies clash by night.

253
Notes

283
Bibliography

297
Index

To

the late Professor T. R. V. M

and

the late Dr. V. Raghavan

with gratitude and affecti

(1975); "Poetic Emotions and Poetic Semantics," *Journal of Aesthetics and Art Criticism* 34 (1976); "Validity in Interpretation: Some Indian Views," *Journal of Aesthetics and Art Criticism* 36 (1978); "The Indian Theory of Suggestion (Dhvani)," *Philosophy East and West* 27 (1977); "The Nature of Poetic Truth: Some Indian Views," *British Journal of Aesthetics* 19 (1979). I thank the editors for permission to reproduce this material.

9

POETIC APPREHENSION AND POETIC TRUTH

Another important concern of the Sanskrit critics is the nature and status of poetic knowledge and the related question of the referentiality of poetic statements. The Indian philosophical schools were also seriously occupied with the general problem of knowledge, truth, and meaning, and their speculations had a vital influence on the literary critics in their own formulations concerning the validity of poetic meanings. Is poetry a fictional discourse? Does it yield valid knowledge about the world? How are poetic meanings apprehended, and what is the ontological status of the objects referred to in poetry? These and other questions, which are also the burning issues in contemporary critical discussions in the West, figured prominently in the criticism of Lollaṭa, Śaṅkuka, Bhaṭṭanāyaka, and Abhinavagupta.

The most contentious issue, however, was the question of imitation in poetry, with the problem of poetic illusion as its corollary. Another important issue, which has a bearing on the problem of truth, is the question of the poetic universal. Are poetic statements statements about particular persons and their dealings, or are they statements about general human nature? This question, as we shall see, has important consequences for determining the validity of poetic statements. If poetic statements are typically about particular persons, they would not be true assertions, considering that most characters and events in literature are fictitious. If, however, it can be shown that they have a universal import, then they could be said to possess a kind of truth value. But, then, one has to demonstrate how precisely poetic statements, which invariably describe particular human situations, come to acquire a universal significance. As this question of poetic universals logically precedes the question of poetic truth, I shall take it up first.

The Question of the Poetic Universal

That poetry deals with universal or representative truths, as opposed to history, whose business is with particular facts, is a well-known dictum of Aristotle's. A poet, Aristotle says, differs from a historian because "the historian relates what happened, the poet what might happen." It is not "the poet's business to relate actual events, but such things as might or could happen in accordance with probability or necessity. . . . Poetry deals with general truths, history with specific events."[1] This distinction, in the form in which it is stated by Aristotle, raises a number of questions. First, if history deals with specific events, so does poetry. The concern of poetry is not with abstract truths stated abstractly. Aristotle's likening of poetry to philosophy seems mistaken. Nor is the concern of poetry for that matter, with general truths exemplified by particular instances. A play or novel need not convey any generalized truths at all; often a good one makes no statements at all about what it presents in the form of an action or a narrative. Poetry, as a presentational mode of expression, is primarily concerned with concrete facts and events of experience. It is necessarily all about "what Alcibiades did or suffered."

Again, a literary work does not typically give generic names to its characters, such as "the miser," "the jealous husband," "the clever slave," "the type of ambitious man who sells his soul to the devil for a life of power and pleasure," and so forth, as Aristotle seems to think, but presents them as particular individuals with a name and a local habitation—Othello, the Moor of Venice, Dr. Faustus of Guttenberg, and so on. Any situation presented in literature is a particular situation, in the form in which it is presented. (One need not consider straightforward moral or other allegories—Everyman, the Seven Deadly Sins, and so on.)

Aristotle makes a further distinction between literature and history on the ground of their structure. An epic or a tragedy has a unified plot structure and arranges its events in a causal sequence. On the other hand, "History has to expound not one action but one period of time and all that happens within this period to one or more persons, however tenuous the connection between one event and the others. The battle of Salamis and that of the Carthaginians in Sicily took place at the same time, but they had no common purpose."[2] What Aristotle says is true of a whole book of history, like the history of ancient Greece or Rome. But does it apply to a particular episode in history, like the battle of Salamis or Agincourt or the death of Julius Caesar, in which events have to be linked together in a necessary causal sequence even as they have to be in a drama centering round that very episode? It appears, then, that a distinction cannot be made between history and literature either on the ground that the events in poetry are more unified than actual historical events or on the ground that poetry presents general truths rather than particulars. Yet it is common experience that poetry is more universal than history. The question, thus, is, How are the particulars of poetry transformed into universal, representative truths so that they acquire a general human significance and relevance?

The answer to this should perhaps be sought in Aristotle's own statement defining "general truth." General truths, Aristotle says, "are the kind of thing which a certain type of person would probably or inevitably do or say."[3] This statement could be interpreted to mean that, although the poet necessarily presents a particular, concrete human action, its significance extends beyond the particular instances to other instances of that type. This extension does not happen in history. A historical proposition like "Caesar took Gaul" is predicated only of Caesar and does not admit of a universal extension, whereas poetic propositions like "Othello strangled Desdemona" may be said to be applicable to all general human situations involving men like Othello.

There seems, however, to be a logical hurdle here. How can a singular proposition, in which something is predicated of a subject who is not a class (or who is a class having only one member), generate an understanding about a whole class of subjects called "men like Othello"? Logically, then, the statement about Othello is as "particular" and specific as the one about Caesar. Aristotle does not provide a solution, nor do his commentators. Thus, Butcher admits that the universal of poetry is not an abstract idea "embodied in a particular example"—that is the method of allegory. It is rather that "the particular case is generalized by artistic treatment."[4] But this is hardly a solution to the problem since the precise nature of this artistic treatment is left undefined.

The Sanskrit critics too recognize that poetic meanings are generalized.[5] But they offer a clearer explanation of the phenomenon than is found in Aristotle's *Poetics.* They state that this generalization, which they call *sādhāraṇīkaraṇa,* is rather a characteristic of the way in which poetic meanings are apprehended than a formal characteristic of poetic statements. But then the question will be, what is it that prompts a generalized apprehension of the particulars of poetry as opposed to the particulars of history? The fact that some or all readers see them that way is not a guarantee that they will necessarily be seen that way; besides, it does not explain the difference between meanings in poetry and meanings in history. One needs a better logic than that to prove the case.

In terms of the *mīmāṃsā* theory, no idea can be read into words unless it is present as the meaning of those words. So one should be able to show that this generalized perception is an aspect of the cognitive meanings of poetic statements. So Abhinavagupta points out that the generalizing or "impersonalizing" of meaning is, in some speech contexts, a feature of verbal cognition. In discussing the Vedic example "Prajāpati cut out his omentum and offered it to the fire," the Mīmāṃsakas have argued that, though this sentence is a declarative, historical statement, it has the force of an injunction in the general context of the Vedic injunctions. Hence, the sentence, by praising the action of Prajāpati, induces in the qualified person, after he has grasped the literal meaning, a second perception that "I should offer fat to the fire."

But how does this second perception arise? The Mīmāṃsaka's answer is that it arises because of the apparent inconsistency of the primary meaning. A factual statement has no place in an injunctive context unless it can somehow be related to that context. That relation, in this case, can only be that of an *arthavāda* (commendation or injunction through commendation). That is, by commending a certain course of action, you are, by implication, prompting the hearer to adopt that course of action. Thus, in the present example, the factual statement undergoes transformations in the process of apprehension in the following two ways: first, it is taken as implied praise; the implied praise is then taken as an implied injunction.

Often, Vedic injunctions, even when they are not commendatory statements, are framed as declarative sentences, like "He offers curds to the fire," "He places the wetted pebbles," "He performs the sacrifice," "He gives gold to Ātreya," and so forth *(juhoti, yajati, upadadhāti, dadāti)*—all in the present indefinite (*laṭ* form). But, since their purport is injunctive in the general context of the Veda, they are transformed into the imperative form *(liṅ)*—"He should offer curds," "He should perform the sacrifice," and so on—on the strength of the maxim "Imperative, even if it is not explicitly stated" (i.e., the present form is sometimes capable of indicating an injunctive force). We also have the familiar expressions in English "If I were you, I would act at once," "If a guy wants something, he goes and gets it," which have the force of "You should act at once."

The literary critics adopt this line of argument and show that the particular statements of literature are transformed into general statements, that is, statements that can be applied potentially to all typical cases. In the words of the texts:

> Just as, from the statement "Having praised the sun god he has attained lasting health," there is first the understanding of its literal meaning, and subsequently there doubtless arises a cognition negating time and other particularities obtained from the sentence, in the form "Whoever praises the

> sun god becomes free from malady; therefore I will also praise the sun god for the removal of my illness," in the same way, even from a poetic statement there is no doubt that the reader gets this kind of perception.[6] For instance, from statements like "They lay by night," "He offered [the omentum] to the fire," there comes to the qualified person . . . immediately after the perception of the literal sense, a second perception of the form "I will lie by night," "I will offer," and so on, negating the particularities of time [person, etc.]. This second perception is of the nature of a transfer [of the literal sense], and is called variously "prompting," "command," etc. In a similar way, from poetic statements also, there comes to the qualified reader another cognition [transcending the words of the poem].[7]

After understanding from the poem that "Umā" or "Hara" said so or did so, there arises in the reader another perception of a different order, eliminating the temporal, personal distinctions assumed by the sentence. In the injunctive context of the Veda, we noted that what departicularized and depersonalized the historical or factual statement and gave it an injunctive force was the general injunctive context of the text. So also, in the case of a literary text, it can be argued that it is the evocative context of the literary utterance that generates this depersonalized second perception that what is being said about a character, Umā or Hara, is really not about that individual character alone but about all those who are like that character.

This is not, of course, to say that the characters lose their particularity; they are invariably seen under the particular descriptions given of them. But the feelings and attitudes they express are apprehended as the general human emotions felt by all persons in their circumstances. This power of generalization must be supposed to inhere in the emotive factors themselves, in other words, in the nature of the facts reported in the literary text. The facts reported in history books, such as "James I succeeded to the throne of England in 1603," "The battle of Trafalgar was fought in 1805," and so forth, cannot be given a general application because of the unique reference of the actions reported, whereas the facts of literature, pertaining to love, hate, sorrow, joy, and so forth, are not events that happen only to particular individuals at a particular place and time. By their very nature they are sharable by all men alike, regardless of the determinations of time and place. Historical reporting does not dwell typically on the feelings of its personae. But, where it does, it is not merely history but drama (e.g., *The Last Days of Pompeii*). So, in emotive statements, events are capable of giving rise to a generalized perception even though they are presented as particular facts: "Othello grew jealous and murdered his wife. All jealous husbands can act like him, and I too would perhaps act like him were I provoked." This meaning can be drawn as an implication from the literal sense of the statement; hence, it is part of the cognitive content of that statement.

The warrant for drawing this implication is provided by the general evocative purpose of statements occurring in literature. That such is the purpose of literary statements may be established by the fact that, in them, emotive events are not stated merely as bare facts but are given adequate treatment through the display of their objects and expressions. This is true not only of longer compositions, like dramas and epics, but of short lyrics as well, in which either a situation is briefly outlined or its bare details given cryptically so that the fuller picture has to be imagined by the reader. The very fact that the poet dwells on the emotional significance, explicit or implicit, of the facts presented is proof enough that the statement is made for the purpose of evoking the emotions. No one would give a detailed picture of an event, such as that of a man murdering his wife, describing motives, circumstances, the feelings of the persons involved, and so forth, and then claim that he is simply "informing" or "reporting" the facts of the case. In crime fiction, too, no doubt, details of motives and circumstances are presented as the facts of the case, but no attempt is made to describe the feelings and responses of the parties concerned. This does not debar it from the designation of literature since the events are not being reported in the context of criminal court proceedings, and the narrator of the novel (or, in a life situation, whoever is telling the story) may be supposed to be presenting the story for the purpose of evoking certain responses—wonder, suspense, and so forth—in the audience. These responses are also implied in the characters of the novel. The evocative purpose is thus implied in the discourse.

Another argument put forward by Abhinavagupta to show that the particulars of literature have a generalizing implication is, "They (the personages of a drama) are no doubt apprehended under a particular description. Even so, particulars appear in their own nature as particulars only when they are felt to be contemporaneous and hence useful in some way to our practical interests. But in drama the characters and events are not seen as being contemporaneous, and hence their particularity is accepted in its generalized form. In poetry, too, the same generalization of the emotive factors takes place."[8] It is this temporal remoteness of events in poetry and the absence of any direct bearing of those events on our practical interests that aids their generalization. I am going to argue below that this remoteness characterizes, not only the facts presented in a drama or novel dealing with historical or legendary characters and events, but also those other forms, such as the lyric, that present events in the present tense. Events in literature are apprehended as accomplished facts and things of the past whatever the tense in which they are presented. It is conditions such as these that permit the reader's cognition that poetic characters like Hamlet and Othello are not particular persons with a historical identity but generic types of men loving, suffering, and so on.

There is, moreover, such a thing as the power of sympathy, which enables the reader to relate himself to the presented emotive situation in a personal way. Once it is felt that the events happening to others like Hamlet or Othello might be happening to oneself and the reader is immersed in that experience, those facts pertaining to Hamlet or Othello may be said to undergo an extension and, being stripped of all particularity, become mine and yours equally. Nonemotive facts or facts occurring in nonemotive contexts, like Caesar's conquering of Gaul, are not amenable to this kind of extension.

Abhinavagupta dwells at length on the phenomenon of sympathy, which abolishes all spatiotemporal and personal distinctions and induces the consent of the reader's or spectator's heart and his identification with the characters and events of the poem or drama. It has to be assumed of course, as Abhinavagupta does, that an adult person has direct knowledge of all sorts of human emotions—love, hate, sorrow, and so on—which are embedded in his mind as memories or impressions, both prenatal and acquired in the course of one's life, and which are potentially present all the time but are spurred into action when suitable conditions—actual or imaginary—present themselves. The emotions depicted in the play or poem are such conditions and are called *bhāvas* because they cause or induce sympathetic vibrations *(hṛdaya-spanda)* in the reader's heart and are conducive to aesthetic relish *(rasana)*.

What the reader contemplates are of course the given mental states—not fear, love, and so forth in the abstract, however, but these emotions as attached to certain objective conditions and residing in a particular locus. Hence, characters are given particular names, like Othello, Macbeth, Rāma, and so on, and shown in a particular set of circumstances that cause in them certain emotive reactions, although the particularity of both the characters and the events is negated in the process of the reader's apprehension. Without a minimum of specification (particularization), there can be no perception of their representative character. Generic attributes cannot be apprehended unless they are exhibited in individuals.[9]

This point is summarized in a text on drama as follows: "The characters such as Rāma convey the notion of certain states of feeling of certain types of heroes, such as those of an elevated nature, and so forth, and they generate feelings like love in the spectators and are relished by them.

They are the causes of rasa, being freed from their particularity." The commentator on the text adds:

> The poets surely do not gain knowledge of the condition of Rāma and others [legendary or historical persons] individually. . . . What, then, do they do? They visualize the mental states of the elevated and other types of heroes in a vivid manner, since these are the common experience of all humanity, and then trace them in specific characters [like Rāma], which simply provide the locus for those mental states. The names like Sītā [occurring in the poem] are deprived of the particularity of their designation as the daughter of Janaka and so on, and become denoters of common womanhood.[10]

Although, however, a lot is said by these critics about the role of sympathy in aesthetic experience, the case for the generalization of poetic meanings need not rest on an appeal to the reader's response, for we have also been able to show that this transformation of the particular into the universal is a feature of the cognitive-semantic situation of the poetic statement. We can therefore conclude that poetry deals primarily with particulars, insofar as its subject matter is concrete human situations and not abstract truths. But, whereas the reference of poetic statements pertains to the particular, the cognition pertains to the universal. That is to say that the particulars of literature are transformed in the cognitive process and understood for their universal import. This, as I said before, is due to the operation of the rule of apparent inconsistency. For, if the characters and events in literature were not generalized, they would not be able to serve the purpose for which they are described, namely, the evocation of moods.

The negation of the particulars of space, time, and person, which is what constitutes the generalizing process, has consequences for certain formal features of literary statements and the way they are translated in the understanding process. The Vedic examples have shown that the tense and person of a sentence can sometimes undergo transformation. The sentence "Prajāpati gave his omentum to the fire," which is in the past indicative and third person, is transformed in the reader's cognition into the imperative mood and first person, in the form "I should offer fat to the fire," in order that it may be related to the injunctive context in which it appears. Similarly, "They are peeling barley" is translated as "Peel barley, I should peel barley." Commands are never in the past tense and have no reference to things already accomplished *(siddha),* only to things that are yet to be accomplished *(sādhya).* They are also not in the present tense since the action to be accomplished has not yet started.

This transformation of tense and person may be seen to occur in literary apprehension too, although the purpose of literary statements is not injunction but evocation. Statements describing an emotive situation may be in the past tense, which is the characteristic tense of narrative reporting, or in the present, which is the normal tense for the lyric. But the mood evoked by them is itself a timeless condition. After understanding the reported events as having happened at some past time to someone called Umā or Hara, the reader has a direct mental perception of the feeling signified by the events.

It must be noted, however, that it is only the mood formulated through the events that is apprehended as an impersonal, timeless category. The events themselves are grasped as being of another person, time, and place. If, for example, the event is one that inspires fear in man or animal —a frightened man or hunted deer—the emotion apprehended from it is "fear in general," uncircumscribed by the sense of time and person. It is not of the form "I am afraid," "He is afraid," or "My friend or enemy or a third person is afraid."[11] The implication of this is that, although, no doubt, the reader is apt to feel a touch of fear, however slight and phenomenologically remote—or he may become actually frightened himself, depending on how sensitive he is—still, as Abhinavagupta explains, he is not totally involved in it, nor is he completely turned back from it. He merely contemplates it as a mental condition that he could feel and others too could feel.[12] This is how the emotion is depersonalized, that is, separated from its locus (the character) and cognized as a generalized state.

All the same, it should be remembered that the events themselves are happening to another person (the character) and that it is he who is involved in the emotive situation, not me or my friend. This sense of pastness and otherness is essential for a detached contemplation of the presented situation; this is what in fact permits the generalization of the emotion. If the presented situation were to produce in me a total delusion that things are happening to me here and now, there would be no generalization. If they are happening entirely to others and have no effect on me, if Alcibiades is the one who is suffering, again there is no generalization. There is only a neutral perception of another person suffering. One might say that it is the peculiar magic of poetic representation that it compels in us a form of identification with the represented emotions that is neither other directed *(paragata)* nor directed entirely toward oneself *(svagata)*. This idea is stated eloquently in the following verse: " 'This is another's only; this is not another's—this is mine; no, this is not mine.' In the gustation of the emotive situation, there is no consciousness of any such distinction."[13]

This consideration leads Abhinavagupta to claim that the aesthetic relish—*rasa* experience—is something transcendental and supramundane. But the distinction made by him between the otherness and pastness of the emotive events and the timeless presentness of the mood contemplated is itself quite clear. What Abhinavagupta means is that, while the events themselves are cast in the mold of time and in other loci, their restrictiveness is what is set aside in the actual apprehension of *rasa*. *Rasa* perception, thus, involves a certain extension that Abhinavagupta likens to the recollection of invariable concomitance *(vyāpti)* between the logical probans ("smoke") and probandum ("fire"). The coextension between smoke and fire was observed by you previously in the kitchen or some other place. But the smoke you are observing now is on the hill. Still, you are able to make an inference as to the presence of fire on the hill through a type of cognition that permits you to apply a perception derived from a past experience to a present instance and thus arrive at a generalization.[14]

In any case, all literary statements are essentially of the nature of reports of past events or finished facts. What Abhinavagupta says about historical or legendary characters and events is also true of all other types of characters and events presented in literature, in whatever person or tense they may appear. Susanne Langer is right in observing that all literature is in the mode of memory. Events in literature come to us in the form of a reality lived and remembered.[15] According to the Indian logicians, in memory an object is thought of as being present at some time, as a "once present condition" *(pūrva-vartamāna-kāla-avacchinnam)*. Since all events reported in a literary text are apprehended as completed experience, irrevocable and final, and therefore as events in the past, and also as events pertaining to a third person removed from the reader in time and place, the use of any particular tense or person will not make a difference for literary apprehension, in the ultimate analysis, that is (though, of course, a variety of stylistic effects may be secured through the use of a particular tense in a composition or through shift in tenses). Thus, whether the facts are presented as happening now ("My heart aches") or as having happened at some time in the past ("A slumber did my spirit seal"), they are apprehended by us as events in the past, in their finished form.

However, according to Langer, there is a difference between the mode of apprehension of what she calls "literature"—which includes all "poetic" forms: lyric, narrative, prose fiction—and the mode of apprehension of "drama." All literature is in the mnemonic mode, whereas drama creates a "virtual future."[16] Drama deals, not with finished realities, but with actions that, though they spring from the past, are directed toward the future. The constant movement, in a drama, is of an imminent future, of actions producing, or threatening to produce, consequences. This view, no doubt, gives a satisfactory account of the element of suspense, which is so vital for the structure of the drama. But it is difficult to understand why the same cannot be said of a novel, verse narrative, or anything that contains a "story" element. Storytelling and narration, Langer says, present life in the perspective of memory, "only depersonalized and objectified"—even as poetry does. But drama, although it is like the poetic art in that it too creates a semblance of life, presents its events in the perspective of things coming.[17]

It is likely that Langer bases this distinction on the fact that the narrative form normally employs the past tense and that therefore there is a finality about the events reported in it. In drama, on the other hand, actions are set in motion and they seem to be happening now—which means that they look forward to a future time for their completion. But it can be argued that both the past tense of the narrative and the present tense of the drama are equally deceptive. For, though events in a story have a finished character, they come alive in the reader's imagination, not as finished facts, but as in some sense happening now—as parts of a developing action. Since they are presented in a causal sequence, they too produce consequential actions, as in a drama. The element of suspense or curiosity as to what will ensue is the same in both forms. In the same way, the present tense of the drama is also deceptive since, in the reading experience, we understand the events not to be taking place literally in the present but as happening at some time in the past.

Langer seems to be thinking of the experience in the theater when she speaks of the dramatic illusion. But, as I shall argue later in this chapter, the reading experience and the theatrical experience differ considerably owing to the difference in their media. In the reading of a drama, be it *Macbeth, Death of a Salesman,* or *Śākuntala,* the action appears removed from us both geographically and historically; it seems a thing of another time and place. The tendency toward the future is there of course, but it exists within a framework of "pastness."

The events of a narrative too are apprehended in this manner even where they are reported in the present tense. Richardson's *Pamela* is, for instance, narrated in the form of letters written in the present. But still we apprehend the events as "happening" at a distant time, as "once happening events," that is, in spite of their present form. The peculiarity of literary experience is that both the sense of the present and the sense of the past are simultaneously active. The presented action, or mood or mental state, as in a lyric, is apprehended as happening now—which accounts for the feeling of immediacy that one has in reading a literary work. It is at the same time sensed as happening at a distant time and place (as it happens in memory). This explains why a story told in the past tense can be retold or paraphrased in both the past and the present tenses. The past tense is used because the events actually happened long ago, and the present tense, called the historic present, too, is justified because the teller of the story is mentally witnessing the things happen.

According to Bhartṛhari, time is single and undivided, metaphysically, and its divisions into tenses a mental construction *(kalpanā)* and something illusory. Yet we accept tense divisions in linguistic usage for carrying on worldly activities.[18] Tenses are purely a matter of verbal usage and depend on how things are cognized and presented in language. The same event or activity, for example, can be presented in both the past and the present tenses. In illustration of this point, Bhartṛhari cites the usage "He kills Kaṃsa," "He ties down Bali," and so on, in which the events referred to were in the past but presented by storytellers in the present tense. As the commentator explains, "That is because the whole story is present in the mind of the tellers at the time of telling and it is evoked in the mind of the hearers also. What figures in the mind is the meaning of words and not outside reality. Thus the storytellers cause the mental Vāsudeva (Krishna, the hero of the acts mentioned) to kill the mental Kaṃsa."[19] "Thus speakers impose on objects a form which is the creation of their own mind."[20]

Again, a linguistic usage may be in the present tense but may actually refer to an event in the future. The Sanskrit word *āśaṃsā* (expectation) implies a present state of mind. But, since it refers to a future object, it is treated by grammarians as possessing future time for purposes of grammatical operations. On the other hand, a desiderative *cikīrṣati* ("He desires to do") is treated as present although the verbal root "to do" refers to the future, for the reason that the desire expressed by the desiderative affix *san* (equivalent of "desires") denotes the present and the affix is the principal and the root secondary.[21] It is shown by all this that linguistic usage in regard to the tenses is inconstant and depends on how a speaker cognizes a particular thing and chooses to express it.

This being the case, formal differences or differences in modes of presentation are to be regarded as no more than formal devices, depending on how the poet wants to present his material, and having no significant bearing on the form of their apprehension. The distinction of subjective/objective, too, does not alter our mode of cognition. Even if the speaker is the poet himself or the lyric subject in propria persona, the cognition is only that of a character (third person) experiencing certain things. Abhinavagupta observes that between drama and poetry there is no essential difference; both forms are essentially dramatic—in the sense that they dramatize an emotive situation so that the reader will contemplate it as though it were happening before his eyes. Although, in the lyric, things are not developed in the fullest detail, the mind supplies the details and dramatizes the speaker and his scene for itself. The voice of the lyric speaker is as much a dramatic voice as that of a character in a play. The intrusive author-narrator in a novel, however, plays a choric role and voices or controls the responses of the reader.

Poetic Truth: Imitation and Illusion

In Sanskrit criticism, there is a lively debate on the nature of poetic truth. In his commentary on Bharata, Abhinavagupta sums up many views on the nature of dramatic representation and argues against the prevalent theories of imitation and illusion.[22] Bharata defined drama by the term *anukaraṇa,* which may be translated as "mimetic reproduction": "Drama is a reproduction of the mental states, actions and conduct of people."[23] Abhinavagupta's predecessors, Lollaṭa and Śaṅkuka, who commented on Bharata's work, understood dramatic representation in mimetic terms and held that aesthetic perception is illusory cognition *(mithyājñāna),* although it does produce real emotions in the spectator.

The connection between the imitation and the illusion theories is obvious. An imitative reproduction of the real, whether in the medium of paint, words, or physical gestures, cannot be the real thing; consequently, the response evoked by it is based on illusion. Abhinavagupta argues that drama, and by extension all poetry *(kāvya),* is not an imitation but a depiction or description in words (or enactment, in the case of theatrical performance) of the life of the emotions that in turn, arouses the latent emotive dispositions of the actor or spectator and causes him to reflect on the presented situation with a degree of sympathetic identification. Poetic experience *(rasa)* is not a case of illusory cognition or false identification but a species of "identical reaction" *(anuvyavasāya)* in the actor or spectator.

Although this debate takes place in the context of theatrical representation, it touches directly or indirectly on some of the crucial questions concerning poetic truth raised in recent critical discussions in the West. Is poetry a fictional discourse, and, if it is, does the unreality attach to the subject matter or to the language? In other words, is there a specifically fictional use of language, and what is the ontological status of literary objects? The Indian philosophical schools too reflected on the general problem of knowledge, truth, and meaning, and the literary critics drew on their theories in their discussion of the nature of poetic knowledge. In what follows, I shall outline Abhinavagupta's arguments and examine some of their implications in the light of the Indian philosophical theories.

Imitation

If, as Bharata said, drama is a reproduction of the emotions in terms of their objects and visible behavioral signs, the question arises as to what precisely the object of that reproduction is and how it may be said to be reproduced in words or in action. Is it the emotions that are imitated or their external manifestations? Again, what exactly is the locus of the so-called dramatic emotion or *rasa?* Does it reside in the represented situation of the drama, or in the person alluded to in the work, or in the actor playing that person's role, or in the spectator, or in all four? Critics before Abhinavagupta debated these problems and offered varying solutions. It was generally assumed by them that aesthetic experience is a unique kind of experience and distinct from all other types *(alaukika),* although they differed in their account of the precise nature of the distinction.

Lollaṭa argued that drama is an imitation of the emotions that are located in the real person, the object of representation, but are attributed to the impersonating actor owing to the similarity in form between him and that person. The resultant illusion is what distinguishes dramatic experience from life experience. For, if the emotion is only attributed to the actor, it must be illusory since the causes that occasioned it in the historical person, Rāma and the like, are not present in the actor. The emotion is a real-life emotion *(laukika)* when it occurs in the imitated object but an aesthetic emotion *(alaukika)* when it is attributed to the actor.[24]

Śaṅkuka accepts Lollaṭa's basic account of dramatic representation as an imitation of the emotions, which can be properly attributed only to the person represented *(anukārya),* namely, the historical Rāma. But he points out that emotions, being mental states, cannot be imitated directly and immediately, but only through their objective signs. Emotions cannot be "perceived"; they can only be inferred from their criteria. So what the actor imitates are the objective signs; from these enacted signs the spectator, in turn, infers the existence of the emotions in the actual hero, as though they were present in the actor himself.[25] *Rasa,* or the dramatic emotion, as distinguished from life emotion, is simply another name for the imitative reproduction of the basic emotion *(sthāyin)* that was originally present in the historical Rāma and that the actor, by his histrionic skill, recreates in himself artificially.[26] But, inasmuch as the spectator's delectable experience springs from the presented situation, this (the imitated action) alone is to be taken as the seat of *rasa,* not the represented person, as Lollaṭa thought, not the impersonating actor *(anukartā)*—because the emotions are only exhibited through the actor and not really present in him or the spectator. The spectator sees the actor as not being different from the person he is imitating (Rāma is objectified in him) and contemplates that person's emotions as exhibited in the actor. He has a dual awareness of the imitator and the imitated; he has the notion "This is that Rāma who was in love, was happy," and so on.

This enacted situation is, however, fictitious since it is only an imitation. The causes and expressions of Rāma's emotions are only assumed in the actor—they are completely nonexistent in him. Hence, they are unreal. But they are not so apprehended by the spectator, who takes the actor for the real person and the imitated emotions for real ones. They are relished by the spectator in the form of an imitation of the basic emotion located in the original character, Rāma. The imitated objective signs from which the emotion is inferred are, however, different from the ordinary logical signs (e.g., "smoke" as the sign, *liṅga,* of "fire") because, although they are unreal, they act as signs toward the emotion in hand. For even from illusory causes sometimes real effects are seen to ensue; for example, real fear, trembling, and so forth can result from a rope mistaken for a serpent.

Here, Śaṅkuka follows a school of Buddhist idealists called Yogācāra, according to whom all knowledge is subjective and illusory, and the only difference between right and wrong knowledge lies in "causal efficacy" *(arthkriyā-sāmarthya)*—the capacity of some knowledge to produce successful practical results. In illustration of this point, the following verse is quoted: "When two people run towards a gem and a lamp scattering their rays at a distance (through two separate key-holes), in the thought that both are gems, there is no distinction in respect of the illusory perception (i.e., between the false perception of the one and the real perception of the other). The distinction lies only in the results achieved."[27] The implication of this is that the perception of both these men was illusory since neither could distinguish between the light of a gem and the light of a lamp. But in one case it produces the desired results (the man who opens the door of the room in which there is the gem finds the gem), whereas in the other case it does not produce the results (the man who opens the door of the room in which the lamp is placed does not get the gem). The first perception is called illusion of the "congruent" type *(saṃvādi-bhrama)* and the other illusion of the "incongruent" or discordant type *(visaṃvādi).* The validity of knowledge is therefore judged, not in virtue of anything intrinsic in knowledge, but by the practical results achieved. In the present case, it is seen that aesthetic relish does result from causes that are entirely fictitious. Even illusive knowledge is thus a type of valid knowledge.[28]

According to Śaṅkuka, then, aesthetic perception is illusory knowledge even though no invalidating cognition appears during our experience at the theater. But, as it still creates a semblance of reality, it is neither strictly illusory nor real but a unique type of experience. In the theater, one does not have the cognition that the actor himself is happy or suffering, or that he is himself Rāma (the imitated person), or that he is not happy, or whether he is Rāma or someone different or someone like him. On the other hand, the cognition is of the form "This man is that very Rāma who was happy." It is thus distinct from both true and false perception and from doubtful knowledge or perception of similarity. It is like the perception of a painted horse *(citra-turaga-nyāya)*. Śaṅkuka says, "There is neither doubt, nor truth, nor error. There is the perception that this man is Rāma. There is also the perception that it is not the very same person. The spectator is unable to decide between the two opposite notions. And he wonders how the felt experience should be accounted for."[29] This, in essence, is a theory of representational illusion based on the analogy of pictorial or plastic representation.

Bhaṭṭanāyaka objects to both these accounts of *rasa* experience on the following grounds. If the knowledge of the character and his condition were derived purely as an inference from the verbal descriptions of the drama, there would be little by way of aesthetic enjoyment to the spectator. Again, if the situation were perceived by him as concerning a third person merely, he would remain totally indifferent to it. The represented emotions cannot also be taken to be happening to the spectator personally because the conditions that produced those emotions in the character are not present in him. Moreover, if the spectator became personally involved in the drama, a pathetic situation on the stage would result only in his own misery, and no aesthetic pleasure can be had. Therefore, Bhaṭṭanāyaka concludes that the *rasa* is realized through a special prompting power, called *bhāvakatva,* inhering in the poetic or dramatic presentation itself, which universalizes the objects and expressions of the emotions presented. The specific aesthetic character of the experienced dramatic emotions consists in this phenomenon of generalization *(sādhāraṇīkaraṇa),* on which Bhaṭṭanāyaka's aesthetic rests. Abhinavagupta takes this concept from Bhaṭṭanāyaka and develops its implications.

But Bhaṭṭanāyaka does argue for dramatic illusion from his own standpoint of Vedāntic metaphysics. The world of a drama is entirely a fabrication of the imagination, and the roles of Rāma and Rāvaṇa, which the actors create in their own persons without at the same time abandoning their identities, have no real existence. In spite of all this, drama is capable of giving rise to aesthetic enjoyment in the spectator, by inducing in him a state of reposeful self-immersion, which, according to Bhaṭṭanāyaka, characterizes *rasa* experience. Further, the illusory world of drama brings home to the spectator the lesson that the world of names and forms is an insubstantial shadow, fabricated by the mind through ignorance.[30]

Abhinavagupta rejects the theory of imitation on the following grounds.

1. While one may distinguish several senses of the term "imitation," Abhinavagupta fixes the focus on its core meaning, namely, "likeness-making" *(sadṛśakaraṇam),* with its implication of a formal, not substantial, likeness, or similarity in difference. The etymology of the Sanskrit equivalent *anukaraṇam* may be explained as "doing or making something in the likeness of, following the nature of, an object, person, or action." Defining the nature of visual representation, Abhinavagupta says,

> It has been claimed by some that the aggregate of pigments, composing the picture of a cow, is itself the cow. If what is meant is that the nature of a cow is manifested by it (the aggregate of pigments), it is certainly untrue. For the quintessential *(pāramārthika)* cow is not manifested by the colors, etc., as objects are revealed by a lamp. All that is accomplished [by the picture] is a particular arrangement [of colors and lines] that is similar to the form of a cow. Those pigments, being arranged into a particular shape that is similar to the formation of the limbs of a cow produce the impression of a likeness to the cow.[31]

Arguing from this position, Abhinavagupta concludes that emotions and mental objects cannot be imitated because not even formal likenesses can be made of them either in the verbal or in the nonverbal presentational medium. Emotions cannot of course be reproduced directly, but can they, as Śaṅkuka contended, be imitated even mediately through their external expressions? Physical gestures and verbal expressions cannot be equated with psychic conditions because they are insentient *(jaḍa),* based on different substrata *(bhinnādhikaraṇa),* and perceived by different organs of perception. Śaṅkuka's analogy of the painted horse is false because the aggregate of physical movements and gestures in the actor does not create a likeness of the form of feeling in the way that the aggregate of paints on the canvas shows a resemblance to the form of a horse. Abhinavagupta also rejects the view that tunes, dance movements, and musical tempi are imitations of anything in real life (except of course in the sense of natural imitation of sounds and motions) because the imitated object, namely, feeling (where feelings may be supposed to be expressed through their medium) and its imitation belong to two different orders of existence.

2. Imitation also implies a distinct knowledge of the original and the copy *(mukhya-amukhya-avalokana)*, as when one holds up a glass of milk and says, "One drinks wine like this," or when we look at a painted horse on the canvas and recognize its similarity to the real animal. Now what is it that is perceived in the actor and that might appear like an imitation? The actor could not be imitating Rāma because no one has seen the historical Rāma, so there is no basis for comparing the reproduction with the original. It is impossible to make an imitation of something whose nature or form is not known to us.

3. Against the contention that no formal likeness can be created, in a visible medium, of invisible things such as mental states, someone may urge that it is the visible signs (behavioral expressions) of the emotions, rather than the emotions themselves, that are the object of the actor's imitation. One might say that imitating the externals is imitating the inner states. But Rāma's actions and gestures are the natural expressions of his own love or sorrow and cannot be dissociated from it. So by imitating them the actor cannot be said to be creating a likeness of Rāma's emotion. Obviously, he cannot also be said to be imitating his own emotion through its visible expressions. He can only be said to be enacting the expressions that are his own as well as those of Rāma—expressions of love or sorrow in general. When such is the case, there can be no question of creating a semblance.

4. Granted that the actor cannot reproduce Rāma's sorrow—Rāma's sorrow is something personal to him—but one might argue that the actor imitates, if not the individual Rāma, then a general notion of sorrow. Even this is inadmissible. If what we have is an enactment or expression of sorrow (through its visible signs), there can be no question of creating a likeness of it. For there is only sorrow, not another thing that is similar to it. Abhinavagupta takes a strong stand against the notion of imitating the universals. General notions of love and sorrow cannot be imitated; they can only be instantiated or exhibited in particular persons. Thus, Rāma is one particular instance of grief-stricken husbands, Othello of jealous husbands, Lear of pitiable old men who have been cruelly abandoned by their children, and so on. These notions may be said to be typified in them. Thus between the characters and actions of a drama and their types in the real world there can be no similarity relation, as between a visual design and its subject, because they are of the same kind *(sajātīya)*.

The same logic applies to the actor acting the role of Rāma. The sorrow that he exhibits is of the same nature as his own, not something that is similar to Rāma's. Moreover, a likeness can be produced only of a particular *(niyata)* object, not of nonspecific *(aniyata)* things or universals. The mind cannot apprehend similarity except in some particular form. So it cannot be said that the actor imitates the sorrow, or its expressions, not of Rāma but of some noble personage. Abhinavagupta sums up the point by saying, "Where generic things are involved there can be no question of one thing being similar to another. . . . What, then, is the sense of reproduction (likeness-making) where generic forms are in question?"[32] Here, Abhinavagupta seems to be following the *mīmāṃsā* view that there is no similarity relation between the universal and the particular. The generic quality of an object, for example, the "pothood" of a pot, cannot be said to be similar to the generic quality of another object of the same species because it is itself the ground of that similarity. Resemblance is not predicated of two identical things. Similarity is always similarity in certain respects and implies difference. In our cognition of things such as a cow or a pot, we cognize different individuals as the same, not as similar. An individual is a complete instance of the universal.[33]

5. From the point of view of the actor, again, there is no awareness in him that he is reproducing the sorrow of Rāma. On the other hand, he has actual experience of the emotional state of a character of a certain description, and he acts out the image of that character constructed from the drama. The process in all this is not that of reproduction but that of an "identical reaction" in which the actor becomes the hero himself. If you argue that the actor is reproducing someone who should have wept in this manner, then his own personality also intervenes so that he might be expressing his own emotions directly. He has the impressions embedded in him, of love, sorrow, and so forth, that had occurred to him previously and that were born of his own observation of life. The spectator's awareness, too, is not that of an imitated emotion but that of a real one. The spectator simply has the notion "This man is immersed in this state." There is no perception of otherness. If the spectator thought that the actor was simply mimicking other people's actions or gestures without having an inward feeling for the things being enacted, or even if the actor himself thought so, the result would be comic laughter, whatever the emotion being depicted. If again, the spectator thought that the dramatic situation was artificial—the actor is only simulating the emotions and their expressions—how could he, as Śaṅkuka maintained, infer real emotions from it? A legitimate inference is possible only from a logical

sign ("smoke") that is recognized to be real, not from one that is known to be a semblance of something else. It is not proper to infer the presence of fire from fog that is perceived as a semblance of smoke.

6. If by imitation you mean doing something or making something following the nature of an object, in obedience to the laws of nature (as Aristotle thought), or "following the ways and actions of the world" *(lokavṛttānusāreṇa),* in the way Bharata defined dramatic presentation—then, every act in real life would have to be regarded as an imitation. However, if you still wish to call drama an imitation for this very reason that it is done in conformity with the ways of the world, there is no harm. When the distinction between the terms is recognized, there will be no cause for quarrel.

7. It follows from the above argument that constructing the plot of a drama according to Bharata's *rasa* formula, according to the rules of propriety and so on, cannot also be regarded as a case of imitation. Making something according to a prescription or formula (compounding a drug, e.g.) cannot be called imitation in any normal sense. When a poem or drama is called a "likeness" of some original—an actual or ideal image—in real life, it can only be in the sense that it is "true to," or reflects, or exemplifies, human action, character, and speech in our world of common experience. It is not the likeness of imitation. Poetry cannot, again, be called imitation because it might be said to "represent" things in the medium of words (a verbal imitation). But, if "represent" is taken in the sense of "describe" or "express," then imitation would have to be extended to every mode of expressing our thoughts by words.[34]

Therefore Abhinavagupta prefers to understand Bharata's term *anukaraṇa,* not as "imitating," but as "relating," "narrating," or "describing" emotive conditions—*bhāvānukīrtanam,* a term Bharata himself used synonymously. Abhinavagupta concludes that drama is in no sense an imitative presentation of the real. It is rather a configuration of the essential elements of emotive life. The poet simply delineates a particular concrete instance of a universal human situation, and the actor and the spectator relive that situation by the power of sympathy. Abhinavagupta agrees with Śaṅkuka that *rasa* arises from the objective situation of the drama, but he asserts that it resides equally in the character, the actor, and the spectator. Otherwise, it will not produce the sympathetic vibration of the heart, without which there is no aesthetic experience.

Illusion

The imitation theory of Lollaṭa and Śaṅkuka led them to believe that theatrical experience is illusory. Since the emotions are falsely attributed to the actor, the spectator suffers an illusion—he takes the semblance for reality. For Lollaṭa, however, this illusion is complete; deluded by the similarity in form and manner between the historical character, Rāma, and the actor playing that role, he has the notion "This is Rāma; he is in love with Sīta." But for Śaṅkuka, it appears that it is not a case of complete delusion. The spectator sees the actor not as Rāma but as a representation of Rāma, even as a horse in a painting is seen, not as a real horse, but as a visual representation or picture of a horse. There is no trompe l'oeil type of effect. But, paradoxically, Śaṅkuka also says that the spectator does not know the actor from the character he is representing; hence, the primary illusion of the actor himself having real emotions is made possible. Again he says that the spectator is not able to decide between the two contradictory notions "He is that Rāma" and "He is not that same person." It seems that what Śaṅkuka means is that, while the spectator implicitly recognizes the fictitious nature of the events on the stage, he still lets himself be persuaded by the spectacle into believing that it is real, in a frame of mind that Coleridge characterized as a "willing suspension of disbelief."[35] Śaṅkuka is, however, quite unequivocal in declaring that the theatrical representation itself is illusory, although it yields a valid aesthetic experience.

Abhinavagupta views the problem of dramatic illusion from the point of view both of stage presentation and of the play itself as a presentation in words. His refutation of the illusion theory is based on the assumption that the focus of the dramatic presentation is the generalized human situation rather than the particular and that the generalizing process is what distinguishes drama from real life. The presented events are contemplated for their general emotive significance alone, freed from all historical determination. However, this process is not due to any sense of illusion; that is, it is not caused by the audience's recognition of the fictitiousness of the work. Rather, it is due to the human focus of the presented situation, which invariably permits us to generalize its meanings and participate in them. The dramatic emotion *(rasa)*, then, is a generalized mood, not a personal emotion directed on particular persons or objects. For instance, the reader does not become fearful of the individual ghost presented in the work—he does not try to run away from it or cry for help—because he knows that in its aspect as a particular object it is unreal. Hence, there is no delusion. As there is also no perception of a semblance between the actor and the historical Rāma or between the character of the drama and a real person in the world, there is no question of taking the semblance for reality, as in the delusive cognition of a conch shell as a piece of silver or of a rope as a serpent.

Śaṅkuka, too, would perhaps admit as much—there is no delusion—

but he would say that the spectator is aware of the semblance but takes it for reality. To this Abhinavagupta objects, "If the spectator has the dual awareness that the person on the stage is both the actor and the character he represents, his mind will be perplexed and he will not get the real experience of the drama."[36] Again, Śaṅkuka's argument that aesthetic experience is neither real nor unreal is untenable. Abhinavagupta asks, If your experience of the drama is not sublated by a subsequent congition, why is it illusory, and, if it is sublated, why is it not illusory?[37] According to Śaṅkuka's logic, it would be a mistaken cognition even in the absence of an invalidating knowledge. Here, anyway, no invalidating cognition occurs. The things in the drama are taken by the spectator or reader as possible and true of the world of our experience.

Abhinavagupta, no doubt, admits the role of theatrical conventions *(nāṭyadharmī)* in concealing the identity of the actor and thereby preventing false identification on the part of the spectator—the notion that whatever is happening is happening to the actor. The awareness that things are not happening to the actor inhibits our tendency to act on them. But he makes it clear that theatrical presentation is not the same thing as the verbal universe created by the drama because of the difference in their mediums—the one is a spectacle *(dṛśya)* and the other a verbal presentation *(śravyakāvya)*, and they have to be judged by different standards.[38] What the theatrical situation, with its illusion-creating devices, conceals is the identity of the actor as a person and the real being of the character superimposed on him—as a separate identity, that is (e.g., Rāma, Duṣyanta, Caesar, and so forth, where such well-known personages are represented). The spectator's mind does not find repose in either of these.[39] All that figures in his mind is the notion that a character of a certain description is being presented. He cognizes the situation, not in the form "This is Olivier and he is acting Hamlet" or "This is that Hamlet who was melancholy," but in the form "This is someone called Hamlet and he is immersed in this state of mind."

This is still illusion, of course, when the identity of the actor is considered—an identity that is concealed by his costume, headdress, and so forth. But the character of the drama himself is not thereby rendered nonexistent because he does exist in the drama as a datum of our consciousness. In fact, as Abhinavagupta points out, it is this mental picture of the character and the situation, which we conjure up from the verbal meanings of the drama, that is the real object of our experience. An imaginative person can visualize this whole world of the drama even without the aid of the stage action. The actor does, however, aid a more vivid realization of the depicted action. But, then, he is not the focus of our attention but simply a medium through which we realize the experience of the drama, even like the idol of a deity, which simply serves as an instrument of meditation and is never mistaken for the deity itself. But, whether in the theater or in our reading experience, Abhinavagupta insists, there is no make-believe or illusion. The knowledge we get is wholly a valid knowledge, and it is of the form "This is Rāma," not of the form "This is not Rāma; this is another."[40]

The following conclusions can be drawn from Abhinavagupta's account of aesthetic experience.

1. Although stage illusion may be admitted, the action of the drama itself is not an illusion, first, because it possesses a certain reality as a verbal presentation. The commentator on the *Daśarūpaka* declares that the characters and events of the drama *(vibhāvādi)* need not necessarily possess an existence in the outside world; they acquire an existential status just by being presented in words. Hence they are not devoid of content.[41] This view reflects the position of the Indian grammarians, according to whom cognition in respect of historical names like Kaṃsa and Nala arises only from their expression in words, as these characters have had no other existence that we know of. So, on hearing about these persons, characterized in a certain way, we form a mental image of them and see them as though they were present before our eyes.[42]

Similar is the case with fictional names. Mr. Pickwick has being and subsists as a verbal presentation, as a man identifiable by some definite characteristics. Gilbert Ryle thinks, however, that, if Mr. Pickwick had no existence in real life, he cannot have any existence at all.[43] I shall argue below that this is a very limited conception of the meaning of "existence." The action of the drama is not an illusion also because it is not so cognized by the reader or spectator, for, if he thought that it was entirely false, how should he experience real emotions? That is, there could be no real emotions from causes recognized to be fictitious; for example, if you thought at the moment of perception that what you saw was in fact a rope and not a serpent, then you would not experience fear. Finally, the situation presented in the drama is not contradicted by experience as in the case of a conch shell seen as silver.

2. Fictional illusion or the "consciousness of fiction" (Dr. Johnson's phrase) is not a condition of aesthetic apprehension, and it is not responsible for the proper aesthetic attitude in the context of literature because the task of depersonalization or transpersonalization is carried out by the emotive situation itself.[44] The inner psychic nature of the spectator will itself cause the sympathetic response. In the theatrical experience, no doubt, the admitted unreality of the dramatic action will induce the necessary sense of distance in the spectator. But, in the reading experience, the very remoteness of the events being reported will prevent too per-

sonal an involvement on the part of the reader. Hence, there is no need to invoke illusion to account for aesthetic distance.[45]

3. Although a literary work creates its own autonomous world with its own system of logical and imaginative relations, it cannot be said that it is independent of the external world so that all considerations of truth and falsity are waived. As a linguistic construction, it cannot, in fact, be without reference to things outside itself. This view is supported both by the realistic epistemology and by the referential theory of language held by most philosophical schools in India, including the grammarians, the Mīmāṃsakas, the Vedāntins, and the logicians. All words must possess an objective reference. Meaning is reference; a self-referential sign is a contradiction in terms. Words are meaningful because they cause cognition of an external world *(bāhyārtha)*. Being a confirmed realist, the Mīmāṃsaka urges that all cognition is objective in character and assumes a real substratum in the external world. The validity of knowledge is judged by us in terms of its faithful presentation of things as they really are.[46]

Like any other type of discourse, literature too must, then, refer to an extralinguistic reality. It cannot be autoreferential or have its own unique class of "poetic" truths. Reference is not, however, to be understood as reference to the observable physical world alone but equally to feelings, concepts, ideas, and all such entities that have a purely mental existence. The referentiality of literature being thus assumed, literary works must be judged, and they are in fact constantly judged by us, for the truthfulness of their reference, for their correspondence with the world of common experience. This truth reference is implied in Bharata's concepts of *lokapramāṇa* (the norms and conventions of the world by which we judge the validity of poetic statements) and *lokadharmī* (or realistic representation). Aesthetic experience is not, as Śaṅkuka thought, an "either-neither," "as if" world in which things are seen to be true though not true. A successful work always fulfills the criteria for truth. We compare the plot of a drama or novel with some general aspects of reality that determine for us that something is plausible or possible.

But this view that literature can make claims to truth has run into considerable difficulties in recent philosophical discussions. The fictional or "no-truth" theories of literature are built around the following arguments: propositions in literature are "only a pseudo-designation" (Ryle), and, hence, the literary use of language cannot be a referring use; the literary mode of speech itself is fictional, an imitation speech act in which the illocutionary force is suspended; or the question of true or false itself does not apply to literature since literature, by its very nature, is nonpredicative and nonassertive and does not make affirmations about anything existing beyond itself, being its own autonomous world with a unique reference.[47]

The speech act model of literature may perhaps be dismissed by saying that literary writing employs all types of sentences—assertive, nonassertive, literal, and metaphorical—and fulfills all meaning conditions and conditions for performing specific illocutionary acts. So it would not be true to say that, in it, the illocutionary functions are suppressed or that the literary use of speech acts is fictional or mimetic or a kind of secondary or "parasitic" use (Austin and Searle). When sentences in fiction behave exactly in the manner in which they do in ordinary speech contexts and are governed by the same rules, there is no warrant for saying that they are parasitic on normal uses. Poetic discourse cannot be called an imitation speech act because the persons in the novel or play or poem are not imitating human utterances—they are, quite simply, making those utterances. There can be only one sense in which it can be called an imitation speech act, and that is that the writer himself pretends to make a speech act in the writing of his poem or novel. But this is absurd. Even in the case of an admitted fiction, such as a story, the storyteller does not pretend to be telling a story or imitating the act of storytelling (assuming that "storytelling" is a distinctive speech act); he is only telling a story.

In any case, what makes a fiction fictional is that the statements made in it are neither true nor false; they do not refer to any existing thing. It all boils down to the question of the truth status of literary statements, then. Here, again, we have to distinguish between the utterances of characters within a work and the work itself, considered as the utterance of its author. The assertions that are directly made by, or attributed to, characters in a novel are fully referential since they refer to things existing in the world of the novel. But, considered as an utterance on the part of the author, the work cannot be a referring act since the things referred to do not exist in the real world; they are only imagined to exist. However, the consideration whether the author is performing a genuine speech act or just pretending, in writing his work, is not critically relevant since that question cannot be settled by appealing to the evidence contained in the work and it does not also change the status of what is in the work.

A distinction should also be made between types of writing that deal with factual (historical or biographical) material and those that deal with invented or fabricated material. It will be readily admitted that Wordsworth's *Prelude,* Keats' "Grecian Urn" ode, or a play about Abraham Lincoln or Henry IV is not fictional in the sense that it makes statements that are neither true nor false. But, in the case of an admitted fiction like *Pickwick Papers* or *Alice in Wonderland,* there can be an argument as to whether sentences occurring in it perform a referring function, that is, whether they refer to things that actually exist or have existed. The answer to this question will depend very much on how we conceive of "existence" and "reference," and it can be attempted from several angles.

First, even on Searle's assumption that "whatever is referred to must exist," it can be argued that statements in a literary work—declaratives or existential propositions about characters and events—do refer to certain persons and states of affairs. But, in terms of the principle of generalization, as noted above, their ultimate reference is not to particular persons or events but to generic types, of which they are instances. (An instance—*vyakti-sāmānya*—is any individual and, according to Indian theories, eternal; a particular individual—*vyaktiviśeṣa*—is noneternal.) Such statements are verifiable in principle, not necessarily as assertions about actual people and things, but in their generic form, as statements about the world and human nature. Thus, in verifying the events in, say, *Othello,* the question to be asked would be, not whether there was or was not a man called Othello who strangled his wife called Desdemona, but whether jealous husbands, of whom Othello is an exemplification, do or do not strangle their wives in bed. The particularity of the names and places mentioned has no real significance or use except as a means of giving a concrete body to the theme depicted. That is, names like "Othello," "Desdemona," and "Iago" have simply the force of *x, y, z* or "Tom," "Dick," and "Harry," and the action too could have taken place in other climes than Venice.[48] In such cases, the test of validity is not correspondence with actual facts but coherence or compatibility with general reality as we know it—what the Indian logicians call *tad-jātīyatva* (consistency with other valid knowledge).

Here someone might object, Can a story about an isolated "jealous husband" be about all jealous husbands? The story itself does not hint at any such general truths. I attempted an answer to this question in talking about the principle of generalization and said that the extension from the particular (the instance) to the general law is a feature of the communicative situation that literature represents.

Nevertheless, Ryle would insist that the fact that a valid law has been exemplified by an imaginary instance does not alter the status of that instance: "The trueness of the general proposition does not in the least degree modify the fictitiousness of the story which purports to describe an instance of the general proposition."[49] We must of course grant that some literary instances are imaginary, in the sense defined by Ryle. But it is possible to quarrel about Ryle's empiricist conception of what it is for an object to be existent or nonexistent. Ryle says that no other sort of evidence than the empirical (meaning by "empirical" "having an existence in the observable world") should be admitted on a question of existence. "Mr. Pickwick" designates no one because there never was such a person.

Searle too understands "fictional" in this sense. Sherlock Holmes can be referred to only as a character in fiction, as he exists only in fiction. Searle takes "exist" to cover "what has existed or what will exist as well as what now exists."[50] Here one might ask, if what "will" exist is also a manner of existing, why could we not admit what "could exist" or what "might have existed" also to the category of existent objects?[51] Why could we not argue that existential propositions in literature too are fully referential because they satisfy Searle's criteria for referring? First, they refer to what has existed (historical novels), or what now exists (social comedies and satires), or what will or could exist or might have existed (Sherlock Holmes, Mr. Pickwick). This is the axiom of existence. Second, characters and events in literature, including fiction, are capable of being identified by an identifying description (the axiom of identification). In other words, the questions Who? What? Which? in respect of them, can be answered satisfactorily, for example, "Hamlet, Prince of Denmark," "Sherlock Holmes, the detective," "Mr. Pickwick, president of the Pickwick Club," and so on.

Even as statements referring to particulars can be validated in their generic form, universal statements about life and human nature, too, can be verified by checking against our experience, for example, "The paths of glory lead but to the grave." Unrestricted generalizations, for example, "What fools these mortals be," can be taken as valid with reference to the context in which they are uttered. Their real force as assertions would be limited by their context; that is, in this case, the context would warrant the conclusion that at least some mortals are fools.

The empiricist account of existence and reference is unnecessarily restrictive also in that it does not allow for the referability of psychic phenomena. Spirits, dragons, monsters, and sea serpents may not have an existence in the outer world, but they are still part of our experience and must be referable. According to Abhinavagupta, even extraordinary incidents, like leaping across the ocean, would seem credible and would evoke appropriate emotional responses because such entities are present in our consciousness and psychic impressions.[52] The test of correspondence, in such cases, should therefore be extended to include the psychic realm also, not merely the world of objects. Thus, Dr. Faustus' covenant with the devil is possible not only *de dicto* or logically (i.e., on our assuming a world in which spirits are present, the world posited by the work) but *de re* because creatures such as ghosts, goblins, devils, and vampires can actually be conceived by us at least in fantasy. The philosopher Rāmānuja held that there is an element of truth in all experience. Even a semblance of truth is a kind of truth because it is an object of experience, for example, dreams, delusions (of a rope as a serpent, of nacre as silver, mirage), visions, and mirror reflections. Such perceptions are no doubt set aside by subsequent knowledge; but at the time of experience they are real. At any rate, such things are the legitimate province of poetry, and poetic propositions about them, too, must be taken to be true descriptions.

The Indian philosophers also draw a distinction between validity and verifiability. Not all knowledge is verifiable by empirical means, yet it is taken to be valid. According to the Mīmāṃsakas, Vedāntins, and grammarians, supersensuous entities or concepts, such as duty *(dharma),* truth, immortality, and so forth, are referring expressions and valid knowledge becasue they are conceivable and nameable. The notion of *dharma* is obtained from the words of the Veda alone and is not corroborated by other means of knowledge. But it does not mean that it is nonexistent or that it is a case of nonapprehension—an empty concept. Its knowledge is got from words, and that is its validity.[53] It is identified via its meaning, not via facts. In sentences like "One who is desirous of heaven should sacrifice to fire," the innate significative capacity of the words themselves conveys the knowledge of *dharma.* Such knowledge is valid in itself as it is not contradicted by other means. Vedic injunctions are therefore the only valid means of knowing *dharma.*[54] For statements to be valid, they need not necessarily be about actual or objective entities, nor do they need to be verified by direct empirical methods. According to the Mīmāṃsakas, historical statements *(bhūtārthavādas),* such as "Then Indra raised his weapon (called Vajra) against the demon Vṛtra," are also not directly verifiable since they are neither obtained from other sources of knowledge nor contradicted by them.[55] Yet they are meaningful existential propositions. Their only validation is the testimony of the word of the Veda.

The same status may be claimed for statements about characters and events in literature, irrespective of whether they are known to be historical or fictitious. It might be argued that assertions about historical events are verifiable in principle, that is, that it is logically possible to verify them. For example, "Cleopatra wore a red dress on her twentieth birthday" could have been verified by a contemporary who saw Cleopatra. But the same could be said of a fictional character like Pickwick or Sherlock Holmes. But in neither case, though, would one come up with any actual evidence. The fact of the matter is that historical accounts are believed to be true because they are supposed to have come from trustworthy sources. Their authority derives from hearsay, from verbal testimony, not from direct perception or inference. They are not doubted as long as they are not incongruous or inconsistent with ordinary human experience. Reports of UFOs and ESP are discredited because they are not thought to be possible. By the same token, a statement about Sherlock Holmes ought to be as authoritative as the one about Cleopatra. Both persons exist for us only in the world created by the words of a text. On the basis of the evidence of the text alone, we cannot tell the difference between history and fiction. Similarly, nonobservation sentences about feelings, sensations, and so forth cannot be directly tested. But their assertive force can be ascertained in conjunction with other statements of observable conditions furnished within the work. Commands, questions, prayers, and exclamations too are unverifiable, but they can be related to their contexts and their expressive (illocutionary) force ascertained.

As for metaphorical statements, as the Vedic exegetes show, they are not ipso facto unverifiable and therefore false since they are not false in their indirect or implied sense, although they are vitiated in their primary sense. They are invariably translated into literal terms to accord with normal modes of speech.[56] Metaphorical statements in the Vedic texts, apparently absurd or baseless, serve to eulogize the sacrificial acts and are thus indirectly related to the main injunctive sentences. For instance, the Veda speaks of "the fist of Indra holding heaven and earth." But, according to *mīmāṃsā,* the Vedic texts themselves do not justify the presumption that gods have material bodies like human beings. So the text should be interpreted figuratively as mere praise of the deity, the sense being that "Indra is such a being that if he had a fist it would be so large as to hold heaven and earth."[57]

One might ask how a statement that is intrinsically false could serve as a serious inducement to the hearer to perform the act that the statement is meant to eulogize. But this objection, says the Mīmāṃsaka, presents no difficulty. For what is required for a statement to serve as a eulogy is that it should carry the force of a eulogy, not that it should be completely and absolutely veracious. This is also the justification for poetic similes and metaphors, which often make impossible assertions or assertions about things that never happened, and also for expressions like the television commercial that states, "If my Blue Bonnet is not the lightest tasting margarine you have ever tasted, I'll eat my bonnet." The absurdity of this statement does not detract from its force as a praise of the product in question.

Jaimini's aphorism says, "On account of the expression being figurative there would be no contradiction." The commentators add, There would be a contradiction of directly perceived facts if the statement was meant to refer to an actual state of affairs. But all that it signifies is praise, and there can be no contradiction in that. What is in question here is not the veracity of the statement, but the fact that a eulogy is meant. Even the mention of an event that never happened serves the purpose of eulogizing."[58] This same logic of the Mīmāṃsaka may be extended to literary statements—not only to metaphorical sentences but to assertions and descriptions as well. Even if the assertions in a fiction cannot be proved true or false, still, as their purpose is to present a situation, such that it carries a certain evocative force, and not to report an actual state of affairs, they can be held to be meaningful and valid *(pramāṇa)*. All this goes to show that verifiability, as the positivists understand that term, is not a condition of the validity of a statement. As Alston argues, a statement must be considered meaningful only if it can be used for the performance of an illocutionary act.[59] The verifiability criterion, if it is taken seriously, will leave out large areas of human discourse as being meaningless.

The Indian logicians too, like some of their Western counterparts, went by the criterion of verifiability, interested as they were in the literal truthfulness of statements rather than in their meaningfulness as speech acts. They held the view of the extrinsic validity of knowledge *(parataḥ-prāmāṇyavāda)*. All experience must be subjected to empirical proof before its validity can be ascertained. The grammarians, the Mīmāṃsakas, and the Vedāntins, however, held the theory of the self-evident validity of all cognition *(svataḥ-prāmāṇya)*, whether derived from sense perception or from words, and its extrinsic invalidity *(parataḥ-aprāmāṇya)*.[60] For the grammarians, all verbal cognition is mental; meaning does not depend on external verification. What figures in the mind is the meaning of words, not outside reality *(bāhyasattā)*. Words move about in their own realm, although not without any relation to outside reality. Words denote only what figures in the mind. Whether the thing in question, for example, "Mr. Pickwick," exists or not is irrelevant. If we demanded external being of things we refer to, then even existential statements like "The pot is there," "The pot is not there," and "The sprout is springing up" would become unintelligible. For to predicate existence of something that is already there is tautology, and to predicate nonexistence of it or to say that what already exists (the sprout) is being born is contradiction. Again, objects with fixed characters are seen to undergo grammatical transformations in ways in which it is not possible for them in the real world (e.g., "He is cooking," "He is performing the act of cooking"). Therefore, the grammarians conclude that verbal meanings take on their own forms according to use and according to how objects are cognized and presented by someone.[61]

The grammarians, concerned as they are with how things are presented in words rather than with things as they are, of course tend to ignore the question of truth. But the Mīmāṃsakas, with their realistic, pragmatic cast of mind, show equal concern for meaning and validity. Validity they define as uncontradictedness *(abādhitatva)*. Statements like "Fire is cold" and "There are hundreds of elephant herds on the tip of my finger" are not valid knowledge because they are contradicted by other means of cognition. But they may be validated as metaphorical statements when a proper context is given to them. "Paolo loved Francesca" should be treated as a historical statement *(purākalpa)* and valid because it is not contradictory to experience. It is possible that Paolo loved Francesca. But "The U.N. is a World Government" is not valid because it is simply false.[62] However, the Mīmāṃsakas as well as the Vedāntins insist that all knowledge is intrinsically valid and does not require corroboration by other means, although it may be proven false due to extrinsic conditions, such as defective perception and fallacious reasoning.[63] Thus, the difference between a false statement, such as the above, and one like "Mr. Pickwick visited Bath" is that the latter brings with it a conviction of its truth and is not set aside by other evidence within the novel.

While Abhinavagupta does not develop some of these implications, his argument presupposes the views of the philosophers, especially the Mīmāṃsakas and the grammarians, in the view that poetic knowledge, like all valid knowledge, possesses a self-evident validity and that it is uncontradicted by experience. Abhinavagupta remarks, however, that the question of truth is, in a sense, irrelevant to poetic judgment, not only because of the self-evident nature of its truth, but also because what is in question is not the ontological status of the fictional object but its representative character.[64] In terms of his doctrine of generalization, it is immaterial whether a given situation or character is actual or fictitious (Pickwick or Henry IV) because this consideration does not alter our apprehension of it as a formula for an emotive experience. Not all plots and characters are fictitious anyway. But, in terms of the theory of *rasa*, the distinction itself is not critically significant. Whether the poem by Elizabeth Barrett Browning "How Do I Love Thee" is considered as a message actually addressed to Robert Browning or simply as a poetic creation, it still remains a poem with the illocutionary force of a declaration of love.[65] As Osborne observes, "neither factual truth in the sense of historicity nor theoretical or metaphysical truth . . . is necessary to a good work of art. You do not judge *Odyssey* a better poem because you believe or do not believe that parts of it were based upon an actual voyage in prehistoric times."[66] It is for this reason perhaps that we as readers do not normally care to investigate the truth of poetic statements, not that the notion of truth is not applicable to them or that we willingly suspend disbelief to go along with the fictional convention or "game" of the poem or drama.

10

THE VALIDITY OF *RASA* AS A THEORETICAL CONCEPT

The central concern of this essay has been the determination of the nature and meaning of "poetry"—understood in the broad Aristotelian sense of that term or in the sense signified by the Sanskrit term *kāvya,* which comprehends all that we call "imaginative" literature. General problems of language, meaning, and interpretation too have been discussed, but only to the extent that they have any bearing on our understanding of literary texts. The problem of definition, most perplexing as it is, is of course crucial to any inquiry of this kind, and, as noted in chapter 3, it occupied the minds of the Sanskrit critics most seriously in their attempts to arrive at a general theory of literature. I have argued that, of all the rival doctrines advanced, the concept of *rasa* alone promises the best definition of literature and one that can account for all its elements and values.

One of the senses in which the term *rasa* is understood is as aesthetic experience in general or as the generalized emotion resulting from a poetic work. Speculation on the nature of aesthetic rapture abounds in Abhinavagupta. But it often takes us beyond the confines of aesthetics. Therefore, in my discussion I have focused on the other, objective sense of the term, the sense that both Bharata and Ānandavardhana emphasize and that Abhinavagupta too, as I showed, recognizes in spite of his ultimate metaphysical concerns—namely, *rasa* as the expressed meaning of the work or, more specifically, as emotive meaning or meaning that conveys information about people's emotions. The primary end of poetry is evocation of feelings—"evocation" understood in the sense of calling to mind rather than the actual arousal of the feelings embodied in the poem. Poetry is preeminently emotive discourse, a presentation of human feelings through their objective conditions, in the manner stipulated by Bharata. The inner life of the psyche—man's strivings and passions, his desires and states of sentience—is its special province.

But here it may be questioned whether the claim for the universality of the *rasa* aesthetic is shared by the *rasa* aestheticians themselves. A more inclusive, composite version of the *rasa* theory—*rasa*-and-*dhvani* rather than *rasa* alone—it may be argued, is the view accepted by them and one that is more in accord with the mainstream of the Sanskrit tradition. The major *rasa* theorists after Bharata, namely, Ānandavardhana and Abhinavagupta, while they clearly prefer a *rasa*-dominant poetry, at least allow for poetry of other sorts. A hierarchy, rather than a monolith, is implied.

I have already pointed out in chapter 3 that the *rasa*-and-*dhvani* position maintained by the *dhvani* critics is at best equivocal and that the essentiality of *rasa* is what these critics themselves finally established, following the authority of Bharata. And, as I stated before, *dhvani* and *rasa* are conceived by them not as alternative principles but as, in a sense, a single principle called *rasa-dhvani,* or emotive suggestion, to which the various other classes of poetry discussed by them are rendered subservient. A close examination of their statements will demonstrate this point and will also clarify the sense in which a hierarchy of poetic classes is recognized by them.

In the *dhvani* system, there are three types of poetry: *(a)* poetry of suggestion, in which the suggested content is the principal theme; *(b)* poetry of "subordinated suggestion," in which the suggested meaning is less important than the expressed or merely subserves the expressed (e.g., in figurative expression, in which suggestion is sometimes found, the suggested is subordinated to the expressed and is merely ornamental) or in which the suggested sense is made explicit through some telltale word or phrase; and *(c)* what may be called "trick writing" or "wit writing," which is predominantly figurative and depends for its effect on mere strikingness or peculiarity of sound or sense, with no element of *rasa* in it.[1] The first type, *dhvani,* is rated the best. Of the second type, Ānandavardhana says that even though, in it, the suggested meaning is less important than the expressed, it too can become full-fledged suggestive poetry provided it expresses the *rasas.*[2] Of the third type, the purely figurative kind (rated inferior or *adhama*), he says, "It is not really poetry; it is but imitation poetry."[3]

The first type, suggested sense, is again divided into three classes: *(a)* suggested idea, *(b)* suggested figure, and *(c)* suggested *rasa.* (According to *dhvani* theory, *rasa* is, as noted before, always a suggested meaning, never directly stated, a notion that I try to refute in chap. 6.) With regard to these, Abhinavagupta is quite emphatic in saying that the *rasa* type alone is the truly suggestive poetry because the other two invariably lead to or culminate in it.[4]

At first sight, Ānandavardhana might give the impression that there are two distinct principles at work in his scheme: *dhvani* and *rasa*. But, in the final analysis, he too admits that *rasa* is the more essential of the two. The following statements will make his position clear. Speaking of the relative importance of the three varieties of suggestive poetry, he says, "Although one can discern other sub-species of the suggestive type (i.e., the suggested idea and the suggested figure), it is only in relation to the basic and transitory emotions that they can be understood, because of the primacy of the latter."[5] Again, he says, "Although many varieties of suggestion [suggestive means] are possible [by which poetic themes can be given an air of novelty], the poet should pay special attention to one particular variety, namely, the delineation of the basic and other emotions."[6] Speaking of the third, purely figurative, type, he says that this class (not being genuine poetry at all) is being listed by him because examples of this type exist in the work of those who compose without regard for the *rasas*. "But according to the principles of poetry laid down here, there can be no poetry of any type that is not poetry of suggestion. For, for mature poets, in the absence of a focus on rasa, poetic activity would be without any charm at all. And, conversely, where there is focus on rasa, there will be no subject that will not become exceedingly charming by being made the accessory of the intended rasa."[7]

Note in the above statement that Ānandavardhana equates *dhvani* and *rasa* in saying that the focus on *rasa* is the true test of poeticality, which, in turn, is only the mode of suggestion. Again, since all manner of subjects are capable of being the bearers of *rasa* (of being given an emotive treatment), he says that "no poetic type can be said to fall outside of the sphere of *dhvani*."[8] Poetry of "subordinated suggestion," he says, comes within the sphere of *dhvani* when viewed from the standpoint of *rasa*, that is, when there is a significant emotive theme in it.[9] In these two passages, too, the close interlinking of the *rasa* and the *dhvani* concepts is evident. Thus, whenever Ānandavardhana or Abhinavagupta speaks of *dhvani,* he seems to think of *dhvani* as modified by or subjected to the overall governance of *rasa*. Thus, when Ānandavardhana says that, "for people with mature intellects, only the suggestive kind will deserve the designation of poetry,"[10] this statement should be understood in the light of another admission by him that, "where the rasas are not the subject matter of discourse, there no manner of poetry is possible."[11] Should there be any lurking doubt about Ānandavardhana's position, it is removed by Abhinavagupta's statements on the essentiality of *rasa*. Speaking of the variety, "subordinated suggestion," Abhinavagupta shows in his analysis of a Sanskrit example that, in this class of poetry, although the suggested (i.e., implied) meaning is of only secondary importance as it serves merely to enhance the charm of the expressed meaning, this expressed meaning itself becomes the instrument of a *rasa* type of suggestion; therefore, suggestion has been held to be the soul of poetry.[12]

It appears, then, that for both Ānandavardhana and Abhinavagupta *rasa-dhvani* (emotive suggestion or evocation) rather than *rasa*-and-*dhvani* is the defining essence of poetry. The *rasa* element informs all types of suggestive poetry. Abhinavagupta states quite explicitly that, when we speak of *dhvani,* what we actually mean is *rasa-dhvani* since that, in fact, is the soul of poetry. Whether you call it *dhvani* or *rasa-dhvani,* that, then, is the sole criterion. These critics no doubt recognize the possibility of poetry of other (inferior) sorts. But they do so in a spirit of toleration. Even suggestive poetry gets mixed up with other types of expressive modes (direct or figurative), and *rasa* too may appear in varying degrees of purity and intensity. Hence, in their classifications, they rank poetry as best, second best, second rate, third rate, and so on. One may call this a "hierarchy." But it is also a monolith inasmuch as all other sorts of poetry and all other elements of poetic language—figure, style, and so forth—must ultimately be subjected to the test of *rasa* and be justified in terms of it. In their concern for finding the one distinguishing mark of poetry, they assume that, once the nature of poetry is understood and standards of excellence set for the ideal type, the lesser orders will take care of themselves.

Bharata, Ānandavardhana, and Abhinavagupta are the *rasa* aestheticians in the main line, and their position with regard to the centrality of the *rasa* concept has been stated. Of the followers of the Rasa-Dhvani school, Mammata clearly recognizes *rasa* as a guiding principle and as a criterion of poetic excellence, although he does not include either *rasa* or *dhvani* in his definition of poetry.[13] The same is true of Hemacandra, who, by his own admission, accepts the view of Abhinavagupta on *rasa.*[14] Jagannātha is the only one among the major critics explicitly to reject *rasa* as a principle of definition that can explain all literature. But his objections have been effectively answered by the *rasa* theorist. As I pointed out in chapter 1, most writers after Abhinavagupta tend to be rather accommodating in dealing with rival theories—perhaps out of respect for the ancients—and, consequently, miss the focus given to critical discussions by Ānandavardhana and Abhinavagupta. They fail to offer a consistent theory of literature. Their definitions are syncretistic, not true definitions. Viśvanātha is the only one to insist on a more rigorous, logically consistent definition in terms of *rasa.* In doing so, he corrects the ambiguities present in the poetic scheme of the Dhvani school.

Bharata's *rasa* doctrine was commented on in diverse ways both before and after Abhinavagupta, and many reformulations and mutations of it appeared in the course of its history. One major mutation occurs in the work of the Vaiṣṇava aestheticians of Bengal, who argued for a distinct devotional *rasa (bhakti)* and offered a completely revamped version of the *rasa* theory. Another instance is Bhoja. Bhoja regards *rasa* as an inalienable condition of poetic beauty. But, at his hands, the *rasa* concept undergoes a significant change. Bhoja makes two points. First, all *rasas* originally spring from and dissolve into one basic or germinal *rasa,* which he calls the supreme ego-sense or eros *(ahaṃkāra, abhimāna, śṛṅgāra),* the root of all *rasas.* Whatever its psychological or metaphysical value, this idea is not of much use to the aesthetician. The second theory he puts forward is that all emotions *(bhāvas),* all emotional expressions, and even the objects of emotion can become *rasas.* According to Bharata, we recall, only the basic emotions (whether eight or nine) could be developed into aesthetic moods. But Bhoja obliterates Bharata's fundamental distinctions in a rather unconscionable way.[15] Such aberrations aside, the *rasa* doctrine has remained faithful, throughout the ages, to the original formulations of Bharata, Ānandavardhana, and Abhinavagupta. The extreme views do not find any significant place in the *rasa* canon. Hence, for all practical purposes, the *rasa* theory may be taken as a unified doctrine.

It has been argued from the standpoint of *rasa* that neither figurative expression, nor the implicative manner, nor a well-marked style, can be considered to be the differentia of literature. In arguing against the *dhvani* theory, I pointed out that even direct statements—descriptions, declarations, and the like—can become effective as a vehicle of feeling in the right context and that indirection or obliqueness of the kind insisted on by the *dhvani* theorist is not a necessary condition of poetic expression.[16] All these formal or semantic devices can of course be important and valuable, but only when they are justified by the meanings that they subserve, and not in isolation. This conclusion, which derives from the definition of literature I have advanced, will have consequences for our evaluation of literature. In evaluating the language and formal organization of a poem or play, we must first consider its meaning, for it is the meaning that gives validation to its style and form.

A properly evaluative judgment of a work of literature will, in terms of the *rasa* theory, consist of explaining how the work achieves success as a presentation of an emotive situation, whether it is consistent with the logic governing that kind of discourse, what the elements in it are that make for its coherence as an emotive utterance, whether the language employed is right for the kind of utterance it aims to be, and so on. All this is summed up in the concept of *rasaucitya,* or propriety in delineating the emotions—which is employed as the single, most inclusive criterion for judging literature. Many other concepts that I have discussed, such as figurative expression, expressional deviation, implicative language, style, and poetic excellences or qualities, have no doubt also been employed as evaluative criteria by their respective protagonists. But I have argued that none of these features are the invariable conditions of poetic speech. Hence, they cannot serve as criteria of evaluation.

Valid criteria for evaluative judgments can be formulated only on the basis of permanent or necessary properties, which all literature must possess, and not on the basis of nonnecessary properties, such as complexity, irony, and so on. Only primary or defining features are capable of generating adequate criteria or general principles of evaluation. The reasons we give for the success or failure of a work are not derived from such variable conditions as the values or significance that certain people see or do not see in particular artworks or styles from age to age. Critical judgment is not a matter of taste, nor is it to be guided by reigning fashions, present concerns, or official attitudes. Hirsch is no doubt right in distinguishing "meaning" from "significance." But I think he is wrong in assuming that criticism has to do with significance, understood in the above sense.[17] A certain age may not see value, say, in Milton and berate him in the light of its own standards, for example, that Milton does not write in the idiom of living speech, that he lacks the ironic sense, and so on. But such statements, in terms of my argument, do not amount to a critical judgment because they wrongly assume that qualities, such as prosaic strength and ironic sense, are the necessary conditions of literature.

Aucitya, translated as "propriety," is understood by the Sanskrit writers as the harmonious adaptation of the poetic means—language, figure, image, and so on—to the poetic end. This end is conceived by the *rasa* theorist as the evocation of *rasa.* Poetic art consists in the securing of language, ideas, and so forth appropriate to this end. While, thus, the final ground of reference in poetic criticism is evocation of aesthetic moods, the only criterion of beauty is appropriateness—the idea that, in poetry, good and bad is to be determined on the ground of appropriateness and inappropriateness and that merits and faults do not obtain abstractly but depend on many interrelated factors, such as suitability of languge to theme, tone, context, and so forth. The guiding principle in the determination of poetic excellences *(guṇas)* and blemishes *(doṣas)* is propriety. Excellences are promoters of the poetic end *(kāvyotkarṣa-hetu),* and blemishes are depressers thereof *(tad-apakarṣa-hetu).*[18]

All writers, from Bharata down, assumed decorum to be a central regulative principle.[19] Bharata treats *aucitya* in relation to the problems of drama and stage presentation.[20] In regard to all the elements of the verbal text, such as diction, figure, style qualities, prosodic patterns, and so on, as well as those of stage performance, such as modes of address, gesture, and intonation, the *Nāṭyaśāstra* is guided by the requirements of dramatic decorum. All the verbal features are to be adapted to the *rasa* treated. Ānandavardhana considers propriety in regard to the style qualities, figures, and diction and propriety of the speaker, the person addressed, and the expressed meaning in relation to the literary medium adopted. But he is emphatic in stating that the sole consideration in deciding the propriety of form and matter is the end of delineating the *rasas,* to which all other features must be subordinated. Whatever promotes *rasa* evocation must be considered to be proper to the composition.[21] Subsequent discussions of poetics by Abhinavagupta, Mammaṭa, Kuntaka, Bhoja, Kṣemendra, and others also assumed *aucitya* as a central principle and as the very life of a literary composition.[22] However, it must be recognized that, as a critical concept, appropriateness cannot stand on its own legs; it has to be propped by another concept or standard of evaluation. Appropriateness presupposes an end to which something may be said to be appropriate. This end, according to the *rasa* theorist, is evocation of moods *(rasa-dhvani).*

Decorum also operates in relation to the various types of poetic composition, for the use of poetic figures and styles as well as the organization of the subject matter have to be guided by the demands of the literary form adopted. This is the familiar theory of genres, with the accompanying theory of poetic styles—high, middle, and low—appropriate to the various genres. Decorum, as developed in Western criticism, after Horace, appeared in close association with genre criticism. In Roman and Neoclassical criticism, the genres (mostly those listed in Horace) were assumed to be fixed categories with both a normative and a prescriptive value attached to them. The mixture of authoritarianism and conservatism that has characterized genre criticism has made it and the accompanying principle of decorum suspicious terms in our century. Croce made the rejection of genres the starting point of his aesthetics. Modern critics have questioned whether the notion of decorum, as it appears in the context of the genre theory, refers to something intrinsic to the nature of the work or to something established by convention. An enlightened theory of poetic genres should therefore recognize that literary forms are not permanent fixtures or rigid categories. They are constantly undergoing significant changes, and new forms are coming into being. It is instructive to remember that, even at the time of Horace, the original Aristotelian kinds had undergone a marked development in subdivision and new kinds were added.

The Sanskrit critics, too, elaborated rules of decorum relating to types of composition. They classified the various types of literature on the basis of such broad and inclusive divisions as prose, verse, or mixed, visible (stage drama) and audible (nondramatic literature), short or long, and so forth. The well-known literary kinds were the short lyric, the stray verse *(muktaka),* a string of two or more verses treating a connected theme, the long descriptive poem, the short poem expounding the goals of man, anecdote, historical prose narrative, prose romance, the long poem (narrative or descriptive), and ten varieties of drama *(daśa-rūpaka).* General guidelines were provided as to the propriety of language and style with respect to the various kinds.[23] But these classifications were never regarded by them as ultimates, and new types were constantly added and old ones redefined. For instance, Bharata treated ten types of drama (with further subdivisions of one of them) and three verbal styles (the grand, the graceful, and the energetic) to be employed according to the propriety of each kind of drama, the type of character, and *rasa.* Subsequent classifications listed eighteen more minor varieties and numerous other divisions of audible poetry. In fact, the types that are listed are so numerous that they might have included all the possible modes and styles of composition known in those days. The Sanskrit poeticians also provided for the mixture and modification of styles to suit the speaker, subject matter, and the particular species of composition.[24] All this points to the extreme flexibility of the Sanskrit theories of poetic kinds and styles.

It is also worth noting that not all generic distinctions are basic and central to the classification of literature. Traditional distinctions, such as lyric and pastoral, are distinctions based on differences in form or subject matter and do not touch the essential quality of the work, namely, its emotive tone. (The same goes for some of the genres in Sanskrit literature, mentioned above.) Besides, some of these genres lack proper definition. The lyric is a case in point. The standard definition of it as "a short poem, employing a single speaker and expressing thought and feeling" does not tell us much about the "kind" of meaning expressed by it. Although these formal features—shortness and the voice of a single speaker (expressing thought and feeling can hardly be a defining feature since all poetry does that)—do to some extent determine the structure of the poem by imposing certain formal restrictions on the expression, they do not describe the fundamental aesthetic character of the poem, which makes it an elegiac outcry, a song of joy or triumph, a lover's complaint, a meditation, or an angry protest. The fact that compositions as diverse as Marvell's "To His Coy Mistress," Wordsworth's "Tintern Abbey," and Arnold's "Dover Beach" can all be lumped together under the common label "lyric" argues against the lyric being a distinct "kind" of poetry. For the qualitative differences that exist between these poems are more significant than any formal likeness they may have.

Similarly, the difference between an epic, such as Homer's *Iliad,* and a "comic-epic," such as his *Margites,* is of greater consequence aesthetically than the difference between an epic and a tragedy (in terms of Aristotle's definition). The basic difference between a narrative and a stage drama is of course important because of the difference in the media involved. But the difference between the narrative and the dialogue forms is not so fundamental in the reading experience. It is common knowledge that a novel can often be rewritten as a dialogue, and vice versa, without affecting the tone of the original. Another trouble with traditional genre theory is that it does not provide for the emergence of new species or new combinations of old ones, with the result that whenever a *Moby Dick,* a *Song of Myself,* or a *Waste Land* has appeared, it has tended to upset the applecart of genre theory.

All this points to the conclusion that generic distinctions, along traditional lines, are neither final nor helpful in identifying the aesthetic character of a work. It is not being argued of course that the distinctions do not exist or that they are immaterial. One always examines them in specific instances, and then one shows how they are significant for the work. Thus, when a work like *Paradise Lost* purports to be an epic poem and fits a certain definition of that species, it ought to be described as such and judged according to the standards applicable to that species. Even so, it must be insisted that what makes that poem an epic is not any superficial formal or stylistic resemblances it may have to, say, the *Aeneid,* such as the epic invocation, the divine machinery, the epic simile, and so forth, which are incidental features, but the fact that it treats a heroic theme. It is the heroic tone, then, that defines its aesthetic character and gives it its distinction as a class of composition. Therefore, a more satisfactory basis for generic distinctions would be the emotions with their distinct and characteristic tones. The distinctions of tragic, comic, heroic, furious, serene, and so on are not, for instance, like the formal distinctions employed in differentiating between an epic, a tragedy, a lyric, and so on. They are more intrinsic to the nature of the work because they go to define the kind of thing it is.[25]

While the fact of a work being a lyric, an epic, or a drama is no doubt also important, as it accounts for some of its technical features, this consideration should come only after the emotive tone, the dominant *rasa,* of the work is identified. Form in poetry (i.e., the gross structure of a poem or play) is also best defined as a curve describing the trajectory of the emotion, its rise, proliferation, and subsidence *(bhāvodaya, bhāva-*

śabalatā, bhāva-śānti).[26] Any form that carries a mood to its completion is organic, anything that begets a feeling connection.[27] The well-known rules of plot construction have their basis, ultimately, in the logic of the emotions themselves. *Rasa* being thus the organizing principle in literature, it should also be the primary criterion by which all formal aspects of a work can be evaluated. Because a given poem deals with a heroic subject, we say that its elevated style and other heightening devices are appropriate to its tone, that the language is best suited to its matter. We further say that a colloquial diction or deflating imagery would be incongruent with that kind of discourse. Thus, in determining generic or fomal propriety, our final court of appeal is not conformity to traditional types but congruity between the poetic idea and the form adopted.

But how can this congruity be established since we denied that there was any necessary connection between style and emotion (chap. 7)? Stylistic devices, we said, are polyvalent. How then can we ascertain whether a given manner fits the matter treated or harmonizes with the emotion? That manner was certainly not demanded by the emotion in question as its only adequate vehicle of expression. Appropriateness of form to matter should therefore draw on an authority outside itself for its own determination. This authority, in Bharata's terminology, is *lokapramāṇa,* or worldly usage. All aspects of a literary presentation must conform to the norms of human discourse. Even as in identifying an emotion by its objects and expressions we ask whether a given set of reactions—looks, gestures, and so forth—are such that could be caused by the object in question and whether the reactions are normal in that state of mind, in the case of judging the fitness of language to emotion we have to ask whether a given set of vocabulary items, images, or syntax is such as is normally used in the expression of that emotion or sanctioned by convention. Even the departures from convention must ultimately draw their sanction from convention. The polyvalency of stylistic forms ought not to stand in the way of our judgment. To illustrate, a man may express his anger in harsh, explosive syllables and broken syntax or in long periods and compound constructions, or he may use soft syllables and simple structures. But, as long as we know that anger can be expressed in any one of these ways and are able to say that a chosen manner is congruent with the norms of that discourse, our judgment is not hampered.

Similar is the case with generic propriety. There is no conformity or invariable association between any particular generic type or formal organization and any given emotion. The tragic emotion, for instance, is as well expressed in a narrative as in a dramatic form. But, in such cases, we look at the particular narrative or drama and try to determine whether the details of its structure and style are in keeping with the emotion treated and also consistent with the general principles of a narrative or a dramatic mode of construction.

Decorum, whether in Indian or Western poetics, is no doubt a relativistic concept, for it can operate only with reference to some other concept or concepts. Appropriateness and relevance of critical reasons are intelligible only in terms of a particular context. One might go so far as to say that all criticism, as evaluation, is committed to a relativistic logic: that is, a judgment as to values is possible only with reference to the values that are given. An evaluation of a poem must assume the same values or ends as are assumed by the poem; it cannot question the worth of the ends themselves. It can at best question the adequacy of the means. All profitable criticism is in fact an evaluation of the means as means, not of the ends. The concept of decorum seems thus to address itself to the central task of criticism by directing attention to this question of means and ends. However, the chief difficulty in applying the concept in practical criticism is that poetic ends are conceived differently by different people; consequently, it appears that a plurality of criteria has to be assumed even if decorum is accepted as the operative principle. The *rasa* theory seeks to remove this difficulty by postulating that there is one single end that is common to all literary discourse, namely, the evocation of moods, and, hence, one single, inclusive criterion—appropriateness in respect of the presentation of the emotions.

I have stated in broad outline the case for *rasa* as a theoretical concept and indicated its usefulness as an instrument of definition and its application to the practical problems of evaluation. I have also argued that *rasa,* understood as the principle of emotive expression, offers a viable basis for mounting a general theory of literature. But the *rasa* theory is by no means alone in arguing for the centrality of the emotions in poetry or in attempting a definition of poetry in those terms. For there are numerous parallels to or variants of this theory in Western criticism, although it is in the Sanskrit tradition that it happens to be developed more fully. As is well known, emotions were at the center of most expressive theories of art. The emotionality of poetic expression was a prime consideration in Longinus' theory of the sublime, in the formulations of the eighteenth-century theorists—John Dennis and Bishop Lowth, to name but two—who were influenced by it, as well as in the theories of many nineteenth-century philosophers and poet-critics, including Wordsworth, J. S. Mill, Burke, and others. It was a commonplace of Enlightenment and Romantic thought that feeling is the essence of poetry and what distinguishes poetry from prose. Thus, John Dennis said, "Passion, then, is the characteristic mark of poetry, and, consequently, must be every where. . . . For without Passion there can be no Poetry, no more than there can be Painting. And tho' the Poet and the Painter describe Action, they must describe it with Passion."[28]

As I have already stated, one of the basic assumptions of the *rasa* theory is that the object of poetry is not to convey information about the world or simply to affirm facts but to exhibit the feeling responses produced in people by the objects and facts of the world. Alexander Smith, a nineteenth-century Scottish philosopher, made the same point when he wrote, "The essential distinction between poetry and prose is this:—prose is the language of *intelligence,* poetry of *emotion.* In prose, we communicate our *knowledge* of the objects of sense or thought—in poetry, we express how these objects *affect* us."[29] This distinction was also the established tenet of the Romantic philosophy of Wordsworth and the Wordsworthians: a mere representation of facts unmodified by feeling is not poetry.[30] Speaking of the language of poetry, Smith observes again that it is not merely referential but also expressive of emotion. That is, although poetry employs words with precisely the same grammatical and verbal import as ordinary prose, in it reference serves to intimate feeling. The "direct object" of a poetic description is "not to convey information, but to intimate a subject of feeling."[31]

Analyzing the line from Gray's "Elegy" "The curfew tolls the knell of parting day," Smith remarks, "The vital character of this line, as constituting it poetry, is, that it is not the mere *fact* or *truth* . . . that the words of the poet aim at communicating, but his emotion in regard to the fact."[32] It is significant that a similar view is expressed by L. A. Reid, in our own time. Reid says that what art embodies are emotive values, which can be perceived as objective qualities of the work, "not facts or ideas as such," or "knowledge that," or "feelings alone" (because feelings in themselves are subjective entities), but "feelings-about-things, or things (facts, ideas, anything)-as felt." "When Tennyson wrote, 'Into the valley of death rode the six hundred,' he was not merely affirming the fact, but was concerned with it as an event moving the feelings."[33]

Many Continental theorists down to Croce had a stake in the emotionality of art, including music. But they were for the most part thinking either of the artist's self-expression or of the reader's or viewer's response. For instance, both Eugene Veron and Tolstoy defined art as the language of the emotions. But Veron focuses on the artist's character and genius, whereas Tolstoy, with his "infection" theory, focuses on the communicative aspect.[34] Kant's theory of disinterested delight as being characteristic of aesthetic attitude has a parallel in Abhinavagupta's aesthetics. But his philosophy of taste is response oriented, although judgments of taste are taken to be valid interpersonally, whereas the emphasis of the *rasa* theory, in the way I project it, is object centered.[35] Bharata, Ānandavardhana, and Abhinavagupta no doubt acknowledge that from the poet to the percipient there is a continuum of experience; neither the intuited feeling of the poet nor the felt experience of the percipient is denied. But, as I argued in chapter 2, their primary concern is with the objectification of emotions through the medium of the work and with establishing criteria for their determination and appraisal. At any rate, for purposes of critical analysis, *rasa* is to be taken as the verbal import of the work rather than as a designation for the poet's or the reader's subjective process.

In our own century, C. J. Ducasse, as does Veron and Tolstoy, defines art in terms of the emotions but holds that objectification, rather than communication, is the concern of artistic activity. He also argues that what the art object conveys is not the raw emotion but a "mental image" of the emotion or "feeling-image."[36] This point is of interest to the *rasa* theorist since he too makes a distinction between life emotions *(bhāvas),* which are the subject matter of the poem, and the aesthetically transformed emotions *(rasas)* that the reader derives from them.

That poetry "always expresses inward states," the "living tissue of feelings and events," is also fundamentally the view of Bergson.[37] One may quarrel with Croce's equation of intuition and expression and his subjectivizing of artistic creation. But his theory of artistic intuition places the emphasis squarely on the emotions. Analyzing an episode from Virgil's *Aeneid,* he remarks that, through all the details of the description, "there runs a feeling, a feeling which is our own no less than the poet's, a human feeling of bitter memories, of shuddering horror, of melancholy, of homesickenss, of tenderness . . . something inexpressible in logical terms, which only poetry can express in full."[38] He remarks further that other things found in poetry, such as reflections, exhortations, polemics, and so forth, are extraneous, nonpoetic elements "merely interpolated into or attached to the poem," unless they happen to be in some way connected with the "image-feelings" themselves.[39] Art is not philosophy, not history, not instruction or oratory, but "contemplation of feeling" or "lyrical intuition."

Dilthey too emphasized the role of feelings in aesthetic theory, arguing from his own phenomenological position. The artistic medium cannot be considered apart from its essential or "nuclear content," its feeling. The poet does not present us with mere objects and objective events; rather, he conveys their "felt or lived qualities" *(erlebnis).*[40]

Susanne Langer is undoubtedly the foremost among the modern aestheticians who have accorded a central place to feeling in the philosophy of art. Her theory of art and literature should be of great interest to the

Indian theorist not only because of certain affinities to the *rasa* concept but because she makes a particular mention of that concept in the context of her discussion of the dramatic form. She understands *rasa* as the "vital feeling" of the work. "Rasa is, indeed, that comprehension of the directly experienced or 'inward' life that all art conveys."[41] According to Langer, a work of art "is an expressive form created for our perception through sense or imagination, and what it expresses is human feeling," the word "feeling" meaning "*everything that can be felt,* from physical sensation, pain, and comfort, excitement and repose, to the most complex emotions, intellectual tensions, or the steady feeling-tones of a conscious human life."[42]

Langer stresses the experiential character of the events and ideas expressed in poetry. Poetry's special mode of expression is "presentational" rather than discursive. Discursive ideas, facts, and events, in themselves, have no place in poetry. They must assume an emotional value. "Were poetry essentially a means of stating discursive ideas, whether directly or by implication, it would be more nearly related to metaphysics, logic, and mathematics than to any of the arts."[43] Poetry may no doubt contain statements of opinions and philosophical or other reflections as its materials. But, Langer says, "Poetic reflections . . . are not essentially trains of logical reasoning, though they may incorporate fragments, at least, of discursive argument." "Of course a poet usually builds a philosophical poem around an idea that strikes him, at the time, as true and important, but not for the sake of debating it. He accepts it and exhibits its emotional value and imaginative possibilities."

In the "Immortality" ode, for example, Wordsworth is essentially expressing the excitement generated by the Platonic idea of reminiscence, not persuading us to a belief in preexistence.[44] According to the *rasa* theory too, even bare statements of facts, ideas, and opinions acquire emotive force, are tinged with some feeling or other, provided there is a context for them. It is not the messages contained in such statements that are of poetic value but people's emotional reactions to those messages. Langer remarks, "There is nothing the matter with an ardent moral idea in poetry, provided the moral idea is used for poetic purposes"; in illustration, she cites lines from Wordsworth and Shakespeare.[45] Likewise, in her analysis of other poetic examples, including Blake's "Tyger" and "The Echoing Green" and a Chinese poem, Langer seeks for the "emotional core" of the poem.[46] Commenting on the Chinese poem, she says, "There is nothing in the whole structure that has not its emotional value."[47] Langer applies the same criterion to prose fiction and drama as well. The novel is essentially "poesis," and "its import is formulated feeling, not sociological or psychological theory."[48]

Langer's thesis that art "is the creation of forms symbolic of human feelings" and that there is an iconic correspondence between the formal features of art works and the forms of feeling has run into considerable difficulties.[49] We need not invoke the "ineffable" forms of feeling with which the art form is supposed to be congruent in order to explain the adequacy of a given articulation of feeling. It is enough that we are able to recognize the expressed feeling by its criteria, namely, its objects and other attendant circumstances, without which it must remain unknowable to an outsider. It may also be questioned whether, in the case of poetry, any resemblance exists between the expressed content and the verbal forms that express it. The feelings presented in a poem are revealed to us directly as verbal meanings. But it is difficult to see how the verbal sign is iconic with what it signifies.

Langer rightly insists on the impersonality of the feeling objectified in the work. A poem is not a symptomatic expression of the poet's actual feelings, although it might have sprung from them; rather, it creates an image or a symbol of feeling, as an object given for contemplation, whose meaning is grasped immediately, not inferred, by the reader. "The feeling expressed by this form" (the symbolic form), she says, "is neither his, nor his hero's, nor ours. It is the meaning of the symbol."[50] Langer's idea of the "virtual" or "semblance" aspect of art is a key idea in her theory. What we have in poetry is virtual experience or an appearance of experience, not a dripping emotion but an "image" or "apparition" of emotion, not actual self-expression but a semblance thereof. This notion accounts for the work's "otherness" from actuality and for the contemplative detachment that is characteristic of our response to it. This the *rasa* theory (as already noted in chap. 9) stresses, although the *rasa* theory is not framed in terms of mimetic illusion (which, at bottom, art is in Langer's view).

Consistently with her theory of virtuality, Langer argues further that what a work of art expresses is not "feeling or emotion actually experienced in response to real events" but "an imagined feeling" or imaginary affect.[51] This no doubt seems true not only of the way the poet conceives his work but also of the way the reader apprehends it. In both cases, feelings are only imagined (if not illusory in the ordinary sense); they do not spring from real events. Langer also draws a distinction between the "emotion presented in the work"—that is, the emotion of the fictive persons in the work—and the emotion presented "by the work," which is "the poetic import of the composition" as a whole, "presented," not "represented," "as the perceptible quality of the created image."[52] This emotion, again, is not any particular emotion, like joy or sorrow, but a perceived "quality" of life, abstracted from its associated conditions;

hence, it is not in need of an objective correlative, as the emotions occurring within the world of the work are.[53] What Langer calls the import of the total work is, then, just "feeling," characterized by a pattern of tensions and resolutions.

The *rasa* theory too distinguishes between the symptomatic emotions occurring within the work *(bhāvas),* presented descriptively through their objective correlates, which the persons in the work are shown as suffering, and the emergent emotional quality or dominant feeling tone of the whole *(rasa),* which we savor. This "feeling that shines through the play itself—the vital feeling of the piece" is, as Langer rightly observes, what is called *rasa.*[54] But there is an important difference: this feeling tone of the whole work that emerges from the welter of presented emotions as a unified impression is not merely "one nameless passage of 'felt life' " or *"elan vital."*[55] (Granted of course that every feeling has its tension pattern, its rhythm of rise, commixture, and subsidence.) It is an emotion of a particular description—tragic, comic, marvelous, heroic, serene, or other—and it is firmly anchored in the concrete emotive situation presented in the work. As Abhinavagupta points out, it lasts only as long as our contemplation of its objective correlatives lasts and cannot be dissociated from them.[56] (There can, in fact, be no nameless, objectless emotions.)

Thus, the *King Lear* emotion is an emotion that is embedded in the *King Lear* situation and is qualitatively the same as that of the protagonists in the play. The details of the drama themselves have led, through careful orchestration, to this focalized mood or flavor that, in this case, is the tragic feeling. The *rasa* theory no doubt insists on the transcendent *(alaukika)* character of our feeling response to the work—which is not quite the same as the response of the persons in the play to their own situations. Our feeling in regard to the work is liberated in the process of apprehension from its constrictions of time, place, and person owing to the reader's distance from the world of the work (see chaps. 3, 9). Thus, *rasa* (now understood as the feeling experience of the reader) is, one might say, a highly refined, aesthetically transformed version of the feeling embodied in the work but, nonetheless, the same in essence and as concrete and particular as the other. That is why we are able to differentiate between kinds of *rasa* experiences corresponding to distinctly different feeling tones of literary works—tragic, comic, heroic, and so on—although, of course, we may also speak of "the *rasa* experience" in general terms to denote the response appropriate to all poetic works.

The question of emotional expression in the arts is fairly central to present-day aesthetic debates. As a recent writer puts it, "A great deal has, and continues to be, written [sic] on the expression of emotion in the arts. It no longer seems plausible to define art as expression, but that it expresses emotion is still thought to be an important fact about art."[57] However, the trouble with emotionalist theories, as the above quote suggests, is that "expressiveness" has been used to define all art in general, whereas, in reality, it does not serve as well in explaining the nature of the nonrepresentational arts, like music, as it does in explaining literature. So much so that philosophers have been forced into some unusual maneuvers in making the term fit all the arts. Ducasse is a case in point. He attempts to assign a distinct emotion to every sensory quality, for example, "the feeling of cerulean blue," which permits him to extend his theory of emotion even to nonrepresentational objects.[58] One would suspect the same sort of maneuver in Langer's elaborate reasoning about the symbolization of feeling in music and architecture. It would also appear that she "spiritualizes" the concrete emotional content of literature so that her formula may fit the other art forms as well. At any rate, the claim that human feeling is the universal subject matter of art is difficult to sustain.[59] As for the *rasa* theory, it is, as I stated in chapter 2, primarily a theory about literature and was not advanced by its proponents as a general theory of the arts, although there was some infusion of that concept into theories of dance and sculpture and, in some degree, music as well.

In any case, the application of *rasa* to literature itself should not present any problem once certain familiar misgivings surrounding emotional expression in the verbal medium are removed. For one thing, as we have seen, emotive theories in the West are often stated in terms of the self-expression of the artist and have incurred the charge of intentional fallacy and private language. But this difficulty has been removed by the insistent arguments of the modern theorists, notably Langer. If emotive qualities are to be attributed to literary works, they must be shown to inhere in the works themselves as their phenomenally objective properties. This is possible only by locating them either in their subject matter or in their formal design or Gestalt character. But, evidently, in poetry, as I have argued in chapter 7, surface properties or compositional features —the sounds of words, metrical form, and syntax—cannot by themselves carry emotive significance; they can do so only in conjunction with the human situation that the work delivers. Emotion is presented to us as verbal meaning, not sensorily as aesthetic surface. Emotive terms can be used, then, only in characterizing the verbal meanings of the work, not its Gestalt.

A great deal has been said in recent aesthetic discussions about how expressive properties may be ascribed to artworks.[60] The problem of making such ascriptions seems to hinge largely on how artworks in general and nonrepresentational works in particular may be said to have these properties. It is suggested that, because sonatas, poems, and paintings cannot be said to have feelings, moods, and attitudes, anthropomorphic properties, such as tenderness, gaiety, sadness, longing, and nostalgia, cannot be ascribed to them except metaphorically. Another implication of this problem is whether expressive properties such as these denote intentional states of persons and whether expression is necessarily an intentional act. Evidently, expressive properties ascribed to musical compositions do not involve an intentional act if the composer is not taken into account. But these problems do not affect expression in literature, and it seems possible not only to ascribe expressive qualities to literary works literally but also to preserve their intentional character.

For one thing, the expressiveness of words, like the expressiveness of natural gestures, and unlike that imputed to music and to some visual art objects that cannot speak for themselves, is more straightforward and is effected directly by the denotative capacity of words. Thus, what we have in literature are descriptions of intentional objects and of the voluntary or involuntary reactions produced by them in persons or sometimes direct utterances expressive of such objects and reactions. Emotive adjectives like "sad," "joyful," and so forth may be used to characterize them. For another, as literature is composed of sentences, which are the illocutionary utterances of persons—the speaker in the lyric, the narrator, or the fictional character—we can call these utterances intentional acts expressive of emotions without committing ourselves to the fallacy of authorial intention.

Moreover, expressiveness in literature is not simply a matter of certain qualities being applicable to whole works or to their parts but involves the performing of speech acts. There are the represented acts of expression—somebody does actually express his emotions in the only way he can: through speech and through action and gesture (where these are reported or described by another person in the poem or play, or by the dramatic speaker of the lyric, or by the narrator of the story). However, we do metaphorically ascribe qualities that belong to the events depicted in the work to the work itself and label it as tragic, comic, or romantic by way of characterizing its overall impression or emotional tone—which may be called its expressive property.

The foregoing brief review of Western theories has revealed that *rasa* is neither a unique concept nor in any way peculiar to Indian thinking but that different versions of it exist in the Western theory as well. However, there is also evident in Western criticism a general resistance to and suspicion of emotions and emotionalist theories. The reasons for this attitude are not far to seek. For one thing, Western criticism, since Aristotle, has emphasized a formalistic, empirical approach to art criticism. Emotive theories are often thought to be in danger of lapsing into subjectivism. Then, again, as Reid points out, because "the word 'emotion' tends to suggest a violent state of feeling . . . there is a tendency among some writers on aesthetics to 'play down' emotion." If emotions are to be expressed in art, they must be present as cognitive meanings. But, Reid goes on to say, "It is important to recognize the part which feeling itself must play even in the cognitive process of apprehending aesthetic meaning."[61] What Reid says accords well with Abhinavagupta's point that *rasa* perception is a special type of awareness, but one that is fundamentally in the cognitive mode.[62]

Besides, the objectivity of the emotions in poetry is fully assured since the emotions, as we have seen, inhere in the words of the poem as their cognitive meanings. Again, the *rasa* theory does not believe that poetry is merely an emotional discharge of the poet; it firmly asserts that poetic creation involves the shaping of the materials of experience into the controlled expression of the poem. Abhinavagupta points out that the poet Vālmīki's grief, aroused by the pitiful cries of the Krauñca bird at the sight of her mate killed by the fowler's arrow, became transformed into a poem only when he contemplated the situation in an aesthetic light, that is, as a thing to be relished, and expressed himself in a form regulated by appropriate word choice, meter, and image. It was not the poet's raw emotion that got into the poem as the pathetic *rasa*. A grief-stricken person does not savor his grief; much less does he spew out a poem in that condition.[63]

Even though, thus, we have removed all doubts in regard to the expression of emotions in poetry, it may still be objected that *rasa* or the emotive element is not the only and defining characteristic or value of poetry. There are other values in poetry besides the emotions—figurative and other formal elements—that are equally important. Granted that poetry contains emotions. But it contains, not only emotions, but ideas, pregnant thoughts, new perceptions, explicit or implicit theses, philosophical reflections, and so forth, for which it is valued by mature readers. It may be interesting to the same or to different people for different kinds of things—for social or cultural criticism, historical information, or moral or religious instruction.

The answer to this objection has already been given in the foregoing pages. It only needs to be reiterated here that to set up *rasa* as the criterion of poeticity is not to rule out of court all other literary interests, concerns, and values. The principle of *rasa* does not operate in isolation from all such values, nor is it incompatible with them. First, it does not eliminate considerations of metaphor, suggestion, formal organization, and so on but works in cooperation with such elements. Abhinavagupta states that it is only when the essential suggestive or evocative element (which is the "soul" of poetry) subsists in a linguistic "body" (consisting of word and meaning) that is enlivened by appropriate style qualities and figures that a composition is given the designation of poetry.[64] What, however, the *rasa* theory insists on is that all such formal or stylistic elements are only a means to the primary end of *rasa* evocation. This is also Langer's position. Commenting on Eliot's theory of poetic expression, she writes, "Sound and structure, imagery and statement all go into the making of a vehicle for the poet's idea, the developed feeling he means to present."[65]

Literature will no doubt contain all sorts of thoughts and observations as they are an inseparable part of human discourse. But it is not the primary aim of literature to state facts as merely an information to be conveyed, as many Western theorists have affirmed.[66] Pure ideational material cannot be of aesthetic interest unless it serves as a source of emotion. Often, no doubt, a writer may write for the avowed purpose of preaching, expounding, or justifying an idea or creed. Milton wrote *Paradise Lost* to justify the ways of God. But his poem does not owe its literary character purely to the ideas it expounds. The theological intent of *Paradise Lost* is certainly a vital fact about the poem. But it does not conflict with its being an epic—the two elements coexist with each other, the theological doctrine simply serving as material for the poet to work on. We know that Milton designed the poem as a Christian epic. But to read the poem simply as doctrinal literature is not to attend to its aesthetic value. As a recent critic has pointed out, Milton was not "writing a work of Christian apologetics." "He was writing an epic poem, retelling the best-known story in the world," and bringing the biblical myth to life.[67] The same holds for *Samson Agonistes* and for the poignant devotional lyrics of Donne, Herbert, Hopkins, or the saint poets of India. The upshot of this argument is that, whatever the ulterior motive of the poet in creating his work, he has made an object that possesses certain aesthetic properties, insofar as it is a work of art at all, and that may be viewed from a distinctly aesthetic point of view and also that, whatever other interests the work may invite, the best way to understand and evaluate it as art is the way that is aesthetically most relevant.

I have treated the *rasa* theory as well as the other categories of Sanskrit criticism, such as metaphor, *dhvani,* figuration, and style, as though they were part of a universal discourse on aesthetics, abstracting them from their moorings. In doing so, I have assumed that aesthetic problems and problems of meaning, truth, and interpretation are the same in all languages and philosophical traditions. But this approach is neither so original nor so unusual. Exponents of Indian philosophy from Radhakrishnan and Murti down to Matilal and Karl Potter have demonstrated that philosophers of both India and the West have addressed the same set of problems—ontological, epistemological, and semantic—and that many Western equivalents exist to the terms and concepts employed by the classical Indian thinkers.[68] Comparisons of Indian and Western aesthetics are still in their nascent stage, although laudable beginnings have been made in this direction in the work of Munro, Deutsch, and Gerow.[69] The fundamental assumption of all comparative studies is that general principles, whether they be of art, logic, or philosophy, have a validity even outside their originating contexts. Thus, Aristotle and Bharata each worked within his own independent tradition, basing his formulations on the literature and the artistic practices with which he was familiar. But the principles of criticism they derived from their respective literatures can be seen to have application across the boundaries of their individual traditions. Western critical norms have sometimes been profitably applied in judging Indian literature, and, similarly, the Sanskrit critical principles too may be applied to Western examples without violating the sanctity of either cultural tradition.[70]

The question whether *rasa* is a culture-bound concept representing a uniquely Indian point of view or a universal concept in aesthetics has been raised in recent discussions.[71] The argument for *rasa* being a culture-bound concept generally rests on the following assumptions: that the concept sprang from a particular set of dramatic and theatrical practices and conventions, that it reflects the peculiar cultural conditions of the Indian people and their sensibilities in contrast to those of a Western audience; and, hence, that the *rasa* type of response would not be a proper response to Western literature. Another criticism is that, because *rasa* is concerned with emotions, it encourages a "saccharine emotionalism" and that the only Western parallels to a *rasa* type of literature are melodrama and the soap opera.

I have already, in effect, answered this last objection. Bharata's *Rasa Sūtra,* combined with the elaborate rules of decorum that he and his successors devised for the structured presentation of emotions in poetry, ensures the work against lapsing into mere emotionalism. It would be a mistake to think that *rasa* in a poem or drama is accomplished simply by putting together a few emotive events. There are the considerations of plot, diction, meter, figure, image, genre, unity of tone, and so on, which are necessary for a successful presentation and to which the Sanskrit critics give the fullest attention. The primary emphasis of the Sanskrit texts is on the craft of making poetry. Nowhere is it suggested that poetry is a mere blowing off of emotional steam. This point has been made before.

Also, none of the examples—Sanskrit or English—that we have considered, and none that the Sanskrit texts themselves cite as illustrations of the various *rasas,* can be said to be guilty of the kind of crude emotionalism that is under attack. Besides, there can be nothing aesthetically wrong with emotionalism or sentimentalism per se (although these terms are often taken in a pejorative sense in Western criticism) as long as the emotions presented are not, to borrow Eliot's words, "in excess of the facts as they appear," are warranted, that is, by the données of the situation described.[72]

It would also not be right to think that the *rasa* theory, with its list of nine basic emotional stereotypes, does not provide for the expression of the subtle nuances of feelings. As I showed in chapter 4, it does provide for the greatest complexity of emotional expression. Moreover, the thirty-three transitory emotions listed by Bharata, although they may not exhaust all possible psychic states (for some of which we have no words), cover a whole range of commonly recognized varieties. Bharata's distinction between primary and fleeting emotions, too, is psychologically valid and finds support in the writings of some Western psychologists.[73]

It may also be noted here that only some of the nine basic emotions have generally been popular with writers, especially of long poems and plays, and they are realized as full-fledged aesthetic moods or *rasas,* pervading entire works and setting the tone for them. Thus, the romantic, heroic, tragic, and comic themes have been traditionally popular with writers. Horror is cultivated in the Gothic romances and the serene sentiment in nature descriptions and devotional works. We do not have many samples of entire works based on disgust as the ruling emotion, except for some poems of Swift. The marvelous sentiment is characteristic of the *Arabian Nights,* fairy tales, science fiction, and the like. But, more often, disgust, rage, and wonder enter as episodes in the larger context of one of the other dominant sentiments. At any rate, the notion that an entire composition could be governed by one dominant mood, which integrates its various strands and gives it unity of impression, is an important tenet of the *rasa* theory, and its truth can be demonstrated. It is of course easier to demonstrate such unity in Homer than in the *Mahābhārata* because of the encyclopedic nature of the latter.

Now for the other argument, namely, that *rasa* is a culture-bound concept and good only for understanding Indian, especially classical, literatures. In chapter 8, I argued that the essential human experience that literature communicates is not historically or culturally conditioned but appeals to what is most basic and elemental in human nature.[74] A similar case has been made in the foregoing pages for the universality of critical concepts in general. If aesthetic experience is universal, the laws derived from it, too, must be universally valid. This truth was taken to be axiomatic by traditional thinkers in the West as well as by the *śāstra-kāras* ("makers of science") of ancient India. One must of course allow for certain elements in any literature that are culturally derived and that are therefore unique to that literature—and also perhaps for some technical principles that have application to that literature alone, for example, theatrical practices, dramatic or poetic conventions, generic types, and so on.

But we must also distinguish between them and the concepts that are formulated at a higher level of generalization, such as those explaining the nature and function of literature and the problems of literary semantics. Aristotle's theory of mimesis, his definition of tragedy, his theory of metaphor, and the concepts in Sanskrit that we have discussed may be rightly classed among such principles, and their validity extends beyond their respective linguistic and cultural boundaries. At any rate, it is difficult to see what is uniquely "Indian" about *rasa* and what the peculiar cultural conditions were that molded it.[75] The very fact that Western criticism too has parallel theories and that Western examples may be examined in the light of *rasa* is proof of its universal applicability.

What James Liu observes in his *Chinese Theories of Literature* is instructive. Liu shows that some of the Chinese theories are valid for other literatures. Speaking of cultural relativism in comparative literature, he says, "Having made due allowances for differences in beliefs, assumptions, prejudices, and ways of thinking, between different cultures and different ages, we must aspire to be transhistorical and transcultural, searching for literary features and qualities and critical concepts and standards that transcend historical and cultural differences. Otherwise we should no longer speak of 'literature' but only of discrete 'literatures,' nor of 'criticism' but only of 'criticisms.' "[76] Monroe Beardsley has also argued that aesthetic principles themselves are not governed by cultural or semiotic conventions and that "cultural criticism," legitimate as it may be in its own field, must "acknowledge, make room for, and preserve the distinctively aesthetic point of view."[77]

While, thus, it may be granted that, as a theoretical concept, *rasa* has validity, not only for Indian, but for other literatures as well, it may still be doubted that it can give a satisfactory account of all literature and all types of literary works. A similar doubt was expressed by Indian critics. Can nature descriptions and the like be explained in terms of *rasa?*[78] I argued in chapters 3 and 8 that even purely objective descriptions presuppose a speaker and his attitude toward the objects described and that they thus get connected to some emotion or other. Otherwise, as human utterances, they must appear quite pointless.

Turning now specifically to the question of how well the *rasa* concept can be applied to Western literature, I think we can safely claim that it can satisfactorily deal with a great bulk of that literature. The most obvious candidates, among the literary forms, for our consideration in this context would be the lyric, satire, drama, and the epic. By its very nature, as an expression of subjective feelings and thought, the lyric is best suited for the application of emotive criteria. The tangled passions of Shakespeare's sonnets, the casuistries of Donne's love poems or the "holy discontent," "the low devout melancholy" of his divine poems, the fervid outpourings of Shelley's or Keats' odes, the quiet ruminations of Wordsworth, the infernal visions of the Romantic "Satanists" and surrealists (Poe, Rimbaud), the complex involutions of the mind in Browning's dramatic monologues, Emily Dickinson's ecstatic notations, the imaginative strainings of Hopkins or Hart Crane, Whitman's songs of celebration, cummings's chants of innocence, the suicidal fantasies of Sylvia Plath—the list could go on and on—these cannot be explained except in terms of an emotive theory of poetry.

Also, aside from the obvious cases of Yeats, Eliot, and Pound,[79] to whose work emotional expression is fairly central, Symbolist and post-Symbolist poetry (both French and English) depends on the rendering of subjective moods and tensions—despair, horror, ennui, or the sense of loss and fear. The eighteenth century in English literature is generally regarded as a moralistic age and an age of reason. But it was also preeminently an age of comedy. It is as comic satire that much of that literature (Dryden's "Mac Flecknoe," Pope's *The Dunciad*) retains its value beyond its contemporary reference. Anger and disgust are the ruling passions of Swift's "tragical" or Juvenalian satire, but they are masked behind a comic-ironic guise, which dictates the general tone of his writings.

No drama—whether tragic or comic-satiric, Greek, Shakespearean, Jacobian, Restoration, or modern (O'Neill, Miller, Tennesse Williams)—can survive without a strong emotional focus or emotional center. Action, dialogue, and character must revolve around that center. There are of course the problem plays and the propaganda plays, in which an ideology is what dictates the theme. But even they normally contain an emotional tension of some sort, generated by the clash of ideas, which is what makes them dramatic in the first place (e.g., the plays of Shaw). There is a perceptible emotional point even in the black comedies of our era, which are often labeled "tragi-comedies." The metaphysical impasse and the very apathy of the characters to that condition, which these dramas portray, are presented as a felt condition of human existence, not as a philosophical view merely.

Usually the novel, as a fictional narrative, is valued for its representation of men and manners or for its moral or sociological comment. But, as Langer has pointed out, it also has an artistic function to fulfill, which is not to expound ideas or to illustrate social or cultural conditions but to formulate a feeling, a sense of lived experience. All literature may in fact be said to be in the "experiential" mode. Thus, the aim of Hawthorne's New England romances or of Faulkner's fables of the South was not to write the cultural history of those places and eras but to voice the agony of a culture. The case of the psychological novel is even more straightforward. There is usually a dominating mood or feeling of life or emotional concern that pervades the narrative and gives the events their direction and structure (e.g., Virginia Woolf's *To the Lighthouse* and *Mrs. Dalloway*)—horror or moral revulsion (Conrad, *Heart of Darkness*); elegiac pining, loneliness, regret for unlived life (James, *The Ambassadors,* "The Beast in the Jungle"); the need to establish human connection (Sherwood Anderson, E. M. Forster); the agonies of self-quest (Joyce, *Portrait of the Artist;* Stephen Crane, *The Red Badge of Courage*). The point of Lawrence's novels is not his theorization merely about individual identity versus sexual mergence but his dramatization of those very polarities. Similarly, Stephen Crane's tragic sense must be seen as the dominant theme of his fiction; it underlies his ideological battles and provides the rationale for his ironic perception. Hemingway is perhaps the purest example of a novelist who sought to record experience exactly the way it was and felt, scrupulously avoiding all discursive thought. Emotion is the very foundation on which his aesthetic rests. The key to his novels and short stories is the emotion-producing event, "the sequence of motion and fact which made the emotion."[80] This, together with his technique of understatement and omission, makes his works perfect examples of what the *dhvani* critics call a suggestive rendering of emotions.

It would thus appear that *rasa,* as a critical instrument and analytic tool, is capable of wide application to literature of diverse kinds. Even so, there is of course room for a good deal of dispute. For one thing, one could quarrel about the scope of the term "literature." In the Western tradition, "literature" encompasses a great variety of things, including the discursive essay, biography, orations, sermons, and so forth. An emotive definition of poetry will obviously not fit these types. It would be foolish to argue that *rasa* can account for Bacon's or Emerson's essays or Jonathan Edwards' sermons. Even though traces of emotion may be found in sermons and orations, such writings are primarily discursive tracts, not emotional expressions. Bacon's essays are considered good literature on grounds other than emotiveness, such as their stylistic symmetries, epigrammatic brilliance, and neat logical structure. Lincoln's "Gettysburg Address" is an oration and good literature by rhetorical standards (although it could become emotionally charged when set in the context of a drama on Lincoln's life). In any case, emotions are not what define the literariness of these writings.

However, in Western criticism, "imaginative literature" or belles lettres is commonly distinguished from mere discursive writing, and emotive criteria are applied to it.[81] In Sanskrit literature too, under the term *kāvya,* a great many varieties of composition were included—historical and gnomic-didactic writing in addition to drama, epic, lyric, and romance. Scriptural and canonical literature and scientific treatises were of course strictly excluded from its purview. However, in the critical tradition stemming from Bharata and the early rhetoricians, only the epic, drama, lyric, and prose romance were accorded the status of *kāvya.* The test of a *kāvya* was believed to be the quality of delight or emotional thrill *(camatkāra),* whether it resulted from some peculiar turn of expression or from *rasa.* Thus, the term *kāvya* came to be applied commonly to imaginative literature, and the *rasa* doctrine was discussed mainly in the context of this type.

We may, then, agree to limit the term "literature" to so-called imaginative literature and show that the theory of *rasa* fits the well-known paradigm or core cases. Even so, there will no doubt be borderline cases in which emotive meaning is not the primarily intended one. A great many kinds of things (sometimes a ridiculous variety of things—antipoetry, antiart, antitheater, and so on) go under the name of literature and art in our age of experimentalism, and applying the *rasa* standards to such instances and pronouncing them worthless and not genuine literature would be prescriptive. But this limitation that the *rasa* theory suffers from is in fact shared by any definitional proposal. No definition of art or literature, however well reasoned, can aspire to cover all conceivable cases, especially because conceptions of art and literature themselves undergo changes and works not hitherto recognized as art come to be regarded as art. This frustration with the problem of definition has led, in our time, to institutional theories or, alternatively, to the conclusion that the search for a universal definition of art or literature is futile and a philosophical dead end. Some influential modern writers on aesthetics have still maintained the traditional belief in the possibility of definition.[82] The *rasa* theory too should then be taken as just another definitional proposal, but one that promises, within the limits aforementioned, to give a reasonably good account of what many people in all ages and countries have thought to be valuable in literature and also one that avoids the shortcomings of other competing theories.

NOTES

CHAPTER I
INTRODUCTION

1. The excellent work of Masson and Patwardhan deserves a special mention in this context. In their detailed and scholarly treatment of the *rasa* theory and Abhinavagupta's philosophy of aesthetics, not only do they illuminate many points of critical interest, but they also emphasize the primacy of the *rasa* principle in the Indian scheme. They do not, however, attempt a conclusive appraisal of the rival schools from that standpoint. See Masson and Patwardhan, *Śānta Rasa and Abhinavagupta's Philosophy of Aesthetics,* and *Aesthetic Rapture.*

2. Gerow, "*Rasa* as a Category of Literary Criticism," 231.

3. Sylvain Lévi, *Le théâtre indien,* quoted in Langer, *Feeling and Form,* 321, n. 25.

4. Both Pandey and Masson/Patwardhan are of course right in tracing Abhinavagupta's views on *rasa* experience to his transcendental theories. Abhinavagupta does equate aesthetic pleasure with spiritual ecstasy. But the point I wish to make here is that, notwithstanding the mysticism, Abhinavagupta's explanations do not fail to make sense at the level of aesthetic psychology.

5. See Munro, *Oriental Aesthetics,* 80–91.

6. Amaladass, in his *Philosophical Implications of Dhvani,* argues that *dhvani* is not merely a semantic concept but a worldview. "The *dhvani*-attitude," he writes, "once perfected enables the reader to grasp the 'inner reality' in every thing, to experience the total significance of the world at large" (209). He reads a metaphysical significance into Ānandavardhana's "body-soul" *(ātma-śarīra)* analogy. In spite of the cogent textual analyses the book provides, one feels that a great deal is being forced on the text. The author himself is aware of this weakness and admits that Ānandavardhana "may not even be conscious of these [philosophical] presuppositions" (9). Moreover, if *dhvani,* as he claims, is a symbol language in the very broad sense in which he understands that term—a symbol may be seen in everything; the world itself is a symbol (162ff.)—then what purpose is served by calling *dhvani* a symbol language since everything else may be called by that name?

7. On the question of the universality of critical concepts, see chap. 10. Eliot Deutsch thinks that *rasa,* for one, is a universal concept capable of explaining aesthetic experience in general (see his *Studies in Comparative Aesthetics,* chap. 1).

CHAPTER 2
RASA: POETRY AND THE EMOTIONS

1. *Nāṭyaśāstra* 6.31, gloss: *rasa iti kaḥ padārthaḥ . . . āsvādyatvāt.*

2. "Abhinavabhāratī," *Nāṭyaśāstra* (BHU ed.) 1, pp. 15–16: *tatra nāṭyam nāma laukika-padārtha-vyatiriktam. . . .*

3. Coomaraswamy, *The Transformation of Nature in Art,* 46, and *The Dance of Śiva,* 41–43.

4. Pandey, *Comparative Aesthetics,* chap. 2.

5. Ibid., 140–142.

6. "Abhinavabhāratī," *Nāṭyaśāstra* 6, p. 670.

7. *Nāṭyaśāstra* 1.121: *sukha-duḥkha-samanvitaḥ.*

8. "Abhinavabhāratī," *Nāṭyaśāstra* 6, p. 652: *tat kāvyārtho rasaḥ.*

9. *Nāṭyaśāstra* 1.112.

10. For an exhaustive account, see Raghavan, *The Number of Rasa-s;* see also chap. 4 below.

11. *Nāṭyaśāstra* 29 contains a detailed discussion of the use of various musical notes and melodic structures for heightening emotional effects.

12. "Locana," *Dhvanyāloka* (Kāvyamālā reprint) 3.4, p. 160: *vibhāvādi saṃyogād hi rasa niṣpattiḥ. . . .*

13. Compare Susanne Langer's theory of dance as emotive gesture (*Feeling and Form,* chap. 11).

14. *Nāṭyaśāstra* 4.268; for Abhinavagupta's views, see "Abhinavabhāratī" on 265–273.

15. "Abhinavabhāratī," *Nāṭyaśāstra* 4.273, p. 435: *anena rasāṅgatvān nṛttasya nāṭyatvaṃ jñeyam.*

16. *Viṣṇudharmottara* 3.35 ("Citrasūtram") and 43: *citra-rasaḥ.*

17. For a discussion of the various aesthetic theories, see Osborne, *Aesthetics and Criticism;* and Sparshott, *The Theory of the Arts.*

18. "Abhinavabhāratī," *Nāṭyaśāstra* 1.5, p. 36: *na hy anena sāmājiko vinīyate.*

19. Ibid., 1.115, p. 134.

20. See Casey, *The Language of Criticism.*

21. Huw Morris-Jones, "The Language of Feelings," in *Aesthetics in the Modern World,* ed. Osborne, 94–104.

22. *Nāṭyaśāstra,* gloss on 6.31.

23. Abhinavagupta, "Locana," *Dhvanyāloka* 1.5, p. 31: *na tu muneś śoka iti mantavyam.*

24. See *Bhāvaprakāśana of Śāradātanaya* (GOS ed.) 1.9, p. 154: *śabdopanīta; Sāhityadarpaṇa* 3.25: *śabdasaṃbhavāt; Nāṭyaśāstra,* "Madhusūdanī," p. 17: *kāvyaśabdasya mukhyatayā pratipādyo arthaḥ rasaḥ.*

25. This is the substance of Dhanika's view although presented in a different context. *Daśarūpaka* (Adyar ed.) 4.37, p. 211.

26. Eliot, *Selected Prose,* 29.

27. Eliot, "Ezra Pound: His Metric and Poetry," in *To Criticize a Critic,* 170, 181.

28. Eliot, *Knowledge and Experience in the Philosophy of F. H. Bradley,* 23.
29. Osborne, "The Quality of Feeling in Art," 105–124.
30. *Daśarūpaka,* pp. 167–168.
31. Hepburn, "Emotions and Emotional Qualities," 81.
32. Osborne, *Aesthetics and Criticism,* 145.
33. Morris-Jones, "The Language of Feelings" (n. 21 above), 99.
34. "Abhinavabhāratī," *Nāṭyaśāstra* 6, p. 625: *sthāyī tu kāvyabalād api nānusaṃdheyaḥ.*
35. Ibid., p. 630: *jaḍatvena, bhinnendriya-grāhyatvena, bhinnādhikaraṇatvena.*
36. "Locana," *Dhvanyāloka* 1.5, p. 33: *prāksaṃviditaṃ paratrānumitaṃ ca.*
37. "Abhinavabhāratī," *Nāṭyśāstra* 6, pp. 668–671, on the nature of *rasa.* Abhinavagupta insists that *rasa* is not produced afresh by the presented situation of the drama: *ata eva vibhāvādayo na niṣpatti hetavo rasasya* (p. 671).
38. Austin, *Philosophical Papers,* 77–78.
39. Donagan, "Wittgenstein on Sensation."
40. Gudmunsen, *Wittgenstein and Buddhism,* 40–42.
41. Wimsatt and Beardsley, "The Affective Fallacy," 38.
42. *Nāṭyaśāstra* 6.31, gloss, p. 678; 7.1, gloss, p. 783.
43. *Nāṭyaśāstra* 7.7.
44. Wimsatt and Beardsley, "The Affective Fallacy," 30.
45. "Abhinavabhāratī," *Nāṭyaśāstra* 6, p. 669: *na tāṭasthyena pratipadyate;* p. 672: *na taṭasthatayā ratyavagamaḥ.*
46. Ibid., p. 669: *anumāna-smṛtyādi-sopānam anāruhyaiva tanmayībhāvocita-carvaṇā-prāṇatayā.*
47. "Locana," *Dhvanyāloka* 2.4, p. 85: *vyutpādanaṃ ca śāsanapratipādanābhyāṃ . . . vilakṣaṇam.*
48. Ibid., 1.21, p. 70: *vibhāvādi-carvaṇādbhuta-puṣpavat . . . evāyaṃ rasāsvādaḥ.*
49. Ibid., 2.4, p. 84: *apratītaṃ hi piśācavad avyavahāryaṃ syāt.*
50. "Abhinavabhāratī," *Nāṭyaśāstra* 6, p. 645.
51. *Rasagaṅgādhara* (BHU ed.) 1:15, Nāgeśa's commentary: *jñānaṃ ca bhāvanārūpam eva.*
52. "Abhinavabhāratī," *Nāṭyaśāstra* 6, p. 646. In Indian logic, the different modes of knowledge *(pramāṇas)* are distinguished according to the means (*karaṇa,* instrument) by which knowledge is produced and according to their operation *(vyāpāra).*
53. "Locana," *Dhvanyāloka* 2.4, pp. 84–85: *pratīyamāna eva hi rasaḥ; pratītir eva viśiṣṭā rasanā; pratītyā eva ca rasyante.*
54. *Sāhityadarpaṇa* 3.20 and gloss.
55. "Locana," *Dhvanyāloka* 1.5, p. 31.
56. See Lewis, *The Poet's Way of Knowledge.* Crane (*The Languages of Criticism and the Structure of Poetry,* 58) points out that for Aristotle poetry "is not itself a mode of knowledge."
57. Vivas, "The Objective Correlative of T. S. Eliot."
58. "Abhinavabhāratī," *Nāṭyaśāstra* 6.38, p. 691: *kavir hi sāmājikatulya eva;*

Dhvanyāloka 3.42, gloss, p. 278: *śṛngārī cet kaviḥ kāvye jātaṃ rasamayaṃ jagat.*

59. "Locana," *Dhvanyāloka* 1.6, p. 34: *nāyakasya kaveḥ śrotuḥ samāno anubhavas tataḥ.*

60. See Krieger, *The New Apologists for Poetry,* 161.

61. See further chap. 4.

62. "Locana," *Dhvanyāloka* 1.4, p. 23: *pratipattuśca rasāveśo rasābhivyaktyaiva . . . pratipattur api rasāveśo na niyataḥ.*

63. McKeon, "Literary Criticism and the Concept of Imitation in Antiquity," 143.

CHAPTER 3
THE ESSENTIALITY OF THE EMOTIONS

1. *atattva-vyavacchedako dharmaḥ.*

2. *Nāṭyaśāstra* (BHU ed.) 6.31, gloss, p. 620: *na hi rasād ṛte kaścid arthaḥ pravartate.*

3. *Kāvyānuśāsanam* (Kāvyamālā ed.), p. 19.

4. *Kāvyaprakāśa* 1.4.

5. Kuntaka, *Vakrokti-Jīvita;* Viśveśvara, *Camatkāracandrikā;* Kṣemendra, *Aucityavicāracarcā.*

6. Daṇḍin, *Kāvyādarśa* 1.10: *iṣṭārtha-vyavacchinnā padāvalī;* Jagannātha, *Rasagaṅgādhara* 1:13: *ramaṇīyārtha-pratipādakaḥ śabdaḥ kāvyam.*

7. See the verse attributed to Bhaṭṭa Tauta, quoted in *Kāvyānuśāsanam,* p. 3.

8. In practice, it led Coleridge to devalue the poetry of wit. But, paradoxically, it also enabled the New Critics to defend the line of wit and denigrate the Romantics. In Richards' hands, imagination undergoes a sea change and becomes a certain structure of meaning rather than a special organ of poetic creation. See Richards, *Coleridge on Imagination.* De, in chap. 1 of *Some Problems of Sanskrit Poetics,* complains that, with their purely technical and scholastic approach, the Sanskrit theorists fail to do justice to the intuitive, imagative aspects of poetic creation. But this scholasticism of the Sanskrit critics seems to me the very precision of their greatness.

9. *Kāvyālāpāṃśca varjayet.* For "the function of literature" *(kāvya-prayojana),* see Mammaṭa, *Kāvyaprakāśa* 1.2.

10. "Abhinavabhāratī," *Nāṭyaśāstra* 1, p. 36: *na hy anena sāmājiko vinīyate;* "Locana," *Dhvanyāloka* 1.1, p. 14: *caturvarga-vyutpatter api ca ānanda eva pāryantikaṃ mukhyaṃ phalam.*

11. A considerable amount of literature in Sanskrit that is predominantly didactic in intent is nevertheless regarded by many as great poetry, e.g., devotional lyrics *(bhakti-kāvya).*

12. Richards, *The Principles of Literary Criticism,* chap. 2.

13. See Coomaraswamy, *The Transformation of Nature in Art,* chaps. 1, 5, and passim.

14. Contra Sukla, *The Concept of Imitation in Greek and Indian Aesthetics.*

15. For Taruṇavācaspati, qualities of style, such as density, looseness, and symmetry, are also figures, in the wider sense of poetic embellishments: *guṇā*

alaṃkārā eva ity ācāryāḥ. See De, *History of Sanskrit Poetics,* 2:83, n. 17. For a clarification of the distinction between *guṇa* and *alaṃkāra,* see Gerow, *A Glossary of Indian Figures of Speech,* 31–32.

16. *Kāvyādarśa* 1.10, 2.1.

17. See Gerow, *A Glossary of Indian Figures of Speech,* 29. His interpretation of the position of the figurationists seems sound.

18. *Vakrokti-Jīvita* 1.6 and gloss.

19. *Kāvyālaṃkāra* 2.85.

20. Ibid., 2.30.

21. Ibid., 1.30.

22. Ibid., 1.36.

23. Ibid., 2.87.

24. Ibid., 2.93. For a discussion of the controversy over this question, see Gerow, *A Glossary of Indian Figures of Speech,* 42–48.

25. *Vakrokti-Jīvita* 1.11–13, and 3.4, gloss (Krishnamoorthy ed.) p. 136. All page references are to this edition.

26. Ibid., 3.4, gloss, p. 136. See also the introduction (p. xxxvi) to De's edition of this work.

27. *Vakrokti-Jīvita* 4.

28. Ibid., 1.6: *sālaṃkārasya kāvyatā.*

29. *Kāvyālaṃkāra* 1.16: *śabdārthau sahitau kāvyam;* Rundrata, *Kāvyālaṃkāra* 2.1: *śabdārthau kāvyam;* and Nāmisādhu's commentary in Chowkhamba ed., p. 17: *dvayasyāpi prādhānya-khyāpanārtham.*

30. *Vakrokti-Jīvita* 1.7, gloss, p. 9: *na śabdasyaiva ramaṇīyatā-viśiṣṭasya kevalasya kāvyatvam, nāpyarthasyeti.*

31. Ibid., 1.7, gloss, p. 10.

32. *Kāvyālaṅkārasūtrāṇi (Chowkhamba ed.), p.* 7, "Kāmadhenu" commentary on 1.1.2; see also 3.1.1–3 and commentary.

33. *Dhvanyāloka* 2.7–8, and "Locana," p. 96; *Kāvyapradīpa* 8.1, and commentary, pp. 274–275.

34. "Locana," *Dhvanyāloka* 1.16, p. 58.

35. This approach to linguistic texts will be supported, not only by *mīmāṃsā,* but by modern speech act and discourse analysis theories. For further discussion of the *mīmāṃsā* view, see chap. 8.

36. Bhaṭṭanāyaka is quoted by Abhinavagupta in "Locana," *Dhvanyāloka* 1.5, p. 32. The word *vyāpāra* in the text is best interpreted as "the activity of *rasana* or *rasa* evocation."

37. Ibid., 1.5, p. 32: *vyāpāro hi . . . dhvananātmā rasanā-svabhāvaḥ. . . .*

38. Ibid., 1.1, p. 14.

39. "Abhinavabhāratī," *Nāṭyaśāstra* 1, p. 69.

40. Ibid., 6, pp. 684–685: *kāvye api nāṭyāyamāne eva rasaḥ . . . kāvyam ca nāṭyam eva.*

41. *Nāṭyaśāstra* 6.31, gloss, p. 620.

42. Ibid., 6.35: *evaṃ bhāvā bhāvayanti rasān abhinayais saha;* see also 7.1–3, and gloss, p. 783: *kāvyārthān bhāvayantīti bhāvāḥ;* "Locana," *Dhvanyāloka* 2.4, p. 85: *kāvyaṃ bhāvakaṃ rasān bhāvayati.*

43. *Nāṭyaśāstra* 7.1, gloss.

44. "Abhinavabhāratī," *Nāṭyaśāstra* 6, p. 652: *tat kāvyārtho rasaḥ;* 7, p. 786: *kāvyasyārthāḥ rasāḥ.*

45. "Locana," *Dhvanyāloka* 2.3, p. 79: *na hi tac chūnyaṃ kāvyaṃ kiṃcid asti . . . rasenaiva sarvaṃ jīvati kāvyam. . . .*

46. *Dhvanyāloka* 3.43, gloss, p. 276: *yatra tu rasādīnām aviṣayatvaṃ sa kāvyaprakāro na saṃbhavaty eva . . . satyam.*

47. "Abhinavabhāratī," *Nāṭyaśāstra* 1, p. 111.

48. *Dhvanyāloka* 2.6, gloss, p. 94.

49. Compare Eliot, *Selected Prose,* 52–53: "In truth neither Shakespeare nor Dante did any real thinking—that was not their job." Thought, as "the material enforced upon each to use as the vehicle of feeling, is of no importance." Yeats too thought that literature differs from scientific writing "in being wrought about a mood" (*Essays and Introductions,* 195).

50. "Locana," *Dhvanyāloka* 1.5, p. 31: *tena rasa eva vastuta ātmā, vastvalaṃkāra-dhvanī tu sarvathā rasaṃ prati paryavasyete.*

51. *Dhvanyāloka* 4.5, gloss, p. 301: *alaṃkārāntara-virahe api; Kāvyaprakāśa* 1.4, gloss: *sphuṭālaṃkāra-virahe api na kāvyatvahāniḥ.* Mammaṭa further says that, where there is no *rasa,* poetic figures merely result in a certain oddity of expression. Sometimes they do not help *rasa* even where it is present (8.67, gloss).

52. *Dhvanyāloka* 2.7, and gloss, p. 95.

53. See Viśvanātha, *Sāhityadarpaṇa* (Kane ed.), text, pp. 3–4, and notes, p. 15.

54. *Dhvanyāloka* 4.6, gloss, p. 302: *anapekṣitārthaviśeṣākṣara-racanaiva. . . .*

55. "Locana," *Dhvanyāloka* 1.18, p. 69: *rasaṃ prati vyañjakatvam.* See further chap. 7.

56. *Dhvanyāloka* 1.5, and gloss, pp. 31–32. Also see n. 50 above.

57. *Sāhityadarpaṇa* 1, p. 5: *vākyaṃ rasātmakaṃ kāvyam.*

58. *Vyaktiviveka* (Chowkhamba ed.), pp. 98–104.

59. Ibid., p. 102: *anubhāvavibhāvānāṃ varṇanā kāvyam ucyate.*

60. Ibid., p. 142.

61. Ibid., p. 104: *teṣām vibhāvādirūpatayā rasābhivyakti-hetutvopagamāt.*

62. *Rasagaṅgādhara* (BHU ed.) 1:44–46.

63. See further chap. 7.

64. Beardsley, *The Possibility of Criticism,* 101.

65. "Abhinavabhāratī," *Nāṭyaśāstra* 1, p. 113.

66. See Dickie, *Aesthetics,* chap. 5, and *Art and the Aesthetic,* chap. 5.

67. Culler, *Structuralist Poetics,* 167.

68. Ellis, *The Theory of Literary Criticism,* 42.

69. For criticism of institutional theories, see Beardsley, "Is Art Essentially Institutional?" in *The Aesthetic Point of View,* 125–143. For an elucidation and defense of Dickie's institutional theory, see Sparshott, *The Theory of the Arts,* 564–565, n. 9.

70. "Abhinavabhāratī," *Nāṭyaśāstra* 6, p. 653. See further chap. 9.

71. On the conditions of emotive meaning, see Alston, *Philosophy of Language,* 47.

72. "Abhinavabhāratī," *Nāṭyaśāstra* 6, p. 647: *pratyaya-gocaratāpādanam.*

73. Kumārila, *Ślokavārttikam,* "Codanāsūtram" 222, 266. The actual result produced is not included in the injunctive affix *(vidhi-liṅ).*

74. Hospers (*Meaning and Truth in the Arts,* 157) says that statements in literature "do not generally function as assertions" and that "their function in the poem is actually an evocative one and not an informative one."

75. For a discussion and defense of the view in question, see Reichert, *Making Sense of Literature,* 169–172.

CHAPTER 4
THE LOGIC OF THE EMOTIONS

1. Charlton, *Aesthetics,* 18.
2. Casey, *The Language of Criticism,* 82.
3. For an elucidation of "cause" and "object," see Charlton, *Aesthetics,* 86.
4. Casey, *The Language of Criticism,* 103.
5. *Nāṭyaśāstra,* gloss on 6.31.
6. See *Nāṭyaśāstra* (BHU ed.) 1.7.3, and gloss, p. 792.
7. Rajachudamani Dikshita, *Kāvyadarpaṇa,* p. 140: *yānyālambya viṣayīkṛtya ratyādayo jāyante.*
8. Compare Charlton, *Aesthetics,* 87. Charlton distinguishes between "material cause" and "formal cause": "That which excites a person's emotion, under whatever description we care to apply, is its material object; it is its formal object under the description . . . under which the person moved thinks of it." The material cause of an emotion, like love, would be a young woman, its formal cause the fact that she appears to a man as an object to be desired.
9. Vidyācakravartin's commentary on *Kāvyaprakāśa* (Dwivedi ed.) 4.28, p. 64: *utpādakaṃ kāraṇam.*
10. *Kāvyapradīpa* (Kāvyamālā ed.), p. 61: *upacārāt tatrāpi vibhāvavyavahāraḥ.*
11. Vidyācakravartin, *Kāvyaprakāśa* 4.28, p. 64: *jātopi anuddīpitas san ajātaprāya eva.*
12. Charlton, *Aesthetics,* 88.
13. *Kāvyaprakāśa* 4.28, gloss: *pratīitiyogya; Kāvyapradīpa,* commentary, p. 61: *prakaṭīkurvanti* (they, the *anubhāvas,* exhibit the feelings).
14. *Daśarūpaka* (Adyar ed.) 4.3, p. 170: *anubhāvo vikāras tu bhāvasaṃsūcanātmakaḥ.*
15. "Abhinavabhāratī," *Nāṭyaśāstra* 6, p. 683: *abhinayā anubhāvā eva.*
16. Ibid., 6, p. 716: *ata eva te abhinayā anubhāvāśca.*
17. *Nāṭyaśāstra* 7.1.
18. Ibid., 7.94, gloss, p. 825.
19. *Daśarūpaka* 4.4, and Dhanika's commentary, p. 173.
20. *Kāvyadarpaṇa,* p. 140; *Kāvyapradīpa,* p. 62.

21. "Abhinavabhāratī," *Nāṭyaśāstra* 6, p. 675.

22. *Nāṭyaśāstra* 7.96–100.

23. "Abhinavabhāratī," *Nāṭyaśāstra* 6, p. 668: *sāmagrī (saṃyogas) tu na vyabhicārī.*

24. Olsen, *The Structure of Literary Understanding,* 30.

25. "Abhinavabhāratī," *Nāṭyaśāstra* 6, p. 675.

26. Ibid.

27. *Nāṭyaśāstra* 6–7.

28. "Marmaprakāśa," *Rasagaṅgādhara* 1:155. For further discussion of *śānta rasa,* see "Abhinavabhāratī," *Nāṭyaśāstra* 6, pp. 762–781, "Śānta Prakaraṇam"; *Dhvanyāloka* (Kāvyamāla reprint) 3.26, gloss, and "Locana," pp. 219–221; *Daśarūpaka* 4.35–36, 45 and commentaries, pp. 202–204, 223; Raghavan, *The Number of Rasa-s,* 1–102; Masson and Patwardhan, *Śānta Rasa and Abhinavagupta's Philosophy of Aesthetics,* 91–143.

29. The details are omitted here due to limitations on space. Bharata's description of each mental state (in *Nāṭyaśāstra* 6–7) is quite detailed.

30. See *Rasagaṅgādhara* (BHU ed.) 1, "Bhāvaprakaraṇam," p. 298: *balanāśajanyaṃ duḥkham eva balāpacayaśabdena vivakṣitam (glāniḥ).*

31. See "Abhinavabhāratī," *Nāṭyaśāstra* 6, p. 781: *evaṃ bhaktāv api vācyam;* Raghavan, *The Number of Rasa-s,* 141–153.

32. The distinction observed between fear and fright (in *Saṅgītaratnākara of Śārṅgadeva,* p. 240) cannot be a qualitative difference; it must be one that is due to the conditions and objects *(upādhis)* that produce it.

33. T. S. Eliot speaks of a distinction between the "dominant tone" of a drama and "a number of fleeting feelings, having an affinity to this emotion" ("Tradition and Individual Talent," in *Selected Prose,* 28). Stephen C. Pepper (*Aesthetic Quality,* 109–110) speaks of "the principle of dominant emotion" and that of "alternative strands" constituting "interlocking action patterns specific to that emotion."

34. "Abhinavabhāratī," *Nāṭyaśāstra* 6, pp. 665–666.

35. Ibid., 6, pp. 665, 722.

36. Compare *Rasagaṅgādhara* 1:158.

37. "Abhinavabhāratī," *Nāṭyaśāstra* 6, pp. 667, 722.

38. Ibid., 6, p. 667.

39. *Daśarūpaka* 4.7: *viśeṣāt ābhimukhyena caranto vyabhicāriṇaḥ; Nāṭyaśāstra* 7.28, p. 802.

40. *Daśarūpaka* 4.7, 34; *Nāṭyaśāstra* 7.127, 129.

41. *Rasagaṅgādhara* 1:158.

42. "Abhinavabhāratī," *Nāṭyaśāstra* 6, p. 666.

43. *Nāṭyaśāstra* 6.31, gloss, p. 677: *nānābhāvopagamāt rasa-niṣpattiḥ.*

44. Ibid., 7.126: *na hy ekarasajaṃ kāvyaṃ kiñcid asti;* 7.132: *vimarde rāgam āyāti.*

45. "Abhinavabhāratī," *Nāṭyaśāstra* 6, p. 721.

46. *Dhvanyāloka* 3.21, 22.

47. Ibid., 3.22, pp. 211–212, gloss and "Locana."

48. Joy or jubilation is no doubt, in terms of Bharata's typology, a transient feeling. But, as it is, in this case, felt in the context of love, one may take love as the dominant theme of the sonnet and its dominant tone.

49. *Nāṭyaśāstra* (GOS ed.) 4.28.22.

50. *Daśarūpaka* 4.34, p. 196: Dhanika's commentary; *Rasagaṅgādhara* 1.204, 211–212; *Dhvanyāloka* 3.25–26, and gloss, pp. 218–219.

51. *Dhvanyāloka* 3.20, gloss, p. 208, and "Locana," pp. 206–207.

52. *Daśarūpaka* 4.34, p. 210: Dhanika's commentary. Some Indian *kāvyas* (long poems) have multiple meanings; i.e., they treat different themes simultaneously through multiple meaning words.

53. Ragahavan, *The Number of Rasa-s,* 161. Bharata's culinary analogy should, therefore, not be pressed too closely.

54. Kames, *Elements of Criticism* 1:151–183.

55. Richards, *The Principles of Literary Criticism,* chap. 32.

56. Ibid., 193.

57. Coleridge, *Biographia Literaria,* vol. 2, chap. 14, p. 174.

58. Richards, *The Principles of Literary Criticism,* 199n.

59. Ibid., 194.

60. Adams, *Strains of Discord,* 13.

61. Compare Nowottny, *The Language Poets Use,* 138.

62. Richards, *Coleridge on Imagination,* 94.

63. Warren, "Pure and Impure Poetry." 87.

64. See Eliot, "Poetry and Philosophy," in *Selected Prose,* 50–52, and *Knowledge and Experience in the Philosophy of F. H. Bradley,* 18–20. In the book on Bradley, Eliot states that thought and feeling are not separate and isolable aspects or phases; rather, they imply each other.

65. See Styan, *The Dark Comedy;* Hofstadter, "The Tragicomic."

66. See Esslin, *The Theatre of the Absurd,* 205.

CHAPTER 5
MODES OF MEANING: METAPHOR

1. *Kāvyaprakāśa* 2.7: *sākṣāt saṃketitam.*

2. Ibid., 2.7, gloss.

3. See further Raja, *Indian Theories of Meaning,* 157–159.

4. Bhartṛhari, *Vākyapadīya* 2.266.

5. *Kāvyaprakāśa* 2.9, gloss, p. 18 (Jha ed.).

6. Mukulabhaṭṭa, *Abhidhāvṛttimātṛkā* (Chowkhamba ed.), Kārikā 1, p. 2.

7. Udayana, *Nyāyakusumāñjali* (Chowkhamba ed.) 3.12, p. 380.

8. Subrahmanya Sastri, *Śābdataraṅgiṇī,* pp. 132–133: *śakye tātparyasya lakṣaṇātva-abhāvāt aśakye tātparyaṃ lakṣaṇā; prayoktur abhiprāyo lakṣaṇā.*

9. Gāgābhaṭṭa, *Bhāṭṭacintāmaṇi* (Chowkhamba ed.), p. 58; Raja, *Indian Theories of Meaning,* 260.

10. *Bhāṭṭacintāmani,* p. 58.

11. "Locana," *Dhvanyāloka* (Kāvyamālā rpt.) 1.21, p. 70.

12. *Laghumañjūṣā,* quoted in *Śābdataraṅgiṇī,* p. 122.

13. *Śābdataraṅgiṇī,* p. 120.

14. See Raja, *Indian Theories of Meaning,* 233–239.

15. "Tantravārttikam," *Mīmāṃsādarśana* (Anandasram ed.), Sūtra, 1.4.22, p. 313: *abhidheyāvinābhūte,* etc. *Kāvyaprakāśa* 2.12: *sādṛśya* and *saṃbandhāntara* are the two bases of classification. Compare Aristotle, *Poetics* 1457b, on metaphor.

16. See the discussion in *Nyāyasiddhāntamuktāvalī* (Chowkhamba ed.), Kārikā 82, p. 285: *lakṣaṇā śakyasaṃbandhaḥ, tātparyānupapattitaḥ;* Jagannātha, *Rasagaṅgādhara* (BHU ed.) 2, pp. 154–157.

17. For a discussion of connotational meanings, see chap. 6.

18. *Kāvyaprakāśa* 2.9, and 2.10, 15–16, gloss. *Pratāparudrīya* (Raghavan ed.), p. 31, Kumārasvāmin's commentary: *anena saṃbandha-anupapatti-prayojanānāṃ trayāṇām api lakṣaṇābījatvam uktam.*

19. *Śābdataraṅgiṇī,* p. 134: *śakyaniṣṭhaḥ aśakyasaṃbandho lakṣaṇā; śakyārthaḥ lakṣyārtha-smārakaḥ.*

20. Kumārila, *Tantravārttika,* quoted in Raja, *Indian Theories of Meaning,* 249, n. 1: *ajahatsvārthāḥ sarvāḥ śabdapravṛttayaḥ.*

21. Evidently, the theory characterized by Beardsley as the supervenience theory of metaphor is wrong. This theory assumes that metaphoric meaning is something extraneous to literal meaning; the literal meaning is overridden. See Beardsley, *Aesthetics,* 136.

22. Beardsley, *Thinking Straight,* (1975), 162. See also *Tantravārttika* (Jha trans.), 1.440–446.

23. *svārthatyāge samāne api saha tenānyalakṣaṇā.* For classifications of *lakṣaṇā* varieties based on degrees of feature cancellation, see Raja, *Indian Theories of Meaning,* 249–254.

24. A term used in logic, "counterpositive" is that whose existence is denied: *yasya abhāvaḥ sa pratiyogī.*

25. See *Rasagaṅgādhara* 2, "Lakṣaṇānirūpaṇam," esp. pp. 168, 192.

26. *Śābdataraṅgiṇī,* p. 134, "Ṭippaṇī"; p. 142.

27. *Bhāṭṭacintāmaṇi,* p. 50. This position of the advocates of the semantics of the word agrees with the view of Max Black, who calls the metaphoric word "focus" and designates the remainder of the sentence the "frame." Metaphoric meaning for Black is the result of an interaction between the focal word and the literal frame. See Black, "Metaphor," 220, 228.

28. For a summary of the various views, see Jayanta Bhaṭṭa, *Nyāyamañjarī* (Bhattacharyya trans.), pp. 318–327.

29. See Raja, "Pāṇini's Attitude towards Lakṣaṇā."

30. *yat paraḥ śabdaḥ sa śabdārthaḥ.*

31. *Śābdataraṅgiṇī,* pp. 127–129.

32. *Abidhāvṛttimātṛkā,* p. 24.

33. *Dīrgha-dīrgha-vyāpāra* has its source in *Mahābhāṣya.* This concept is later attributed to the Prābhākara school of *mīmāṃsā.* But this school does recognize the activity of *lakṣaṇā.*

34. *Vākyapadīya* 2.304–313; Raja, *Indian Theories of Meaning,* 272–273.

35. *Vākyapadīya* 2.336; Iyer, *Bhartṛhari,* 197–198.
36. *Vyaktiviveka* (Chowkhamba ed.), pp. 114, 121, 140, 147.
37. *Śābara-Bhāṣya* (Jha trans.) 1:156.
38. "Locana," *Dhvanyāloka* 1.21, p. 66.
39. Tindall, *The Literary Symbol,* 5, 12.
40. Eliot, "Hamlet," in *Selected Prose,* 102.
41. Tindall, *The Literary Symbol,* 12, 13.
42. *Kāvyaprakāśa* 2.11, and gloss.
43. Bādarāyaṇa, *Vedānta Sūtras* 1.4.1: *śarīra-rūpaka-vinyasta-gṛhīte darśayati;* 1.2.24: *rūpopanyāsācca.* For an explanation of the symbolism of the sacrificial animal with four horns *(catvāri sṛngā),* see also *Śābara-Bhāṣya* (Jha trans.) 1:77, 83.
44. Levin (*The Semantics of Metaphor,* chap. 7, esp. pp. 127, 132) says that "nonexistent" entities and personified objects described in poetry should be construed "phenomenalistically" or literally and that they call for a "shift in world orientation." While this is true of poetic statements of the "mythical" kind, it is not, as Levin argues, true of poetic metaphor in general. All metaphors, including poetic metaphors, can be interpreted figuratively.
45. See Beardsley, *The Aesthetic Point of View,* chap. 15; and also Searle, "Metaphor." Searle's account of metaphor is remarkably close to the Indian theory.
46. See further chap. 8.
47. Cohen, "Notes on Metaphor."
48. Margolis, *Art and Philosophy,* chap. 13, esp. pp. 290, 301–302, 305.
49. Cohen, "Notes on Metaphor," 252–254.
50. See chap. 8.
51. Margolis, *Art and Philosophy,* 297.
52. Davidson ("What Metaphors Mean") argues that a metaphor "doesn't say anything beyond its literal meaning" and that what distinguishes it is an effect of its use. There is no such thing as a metaphorical "meaning." For Derrida, on the other hand, all meaning is metaphorical; there is simply no literal meaning. For a critique of these extreme views and a defense of the literal-metaphorical distinction, see Novitz, "Metaphor, Derrida, and Davidson."

CHAPTER 6
SUGGESTION

1. *Kāvyaprakāśa* (Jha ed.) 2.10, gloss, p. 22.
2. "Locana," *Dhvanyāloka* (Kāvyamālā reprint) 3.33, p. 238: *arthāntaratvaṃ saṃbandhi-saṃbandhatvam anupayukta-samayatvam iti vyaṅgyatāyāṃ nibandhanam;* also gloss on the Kārikā, p. 234: *abhidheya-sāmarthyākṣiptaḥ saṃbandhi-saṃbandhī.*
3. *Kāvyaprakāśa* 2.18.
4. See Subrahmanya Sastri, *Śābdataraṅgiṇī,* p. 152; Rajachudamani Dikshita, *Kāvyadarpaṇa,* pp. 75–80.
5. *Dhvanyāloka* 1.20: *mukhyāṃ vṛttiṃ parityajya. . . .*

6. *Kāvyaprakāśa* 3.23.
7. Ibid., 2.14–18; *Kāvyapradīpa* (Kāvyamālā ed.), pp. 39–42.
8. *Kāvyadarpaṇa,* p. 80.
9. On "connotation," see Beardsley, *Aesthetics,* 125, 150–151, and *Thinking Straight* (1950), chap. 3, (1975), chap. 5.
10. *Vākyapadīya* 2.120–134; Iyer, *Bhartṛhari,* 228–232.
11. Beardsley distinguishes between "necessary" properties, which are "designated," and "nonnecessary" or "attendant" properties, which are "connoted." See *Thinking Straight* (1975), 162.
12. Beardsley, *Thinking Straight* (1950), 70.
13. *Dhvanyāloka* 3.33, gloss, p. 246: *prakaraṇādyavacchedena tasya pratīter itarathā tvapratīteḥ.*
14. *Arthasaṃgraha* (Nirnayasagar ed.), p. 55: "prakaraṇa-nirūpaṇam."
15. See "Tantravārttikam" (Sanskrit text) on *Jaimini Sūtra,* 2.2.48, *Mīmāṃsā-darśanam* (Anandasram ed.), pp. 444–445.
16. *Śabdataraṅgiṇī,* p. 143; Gadādhara, *Śaktivāda,* pp. 2–3; *Nyāyamañjarī* (Bhattacharyya trans.), pp. 101–102.
17. "Locana," *Dhvanyāloka* 1.5, p. 32: Bhaṭṭanāyaka's objection: *sarvatra tarhi kāvya-vyavahāraḥ syāt;* 1.4, p. 20; 1.13, p. 39.
18. *Dhvanyāloka* 3.33, gloss and "Locana," p. 244.
19. Ibid., 1.4, gloss, p. 19.
20. "Locana," *Dhvanyāloka* 1.4, pp. 19–20.
21. This was Bhaṭṭanāyaka's objection, cited in "Locana" on the example, *Dhvanyāloka,* p. 23.
22. *Dhvanyāloka* 1.16, gloss and "Locana," pp. 58–59.
23. Ibid., 1.21: *vācakatvāśrayeṇaiva guṇavṛttir vyavasthitā;* and "Locana"; 1.13, gloss, p. 40. The figurative categories are *vācya-vācaka-mātrāśrayiṇaḥ,* based on the relation of the conventional sense to the denotative word. See also ibid., 2.27.
24. Ibid., 1.16, p. 54.
25. Ibid., 2.26.
26. Ibid., 2.28, gloss, pp. 134–135.
27. Udbhaṭa, *Kāvyālaṃkāra-Sāra-Saṃgraha* (BORI ed.), pp. 85–89, Indurāja's commentary.
28. "Locana," *Dhvanyāloka* 2.21, p. 66.
29. *Dhvanyāloka* 3.33, gloss, p. 241, and "Locana": *yad ubhayāśrayatvena vyavasthānat tadubhaya-vailakṣaṇyam.*
30. *Kāvyādarśa* 2.310; *Kāvyaprakāśa* 9.84; *Kāvyālaṃkāra-Sāra-Saṃgraha* 4.9.
31. *Kāvyaprakāśa* 2.19.
32. On unity of meaning, see further chap. 8.
33. *Vākyapadīya* 2.314–316; Raja, *Indian Theories,* 48–59.
34. Empson, *Seven Types of Ambiguity,* 151–158.
35. Ibid., 151, 157.
36. *Rasagaṅgādhara* (BHU ed.) 2:29–31.
37. *Vākyapadīya* (Iyer trans.) 2.300–303 and notes, pp. 130–131.
38. Empson, *Seven Types of Ambiguity,* 77.

39. Ibid., 103.

40. Empson, *The Structure of Complex Words,* 54. According to Empson, "harbor" is the major or "head sense" of "port" and "drink" the minor sense. In any case, what is important is that the two senses must be related somehow, and the implied metaphor is what relates them.

41. See the discussion in Appaya Dīkṣita, *Vṛttivārttika* (Kāvyamālā ed.), pp. 12-13, 15. Also Jagannātha, *Rasagaṅgādhara* 2, "Nānārthaśabdaprakaraṇam," pp. 15-44; *Śābdataraṅgiṇī,* pp. 148, 150.

42. *Dhvanyāloka* 2.22, gloss, p. 121: *asaṃbaddhārtha-abhidhāyitvaṃ mā prasāṅkṣīt. . . .*

43. *yat paraḥ śabdaḥ sa śabdārthaḥ.* See also *Tantravārttika,* n. 15.

44. "Locana," *Dhvanyāloka* 1.4, p. 19: *vākyārthe tātparya śaktiḥ parasparānvite;* 2.28, p. 141: *ata eva samāptāyām eva abhidhāyām.*

45. According to Abhinavagupta, there are thus four categories of meaning: word meaning *(abhidhā),* sentence meaning *(tātparya),* secondary meaning *(lakṣaṇā),* and suggestion *(vyañjanā).* See "Locana," *Dhvanyāloka* 1.4, pp. 19-20.

46. *Daśarūpaka* (Adyar ed.), p. 206: Dhanika's commentary.

47. See the discussion in *Kāvyaprakāśa* (Jha ed.), v. 47, gloss, pp. 143, 145. Most of Beardsley's examples under "Suggestion and Slanting" (*Thinking Straight* [1975], 169-172) would be subsumed under implicit assumptions and so forth and would not be regarded as suggestion in terms of the *dhvani* theory.

48. *Vākyapadīya* 2.445ff. Bhartṛhari does not, however, recognize elliptical sentences. For him, even single-word utterances like "Tree!" make complete sentences (1.325-326). Compare Wittgenstein, *Philosophical Investigations,* 19-20.

49. *Kāvyapradīpa,* pp. 158-159.

50. *Vākyapadīya* 2.310; 2.314: *na rūpādeva kevalam.*

51. *Kāvyaprakāśa* 5.47, gloss, p. 144: *upātta-śabdārtha eva tātparyam.* This is also the Nyāya view of purport. See Raja, *Indian Theories of Meaning,* 220-221.

52. *Daśarūpaka,* p. 212: *tātparyaṃ na tulādhṛtam.*

53. *Pratāparudrīya,* p. 29: *tātparyārthopi vyaṅgyārtha eva, na punaḥ pṛthagbhūtaḥ;* also commentary on p. 30. Bhoja, too, identifies *tātparya* with *dhvani.* See Raghavan, *Bhoja's Sṛṅgāra Prakāśa,* 157. See also Bahurūpamiśra's commentary on *Daśarūpaka* (Varanasi ed.) 4.37, pp. 122, 124.

54. See nn. 17 and 18 above.

55. *Dhvanyāloka* 1.4, gloss, pp. 29-30.

56. *Sāhityadarpaṇa* (Chowkhamba ed.), 5.1, gloss, p. 338: *na ca saṃketito rasādiḥ. . . .*

57. *Kāvyaprakāśa* 4.25, gloss, p. 50: *na khalu vibhāvānubhāva-vyabhicāriṇa eva rasaḥ, api tu rasas tair iti.*

58. *Dhvanyāloka* 3.33, gloss, pp. 236-237; 2.3, gloss, p. 81: *rasādir artho hi saheva vācyenāvabhāsate.*

59. See Beardsley, *Aesthetics,* 121-122, 147-148; Empson, *The Structure of Complex Words,* chap. 1.

60. The term "import" corresponds to the Sanskrit *pratīyamānārtha,* or whatever is implied, while "purport" *(tātparya)* is understood as the comprehensive intent of a sentence, whether explicit or implied.

61. *Dhvanyāloka* 3.16, gloss, p. 197: *na tu (nanu) cārthasāmarthyākṣepyā rasādayaḥ*. . . . Compare Beardsley, *Thinking Straight* (1975), 181–182: "The emotive force of a term . . . depends in large part upon its meaning."

62. "Locana," *Dhvanyāloka* 3.4, p. 161: *tena rasapratītir vibhāvāder eva*. . . .

63. For example, Stern, quoted in Empson, *The Structure of Complex Words*, 22.

64. *Dhvanyāloka* 3.16, gloss, p. 198: *rasādi-samarpaṇa-sāmarthyam eva naisargikaṃ śabdānāṃ viśeṣa iti;* also "Locana" on p. 197; and "Dīdhiti" commentary in Chowkhamba ed., pp. 349–351.

65. *Dhvanyāloka* 2.23, gloss, p. 124: *śabdavyāpāraṃ vinaiva.*

66. Empson, *The Structure of Complex Words*, 55.

67. *Dhvanyāloka* 3.33, gloss, p. 251: *ataśca vyaṅgyapratītir liṅgapratītir eva*. . . . See also Jagadīśa, *Śabdaśaktiprakāśikā* (Chowkhamba ed.), pp. 144–154; Gadādhara, *Śaktivāda* (Chowkhamba ed.), pp. 2–3.

68. *Vyaktiviveka* (Chowkhamba ed.), p. 70: *vastusvabhāva evāyam; Kāvyadarpaṇa*, p. 144: *vastusvabhāvāyattam.*

69. *Daśarūpaka* 4.37; "Laghutīkā," p. 214: *rasoddeśena prayuktānaṃ (vākyānāṃ) rasaparatvam eva bhavati.*

70. *Daśarūpaka*, pp. 211–212: Dhanika's commentary.

71. *Kāvyālaṃkāra-Sāra-Saṃgraha*, p. 89: *ataśca rasādiṣu abhivyañjakatvasya na arthāntaratā.*

72. *Dhvanyāloka* 3.33, gloss, p. 228: *tatpratītyoḥ kāryakāraṇabhāvena vyasvasthānāt.*

73. *Kumārasaṃbhava* 4.1–4.

74. "Locana," *Dhvanyāloka* 2.3, p. 80: *vibhāvānubhāvau tāvat svaśabdavācyau eva.*

75. *Dhvanyāloka* 1.13.

76. See further chap. 7.

77. *Dhvanyāloka* 3.33, gloss, p. 250: *tathaiva vyañjakatvaṃ vācakānāṃ śabdānāṃ avācakānāṃ ca gītadhvanīnāṃ aśabdarūpāṇāṃ ca ceṣṭādīnāṃ*. . . .

78. Beardsley, *Aesthetics*, 283.

79. See ibid., chap. 7.

80. Jesperson, *The Philosophy of Grammar*, 309.

81. Pound, *Selected Poems*, 55.

82. Beardsley, *Aesthetics*, 123.

83. *Dhvanyāloka* 3.33, gloss, 251.

84. Beardsley, *Aesthetics*, 123, 126.

85. Ibid., 125.

86. Ibid., 127, 128.

87. Bhaṭṭanāyaka, quoted in "Locana," *Dhvanyāloka* 1.1, p. 14: *aṅgatvaṃ (aṃśatvaṃ) na rūpatā.*

CHAPTER 7
STYLE AND MEANING

1. Daṇḍin, *Kāvyādarśa* 1.101; 2.368: *anantam alaṃkriyānām.*

2. This is true of the Russian Formalists and the Prague school, of the neo-

Firthian school of linguistics, as well as of such others as A. A. Hill and Samuel Levin *(Linguistic Structures in Poetry)*. For other references, see below.

3. *Vakrokti-Jīvita* (Krishnamoorthy ed.) 1.10, and gloss, p. 20.

4. See Lemon and Reis, trans., *Russian Formalist Criticism;* Garvin, trans., *A Prague School Reader on Esthetics, Literary Structure, and Style.*

5. Shklovsky, "Art as Technique," in Lemon and Reis, *Russian Formalist Criticism,* 18.

6. *Vakrokti-Jīvita* 1.6, and gloss: *sālaṃkārasya kāvyatā;* 1.10: *tayoḥ punar alaṃkṛtir vakroktir eva.*

7. *Kāvyādarśa* 1.101–102.

8. Lahiri, *Concepts of Rīti and Guṇa in Sanskrit Poetics,* 58. This is the view expressed by Taruṇavācaspati. See Raghavan, *Bhoja's Śṛṅgāra Prakāśa,* 293–294.

9. *Kāvyālaṅkāra-Sūtrāṇi* (Chowkhamba ed.) 1.2.8: *viśeṣo guṇātmā.*

10. Bharata was the first writer to specify the ten style qualities. After him, Bhāmaha mentions three qualities as the general characteristics of good poetry, but he does not connect them to poetic style. Daṇḍin, Vāmana, and Rudraṭa list the qualities as ten. Subsequent writers add to the list. In Bhoja, there are twenty-four qualities of sound and as many of sense.

11. *Kāvyālaṅkāra* 1.2.7, "Kāmadhenu" commentary, p. 15: *artheṣu aupacārikī rītir aṅgīkartavyā.*

12. *Kāvyālaṅkāra* 1.2.6.

13. Ibid., 3.1.1–3: *kāvyaśobhāyāḥ kartāro dharmā guṇāḥ. tadatiśaya-hetavas tu alaṃkārāh. pūrve nityāh.*

14. *Sāhityadarpaṇa* 9.1: *padasaṃghaṭanā rītiḥ;* Rudraṭa, *Kāvyālaṅkāra* (Chowkhamba ed.), Nāmisādhu's commentary on 2.6, p. 23: [*rītayaḥ*] *śabdāśrayā guṇā iti.*

15. See *Dhvanyāloka* (Kāvyamālā ed.) 3.46–47. "Locana" on these Kārikās (p. 290) states that all style features resolve into characteristic qualities of the *rasas: ritir hi guṇeṣveva paryavasāyitā . . . guṇāśca rasaparyavasāyina eveti.*

16. For Jagannātha, too, the structural beauty of a composition can be a matter of independent interest, regardless of whether *rasa* is present in it. Style qualities are also not the exclusive properties of the *rasas (rasamātra-dharmāḥ).* See *Rasagaṅgādhara* (BHU ed.) 1.234, 381.

17. "Locana," *Dhvanyāloka* 1.2, p. 15.

18. *Sāhityadarpaṇa* 1.3; see also *Dhvanyāloka* 3.2–4.

19. "Locana," *Dhvanyāloka* 1.5, p. 31: *tena rasa eva vastuta ātmā. . . .* The *dhvani* critics to not of course say that suggestion is a formal embellishment. They rather maintain equivocally that all suggestion must culminate in *rasa* while yet declaring that it is the soul of poetry.

20. Darbyshire, *A Description of English,* 159.

21. Ohmann, "Generative Grammars and the Concept of Literary Styles," in *Linguistics and Literary Style,* ed. Freeman, 268.

22. Enkvist, "On Defining Style," in *Linguistics and Style,* ed. Spencer, 28ff.

23. Compare Hirsch, "Stylistics and Synonymity," in *The Aims of Interpretation,* 56: "Normally by style we mean the linguistic form of an utterance considered apart from meaning."

24. Compare Beardsley's discussion of this question in *Aesthetics,* 134–144, 430–436. Although Beardsley does not favor the literalist view of metaphor, he does admit that metaphor can be analyzed and paraphrased.

25. Beardsley, "Verbal Style and Illocutionary Action," in *The Concept of Style,* ed. Lang, 161.

26. Ibid., 158–159.

27. Beardsley, *Aesthetics,* 223.

28. *Aṣṭādhyāyī,* a book of descriptive grammar, by Pāṇini (ca. 400 B.C.); commentaries of Kātyāyana (ca. 300 B.C.), Patañjali (ca. 150 B.C.: *Mahābhāṣya*), and Kayyaṭa (ca. A.D. 1000).

29. *Ślokavārattika,* "Pratyakṣa-Sūtram," vv. 185, 208.

30. *Nyāya-Mañjarī* (Bhattacharyya trans.), pp. 322–324.

31. *Vākyapadīya* 2.434.

32. Wittgenstein, *Philosophical Investigations,* 244.

33. Kenny, *Wittgenstein,* 183.

34. "Locana," *Dhvanyāloka* 3.3–4, p. 161. See n. 52 below.

35. Compare Richard Ohmann's view of style as "epistemic choice." For Ohmann, style features correlate with certain conceptual orientations; they are a key to a writer's mode of experience. See "Prolegomena to the Analysis of Prose Style," 398–411.

36. See Ogden and Richards, *The Meaning of Meaning,* chap. 1; Beardsley, *Aesthetics,* 228; Black, "Language and Reality," 729.

37. Hymes, "Phonological Aspects of Style."

38. Ibid., 113.

39. Sparshott, *The Structure of Aesthetics,* 346.

40. Compare Nowottny, *The Language Poets Use,* 14. Nowottny remarks that, though the sound structure cannot "mean or do by itself," it does so "in conjunction with the sense." The "sound-structure makes the reader feel . . . what the sense of the words calls up."

41. Hymes, "Phonological Aspects of Style," 110.

42. Beardsley, *Aesthetics,* 235.

43. Davie, *Articulate Energy,* chap. 7.

44. Leech, "Linguistics and the Figures of Rhetoric," 146.

45. It is debatable whether Bacon's essays should be regarded as literature in the sense that Shakespeare's plays or Donne's poems are literature. However, in terms of the theory of literature I am defending here, they should be classed as discursive writing rather than as literature proper.

46. For a discussion of the stylistic aspects of syntax, see Turner, *Stylistics,* chap. 3.

47. "Locana," *Dhvanyāloka* 3.1, p. 150: *śabdastu na kadācid vyaṅgyaḥ, api tu vyañjaka eveti.*

48. *Dhvanyāloka* 3.2.

49. Ibid., 3.3–4.

50. "Locana," *Dhvanyāloka* 1.4, p. 18: *arthasāmarthyāt pratīyamānāvagatiḥ. śabdaśaktiḥ kevalam avāntara-karaṇa iti.*

51. Ibid., 3.3–4, p. 163: *vibhāvādi-saṃyoga-prāṇatvāt;* 3.16, p. 189: "Rasa is

manifested by all the elements of a composition, ranging from phonemes to the entire work—either directly through the description of the emotive factors *(vibhāvādi-pratipādana-dvāreṇa)* or indirectly through the suggestive power of phonemes, words, etc."

52. Ibid., 3.3–4. pp. 160–161: *yadyapi vibhāvānubhāva-vyabhicāri-pratīti-saṃpad eva . . . sahakāryeva. . . . na tu varṇair eva rasābhivyaktiḥ. . . . tena vibhāvādayo yadā viśiṣṭena kenāpi padenārpyamāṇāḥ rasa-camatkāra-vidhāyino bhavanti tadā padasyaivāsau mahimā samarpyata iti bhāvaḥ.*

53. *Dhvanyāloka* 3.6, and gloss, p. 165.

54. Hill, *Constituent and Pattern in Poetry,* 27.

55. Hill, "Poetry and Stylistics," in *Essays on the Language of Literature,* ed. Chatman and Levin, 391.

56. Compare Sinclair's "Taking a Poem to Pieces," an analysis of Philip Larkin's "First Sights." Sinclair shows how the grammatical and other patterns in the poem give it an "exceptionally good fit." But nothing is said about the meaning of the poem and its intrinsic interest.

57. *Dhvanyāloka* 2.17, gloss, p. 106: *tasmān na teṣāṃ bahiraṅgatvaṃ rasābhivyaktau.*

58. Ibid., 3.4, gloss, p. 163.

59. Ibid., 3.4, gloss and "Locana," p. 163.

60. Homer, *The Iliad,* 409.

61. Darbyshire, *A Description of English,* 91–97.

62. Hirsch ("Stylistics and Synonymity," in *The Aims of Interpretations,* 67) observes, "We cannot, in fact, decide whether a trait of style is part of meaning until we know what the meaning is. Our knowledge of meaning determines the semantic functionality of style, not vice versa."

63. Compare Fowler, "Linguistic Theory and the Study of Literature," in *Essays on Style and Literature,* 11.

64. Rulon Wells ("Nominal and Verbal Style," 215) observes that "underlying the very notion of style is a postulate of *independence of matter from manner*" and "the so-called fitness of manner to matter, or consonance with it."

65. On the problem of paraphrase, see Beardsley, *Aesthetics,* 432–437. Beardsley observes that "there is no conclusive argument against the possibility, in principle, of paraphrase" (435). The "use" theorist of language would of course reject paraphrasability, for to say that meaning is translatable into alternative signs is to imply that there is a "meaning" as distinct from "use." See, e.g., Robinson, *The New Grammarians' Funeral,* 115–116. Robinson's objections to paraphrasability stem from his rejection of semantic universals and of the referentiality of language. The most widely held Indian view on this question, except for the Buddhist argument, is that all words are referential and mean the universal. According to Bhartṛhari, even nonreferring expressions--articles, prepositions, and so forth—have referential meanings: they refer to notions of time, position, relation, and so on. For a fuller discussion, see Raja, *Indian Theories of Meaning,* 69–94.

66. On the question of synonymy and semantic characterization, see Harris, *Synonymy and Linguistic Analysis.*

CHAPTER 8
THE LOGIC OF INTERPRETATION

1. For a clarification of these terms, see Beardsley, *Aesthetics,* 129–130, 401–404, and "Some Problems of Critical Interpretation," 352–353; Sparshott, *The Concept of Criticism,* chap. 21, and *The Theory of the Arts,* 246–262.

2. Hirsch, *Validity in Interpretation,* 8, 57, 211.

3. Mādhava Āchārya, *Sarva-Darśana-Saṃgraha* (Cowell and Gough trans.), p. 184.

4. *Jaimini Sūtra* 1.2.40: *aviśiṣtas tu vākyārthaḥ.*

5. *Śābara-Bhāṣya,* Sūtra 1.3.30: *ya eva laukikāḥ . . . ta eva vaidikāḥ;* (Jha trans.) 1:116–117.

6. *Jaimini Sūtra* 10.3.44: *śabdārthaś cāpi lokavat; Śābara-Bhāṣya* (Jha trans.) 1:144.

7. Kumārila, *Ślokavārttika* (Jha trans.), "Saṃbandhākṣepa," v. 11, p. 255.

8. Raja, *Indian Theories of Meaning,* 20.

9. *Jaimini Sūtra* 1.1.5: *anapekṣatvāt; Śābara-Bhāṣya* (Jha trans.), p. 9.

10. *Śābara-Bhāṣya,* Sūtra 1.1.5: *śāstraṃ śabdavijñānād asannikṛṣṭe arthe jñānam;* (Jha trans.), p. 15.

11. *Śābara-Bhāṣya,* Sūtra 1.1.2; (Jha trans.) 1:4.

12. *Ślokavārttikam* (Sanskrit text), "Śabda," vv. 93–94; Jayanta Bhaṭṭa, *Nyāyamañjarī* (Bhattacharyya trans.), pp. 316–324.

13. *Ślokavārttikam,* "Saṃbandhākṣepa," v. 1: *svārthe vaktranapekṣatvāt padārtha-padabuddhivat.*

14. *Nyāyamañjarī,* p. 484.

15. Udayana, *Nyāyakusumāñjali* (Chowkhamba ed.), p. 513: *svatantra-puruṣa-praṇītatvaṃ hi pauruṣeyatvam.*

16. *Nyāyadarśana* (Chowkhamba ed.) 2.1.53, and Vātsyāyana's commentary, pp. 319–320; Ṣastri, *A Primer of Indian Logic,* 30.

17. *Ślokavārttikam,* "Autpattika Sūtra," v. 16, and "Śabda," v. 52.

18. Jha, *The Prābhākara School of Pūrva Mīmāṃsā,* 65.

19. On poetic truth, see further chap. 9.

20. *Nyāyamañjarī,* p. 326.

21. Āpadeva, *Mīmāṃsānyāyaprakāśa,* p. 2.

22. *Śābara-Bhāṣya* (Jha trans.) 1:9.

23. *Sabdaprāmāṇikā vayam. yac chabda āha tad asmākaṃ pramāṇam.*

24. Hirsch, *Validity in Interpretation,* 27, 78, 91.

25. Vācaspati Miśra, *Bhāmatī* on "Brahma Sūtra," 1.1.1: *na hy āgamāḥ sahasramapi ghaṭaṃ paṭayitum īśate.*

26. Hirsch, *Validity in Interpretation,* 3.

27. Wimsatt and Beardsley, "The Intentional Fallacy," 5.

28. Kumārila, *Tantravārttika* (Jha trans.) 2:994–999.

29. "Tantravārttikam" (Sanskrit text) on *Jaimini Sūtra* 3.1.13, *Mīmāṃsādar-śanam* (Anandasram ed.), p. 67: *puruṣa-sthānīyo hi vede vidhāyakaḥ, puru-ṣecchā-sthānīyaṃ vidhitvam.*

30. See Booth, *The Rhetoric of Fiction,* esp. 71–76.

31. On the question of intention, see Reichert, *Making Sense of Literature,* chap. 3; Anscombe, *Intention.*

32. On meaning and intention, see Searle, *Speech Acts,* 42–50.

33. Alston, *Philosophy of Language,* 41.

34. Searle, *Speech Acts,* 48.

35. Close, "*Don Quixote* and 'The Intentional Fallacy,' " 38. See also Skinner, "Motives, Intentions, and the Interpretation of Texts."

36. Compare Black, "Meaning and Intention"; Dickie, "Meaning and Intention"; Sparshott, *The Concept of Criticism,* 169, and *The Theory of the Arts,* 249; Beardsley, *The Possibility of Criticism,* chap. 1, and *The Aesthetic Point of View,* chap. 11.

37. *Bhāṭṭacintāmaṇi,* p. 52.

38. Ibid.: *tatpratītīcchayā vaktrā anusaṃhitatvam; Śābdataraṅgiṇī,* p. 42: *tātparyaṃ tadartha-pratītīcchayā uccaritatvam.*

39. *Nyāyakośa,* quoted in Raja, *Indian Theories of Meaning,* 177 n. 1: *tātparya-niścayaḥ kāraṇam.*

40. *Śābdataraṅgiṇī,* p. 132: *aśakye tātparyam.*

41. See the discussion in Appayya Dīkṣita, *Vṛttivārttika,* p. 15; *Nyāyasiddhāntamuktāvalī* (Chowkhamba ed.), pp. 315–316.

42. Jagadīśa, *Śabdaśaktiprakāśikā* (Chowkhamba ed.) and "Rāmabhadrī," p. 27: *tātparyānumāpakatvena prakaraṇa-jñānasya hetutvam* (my summation).

43. *Bhāṭṭacintāmaṇi,* p. 52: *tajjñānāsaṃbhavāt.*

44. Nārāyaṇa, *Mānameyodaya,* p. 109: *vākyārtha-nirūpaṇa-purassarameva nirūpaṇīyam iti.*

45. *Bhāṭṭacintāmaṇi,* p. 52: *taddhetor iti nyāyena tasya vaiyarthyāt.*

46. *Mānameyodaya,* p. 108.

47. Ibid., p. 107: *svamartham abhidhātuṃ kiṃ samarthā na padāvalī.*

48. Bhāṭṭacintāmaṇi, p. 52: *Siddhāntamuktāvalī,* p. 316.

49. *Vedāntaparibhāṣā,* p. 82.

50. Compare Maxwell, *Maxwell on the Interpretation of Statutes,* 28: "The object of all interpretation is to discover the intention of parliament, 'but the intention of parliament must be deduced from the language used.' " See also Wittgenstein, *Philosophical Investigations,* par. 337: "An intention is embedded in its situation, in human customs and institutions."

51. See *Dhvanyāloka* (Kāvyamālā reprint) 3.33, gloss, p. 252.

52. *Vākyapadīya* 2.433: *atyanta-yata-śaktitvāc chabda eva nibandhanam.*

53. *Jaimini Sūtra* 1.2.30: *avyavasthā vidhīnāṃ syāt.*

54. Ibid., 2.1.46: *arthaikatvād ekaṃ vākyaṃ sākāṅkṣaṃ ced vibhāge syāt.* For elucidation of *artha* in the *Sūtra,* see *Śābara-Bhāṣya* (Jha trans.) 1:213–215. There is also the *mīmāṃsā* maxim: *ekārtha-pratipādakatvaṃ vākyam.*

55. *Jaimini Sūtra* 2.1.47: *sameṣu vākyabhedaḥ syāt.*

56. For a discussion of the various views, see Subba Rao, *The Philosophy of a Sentence and Its Parts.*

57. For modern discussions, see Kinneavy, *A Theory of Discourse.*

58. *Jaimini Sūtra* 1.1.2: *codanālakṣaṇo artho dharmaḥ.*

59. Ibid., 1.2.1: *āmnāyasya kriyārthatvād ānarthakyaṃ atadarthānām.*

60. Ibid., 1.2.7: *vidhinā tvekavākyatvāt stutyarthena vidhīnāṃ syuḥ.*

61. Śaṅkara, in his commentary on *Brahma Sūtras,* contests this position and declares that the purport of the Vedānta texts *(brahma-vākyas)* is just to impart right knowledge of Brahman—which aim should be regarded as an end in itself. See *The Vedānta Sūtras of Bādarāyaṇa* (Thibaut trans.), 1.21–44: Sūtras 1.1.3–4.

62. *Kāvyānuśāsana,* p. 74: gloss.

63. *Jaimini Sūtra* 1.3.26: *anyāyas cānekaśabdatvam.*

64. "Tantravārttikam" 1.3.26, *Mīmāṃsādarśanam,* p. 214: *tenaikenaiva siddhe arthe dvitīyādi ca niṣphalam.*

65. "Śābara-Bhāṣyam" (Sanskrit text) 3.2.1, *Mīmāṃsādarśanam,* p. 126: *anyāyas cānekārthatvam.*

66. *sakṛd uccaritaś śabdaḥ sakṛd evārthaṃ gamayati.*

67. "Śābara-Bhāṣyam" 3.3.14, *Mīmāṃsādarśanam,* p. 221: *ekārthavṛttitvād vāco yugapad asaṃbandhāt. . . .*

68. See Bhaṭṭa Śaṅkara, *Mīmāṃsābālaprakāśa* (Chowkhamba ed.) 2.131–147.

69. *anekārthatvam ekārthatvena bādhyate; anekaśabadatvam ekaśabdatvena bādhyate.*

70. *aṅgaṃ pradhānena bādhyate.*

71. *śrutyā lakṣaṇā bādhyate.*

72. *anuṣaṅgeṇa adhyāhāro bādhyate.*

73. *rūdhyā yogo bādhyate.*

74. *sakṛt śrutasya mukhya-gauṇatvānupapatteh.*

75. *Vākyapadīya* (Iyer trans.) 2.251, p. 109 and exegetical note.

76. *Dhvanyāloka* 3.33, gloss, p. 246: *śabdātmani tasya aniyatatvam, na tu sve viṣaye vyaṅgyalakṣaṇe.*

77. Ibid., p. 237: *guṇapradhāna-bhāvena tayor vyasvasthānāt.*

78. See "Locana," *Dhvanyāloka* 2.28, p. 142. Abhinavagupta uses this analogy to suggest that the poet's words are replete with the richest meanings: *mahākavivāco asyāḥ kāmadhenutvāt.*

79. "Tantravārttikam" on Sūtra 1.3.26, *Mīmāṃsādarśanam,* p. 213: *sāmarthyaṃ sarvabhāvānām arthāpatyā avagamyate.*

80. "Śābarabhāṣyam" 10.5.56, *Mīmāṃsādarśanam,* pp. 423–424: *na ānarthakyam āpatatīty aśabdārthaḥ kalpanīyah.* See also Devasthali, *Mīmāṃsā,* 81.

81. *Jaimini Sūtra* 3.3.14: *śruti-liṅga-vākya-prakaraṇa-sthāna-samākhyānāṃ samavāye pāradaurbalyam, arthaviprakarṣāt.* The six principles of construction are direct assertion, indicative sign, sentence context, situational context, order of sequence, and name or etymological meaning. These terms have a progressively diminishing strength. Thus, the indicated or implied sense of a word or sentence is less authoritative than direct assertion and so on. For a detailed exposition, see Sarkar, *The Mīmāṃsā Rules of Interpretation as Applied to Hindu Law,* 5–7, 70–71, 101–160.

82. Patañjali, *Mahābhāsya: vyākhyānato viśeṣa-pratipattir na hi saṃdehād alakṣaṇam* (quoted in Raja, *Indian Theories of Meaning,* 31 n. 2).

83. *Jaimini Sūtra* 1.4.24: *saṃdigdheṣu vākyaśeṣāt.*

84. See Raja, *Indian Theories of Meaning,* 184.

85. Hirsch, *Validity in Interpretation,* 224.

86. Ibid., 203.
87. Ibid., 173–175.
88. Ibid., 201.
89. Culler, *Structuralist Poetics,* 30. For a general discussion of contemporary theories, see Ray, *Literary Meaning;* Fokkema and Kunne-Ibsch, *Theories of Literature in the Twentieth Century.*
90. Culler, *Structuralist Poetics,* 121; see also 130: "Literature is something other than a statement about the world." Culler favors Frye's view that "poems can only be made out of other poems" (30) and that they can be explored within the institution of literature; one need not move "from poem to world" (119).
91. Reichert, *Making Sense of Literature,* 167.
92. Contra Skinner, "Hermeneutics and the Role of History," 228; Close, "*Don Quixote* and 'The Intentional Fallacy,' " n. 35.
93. Ṣcholes, *Structuralism in Literature,* 10.
94. Frye, *Anatomy of Criticism,* 140, 190.
95. Hirsch, *Validity in Interpretation,* 240. Juhl, too, argues that textual features like coherence and complexity are not sufficient in themselves to warrant an interpretation, without those features also being evidence of the author's intention. (see "The Appeal to the Text," and *Interpretation,* chap. 4). For refutation of Juhl's thesis, see Beardsley, "Some Problems of Critical Interpretation," 353–354.
96. Hirsch, *Validity in Interpretation,* 240.
97. Jauss, "Literary History as a Challenge to Literary Theory," 24–25.
98. See Iser, *The Implied Reader,* 274–294; Fokkema and Kunne-Ibsch, *Theories of Literature in the Twentieth Century,* chap. 5.
99. See Ray, *Literary Meaning,* 125–126 (on Eco), 175–176, 178 (on Barthes); Culler, *Structuralist Poetics,* 243, 122, 123–124, 127, 247.
100. For a critique of Derrida, Barthes, and Eco, see Sparshott, *The Theory of the Arts,* 510–511. See also Abrams, "The Deconstructive Angel," and "How to Do Things with Texts."
101. Barbara Johnson, *The Critical Difference,* 79–109.
102. de Man, *Allegories of Reading,* 10–12.
103. Holland, *The Dynamics of Literary Response,* and *5 Readers Reading;* Fish, *Self-consuming Artifacts,* and *Is There a Text in This Class?* For a discussion of these theories, see Ray, *Literary Meaning,* chap. 5, 12; Culler, *On Deconstruction,* 39–41, 64–65, 65–75.
104. Fish, *Self-consuming Artifacts,* 386–387.
105. Reichert, *Making Sense of Literature,* 5–6.
106. Margolis, *The Language of Art and Art Criticism,* 85–86, 91–94, and *Art and Philosophy,* chap. 7. For a critique of Margolis, see Beardsley, *The Possibility of Criticism,* 42–44.
107. Weitz, *Hamlet and the Philosophy of Literary Criticism.*
108. Reichert, *Making Sense of Literature,* 116. The intentionalist too subscribes to the view that there can be only one correct interpretation of a literary work. See Hirsch, *Validity in Interpretation,* 44–47, 230; Juhl, *Interpretation,* chap. 8, esp. 198, 221–223. For Hirsch, meaning is necessarily self-identical and

univocal and requires an author's determining will (46–47). For Juhl, a literary work, being a speech act, cannot have "logically incompatible meanings" (221). Juhl's argument is sound except that he insists that the speaker is the real, historical author. The view that I uphold is that this speaker could be any person appropriate to the context and that the speech act can make sense purely in terms of the logic of the discourse in which it occurs, without appealing to the real speaker.

109. Reichert, *Making Sense of Literature,* 113–115.

110. Weitz (*Hamlet and the Philosophy of Literary Criticism,* 277) admits that some evaluative criteria stand alone and need no justification.

111. See Beardsley, *Aesthetics,* 456.

112. *ihānvaya-mukhenaiva sarvaṃ vyākhyāyate mayā, nāmūlaṃ likhyate kiñcit, nānapekṣitam ucayate.* Mallinātha prefaces his commentaries on Kālidāsa's poetic works with this verse.

113. On critical pluralism, compare Fowler, *The Languages of Literature,* 99. See also Stern, "Occlusions, Disclosures, Conclusions," 160: "Any theory of literature based on the fugitiveness of meanings collapses."

114. Krieger, "Meditation, Language, and Vision in the Reading of Literature," 231.

CHAPTER 9
POETIC APPREHENSION AND POETIC TRUTH

1. Aristotle, *Poetics* 9.1451b, in *Aristotle on Poetry and Style,* 18.

2. Ibid., 23 (p. 49).

3. Ibid., 9.1451b (p. 18).

4. Butcher, *Aristotle's Theory of Poetry and Fine Art,* 194.

5. The doctrine of "generalization" *(sādhāranīkaraṇa)* was first propounded by Bharata. According to Bharata's account of the mythical origins of drama, when the gods staged a play, composed by Bharata himself, in which the demons were shown to be defeated by the gods, the demons protested bitterly to Brahma that the play was designed to slander them. Brahma pacified them by saying that the play was neither about the gods nor about the demons exclusively but a representation of general humanity, their actions and mental states. See *Nāṭyaśāstra* 1.55–106.

6. *Kāvyānuśāsana* (Kāvyamālā ed.), gloss, p. 74.

7. "Abhinavabhāratī," *Nāṭyaśāstra* (BHU ed.) 6, p. 652.

8. Ibid., 1.107: *etādṛśaṃ te rāmādayo . . . vibhāvādīnāṃ jātaḥ.* My paraphrase of this passage is based on the text adopted by Gnoli, *The Aesthetic Experience According to Abhinavagupta,* 89.

9. "Abhinavabhāratī," *Nāṭyśāstra* 1, p. 122: *rāmādiśabdasya atropayogāt . . . viśeṣaleśopakrameṇa ca vinā pratyakṣāpravṛtteḥ.*

10. *Daśarūpaka* (Adyar ed.) 4.40, and Dhanika's commentary, pp. 218–219.

11. "Abhinavabhāratī," *Nāṭyaśāstra* 6, pp. 653–654.

12. Ibid., 6, p. 654.

13. *Sāhityadarpaṇa* 3.12: *parasya na parasyeti. . . .*

14. "Abhinavabhāratī," *Nāṭyaśāstra* 6, p. 564: *vyāptigraha iva dhūmāgnyoḥ.*

15. Langer, *Feeling and Form,* chap. 15.

16. Ibid., chap. 17.

17. Ibid., chaps. 16 and 17, esp, 291, 321.

18. *Vākyapadīya* 3: *Kālasamuddeśa* (chapter on time) (Sharma trans.), vv. 38, 49, and Helārāja's commentary, pp. 67, 74.

19. *Vākyapadīya* (Iyer trans.), 3.1.7.5, and note, p. 151.

20. Ibid., 3.1.7.6, p. 152.

21. Ibid., 3, *Kālasamuddeśa, vv.* 103–104, and commentary, pp. 129–130.

22. The relevant comments in "Abhinavabhāratī" will be found in *Nāṭyaśāstra* 1, 6; and also in *Kāvyānuśāsana,* pp. 68–79; "Locana," *Dhvanyāloka* 2, pp. 82–84.

23. *Nāṭyaśāstra* 1.112.

24. *Kāvyapradīpa* (Kāvyamālā ed.), p. 63, Vaidyanātha's commentary: *dharmyaṃśe laukika āropyāṃśe tvalaukikaḥ. . . .*

25. "Abhinavabhāratī," *Nāṭyśāstra* 6, p. 625: *anukartṛsthvena liṅgabalataḥ pratīyamānaḥ. . . .*

26. "Abhinavabhāratī," *Nāṭyaśāstra* 6, p. 625: *mukhya-rāmādigata-sthāyyanukaraṇa-rūpaḥ.*

27. Dharmakīrti, *Pramāṇavārttika* 2.57, quoted in "Abhinavabhārtī," *Nāṭyaśāstra* 6, p. 627.

28. Mahimabhaṭṭa (*Vyaktiviveka* [Chowkhamba ed.], 1, pp. 76–78) argues that it is useless to consider the question of true or false in the case of poetic presentations because the ultimate aim of poetry is not to make any assertions but merely to cause a certain type of cognition that is its own proof: *pratītimātraparamārthaṃ kāvyādi.*

29. "Abhinavabhāratī," *Nāṭyaśāstra,* 6, p. 628 (my paraphrase).

30. Ibid., 1, pp. 24–25.

31. Ibid., 6, p. 639.

32. Ibid., 1, pp. 117–120: *sajātīyān eva, na tu tatsadṛśān. sādhāraṇarūpasya kaḥ kena sadṛsārthaḥ. sāmānyātmakatve ko anukarārthaḥ.*

33. Kumārila, *Ślokavārttika,* "Vanavāda," v. 48.

34. Compare Twining, *Aristotle's Treatise on Poetry,* 21.

35. Coleridge, *Biographia Literaria,* chap. 19, p. 169.

36. "Abhinavabhāratī," *Nāṭyaśāstra* 1, p. 109: *ubhaya-darśanākulatayā . . . tad dhīsaṃpattyabhāvāt.*

37. Ibid., 6, p. 634.

38. "Locana," *Dhvanyāloka* 2.4, p. 84: *upāya-vailakṣaṇyāt.*

39. "Abhinavabhāratī," *Nāṭyaśāstra* 6, p. 660: *svarūpe viśrāntyabhāvāt.* Here the reading is uncertain. See Gnoli, *The Aesthetic Experience According to Abhinavagupta,* 66, n. 1.

40. "Abhinavabhāratī," *Nāṭyaśāstra* 6, p. 676: *tena rāma ityeva pratītiḥ, na tu ayaṃ na rāmaḥ anyoyam iti.* Contrast Dr. Johnson: "A play read, affects the mind like a play acted. It is therefore evident, that the action is not supposed to be real" ("Preface to Shakespeare," in *Samuel Johnson,* 256).

41. *Daśarūpaka* 4.2, p. 168, Dhanika's commentary.

42. See *Vākyapadīya* (Iyer trans.) 3.1.7.5, p. 151. This verse is quoted by the commentator on *Daśarūpaka,* p. 168.

43. Ryle, "Imaginary Objects," 23.

44. "Abhinavabhāratī," *Nāṭyaśāstra* 6, p. 672: *sādhāranī-bhāvaśca vibhāvādibhir iti.*

45. Compare Bullough, " 'Psychical Distance' as a Factor in Art and an Aesthetic Principle," 350. Bullough says that "it is Distance which primarily gives to dramatic action the appearance of unreality and not *vice versa.*" The point of my argument is, however, that even this "appearance of unreality" is not an invariable factor in literary experience. Sparshott (*The Structure of Aesthetics,* 220) points out that "we may certainly read a true narrative for its aesthetic qualities." Some Indian critics, who followed the Vedānta epistemology, argued that *rasa* experience is erroneous cognition *(bhrama),* in which, owing to the power of illusion, one identifies oneself with the characters of the drama. Without assuming such a power, the phenomenon of "generalization" cannot be explained. See *Rasagaṅgādhara* (BHU ed.), 1, 131–146. On Indian theories of error, see *Vibhramaviveka of Maṇḍana Miśra* (Sastri ed.), pp. i–xxv.

46. *Mīmāṃsābālaprakāśa* (Chowkhamba ed)., p. 6: *prāmāṇyaṃ hi arthatathātvarūpa-viṣayadharmaḥ.*

47. There has been an enormous amount of scholarly writing, in recent times, on the subject of truth in literature. But a convenient review of the various theories may be found in Margolis, *Art and Philosophy,* chap. 12.

48. See n. 9 above.

49. Ryle, "Imaginary Objects," 42.

50. Searle, *Speech Acts,* 77, n. 1. For a criticism of Searle's "axiom of existence," see Margolis, *Art and Philosophy,* 258–259. Margolis argues that "existence is not actually required for the success of reference." "What is true, then, need not be true of the actual world; and what we are referring to, when we are successful, need not exist in the actual world" (260).

51. A thing "will" exist or it "might have" existed only because it is possible for it to exist. So what is involved here is a possibility statement.

52. "Abhinavabhāratī," *Nāṭyaśāstra* 6, p. 659; "Locana," *Dhvanyāloka* 2.4, p. 84: *citra-vāsanā-viśiṣṭatvāc cetasaḥ.* On presenting unlikely things in poetry, compare Aristotle, *Poetics* 25, in *Aristotle on Poetry and Style,* p. 60.

53. Kumārila, *Ślokavārttikam,* "Autpattika-sūtram," v. 9.

54. *Ślokavārttikam,* "Codanā-sūtram," v. 1: *dharme pramāṇam;* "Autpattika-sūtram," v. 10: *abādho avyatirekeṇa svatas tena pramāṇatā.*

55. *Arthasaṃgraha,* p. 123.

56. See *Śābara-Bhāṣya* (Jha trans.) 1:50, 59–60; *Vedāntaparibhāṣā* (Adyar ed.), p. 68.

57. Jha, *Pūrva-Mīmāṃsā in Its Sources,* 296.

58. *Mīmāṃsā Sūtras* 1.2.10; *Śābara-Bhāṣya* (Jha trans.) 1:59; *Tantravārttika* (Jha trans.) 1:40–43. Compare Rājaśekhara, *Kāvyamīmāṃsā* (GOS ed.), p. 25 and notes, pp. 166–168: *nāsatyamasti kiñcana kāvye stutyartham arthavādoyam* (as emended by the editor). Here, the question at issue is that poetry tells lies. In

reply, it is pointed out that, if poetry is to be rejected on that score, then the study of the Vedas and the Śāstras must also be abandoned because they too contain plenty of exaggerations and metaphoric distortions. As a matter of fact, however, both in the Vedas and in poetry what appear to be lies serve only as commendations—of the prescribed actions in the Veda and of poetic assertions.

59. Alston, *Philosophy of Language,* chap. 4.

60. See Chatterjee, *Nyāya Theory of Knowledge,* chap. 5; *Ślokavārttikam,* "Codanāsūtra," passim; *Vibhramaviveka* (see n. 44 above).

61. See Iyer, *Bhartṛhari,* 208, 241, 287, 291. The grammarians, the Mīmāṃsakas, and the Vedāntins recognize that empty subject terms like "the rabbit's horn" and "sky flower," and fanciful statements like "Fire is born out of water" yield verbal knowledge even though they are contradictory to experience. See *Ślokavārttikam,* "Codanāsūtra" v. 6: *atyantāsatyapi jñānam arthe śabdaḥ karoti hi; Vākyapadīya* 1.130. The critic Jagannātha *(Rasagaṅgādhara* 2:170–171) argues that knowledge arising from mere fancy and from words is not affected by contradictory cognition. The Buddhists believe that language creates fictions and that the cognition of fictitious entities is still a valid cognition. See Matilal, *Epistemology, Logic, and Grammar in Indian Philosophical Analysis,* chap. 4. and *Logic, Language and Reality,* chaps. 2.1, 2.2.

62. Beardsley (*Aesthetics* 141) gives this example to demonstrate the weakness of the possibility theory. The account given here of "possibility" is, however, different from Beardsley's.

63. "A cognition is valid until it is proven false, i.e., found to be defective" *(doṣābhāvāt pramāṇatā): Ślokavārttikam,* "Codanāsūtra" v. 6; *Vedāntaparibhāṣā,* p. 65.

64. "Abhinavabhāratī," *Nāṭyaśāstra* 1, pp. 113–114; *Dhvanyāloka* 3.33, gloss and "Locana," pp. 253–254. "Locana" makes the point that one does not look for proof of poetic statements since delectation is the sole end toward which they are directed: *na hi teṣāṃ vākyānāṃ . . . prāmāṇyam anviṣyate. pratītimātraparyavasāyitvāt.*

65. Contrast Ohmann, "Speech Acts and the Definition of Literature."

66. Osborne, *Aesthetics and Criticism,* 91.

CHAPTER 10
THE VALIDITY OF *RASA* AS A THEORETICAL CONCEPT

1. *Dhvanyāloka* 4.42, gloss, p. 275: *rasa-bhāvādi-tātparya-rahitam.*

2. Ibid., 3.41, p. 268: *rasādi-tātparya-paryālocanayā.*

3. Ibid., 3.42, gloss, p. 275: *na tan mukhyaṃ kāvyam. kavyānukāro hy asau.*

4. Ibid., 1.5, "Locana," p. 31: *vastvalaṅkāra-dhvanī tu sarvathā rasaṃ prati paryavasyete.*

5. Ibid., 1.5, gloss, p. 33: *pratīyamānasya cānya-prabheda-darśanepi rasabhāva-mukhenaiva upalakṣaṇam.* The primacy of *rasa* is insisted on again in the following passage, in which Ānandavardhana says that the designation *dhvani* is given only to a poem in which the emotions, in all their forms and stages (of rise, subsidence, etc.), are treated as the principal theme and the word, meaning, fig-

ures, and qualities, each in its own distinct form, contributes to *rasa* evocation: *rasa-bhāva-tad-ābhāsa-tat-praśama-lakṣaṇaṃ mukhyam artham anuvartamānā yatra śabdārthālaṃkārā guṇāśca dhvanyapekṣayā ca vibhinna-rūpā vyavasthitās tatra kāvye dhvanir iti vyapadeśaḥ* (ibid., 2.4, gloss, p. 86).

6. Ibid., 4.5, p. 298.

7. Ibid., 3.43, gloss, pp. 277–278: *idānīṃtanānāṃ tu nyāyye . . . na praguṇībhavati.*

8. Ibid., 3.43, gloss, p. 279: *sthite caivaṃ . . . na dhvani-dharmatām atipatati.*

9. Ibid., 3.43, gloss, p. 279.

10. Ibid.

11. Ibid., 3.43, gloss, p. 276.

12. Ibid., 3.35, "Locana," pp. 256–257: *yadyapi vācyasya prādhānye'pi. . . .*

13. *Kāvyaprakāśa* 7.49, 8.66.

14. *Kāvyānuśāsana,* gloss, p. 79: *etanmatam eva vāsmābhir upajīvitaṃ veditavyam.*

15. Raghavan has offered a forceful criticism of Bhoja's views. See his *Bhoja's Sṛṅgāra Prakāśa,* chap. 19, esp. 442, 447–448, 486.

16. See chap. 3. Compare Hospers, *Meaning and Truth in the Arts,* 128–129.

17. Hirsch, *Validity in Interpretation,* 8, 38, 57, 63, 211.

18. Viśvanātha, *Sāhityadarpaṇa* (Kane ed.) 1.3, pp. 5–6; Kṣemendra, *Aucityavicāracarcā,* Kārikā 6; Mammaṭa, *Kāvyaprakāśa* 7.1; for a fuller discussion of the theory of poetic virtues and blemishes, see Raghavan, *Bhoja's Sṛṅgāra Prakāśa,* chaps. 15, 16; Bechan Jha, *Concept of Poetic Blemishes in Sanskrit Poetics.*

19. The concept of decorum had a respectable ancestry in Western poetics too. See Tuve, *Elizabethan and Metaphysical Imagery,* chap. 9.

20. *Nāṭyaśāstra* 16, 17, 19, 22.

21. *Dhvanyāloka* 3.14, and gloss.

22. For a fuller discussion, see Raghavan, *Bhoja's Sṛṅgāra Prakāśa,* chap. 12, and *Studies on Some Concepts of the Alaṃkāra Śāstra,* "Aucitya"; *Aucityavicāracaracā* 5: *aucityaṃ rasa-siddhasya sthiraṃ kāvyasya jīvitam.*

23. *Dhvanyāloka* 3.7–9, and "Locana."

24. *Sāhityadarpaṇa* 9.5.

25. Aristotle's distinction between tragedy and comedy must, in the final analysis, receive its sanction only in these terms, although Aristotle also uses other bases of difference, such as the social status of the men imitated, their moral nature, and so forth. His distinction between tragedy and the epic is, however, based on purely formal differences and, hence, will not hold good for poems with structures of other kinds. The real distinction of the epic from tragedy would be that the epic treats the heroic emotion, whereas tragedy treats the pathetic emotion. (An epic may of course admit an intermixture of the tragic, as in the *Iliad,* and vice versa.) As Crane (*The Languages of Criticism and the Structure of Poetry,* 65) observes, formal differentiation must remain inconclusive because formal possibilities are indefinite in number. But this should not lead to a diversity of critical languages, as Crane thinks. It points only to the inadequacy of purely formal criteria.

26. See Chari, " 'Structure' and 'Rhythm' in Sanskrit Dramatic Theory."

27. Pepper (*The Basis of Criticism in the Arts,* p. 79) observes that Coleridge conceived of organic form in terms of feeling connections. Where we "recognize a feeling connection, there is organic form."

28. Quoted in Abrams, *The Mirror and the Lamp,* 75.

29. Quoted in ibid., 149.

30. Ibid., 298.

31. Quoted in ibid., 153.

32. Quoted in ibid.

33. Rader, *A Modern Book of Esthetics,* 182–183.

34. Ibid., 48-66.

35. On Kant, see Deutsch, *Studies in Comparative Aesthetics,* 16; Beardsley, *Aesthetics from Classical Greece to the Present,* 213.

36. Rader, *A Modern Book of Esthetics,* 67–70.

37. Bergson, "Laughter" in Rader, *A Modern Book of Esthetics,* 76–77.

38. Rader, *A Modern Book of Esthetics,* 81.

39. Ibid.

40. Muller-Vollmer, *Towards a Phenomenological Theory of Literature,* 100.

41. Langer, *Feeling and Form,* 323.

42. Langer, *Problems of Art,* 15; also 25.

43. Langer, *Feeling and Form,* 227.

44. Ibid., 219.

45. Ibid., 233.

46. Ibid., 226.

47. Ibid., 216.

48. Ibid., 287.

49. Ibid., 40. For a critique of Langer's theory, see Casey, *The Language of Criticism,* 62–72; Dickie, *Aesthetics,* 78–84.

50. Langer, *Feeling and Form,* 211.

51. Ibid., 181.

52. Langer, *Mind,* 1:116–117.

53. Ibid., 116–117, 118.

54. Langer, *Feeling and Form,* 323.

55. Ibid., 374.

56. *Nāṭyaśāstra* 1, p. 671: "Abhinavabhāratī" on *Rasa Sūtra.* Abhinavagupta argues that *rasa* is not strictly produced by the presented situation and does not ensue from it as an effect from its cause, unlike ordinary effects, which continue even after their causes have dissipated: *tad bodhāpagame'pi rasa-saṃbhava-prasaṅgāt.* Also, *Kāvyaprakāśa* (Dwivedi ed.) 4.28, gloss, p. 70: *vibhāvādi-jīvitāvadhiḥ;* Vidyācakravartin's commentary, p. 72: *yāvad eva vibhāvādi-pratītiḥ tāvad eva carvaṇā.*

57. Stecker, "Expression of Emotions in (Some of) the Arts," 409. For other discussions of the place of emotions in art, see Charlton, *Aesthetics,* chap. 4; Barwell, "How Does Art Express Emotion?"

58. Quoted in Margolis, *Art and Philosophy,* 192.

59. See Dickie, *Aesthetics,* 81–82.

60. See Beardsley, *The Aesthetic Point of View,* chap. 6; Margolis, *Art and*

Philosophy, chap. 9; Sircello, *Mind and Art;* Tormey, *The Concept of Expression.*

61. Reid, *Ways of Knowledge and Experience,* 79.

62. See chap. 2, nn. 49, 50.

63. *Dhvanyāloka* 1.5, gloss and "Locana," pp. 31–32.

64. Ibid., 1.4, "Locana," p. 20: *guṇālaṃkāraucitya . . . kāvya-rūpatā-vyavahāraḥ.*

65. Langer, *Mind,* 113.

66. See the discussions of Alexander Smith, Croce, Langer, and Reid above.

67. Gardner, *A Reading of Paradise Lost,* 16.

68. Comparisons between Indian and Western ideas are pervasive in the writings of Radhakrishnan, Dasgupta, and Murti, among others. But see esp. Matilal and Shaw, eds., *Analytical Philosophy in Comparative Perspective.*

69. See Munro, *Oriental Aesthetics,* and also his *Form and Style in the Arts,* in which he examines both Western and Oriental art objects by way of illustrating the principles of art formulated by him. For Deutsch, see n. 35 above. Gerow *(A Glossary of Indian Figures of Speech)* provides copious English examples to illustrate the various rhetorical figures in Sanskirt. Comparisons abound also in Masson and Patwardhan, *Śānta Rasa,* i–xvii and passim. Rayan *(Suggestion and Statement in Poetry)* uses concepts from Sanskrit poetics to illuminate poetic practice and critical ideas in English.

70. Wells' *The Classical Drama of India* is an excellent study that provides a just and balanced appreciation of the Sanskrit dramatic practice from the point of view of comparative literature. Comparisons of Indian and Western dramatic principles and practices are also found in Wilson, *On the Dramatic System of the Hindus;* and Keith, *The Sanskrit Drama in its Origin, Development, Theory and Practice.* Another fine and systematic comparative study is Acharya, *The Tragicomedies of Shakespeare, Kālidāsa and Bhavabhūti*—a work that seeks to demonstrate that "at the highest level of poetic experience all barriers that divide people disappear, revealing the essential unity of art and the unity of poetic experience itself" (xiv).

71. See Baumer and Brandon, eds., *Sanskrit Drama in Performance,* 211–213; and the work of Deutsch and Gerow in the section on *rasa.*

72. Eliot, "Hamlet and His Problem," in *Selected Prose,* 102.

73. Gary Collier *(Emotional Expression)* discusses all aspects of emotional expression, both verbal and physical, touched on in Bharata. He lists two major groupings of emotions, one of six and the other of eight, that include most of the eight basic emotions of Bharata. This book should be of immense interest to students of Indian dramatic theory.

74. See sections on "Contextualization" and "Historicity versus Determinacy."

75. Gerow ("*Rasa* as a category of Literary Criticism," 251) reaches the same conclusion. He writes, "There is little that can be said to be necessarily 'Indian' about *rasa;* it just happens that this view of art has had a rather more full development in India than in the West." The Tantric concept of enjoyment *(bhoga)* as the quintessence of spiritual experience, which furnished the basic vocabulary for

Abhinavagupta's description of *rasa* experience, may no doubt be something peculiarly Indian. But it in no way limits the *rasa* experience to the Indian mind; it only elevates it to the level of the transcendental. Parallels to such a conception of art, too, are not lacking in the Western tradition.

76. Liu, *Chinese Theories of Literature,* 140; also 2. Liu believes that a universal theory of literature is possible.

77. Beardsley, *The Aesthetic Point of View,* 370. See also Deutsch, *Studies in Comparative Aesthetics,* 60, 74. Deutsch believes that it is possible to formulate "certain universal and enduring principles of aesthetic validity" or "standard[s] of aesthetic judgement" that are not "culture-conditional or culture-bound."

78. See Kirshnamoorthy, *Essays in Sanskrit Criticism,* chaps. 7, 16. Krishnamoorthy argues that *rasa* "cannot serve as a sole canon of Sanskrit literary criticism" (73). But most of his objections have been answered in the foregoing pages.

79. See Pound, *Literary Essays of Ezra Pound,* 48–52.

80. Hemingway, *Death in the Afternoon,* 2.

81. See Wellek and Warren, *Theory of Literature,* 9–14. The term "imaginative literature" is not without its difficultires. It is often equated with "fiction." But fictionality cannot be a necessary condition for all works of literature.

82. See Rader, *A Modern Book of Esthetics,* 17–20 (editor's introduction); Margolis, *Art and Philosophy,* chap. 5.

BIBLIOGRAPHY

SANSKRIT TEXTS AND TRANSLATIONS

Abhinavagupta. "Abhinavabhāratī" [commentary on Bharata's *Nāṭyaśāstra*]. See Bharata.

———. "Locana" [commentary on Ānandavardhana's *Dhvanyāloka*]. See Ānandavardhana.

Ānandavardhana. *Dhvanyāloka*. Edited with an introduction, English translation, and notes by K. Krishnamoorthy. Dharwar: Karnatak University, 1975.

———. *Dhvanyāloka of Ānandavardhana*, Udyotas I, II. Edited with an English exposition by Bishnupada Bhattacharya. 2 vols. Calcutta: Firma K. L. Mukhopadhyay, 1956–1972.

———. *Dhvanyāloka*, Udyota I, with "Locana," "Upalocana," and "Kaumudī" commentaries. Edited by S. Kuppuswamy Sastri. Madras: Kuppuswami Sastri Research Institute, 1944.

———. *Dhvanyāloka*, with "Dīdhiti" commentary (Hindi ed.), Varanasi: Chowkhamba Sanskrit Series, 1964.

———. *Dhvanyāloka*, with "Locana" by Abhinavagupta. Bombay: Nirnayasagar Press, 1935. Reprint. New Delhi: Munshiram Manoharlal, 1983.

Āpadeva. *Mīmāṃsānyāyaprakāśa: Āpadevī*. Bombay: Nirnayasagar Press, 1943.

Appaya Dīkṣita. *Citramīmāṃsā*. Varanasi: Vanivihar, 1965.

———. *Vṛttivārttikam*. 3d ed. Bombay: Nirnayasagar Press, 1940.

Bādarāyaṇa. *The Vedānta Sūtras of Bādarāyaṇa, with the Commentary of Śaṅkara*. Translated by George Tibaut. 2 vols. 1890. Reprint. New York: Dover Publications, 1962.

Bhāmaha. *Kāvyālaṅkāra of Bhāmaha*. Edited with an English translation and notes by P. V. Naganatha Sastri. Delhi: Motilal Banarsidass, 1970.

Bharata. *Nāṭyaśāstra*. Vol. 4. Baroda: Oriental Institute, 1964.

———. *The Nāṭyaśāstra*, chaps. 1–27. Edited with translation by Manomohan Ghosh. 2 vols. Calcutta: Manisha Granthalaya, 1967.

———. *Nāṭyaśāstra*, with "Abhinavabhāratī" by Abhinavagupta. Edited, with Sanskrit commentary "Madhusūdanī" and Hindi translation, by Madhusudana Shastri. 3 vols. Varanasi: Banaras Hindu University (BHU), 1971–1981.

Bhartṛhari. *The Kālasamuddeśa of Bhartṛhari's Vākyapadīya*, with Helārāja's commentary. Translated by Peri Sarveswara Sharma. Varanasi: Motilal Banarsidass, 1972.

———. *The Vākyapadīya*, cantos 1, 2. Edited with English translation and notes, by R. Raghavan Pillai. Varanasi: Motilal Banarsidass, 1971.

———. *The Vākyapadīya of Bhartṛhari,* chap. 2. English translation with exegetical notes by K. A. Subramania Iyer. Delhi: Motilal Banarsidass, 1977.

———. *The Vākyapadīya of Bhartṛhari,* chap. 3, pt. 1. English translation with notes by K. A. Subramania Iyer. Poona: Deccan College, 1971.

———. *The Vākyapadīya of Bhartṛhari,* chap. 3, pt. 2. English translation with exegetical notes by K. A. Subramania Iyer. Delhi: Motilal Banarsidass, 1974.

Bhaṭṭanāyaka. *Fragments of Bhaṭṭanāyaka.* Edited by T. R. Chintamani. *Journal of Oriental Research* (Madras) 1 (1927): 267–277.

Bhaṭṭa Śaṅkara. *Mīmāṃsābālaprakāśa.* 2 pts. Benares: Chowkhamba Sanskrit Series, 1902.

Bhoja. *Saraswatī-Kaṇṭhābharaṇa.* Edited by Arundoram Borooah. 1883. Reprint. Gauhati: Publication Board, Assam. 1969.

———. *Sṛṅgāraprakāśa.* Edited by Josyer, 4. vols. Mysore: Coronation Press, 1955–1975.

Daṇḍin. *Kāvyādarśa.* Edited with commentary by Pandit Rangacharya Raddi Shastri. 2d ed. Poona: Bhandarkar Oriental Research Institute, 1970.

Dhanaṃjaya. *The Daśarūpaka of Dhanaṃjaya,* with the commentary "Avaloka" by Dhanika and the subcommentary "Laghutīkā" by Bhaṭṭanṛsiṃha. Edited by T. Venkatacharya. Madras: Adyar Library and Research Centre, 1969.

———. *The Daśarūpaka of Dhanañjaya,* with the commentary "Daśarūpakadīpikā" by Bahurūpamiśra. Edited, with Hindi translation, by A. N. Pandey. Varanasi: Bharatiya Vidya Prakashan, 1979.

Dharmarāja Adhvarin. *Vedāntaparibhāṣā.* 1942. Reprint. Madras: Adyar Library and Research Centre, 1971.

Dharmasūri. *Sāhityaratnākara.* Edited by K. Rajanna Sastri. 2 vols. Hyderabad: Sanskrit Academy, 1972.

Gadādhara. *Śaktivāda.* Benares: Chowkhamba Sanskrit Series, 1929.

Gāgābhaṭṭa. *Bhāṭṭacintāmaṇi: Tarkapāda.* Benares: Chowkhamba Sanskrit Series, 1934.

Gotama. *Nyāyadarśanam,* with the Bhāṣya of Vātsyāyana. 2d. ed. Varanasi: Chowkhamba Sanskrit Series, 1970.

Govinda (Thakkura). *Kāvyapradīpa,* with the commentary of Vaidyanātha Tatsat. Kāvyamālā, 3d ed. Bombay: Nirnayasagar Press, 1933.

Hemacandra. *Kāvyānuśāsanam.* Kāvyamālā, 2d ed. Bombay: Nirnayasagar Press, 1934.

Jagadīśa Tarkālaṅkāra. *Śabdaśaktiprakāśikā.* 2d ed. Varanasi: Chowkhamba Sanskrit Series, 1973.

Jagannātha. *Rasagaṅgādhara,* with "Marmaprakāśa" by Nāgeśa. Edited, with Sanskrit commentary and Hindi translation, by Madhusudana Shastri. 3 vols. Varanasi: Banaras Hindu University (BHU), 1964–1970.

Jaimini. *Mīmāṃsādarśanam,* with *Śābarabhāṣya* and *Tantravārttika.* 6 pts. Poona: Anandasram, 1970–1974.

———. *Mīmāṃsā Sūtras of Jaimini.* Translated by Mohan Lal Sandal. 2 vols. 1923–1925. Reprint. Delhi: Motilal Banarsidass, 1980.

Jayanta Bhaṭṭa. *Nyāyamañjarī*. Varanasi: Chowkhamba Sanskrit Series, 1971.

———. *Nyāya-Mañjarī: The Compedium of Indian Speculative Logic*. Vol. 1. Translated by J. V. Bhattacharyya. Delhi: Motilal Banarsidass, 1978.

Kṛṣṇayajva. *Mīmāṃsāparibhāṣā*. Bombay: Nirnayasagar Press, 1950.

Kṣemendra. *Aucityavicāracarcā*. Hindi ed. Ramnagar, Varanasi: Harihara Prakashan, n.d.

Kumārila. *Ślokavārttika*. Translated by Ganganath Jha. 1908. Reprint. Delhi: Sri Satguru Publications, 1983.

———. *Ślokavārttikam*. Varanasi: Tara Publications, 1978.

———. *Tantravārttika*. Translated by Ganganath Jha. 2 vols. 1924. Reprint. Delhi: Sri Satguru Publications, 1983.

Kuntaka. *The Vakrokti-Jīvita*. Edited by Sushil Kumar De. 3d ed., rev. Calcutta: Firma K. L. Mukhopadhyay, 1961.

———. *Vakrokti Jīvita of Kuntaka*. Edited and translated by K. Krishnamoorthy. Dharwar: Karnatak University, 1977.

Laugākṣi Bhāskara. *Arthasaṃgraha*. 5th ed. Bombay: Nirnayasagar Press, 1950.

Mādhava Āchārya. *Sarva-Darśana-Saṃgraha*. Translated by E. B. Cowell and A. E. Gough. 7th ed. Varanasi: Chowkhamba Sanskrit Series, 1978.

Mahimabhaṭṭa. *Vyaktiviveka*, with Ruyyaka's commentary. Edited, with Hindi translation, by Rewaprasada Dwivedi. Varanasi: Chowkhamba Sanskrit Series, 1964.

Mammaṭa. *Kāvyaprakāśa of Mammaṭa*, with "Bālabodhinī" commentary by Vamanacharya Jhalakikar. 7th ed., rev. Poona: Bhandarkar Oriental Research Institute, 1965.

———. *The Kāvyaprakāsha of Mammaṭa with English Translation*. Rev. ed. Edited by Ganganath Jha. Varanasi: Bharatiya Vidya Prakashan, 1967.

———. *Kāvya Prakāsh or The Poetic Light*, with translation and Vidyācakravartin's commentary. Edited by R. C. Dwivedi. 2 vols. Delhi: Motilal Banarsidass, 1966–1970.

Maṇḍana Miśra. *Vibhramaviveka of Maṇḍana Miśra*. Edited by S. Kuppuswami Sastri. *Journal of Oriental Research* (Madras) 1 (1932).

Mukula Bhaṭṭa. *Abhidhāvṛttimātṛkā*, with Hindi translation and explanation. Edited by Rewaprasada Dwivedi. Varanasi: Chowkhamba Vidyabhavan, 1973.

Nārāyaṇa. *Mānameyodaya of Nārāyaṇa: An Elementary Treatise on the Mīmāṃsā*. Edited with an English translation by C. Kunhan Raja and S. S. Suryanarayana Sastri. 2d ed. Madras: Adyar Library and Research Institute, 1975.

Rajachudamani Dikshita. *Kāvyadarpaṇa*. Vol. 1. Edited by S. Subrahmanya Sastri. Srirangam: Sri Vani Vilas Press, n.d.

Rājaśekhara. *Kāvyamīmāṃsā*. 3d ed. Baroda: Oriental Institute, 1934.

Rudraṭa. *Kāvyālaṅkāra*. Hindi ed., with Nāmisādhu's commentary. Varanasi: Chowkhamba Vidyabhawan, 1966.

Ruyyaka. *Alaṃkāra-Sarvasva*. Edited by S. S. Janaki and V. Raghavan. Delhi: Meharchand Lachmandas, 1965.

Śabara. *Śābara-Bhāṣya*. Translated by Ganganath Jha. 3 vols. 1933. Reprint. Baroda: Oriental Institute, 1973.

Sāgarānandi. *Nāṭakalakṣaṇaratnakośa*. Hindi ed. Varanasi: Chowkhamba Sanskrit Series, 1972.

Śāradātanaya. *Bhāvaprakāśana of Sāradātanaya*. Gaekwad's Oriental Series (GOS), 2d ed. Baroda: Oriental Institute, 1968.

Śārṅgadeva. *Saṅgītaratnākara of Śārṅgadeva,* vol. 4, chapter on dancing. Translated by K. Kunjanni Raja and Radha Burnier. Madras: Adyar Library and Research Institute, 1979.

Siṃhabhūpāla. *The Rasārṇavasudhākara of Siṃhabhūpāla*. Edited by T. Venkatacharya. Madras: Adyar Library and Research Centre, 1979.

Subrahmanya Sastri, V. *Śābdataraṅgiṇī*. Madras: Sanskrit Education Society, 1969.

Tatacharya, D. T. *Rūpakapariśuddhi*. Tirupati: Tirumalai Tirupati Devasthanams Press, 1946.

Udayana. *Nyāyakusumāñjali*. Varanasi: Chowkhamba Sanskrit Series, 1957.

Udbhata. *Kāvyālaṃkāra-Sāra-Saṃgraha,* with Induraja's commentary. Edited by N. D. Banhatti. Poona: Bhandarkar Oriental Research Institute (BORI), 1925.

———. *Udbhata's Commentary on the Kāvyālaṃkāra of Bhāmaha*. Edited by Raniero Gnoli. Roma: Instituto Italiano per il Medio ed Estremo Oriente, 1962.

Upadhyaya, Vacaspati. *Mīmāṃsā Darśana Vimarśaḥ: Studies in Mīmāṃsā Philosophy* (in Sanskrit). Delhi: Bharatiya Vidya Prakashan, 1976.

Vāmana. *Kāvyālaṅkārasūtrāṇi,* with "Kāmadhenu" commentary of Tippa Bhūpāla Hindi ed. Varanasi: Chowkhamba Sanskrit Series, 1971.

Vidyānātha. *Pratāparudrīya of Vidyānātha,* with "Ratnāpaṇa" of Kumārasvāmin. Edited by V. Raghavan. Madras: Sanskrit Education Society, 1970.

Viṣṇudharmottara-Purāṇa: Third Khaṇḍa. Vol. 1. Edited by Priyabala Shah. Baroda: Oriental Institute, 1958.

Viśvanātha. *Sāhityadarpaṇa,* chaps. 1, 2, 10. Edited by P. V. Kane. 5th ed. Delhi: Motilal Banarsidass, 1965.

———. *Sāhityadarpaṇa* Hindi ed. Varanasi: Chowkhamba Vidyabhawan, 1976.

Visvanātha Pañcānana Bhaṭṭācārya. *Nyāyasiddhāntamuktāvalī,* with "Dinakarī" and "Rāmarudrī" commentaries. Varanasi: Chowkhamba Sanskrit Series, 1972.

Visveśvara. *Camatkāracandrikā*. Edited by P. Sarasvati Mohan. Delhi: Meharchand Lachmandas, 1972.

WORKS IN ENGLISH

Abrams, M. H. *The Mirror and the Lamp: Romantic Theory and the Critical Tradition*. New York: Norton, 1958.

———. "The Deconstructive Angel." *Critical Inquiry* 3 (1977): 425–438.

———. "How to Do Things with Texts." *Partisan Review* 46 (1979): 566–588.

Acharya, P. B. *The Tragicomedies of Shakespeare, Kālidāsa and Bhavabhūti*. New Delhi: Meharchand Lachmandas, 1978.

Adams, Robert P. *Strains of Discord: Studies in Literary Openness*. Ithaca, N.Y.: Cornell University Press, 1958.

Alston, William P. *Philosophy of Language*. Englewood Cliffs, N.J.: Prentice-Hall, 1964.

Amaladass, Anand, S. J. *Philosophical Implications of Dhvani: Experience of Symbol Language in Indian Aesthetics*. Vienna: De Nobili Research Library, 1984.

Anscombe, G. E. M. *Intention*. Oxford: Basil Blackwell, 1958.

Aristotle. *Aristotle on Poetry and Style*. Trans. G. M. A. Grube. Indianapolis: Bobbs-Merrill, 1958.

Austin, J. L. *Philosophical Papers*. Oxford: Clarendon, 1961.

Barwell, Ismay. "How Does Art Express Emotion?" *Journal of Aesthetics and Art Criticism* (Winter 1986): 175–181.

Baumer, Rachel Van M., and James R. Brandon, eds. *Sanskrit Drama in Performance*. Honolulu: University of Hawaii Press, 1981.

Beardsley, Monroe C. *Thinking Straight: A Guide for Readers and Writers*. New York: Prentice-Hall, 1950.

———. *Aesthetics: Problems in the Philosophy of Criticism*. New York: Harcourt, Brace & World, 1958.

———. *Aesthetics from Classical Greece to the Present*. New York: Macmillan, 1966.

———. "Textual Meaning and Authorial Meaning." *Genre* 1 (1968): 169–181.

———. *The Possibility of Criticism*. Detroit: Wayne State University Press, 1970.

———. *Thinking Straight: Principles of Reasoning for Readers and Writers*. 4th ed. Englewood Cliffs, N.J.: Prentice-Hall, 1975.

———. "Some Problems of Critical Interpretation.' *Journal of Aesthetics and Art Criticism* 36 (1978): 351–360.

———. *The Aesthetic Point of View: Selected Essays*. Edited by Michael J. Wreen and Donald M. Callan. Ithaca, N.Y.: Cornell University Press, 1982.

Bhatt, Govardhan P. *Epistemology of the Bhaṭṭa School of Pūrva-Mīmāṃsā*. Varanasi: Chowkhamba Sanskrit Series, 1962.

Black, Max. "Metaphor." In *Philosophy Looks at the Arts: Contemporary Readings in Aesthetics,* edited by Joseph Margolis, 218–235. New York: Scribners, 1962.

———. "Language and Reality." In *Problems in the Philosophy of Language,* edited by M. Olshewsky, 719–729. New York: Holt, Rinehart & Winston, 1969.

———. "Meaning and Intention: An Examination of Grice's Views." *New Literary History* 4 (1973): 257–279.

Booth, Wayne C. *The Rhetoric of Fiction*. Chicago: University of Chicago Press, 1961.

Brough, J. "Some Indian Theories of Meaning." *Transactions of the Philological Society* (London) (1953), 161–176.

Bullough, Edward. " 'Psychical Distance' as a Factor in Art and an Aesthetic Principle." 1913. In *A Modern Book of Esthetics,* edited by Melvin Rader, 5th ed., 347–362. New York: Holt, Rinehart & Winston, 1979.

Butcher, S. H. *Aristotle's Theory of Poetry and Fine Art*. London: Macmillan, 1923.

Casey, John. *The Language of Criticism*. London: Methuen, 1966.

Chari, V. K. "The Rasa Theory: Theology or Aesthetics?" In *The Sacred and the Secular in India's Performing Arts: Ananda K. Coomaraswamy Centenary Essays,* edited by V. Subramaniam, 47–61. New Delhi: Ashish Publishing House, 1980.

———. " 'Structure' and 'Rhythm' in Sanskrit Dramatic Theory (Illustrated by the Drama of *Śākuntala*)." *Adyar Library Bulletin* 44–45 (1980–1981): 120–131.

Charlton, W. *Aesthetics*. London: Hutchinson University Library, 1970.

Chatman, Seymour, and Samuel R. Levin, eds. *Essays on the Language of Literature*. Boston: Houghton Mifflin, 1967.

Chatterjee, Satischandra. *The Nyāya Theory of Knowledge*. 1939. Reprint. Calcutta: University of Calcutta, 1965.

Close, A. J. "*Don Quixote* and 'The Intentional Fallacy.' " *British Journal of Aesthetics* 12 (1972): 19–39.

Cohen, Ralph, ed. *New Directions in Literary History*. Baltimore: Johns Hopkins University Press, 1974.

Cohen, Ted. "Notes on Metaphor." *Journal of Aesthetics and Art Criticism* 34 (1976): 249–259.

Coleridge, Samuel Taylor. *Biographia Literaria*. Edited by George Watson. 2 vols. London: Dent, Everyman's Library, 1967.

Collier, Gray. *Emotional Expression*. Hillsdale. N.J.: Lawrence Erlbaum Associates, 1985.

Coomaraswamy, Ananda K. *The Transformation of Nature in Art*. 1934. Reprint. New York: Dover Publications, 1956.

———. *The Dance of Śiva*. Indian ed., rev. New Delhi: Sagar Publications, 1982.

Coward, Harold. *Sphoṭa Theory of Language*. Delhi: Motilal Banarsidass, 1980.

Crane, R. S. *The Languages of Criticism and the Structure of Poetry*. Toronto: University of Toronto Press, 1953.

———, ed. *Critics and Criticism*. Abridged ed. Chicago: University of Chicago Press, 1957.

Culler, Jonathan. *Structuralist Poetics: Structuralism, Linguistics and the Study of Literature*. London: Routledge & Kegan Paul, 1980.

———. *On Deconstruction: Theory and Criticism after Structuralism*. Ithaca, N.Y.: Cornell University Press, 1982.

Darbyshire, A. E. *A Description of English*. Indian ed. New Delhi: Arnold-Heineman, 1979.

Datta, D. M. *The Six Ways of Knowing: A Critical Study of the Vedanta Theory of Knowledge*. 2d ed., rev. Calcutta: University of Calcutta, 1972.

Davidson, Donald. "What Metaphors Mean." *Critical Inquiry* 5 (1978): 31–47.

Davie, Donald. *Articulate Energy: An Inquiry into the Syntax of English Poetry*. London: Routledge & Kegan Paul, 1955.

De, Sushil Kumar. *Some Problems of Sanskrit Poetics*. Calcutta: Firma K. L. Mukhopadhyay, 1959.

———. *History of Sanskrit Poetics*. 2d ed., rev. 2 vols. in 1. Calcutta: Firma K. L. Mukhopadhyay, 1960.

———. *Sanskrit Poetics as a Study of Aesthetics.* Berkeley: University of California Press, 1963.

de Man, Paul. *Allegories of Reading: Figural Language in Rousseau, Nietzsche, Rilke, and Proust.* New Haven, Conn.: Yale University Press, 1979.

Deutsch, Eliot. *Studies in Comparative Aesthetics.* Honolulu: University of Hawaii Press, 1975.

Devasthali, G. V. *Mīmāṃsā: The Vākya-Śāstra of Ancient India.* Bombay, 1959.

Dickie, George. "Meaning and Intention." *Genre* 1 (1968): 182–189.

———. *Aesthetics: An Introduction.* Indianapolis: Bobbs-Merrill, 1972.

———. *Art and the Aesthetic: An Institutional Analysis.* Ithaca, N.Y.: Cornell University Press, 1974.

Dimock, Edward C., et al. *The Literatures of India: An Introduction.* Chicago: University of Chicago Press, 1974.

Donagan, Alan. "Wittgenstein on Sensation." In *Wittgenstein: The Philosophical Investigations: A Collection of Critical Essays,* edited by George Pitcher, 324–351. New York: Doubleday, 1966.

D'Sa, Francis X., S. J. *Śabdaprāmāṇyam in Śabara and Kumārila: Towards a Study of the Mīmāṃsā Experience of Language.* Vienna: De Nobili Research Library, 1980.

Edgerton, F. "Indirect Suggestion in Poetry: A Hindu Theory of Literary Aesthetics." *Proceedings of the American Philosophical Society* 76 (1936): 687–706.

Eliot, T. S. *Selected Prose.* Harmondsworth: Penguin, 1963.

———. *Knowledge and Experience in the Philosophy of F. H. Bradley.* New York: Farrar, Straus, 1964.

———. *To Criticize a Critic.* London: Faber & Faber, 1965.

Ellis, John. *The Theory of Literary Criticism: A Logical Analysis.* Berkeley: University of California Press, 1974.

Empson, William. *The Structure of Complex Words.* London: Chatto & Windus, 1951.

———. *Seven Types of Ambiguity.* New York: Noonday Press, Meridian Books, 1955.

Esslin, Martin. *The Theatre of the Absurd.* Garden City, N.Y.: Doubleday, 1961.

Fish, Stanley. *Self-consuming Artifacts: The Experience of Seventeenth-Century Literature.* Berkeley: University of California Press, 1972.

———. *Is There a Text in This Class?* Cambridge, Mass.: Harvard University Press, 1980.

Fokkema, D. W., and Elrud Kunne-Ibsch. *Theories of Literature in the Twentieth Century: Structuralism, Marxism, Aesthetics of Reception, Semiotics.* London: Hurst, 1977.

Fowler, Roger. *The Languages of Literature: Some Linguistic Contributions to Literature.* London: Routledge & Kegan Paul, 1971.

———, ed. *Essays on Style and Language: Linguistic and Critical Approaches to Literary Style.* New York: Humanities, 1966.

Freeman, Donald C., ed. *Linguistics and Literary Style.* New York: Holt, Rinehart & Winston, 1970.

Frye, Northrop. *Anatomy of Criticism: Four Essays.* 2d ed. New York: Atheneum, 1966.

Gachter, Othmar. *Hermeneutics and Language in Pūrvamīmāṃsā: A Study in Śābara Bhāṣya.* Delhi: Motilal Banarsidass, 1983.

Gardner, Helen. *A Reading of Paradise Lost.* Oxford: Clarendon Press, 1965.

Garvin, Paul L., trans. *A Prague School Reader on Esthetics, Literary Structure, and Style.* Washington, D.C.: Georgetown University Press, 1964.

Gerow, Edwin. *A Glossary of Indian Figures of Speech.* The Hague: Mouton, 1971.

———. "Indian Poetics." In *The Literatures of India: An Introduction,* by Edward C. Dimock et al., 118–143. Chicago: University of Chicago Press, 1974.

———. *Indian Poetics.* Vol. 5, fasc. 3 of *A History of Indian Literature.* Edited by Jan Gonda. Wiesbaden: Otto Harrassowitz, 1977.

———. "*Rasa* as a Category of Literary Criticism: What Are the Limits of Its Application?" In *Sanskrit Drama in Performance,* edited by Rachel Van M. Baumer and James R. Brandon, 226–257. Honolulu: University of Hawaii Press, 1981.

Gnoli, Raniero. *The Aesthetic Experience According to Abhinavagupta.* 2d ed. Varanasi: Chowkhamba Sanskrit Series, 1968.

Gudmunson, Chris. *Wittgenstein and Buddhism.* London: Macmillan, 1977.

Harris, Roy. *Synonymy and Linguistic Analysis.* Toronto: University of Toronto Press, 1973.

Hemingway, Ernest. *Death in the Afternoon.* New York: Scribner's, 1932.

Hepburn, Ronald W. "Emotions and Emotional Qualities: Some Attempt at Analysis." In *Aesthetics in the Modern World,* edited by Harold Osborne, 94–104. London: Thames & Hudson, 1968.

Hill, Archibald A. *Constituent and Pattern in Poetry.* Austin: University of Texas Press, 1976.

Hirsch, E. D., Jr. *Validity in Interpretation.* New Haven, Conn.: Yale University Press, 1967.

———. *The Aims of Interpretation.* Chicago: University of Chicago Press, 1976.

Hofstadter, Albert. "The Tragicomic: Concern in Depth." *Journal of Aesthetics and Art Criticism* 24 (1965): 295–302.

Holland, Norman N. *The Dynamics of Literary Response.* New York: Norton, 1975.

———. *Five Readers Reading.* New Haven, Conn.: Yale University Press, 1975.

Homer. *The Iliad.* Translated by E. V. Rieu. Harmondsworth: Penguin, 1963.

Hospers, John. *Meaning and Truth in the Arts.* 1946. Reprint. Hamden, Conn.: Archon, 1964.

Huprikar, G. S. *The Problem of Sanskrit Teaching.* Kolhapur: Bharat Book Stall, 1948.

Hymes, Dell H. "Phonological Aspects of Style: Some English Sonnets." In *Style in Language,* edited by Thomas A. Sebeok, 109–131. New York: Technology Press of MIT, 1960.

Ingalls, Daniel H. H. *An Anthology of Sanskrit Court Poetry: Vidyākara's "Subhāṣitaratnakośa."* Cambridge, Mass.: Harvard University Press, 1965.

Iser, Wolfgang. *The Implied Reader.* Baltimore: Johns Hopkins University Press, 1974.

Iyer, K. A. Subramania. *Bhartṛhari: A Study of the Vākyapadīya in the Light of the Ancient Commentaries.* Poona: Deccan College, 1965.

Jauss, Hans Robert. "Literary History as a Challenge to Literary Theory." In *New Directions in Literary History,* edited by Ralph Cohen, 11–44. Baltimore: Johns Hopkins University Press, 1974.

Jesperson, Otto. *The Philosophy of Grammar.* New York: Holt, 1924.

Jha, Bechan. *Concept of Poetic Blemishes in Sanskrit Poetics.* Varanasi: Chowkhamba Sanskrit Series, 1965.

Jha, Ganganath. *The Prābhākara School of Pūrva Mīmāṃsā.* 1911. Reprint. Delhi: Motilal Banarsidass, 1978.

———. *Pūrva-Mīmāṃsā in Its Sources.* 2d ed. Varanasi: Banaras Hindu University, 1964.

Johnson, Barbara. *The Critical Difference: Essays in the Contemporary Rhetoric of Reading.* Baltimore: Johns Hopkins University Press, 1980.

Johnson, Samuel. *Samuel Johnson: Rasselas, Poems and Selected Prose.* Edited by Bertrand H. Bronson. New York: Holt, Rinehart & Winston, 1965.

Juhl, P. D. "The Appeal to the Text: What Are We Appealing To?" *Journal of Aesthetics and Art Criticism* 36 (1978): 277–287.

———. *Interpretation: An Essay in the Philosophy of Literary Criticism.* Princeton, N.J.: Princeton University Press, 1980.

Kames, Lord [Henry Home]. *Elements of Criticism.* 3 vols. 1762. Reprint. New York: Johnson Reprint Corp., 1967.

Kane. P. V. *History of Sanskrit Poetics.* 4th ed. Delhi: Motilal Banarsidass, 1971.

Keith, A. Berriedale. *A History of Sanskrit Literature.* 1920. Reprint. London: Oxford University Press, 1966.

———. *The Sanskrit Drama in Its Origin, Development, Theory and Practice.* 1924. Reprint. London: Oxford University Press, 1959.

Kenny, Anthony. *Wittgenstein.* London: Penguin, 1973.

Kinneavy, James L. *A Theory of Discourse.* New York: Prentice-Hall 1971.

Krieger, Murry. *The New Apologists for Poetry.* Bloomington: Indiana University Press, 1956.

———. "Meditation, Language, and Vision in the Reading of Literature." In *Interpretation: Theory and Practice,* edited by Charles S. Singleton, 211–242. Baltimore: Johns Hopkins University Press, 1969.

Krishnamachariar, M. *History of Classical Sanskrit Literature.* Reprint. Delhi: Motilal Banarsidass, 1970.

Krishnamoorthy, K. *Essays in Sanskrit Criticism.* Dharwar: Karnatak University, 1964.

———. *Dhvanyāloka and Its Critics.* Mysore: Kavyalaya Publishers, 1968.

Lahiri, P. C. *Concepts of Rīti and Guṇa in Sanskrit Poetics.* 1937. Reprint. New Delhi: Oriental Books Reprint Corp., 1974.

Lang, Berel, ed. *The Concept of Style.* Philadelphia: University of Pennsylvania Press, 1979.

Langer, Susanne K. *Feeling and Form.* New York: Scribner's, 1953.

———. *Problems of Art.* New York: Scribner's, 1957.

———. *Mind: An Essay on Human Feeling*. Vol. 1. Baltimore: Johns Hopkins University Press, 1967.

Leech, G. N. "Linguistics and the Figures of Rhetoric." In *Essays on Style and Language: Linguistic and Critical Approaches to Literary Style,* edited by Roger Fowler. New York: Humanities, 1966.

Lemon, Lee T., and Marion J. Reis, trans. *Russian Formalist Criticism: Four Essays*. Lincoln: University of Nebraska Press, 1965.

Levin, Samuel R. *Linguistic Structure in Poetry*. The Hague: Mouton, 1962.

———. *The Semantics of Metaphor*. Baltimore: Johns Hopkins University Press, 1977.

Lewis, C. Day. *The Poet's Way of Knowledge*. Cambridge: Cambridge University Press, 1957.

Liu, James J. Y. *Chinese Theories of Literature*. Chicago: University of Chicago Press, 1975.

McKeon, Richard. "Literary Criticism and the Concept of Imitation in Antiquity." In *Critics and Criticism,* edited by R. S. Crane, 117–145. Abridged ed. Chicago: University of Chicago Press, 1957.

Margolis, Joseph. *The Language of Art and Art Criticism*. Detroit: Wayne State University Press, 1965.

———. *Art and Philosophy: Conceptual Issues in Aesthetics*. Atlantic Highlands, N.J.: Humanities, 1980.

———, ed. *Philosophy Looks at the Arts: Contemporary Readings in Aesthetics*. New York: Scribner's 1962. Rev. ed. Philadelphia: Temple University Press, 1978.

Masson, J. L. and M. V. Patwardhan. *Śānta Rasa and Abhinavagupta's Philosophy of Aesthetics*. Poona: Bandarkar Oriental Research Institute, 1969.

———. *Aesthetic Rapture: The Rasādhyāya of the Nāṭyśāstra*. With translation and notes. 2 vols. Poona: Deccan College, 1970.

Matilal, Bimal Krishna. *Epistemology, Logic, and Grammar in Indian Philosophical Analysis*. The Hague: Mouton, 1971.

———. *Logic, Language and Reality: An Introduction to Indian Philosophical Studies*. Delhi: Motilal Banarsidass, 1985.

———. *Perception: An Essay on Classical Indian Theories of Knowledge*. Oxford: Clarendon Press, 1986.

Matilal, Bimal Krishna, and Jayasankar Lal Shaw, eds. *Analytical Philosophy in Comparative Perspective: Exploratory Essays in Current Theories and Classical Indian Theories of Meaning and Reference*. Dordrecht: D. Reidel Publishing Co.

Maxwell, Peter Benson. *Maxwell on the Interpretation of Statutes,* edited by P. St. J. Langan. Indian ed. Bombay, 1976.

Mohan, G. B. *The Response to Poetry: A Study in Comparative Aesthetics*. New Delhi: People's Publishing House, 1968.

Muller-Vollmer, Kurt. *Towards a Phenomenological Theory of Literature: A Study of Wilhelm Dilthey's Poetik*. The Hague: Mouton, 1963.

Munro, Thomas. *Form and Style in the Arts: An Introduction to Aesthetic Morphology*. Cleveland: Press of Case Western Reserve University, 1970.

———. *Oriental Aesthetics.* Cleveland: Press of Case Western Reserve University, 1965.

Novitz, David. "Metaphor, Derrida, and Davidson." *Journal of Aesthetics and Art Criticism* 44 (1985): 101–114.

Nowottny, Winifred. *The Language Poets Use.* 4th ed. London: Athlone, 1972.

Ogden, C. K., and I. A. Richards. *The Meaning of Meaning.* 8th ed., rev. New York: Harcourt, Brace & World, 1946.

Ohmann, Richard. "Prolegomena to the Analysis of Prose Style." In *Essays on the Language of Literature,* edited by Seymour Chatman and Samuel R. Levin. Boston: Houghton Mifflin, 1967.

———. "Speech Acts and the Definition of Literature." *Philosophy and Rhetoric* 4 (1971): 1–19.

Olsen, Stein Hugo. *The Structure of Literary Understanding.* Cambridge: Cambridge University Press, 1978.

Olshewsky, Thomas M., ed. *Problems in the Philosophy of Language.* New York: Holt, Rinehart & Winston, 1969.

Ortony, Andrew, ed. *Metaphor and Thought.* Cambridge: Cambridge University Press, 1979.

Osborne, Harold. *Aesthetics and Criticism.* London: Routledge & Kegan Paul, 1955.

———. "The Quality of Feeling in Art." In *Aesthetics in the Modern World,* edited by Harold Osborne, 105–124. London: Thames & Hudson, 1968.

———, ed. *Aesthetics in the Modern World.* London: Thames & Hudson, 1968.

Pandey, K. C. *Comparative Aesthetics.* Vol. 1, *Indian Aesthetics.* 2d ed. Varanasi: Chowkhamba Sanskrit Series, 1959.

Pandeya, A. C. *The Problem of Meaning in Indian Philosophy.* Delhi: Motilal Banarsidass, 1963.

Pepper, Stephen C. *Aesthetic Quality: A Contextualist Theory of Beauty.* 2d ed. New York: Scribner's, 1938.

———. *The Basis of Criticism in the Arts.* Cambridge, Mass.: Harvard University Press, 1956.

Pitcher, George, ed. *Wittgenstein: The Philosophical Investigations: A Collections of Critical Essays.* New York: Doubleday, 1966.

Potter, Karl H., ed. *Encyclopedia of Indian Philosophies.* Vol. 2, *Indian Metaphysics and Epistemology: The Tradition of Nyāya-Vaiśeṣika up to Gaṅgeśa.* Indian ed. Delhi: Motilal Banarsidass, 1977. Vol. 3, pt. 1, *Advaita Vedānta up to Śaṃkara and His Pupils.* Indian ed. Delhi: Motilal Banarsidass, 1981.

Pound, Ezra. *Selected Poems.* New York: New Directions, 1957.

———. *Literary Essays of Ezra Pound.* New York: New Directions, 1968.

Rader, Melvin. *A Modern Book of Esthetics: An Anthology.* 5th ed. New York: Holt, Rinehart & Winston, 1979.

Raghavan, V. *Bhoja's Sṛṅgāra Prakāśa.* Madras, 1963.

———. *The Number of Rasa-s.* 2d ed., rev. Madras: Adyar Library and Research Centre, 1967.

———. *Studies on Some Concepts of the Alaṃkāra Śāstra.* 2d ed., rev. Madras: Adyar Library and Research Centre, 1973.

Raja, K. Kunjunni. "Pāṇini's Attitude towards Lakṣaṇā." *Adyar Library Bulletin* 29 (1965): 177–187.

———. *Indian Theories of Meaning*. 2d ed. Madras: Adyar Library and Research Centre, 1969.

Ray, William. *Literary Meaning: From Phenomenology to Deconstruction*. Oxford: Basil Blackwell, 1984.

Rayan, Krishna. *Suggestion and Statement in Poetry.* London: Athlone Press, 1972.

Reichert, John. *Making Sense of Literature*. Chicago: University of Chicago Press, 1977.

Reid, Louis Arnaud. *Ways of Knowledge and Experience*. London: Allen & Unwin, 1961.

Richards, I. A. *Coleridge on Imagination*. 1924. Reprint. New York: Harcourt, Brace & World, 1935.

———. *The Principles of Literary Criticism*. 1924. Reprint. London: Routledge & Kegan Paul, 1970.

Robinson, Ian. *The New Grammarians' Funeral: A Critique of Noam Chomsky's Linguistics*. Cambridge: Cambridge University Press, 1978.

Ryle, Gilbert. "Imaginary Objects." *Proceedings of the Aristoteiian Society,* Vol. 12 suppl. (1933): 18–43.

Sankaran, A. *Some Concepts of Literary Criticism in Sanskrit*. 1926. Reprint. New Delhi: Oriental Books Reprint Corp., 1973.

Sarkar, K. L *The Mīmāṃsā Rules of Interpretation as Applied to Hindu Law*. Calcutta, 1909.

Sastri, Gaurinath. *The Philosophy of Word and Meaning: Some Indian Approaches with Special Reference to the Philosophy of Bhartṛhari*. Calcutta: Sanskrit College, 1959.

Sastri, Kuppuswami. *Highways and Byways of Literary Criticism in Sanskrit*. Madras: Kuppuswami Sastri Research Institute, 1945.

———. *A Primer of Indian Logic,* 3d ed. Madras: Kuppuswami Sastri Research Institute, 1961.

Satchidananda Murty, K. *Revelation and Reason in Advaita Vedanta*. New York: Columbia University Press, 1959.

Saxena, S. K. *Aesthetical Essays: Studies in Aesthetics, Hindustani Music and Kathak Dance,* Delhi: Chanakya Publications, 1981.

Scholes, Robert. *Structuralism in Literature: An Introduction*. New Haven, Conn.: Yale University Press, 1974.

Searle, John R. *Speech Acts: An Essay in the Philosophy of Language*. 1969. Reprint. London: Cambridge University Press, 1974.

———. "Metaphor." In *Metaphor and Thought,* edited by Andrew Ortony, 92–123. Cambridge: Cambridge University Press, 1979.

Sebeok, Thomas A., ed. *Style in Language*. New York: Technology Press of MIT/Wiley, 1960.

Sharma, Mukund Madhav. *The Dhvani Theory in Sanskrit Poetics*. Varanasi: Chowkhamba Sanskrit Series, 1968.

Sinclair, J. McH. "Taking a Poem to Pieces." In *Linguistics and Literary Style,* edited by Donald Freeman. New York: Holt, Rinehart & Winston, 1970.

Singleton, Charles S., ed. *Interpretation: Theory and Practice.* Baltimore: Johns Hopkins University Press, 1969.

Sircello, Guy. *Mind and Art: An Essay on the Varieties of Expressions.* Princeton, N.J.: Princeton University Press, 1972.

Skinner, Quentin. "Motives, Intentions, and the Interpretation of Texts." *New Literary History* 3 (1972): 393–408.

———. "Hermeneutics and the Role of History." *New Literary History* 7 (1975): 209–232.

Sparshott, Francis E. *The Structure of Aesthetics.* Toronto: University of Toronto Press, 1963.

———. *The Concept of Criticism: An Essay.* Oxford: Clarendon, 1967.

———. *The Theory of the Arts.* Princeton, N.J.: Princeton University Press, 1982.

Spencer, John, ed. *Linguistics and Style.* London: Oxford University Press, 1964.

Staal, J. F. "Sanskrit Philosophy of Language." In *Current Trends in Linguistics,* vol. 5, *Linguistics in South Asia,* 499–531. The Hague: Mouton, 1969.

———, ed. *A Reader on Sanskrit Grammarians.* Cambridge, Mass.: MIT Press, 1972; Delhi: Motilal Banarsidass, 1985.

Stallman, R. W., ed. *Critiques and Essays in Criticism.* New York: Ronald, 1949.

Stecker, Robert. "Expression of Emotions in (Some of) the Arts." *Journal of Aesthetics and Art Criticism* 42 (1984): 409–418.

Stern, J. P "Occlusions, Disclosures, Conclusions." *New Literary History* 5 (1973): 149–168.

Styan, J. L *The Dark Comedy: The Development of Modern Comic Tragedy.* London: Cambridge University Press, 1962.

Subba Rao, Veluri. *The Philosophy of a Sentence and Its Parts.* New Delhi: Munshiram Manoharlal, 1969.

Subramaniam, V., ed. *The Sacred and the Secular in India's Performing Arts.* New Delhi: Ashish Publishing House, 1980.

Sukla, Ananta Charana. *The Concept of Imitation in Greek and Indian Aesthetics.* Calcutta: Rupa & Co., 1977.

Tindall, William York. *The Literary Symbol.* Bloomington: Indiana University Press, 1955.

Tormey, Alan. *The Concept of Expression: A Study in Philosophical Psychology and Aesthetics.* Princeton, N.J.: Princeton University Press, 1971.

Turner, G. W. *Stylistics.* Harmondsworth: Penguin, 1975.

Tuve, Rosemond. *Elizabethan and Metaphysical Imagery: Renaissance Poetic and Twentieth-Century Critics.* 1947. Chicago: University of Chicago Press, 1961.

Twining, Thomas. *Aristotle's Treatise on Poetry.* 1789. Facsimile ed. New York: Garland, 1971.

Vivas, Eliseo. "The Objective Correlative of T. S. Eliot." In *Critiques and Essays in Criticism,* edited by R. W. Stallman, 389–400. New York: Ronald, 1949.

Walimbe, Y. S. *Abhinavagupta on Indian Aesthetics.* Delhi: Ajanta Publications, 1980.

Warder, A. K. *Indian Kāvya Literature.* Vol. 1, *Literary Criticism.* Delhi: Motilal Banarsidass, 1972.

———. *The Science of Criticism in India.* Madras: Adyar Library and Research Centre, 1978.

Warren, Robert Penn. "Pure and Impure Poetry." In *Critiques and Essays in Criticism,* edited by R. W. Stallman, 85–104. New York: Ronald, 1949.

Weitz, Morris. *Hamlet and the Philosophy of Literary Criticism.* 1964. Cleveland: Meridian, 1966.

Wellek, René, and Austin Warren. *Theory of Literature.* New York: Harcourt, Brace, Harvest, 1956.

Wells, Henry W. *The Classical Drama of India: Studies in Its Values for the Literature and Theatre of the World.* London: Asia Publishing House, 1963.

Wells, Rulon. "Nominal and Verbal Style." In *Style in Language,* edited by Thomas S. Sebeok, 213–220. New York: Technology Press of MIT/Wiley, 1960.

Wilson, Horace Hayman. *On the Dramatic System of the Hindus.* Reprint. Calcutta: Sanskrit Pustak Bhandar, 1971.

Wimsatt, W. K., and Monroe C. Beardsley. "The Affective Fallacy." In *The Verbal Icon: Studies in the Meaning of Poetry,* ed. W. K. Wimsatt, 21–39. Lexington: University of Kentucky Press, 1967.

———. "The Intentional Fallacy." In *The Verbal Icon: Studies in the Meaning of Poetry,* ed. W. K. Wimsatt, 3–18. Lexington: University of Kentucky Press, 1967.

Wittgenstein, Ludwig. *Philosophical Investigations,* translated by G. E. M. Anscombe. 1958. Oxford: Blackwell, 1974.

Yeats, William Butler. *Essays and Introductions.* 1916. Reprint. London: Macmillan, 1971.

INDEX

Abhinavagupta, 12, 31, 37, 195, 230, 231; on basic and transitory emotions, 59–61; on *bhakti rasa,* 58; on the conditions and nature of *rasa* expression, 51, 54, 55, 246; on dance, 14–15; on decorum of the emotions, 233; on drama as poetry, 3, 206–207; on emotive connotations, 120–121; on the essentiality of *rasa,* 40, 42, 229–230; on evocation, 5, 39–40, 45, 46; on generalization of meaning and emotions, 5, 198–199, 200, 201, 203, 204, 210; on imitation and his refutation of it, 33, 207, 211–214; on the moral function of poetry, 32; and mysticism, 6, 11, 227, 253 n. 4; on the nature of *rasa* experience, 238–239, 242; on the objectivity of poetic perception, 28; on the organization of feeling tones, 62; on poetic illusion and his refutation of it, 215–217; on poetic truth, 221, 225, 227 n. 64; on *rasa* perception as a cognitive process, 20–21, 23–25, 119–120, 245, 279 n. 56; on *rasa* as a poetic principle, 3, 228; and *rasa* not a religious attitude, 11; on *śānta rasa,* 56–57; on style, 150, 154; on suggestion, 97, 143; on suggestiveness of music, 14

Absurd drama (black comedy), 73–74, 250

Aesthetic attitude, 44

Aesthetic emotion, 19, 33

Aesthetic of irony, the, 69–74

Ākāṅkṣā (incompleteness of meaning). *See under* Mīmāṃsā

Alaṃkāra. See Figurative language

Ānandavardhana, 3, 11, 12, 31, 37, 230, 231; on concordant and discordant emotions, 65; on decorum of the emotions, 233; on emotive connotations, 121; on the essentiality of *rasa,* 40, 42; on figurative language, 41, 157; on the nature of poetic experience, 239; on the objectivity of poetic emotions, 20; on the primacy of *rasa,* 229–230; on *rasa* as a poetic principle, 3; on suggestion of emotive meanings, 120 (*see also* Suggestion: and emotive meaning); on suggestion and inference, 130; on suggestion as a semantic function, 102; on the suggestiveness of music, 13–14

Anderson, Sherwood, 251

Aristotle, 28, 244, 247, 249; on imitation, 214; on poetic kinds, 278 n. 25; on poetry and history, 196–197; on tragedy, 70; *Poetics,* 12

Arnold, Matthew, "Dover Beach," 234

Austin, J. L., 7, 21, 219

Bacon, F., 251–252; "Of Study," 153

Barthes, Roland, 189

Bateson, F. W., 186–187

Beardsley, Monroe C., 3, 7; on cultural criticism, 249; on metaphor, 93; on the poem as an illocutionary act, 43; on style, 146–147; on suggestion, 130, 131; on word connotations, 83, 101

Beckett, Samuel, *Waiting for Godot,* 73

Bell, Clive, 16

Bergson, H., 239

Bhāmaha: on deviant expression, 31, 35; on style, 137

Bharata, 47, 48, 124, 125, 230, 231, 252; on the criteria of emotional expression, 17, 49–55; on decorum of the emotions, 232–233, 234, 236; on the essentiality of *rasa,* 30, 40; on generalization, 274 n. 5; on imitation, 207, 208, 214; on the nature of poetic experience, 239; on organization of feeling tones, 62; on *rasa* and dance, 14–15; and theory of dramatic emotions, 3, 11; and typology of emotions, 13, 55–61, 248

Bhartṛhari: on meaning, 150, 176; on metaphorical meaning, 88, 89; his meta-

physics, 6; on sentence meaning, 115, 116; on time and language, 206; on unity of meaning, 110, 180
Bhaṭṭanāyaka, 195; on the cognition of *rasa,* 23–24, 210; on dramatic illusion, 210–211; on evocation *(bhāvanā),* 5, 39, 46, 210; on generalization, 210
Bhoja, 233; and theory of *rasa,* 231
Blake, W., "The Tiger," 53, 240; "The Echoing Green," 240
Brooks, Cleanth, 186–187
Brown, Sir Thomas, 40
Browning, Elizabeth Barrett, "How Do I Love Thee," 47, 225
Browning, Robert, 250; "Serenade at the Villa," 148
Buddhist theory of illusion, 209
Burke, Edmund, 237
Butcher, S. H., 197

Casey, John, 48
Cervantes, *Don Quixote,* 171, 185
Charlton, W., 50
Citrakāvya: visual poetry, 158–159; "trick-writing," 228, 229
Close, A. J., 171
Cohen, Ted, 93
Coleridge, S. T.: on imagination, 70–71; on poetic truth, 215
Concrete poetry, 159
Conrad, Joseph, "Heart of Darkness," 251
Context. *See under* Interpretation; Logic; *Mīmāṃsā*
Contextual factors *(prakaraṇādi),* 109
Coomaraswamy, A. K., 6, 11
Crane, Hart, 250
Crane, Stephen, "The Open Boat," 47; *The Red Badge of Courage,* 251
Croce, B.: on emotions, 238, 239; on genres, 233
Culler, Jonathan, 45, 184–185
cummings, e. e., 147, 158, 250

Daṇḍin, 138; his definition of poetry, 34
Davie, Donald, 152
Deconstruction, 7. *See also under* Interpretation
Decorum *(aucitya).* See under *Rasa*
Definition of poetry: criteria of, 31–34; the problem of, 29–31
de Man, Paul, 190–191
Dennis, John, 237–238
Deutsch, Eliot, 247, 253 n. 7, 281 n. 77
Deviant expression *(vakrokti),* 31, 35–36, 135–137
Dhanika: on evocation, 5
Dhvani. See Suggestion
Dickie, George, 44
Dickinson, Emily, 250; "After Great Pain a Formal Feeling Comes," 55
Dilthey, W., 239
Donne, J., 58, 94, 246, 250
Dryden, J., "Mac Flecknoe," 250
Ducasse, C. J., 239

Eliot, T. S., 16, 246, 250; on dominant and fleeting feelings, 260 n. 33; on emotions, 12, 18, 73; on irony, 69; on "objective correlative," 90; "The Love Song of J. Alfred Prufrock," 71, 95; "The Waste Land," 50, 71, 235
Ellis, John, 45
Edwards, Jonathan, 251
Emerson, R. W., 251
Emotive aesthetics, emotive meaning. See *Rasa*
Empson, William, 109–111, 112, 122
Enkvist, N. E., 145
Evaluation, 231–237
Evocation, *(bhāvanā),* 5, 45, 46, 210. See also under *Rasa*
Expressiveness: in the arts, 243; in dance, 14–15; in literature, 243–244; in music, 13; in painting and sculpture, 15

Faulkner, William, 251
Fictionality, 33, 217, 218, 219. *See also* Poetic illusion
Figurative language *(alaṃkāra),* 29, 31, 75; and metaphorical meaning (*see* Suggestion, and metaphorical meaning); poetry as, 34–36, 41; and *rasa,* 41, 157; and suggestion (*see* Suggestion, and figurative expression)
Fish, Stanley, 191
Forster, E. M., 251
Frye, Northrop, 16, 186

Generalization of meaning, of emotions *(sādhāraṇīkaraṇa). See* Poetic universal.

See also under Abhinavagupta; *Mīmāṃsā*
Genres, theory of, 233–236; the emotions as basis for generic distinctions, 235
Gerow, Edwin, 1, 2–3, 247
Gray, Thomas, "Elegy," 238
Gudmunsen, Chris, 22

Hardy, Thomas, 185
Hawthorne, N., 251; *The Scarlet Letter,* 91
Hemacandra: definition of poetry of, 30; on *rasa,* 230
Hemingway, E., 47, 130, 251
Herbert, George, 58, 246
Hill, A. A., 155–156
Hirsch, E. D., 3; on authorial intention, 168; on interpretation, 183, 186; on "meaning" and "significance," 162, 232; on style and meaning, 267 n. 23, 269 n. 62; on unity of interpretation, 273 n. 108
Holland, Norman, 191
Homer, the *Iliad,* 69, 151, 157–158, 235; *Margites,* 151, 235; the *Odyssey,* 226
Homonymous words, 96, 107–113
Hopkins, Gerard Manley, 58, 246, 250; "The Windhover," 53
Horace, 233
Hulme, T. E., 128
Hymes, Dell H., 151–152

Imagination *(pratibhā),* 32, 256 n. 8
Imitation *(anukaraṇa),* theory of, 33–34, 208–214
Indurāja, 124
Institutional theories, 44–45
Intention. *See under* Logic; *Mīmāṃsā;* Vedānta
Interpretation: aspect seeing, 191; context as determinant of meaning and, 183–184; contextualization, the limits of, 184–186; and criteria of verification, 186–187; and deconstruction, 189–191; historicity of the text and, 187–188; and intertextuality, 184–185; and phenomenological and reception theories, 188–189, 191; and reader-oriented theories, 191; and rules of interpretation: their admissibility, 182–183; the scope of the term, 161–162; unity of, 189–192, 193. See also under *Mīmāṃsā*

Intertextuality. See under Interpretation
Ionesco, E., *The New Tenant,* 74
Irony, the aesthetic of, 69–74

Jagannātha: his objection to *rasa,* 43, 230; on basic and transitory emotions, 61
Jaimini, 75, 163, 177, 224; his *Mīmāṃsā Sūtras,* 162
James, Henry, *The Ambassadors,* 251; "The Beast in the Jungle," 251
Jesperson, Otto, 129
Johnson, Barbara, 190
Johnson, Dr. Samuel, 217
Joyce, James, *Portrait of the Artist,* 251

Kālidāsa, *Śākuntala,* 62, 205; *Kumārasaṃbhava,* 121
Kames, Lord, 69
Kant I.,: on aesthetic attitude, 44, 238
Kayyaṭa, 162
Keats, J., 250; "On First Reading Chapman's Homer," 53
Kṣemendra, 233
Kumārila: on impersonality of the word, 165; on intention, 168–169, 170; on secondary meaning, 83; on truth and meaning, 166
Kuntaka: on decorum of the emotions, 233; on deviant expression, 31, 35–36, 135–137; on figuration, 34–35; on *sāhitya,* 36

Langer, Susanne, 16, 243, 251; on the primacy of feeling in art, 239–242, 246; mimetic theory of language of, 151, 152; on tense in literature, 204–205
Lawrence, D. H., 251
Leavis, F. R. 16
Leech, G. N., 152–153
Lincoln, Abraham, "Gettysburg Address," 252
Liu, James, *Chinese Theories of Literature,* 249
Logic, the school of (Nyāya): on context, 172–173; on impersonality *(apauruṣeyatva)* of texts, 163; on intention, 79, 165–166, 171–172, 174; on metaphorical meaning, 79, 85; on purport *(tātparya),* 79, 113, 116, 172; on suggestion, 102–103, 122–123; on validity, 224
Lollaṭa, 195, 207, 208

Longinus, 12, 237
Lorca, "Hunter," 54–55
Lowth, Bishop, 237

Mahimabhaṭṭa: on metaphorical meaning, 87, 88–89; on *rasa,* 23, 31, 42; on suggestion, 42, 123
Mallarmé, S., "The Swan," 92
Mammaṭa: on decorum of the emotions, 233; definition of poetry of, 30; on *rasa,* 230; on suggestion, 99, 108
Margolis, Joseph, 94, 191–192
Marvell, Andrew, "The Garden," 56; "To His Coy Mistress," 234
Masson, J. L., 6; and M. V. Patwardhan, 253 nn. 1, 4
Matilal, Bimal Krishna, 247
Melville, H., *Billy Budd,* 190; *Moby Dick,* 91, 100, 235
Metaphorical (secondary) meaning *(lakṣaṇā),* 75, 76; and allegory, 93; conditions of, 78–85; and figuration, 105; the focus of, 85–87; incompatibility of literal meaning *(mukhyārtha-bādha, anupapatti),* 78–80, 104; and inference, 87, 88–89, 90; and irony, 84, 86; and literal-metaphorical distinction, 93–94, 263 n. 52; the motive for, 81–82, 97–99; and myth, 93; nature of, 77, 82–84; and relation to primary meaning, 80–81; and simile, 84–85; and symbol, 90–92; translatability of, 145, 223; as verbal meaning, 87–90
Mill, J. S., 237
Miller, Arthur, 250; *Death of a Salesman,* 205
Milton, J., 232; *Paradise Lost,* 235, 246; *Samson Agonistes,* 73, 246
Mīmāṃsā: on *ākāṅkṣā* (incompleteness of meaning), 76, 114, 115; on autonomy of verbal meaning, 164–165; the Bhāṭṭa school of, 85, 166, 171, 173, 174; on generalization of meaning, 5, 198; on the impersonality of the word *(apauruṣeyatva),* 165–170; on intention, 93, 168–169, 170, 171, 173–175; on multiple meaning, 179–180; the Prābhākara school of, 85, 166, 171, 174; rules of interpretation, 6, 94, 179–182; as a school of thought, 162; and theory of context, 102, 174, 183–184; and theory of interpretation, 161, 162, 163, 192–194; and theory of language, 3, 4–5, 148–149, 164–165, 184, 197, 218; and theory of metaphor, 85–86; and theory of purport, 79, 113–114, 124, 130; and theory of sentence types, 176–178; and theory of verbal prompting (*bhāvanā,* evocation), 5, 45, 46; and unity of meaning, 5, 108–109, 110, 176–182; and *vākyaśeṣa* (the remainder of the sentence), 115, 124, 130, 181–182; on the validity of propositions, 222–224; and view of similarity, 213
Moral function of poetry, 32–33
Monro, Thomas, 247
Murry, Middleton, 16
Murti, T. R. V., 247

Nāgeśa, 80

O'Casey, Sean, *Juno and the Paycock,* 73; *The Plough and the Stars,* 73
Ohmann, Richard, 144–145
O'Neill, Eugene, 250
Osborne, Harold, 18–19, 20, 225–226

Pandey, K. C., 6, 11, 253 n. 4
Pāṇini, 162; on metaphorical meaning, 87
Paronomasia. *See* Homonymous words
Patañjali, 162; on metaphorical meaning, 87
Person, place, time in literature, 202–206
Picture theory of language, 149–150
Pinter, Harold, *The Birthday Party,* 74
Plath, Sylvia, 250
Plato, 12, 28, 151
Poe, Edgar Allan, 250; "The Fall of the House of Usher," 50; "Annabel Lee," 118; "The Raven," 152
Poetic illusion, 214–226. *See also* Poetic truth
Poetic structure, 235–236
Poetic truth, 6, 195, 207, 275 n. 28, 276 nn. 45, 58, 277 n. 64; and Indian theories of truth and validity, 222–225, 277 n. 61; and poetry as imitation speech act, 218, 219; and referentiality of poetic statements, 218, 219–220; and truth vs. reference in poetry, 220–222

Poetic universal, 6, 195, 196–207
Poetry as emotive meaning. See *Rasa:* as a general theory of poetry
Poetry and history, 40, 196–197
Pope, A., "The Rape of the Lock," 106, 153, 185; *The Dunciad,* 111, 151, 250; translation of Homer of, 151
Potter, Karl, 247
Pound, Ezra, 128, 129, 250; "The Jewel Stairs' Grievance," 130
Prague school, the, 136
Primary meaning *(abhidhā),* 75; conditions of, 76–77
Purport *(tātparya),* theory of. *See under* Logic; *Mīmāṃsā;* Suggestion

Radhakrishnan, S., 247
Rāmānuja, 222
Rasa: as aesthetic relish, 19, 33, 242; affective reference in, 23–24, 27; cognitive status of, 23–25, 26–27 (*see also* Abhinavagupta: on *rasa* perception); and cognitive theories, 25–26; and concordant and discordant emotions, 63–69; criteria for expressing emotions in poetry, 48, 49–55; and dance, 14–15; and decorum of the emotions *(rasaucitya),* 20, 70, 231–237; and durable (basic) and transitory emotions, 55–61; emotive meaning (*see* Suggestion: and emotive meaning; Style: and emotion); as an evaluative criterion, 231–237; and evocation of emotions as the end of poetry, 5, 39–40, 103, 227, 232, 238 (*see also* Evocation); and expressionistic doctrines, 15–17; and figuration, 41, 157; as a general theory of poetry, 1, 3, 12–13, 29, 39–47, 48, 107, 131, 143, 227–228; as the meaning of the poem, 19, 20, 51, 119–121, 227, 239; and music, 13–14; and mutations of the doctrine, 231; number and typology of emotions and, 55–59, 248 (*see also under* Bharata); objections to the theory of, 29, 43, 228, 230, 244–245, 247; objective emphasis of, 17–20, 28, 239, 245, 247–248; and organization of feeling tones, 62–63; and painting and sculpture, 15; as a principle of definition, 31, 39–44, 46–47, 227, 230, 251–252; and the religious emotion, 58–59; *śānta rasa* (quietude), 56–57; theological interpretations of, 6, 10–11; unity of tone, 63, 66–68; universality of the concept, 2–3, 228, 248–251, 280 n. 75; various senses of, 9–10; Western parallels to the theory of, 237–242
Reception aesthetic. *See* Interpretation: phenomenological and reception theories
Richards, I. A., 12, 69–71
Richardson, S., *Pamela,* 205
Reichert, John, 185, 192
Reid, L. A., 238, 245
Rimbaud, A., 250; "The Drunken Boat," 92, 128
Rīti. See Style
Russian Formalism, 136
Ryle, Gilbert, 217, 218, 220

Śabara, 75; on the autonomy of the text, 166; on metaphorical meaning, 89
Sāhitya (harmony of word and meaning), 36, 137, 149
Śaṅkuka, 195; on poetic emotions, 20, 21, 23, 123; on poetic imitation and illusion, 207, 208–210, 211, 213, 215–216, 218
Sanskrit criticism: objective, analytic approach of, 28; as a science *(śāstra),* 3–4; its scholastic spirit, 256 n. 8; schools of, 1–2, 12, 31, 36–37; as not theology or metaphysics, 6, 11; universality of principles of, 6
Śāstra (scientific inquiry): argumentative style of, 8; components of, 4; literary criticism as, 4
Searle, John R., 7, 219, 220, 221
Shakespeare, 46, 65, 73, 185, 240; *Hamlet,* 62–63, 71, 110, 117, 118, 186, 192; *King Lear,* 27, 111; *Macbeth,* 105; *Othello,* 66, 69, 118, 152; *Romeo and Juliet,* 72; sonnets, 63, 73, 109, 250
Shaw, Bernard, 250
Shelley, P. B., 250
Smith, Alexander, 238
Socrates, 151
Sophocles, *Oedipus Rex,* 69
Sparshott, F. E., 3
Speech acts, 7, 170
Stevens, Wallace, "Anecdote of a Jar," 40; "Thirteen Ways of Looking at a Blackbird," 40, 191
Structuralism, 184–185, 189

Style *(rīti):* as deviation, 134, 135–137; and emotion, 133, 143, 144, 148, 149–158; and figuration, 132–137, 138, 140, 157; graphological aspects of, 158–160; and illocutionary meaning, 146–148; lexical aspects of, 156–158; not linguistic form per se, 144–145; not a meaning-expressing function, 145–148; meaning and scope of, 141–149; as ornament, 137, 144, 148, 160; phonological aspects of, 151–156; poetry as, 36–37, 41, 133, 140; polyvalency of, 150; style qualities, 139–140; and suggestion, 140, 142, 143; and synonymy, 148–149

Suggestion *(dhvani):* conditions of, 97; connotational meaning as, 100–102; as a contextual function, 101–103, 112; as a worldview, 253 n. 6; and emotive meaning *(rasadhvaṇi),* 117–127; and figurative expression, 103–107; in gesture, 126, 127; of homonymous expressions, 96, 107–108, 112–113; and imagism, 128, 129, 130; as indirection, 105, 124; and inference, 122–123, 130; and metaphorical meaning, 81, 96–103; poetry as, 2, 37–39, 153; and primary meaning, 107–126; and purport, 113–117, 119, 123–124, 130; and style (*see* Style: and suggestion); as subordination of literal meaning, 125; as supernumerary meaning, 75, 99–100, 103, 107, 112, 117, 124, 126; by suppression, 129, 130; and symbolist theory, 127–130; types of, 95–97, 228–229; as a verbal function, 99

Swift, J., 250; "An Argument against Abolishing Christianity," 170; *Gulliver's Travels,* 170; "A Modest Proposal," 170

Symbolist poetry, 250

Taupin, Rene, 129

Taylor, Edward, 58

Tennyson, A., 238; "Break, Break, Break," 53; "Home They Brought the Warrior Dead," 55

Thomas, Dylan, 147

Tolstoy, L., 238

Twain, Mark, *Tom Sawyer,* 186

Udbhaṭa, 124

Unity of meaning. *See under* Mīmāṃsā

Universality of critical concepts, 6, 246–247

Vāmana, 31; definition of poetry of, 140; on *riti,* 36–37, 138–140

Vātsyāyana, *Kāmasūtra,* 62

Vedānta: on intention, 173, 174; on purport, 174

Veron, Eugene, 238

Verbal meaning: autonomy of, 4, 164–165, 184; determinacy of, 7, 187, 188–189; and dualism of word and meaning, 149; impersonality of, 4, 165–170; limits of, 188–189; paraphrasability of, 160, 269 n. 65; and referentiality of words, 5, 184, 269 n. 65; and synonymity, 148–149; theory of, 4–5; unity of (see under *Mīmāṃsā)*

Virgil, Aeneid, 235, 239

Viśvanātha, on *rasa,* 31, 42, 230

Warren, Robert Penn, 72

Witz, Morris, 192

Whitman, W., 128, 250; "Song of Myself," 235; "When Lilacs Last in Dooryard Bloom'd," 91

Williams, Tennesse, 250

Wimsatt, W. K., and Monroe C. Beardsley, 22, 23, 168, 170

Winters, Yvor, 16

Wittgenstein, L., 16, 47; on aspect seeing, 191; on emotions, 21–22, 48

Woolf, Virginia, *To the Lighthouse,* 251; *Mrs. Dalloway,* 251

Wordsworth, W., 40, 69, 185, 237, 238, 250; "Immortality" ode, 240; "Michael," 157; "A Slumber Did My Spirit Seal," 53, 186–187; sonnet "Composed upon Westminister Bridge," 105, 151; "1801," 118; "Tintern Abbey," 56–57, 234

Yeats, William Butler, 250; "Among School Children," 190–191; "Second Coming," 92; "Sailing to Byzantium," 157

Yogyatā (logical consistency), 77, 93